MAN THE ARTIST His creative imagination

The Macdonald Illustrated Library

MAN THE ARTIST

HIS CREATIVE IMAGINATION

Editorial Board

Sir Gerald Barry

Dr. J. Bronowski

James Fisher

Sir Julian Huxley

Designed by Hans Erni

Macdonald : London

First published in 1964
by Macdonald & Co. (Publishers) Ltd.
Gulf House, 2 Portman Street, London W 1

© *Aldus Books Limited, London, 1964*
Set in England by Hazell Watson & Viney Ltd.
Printed in Italy

The arts make up the subject of this latest volume in a library of modern knowledge for the family.

Our Aldus team of international artists, writers, designers, and editors have found hard work, but much enjoyment, too, in compiling this volume's predecessors— *Science*, *Nature*, *Geography*, *History*, *Technology*, and *Man in Society*. But never have they disputed together so deeply and enjoyed themselves so much as with *Man the Artist*. Art, of the great disciplines, most liberates the human mind and imagination; art provokes the deepest arguments, promotes the freest judgments.

The editorial board of this series, and those whom they advise, are a catholic mixture. Some are artists who like science; some, writers who like everything; others, scientists who like art. It is still fashionable for those on the side of the humanities—literature, language, poetry, the graphic arts, the stage, the screen—to discern a philistinism in scientists, the sort of philistinism that caused the architect Frank Lloyd Wright to say that "Science may produce a civilization but not a culture. Man's life under science alone stays sterile." Yet Wright, most imaginative of engineers, was himself a scientist.

The best scientists, after all, arrange their work, organize and communicate it, with the same surprising logic and free play of the spirit (which some would more simply call imagination) common to dedicated artists. The world is too full and exciting for any outward-looking and forward-looking worker to build a narrow, specialized box to hide in. Such holes are strictly for the pigeons.

Readers familiar with the series will find fewer original works than usual by our chief artist-designer, Hans Erni. This is for an obvious reason. Our illustrations—drawn from the great masters of past and present—have invited themselves into the book. The problem was what to turn away. There was no necessity for an Erni to provide pictures to usher in the chapters.

As in all our volumes, a systematic presentation of the subject is followed, with a copious index to encourage conventional encyclopedic reference. We have tried, as always, to make the kind of information and its flow fit the leading streams of educational curriculums. But this book is not meant to be just "additional reading" for school library shelves. We hope that our readers will like it for itself, and find their enthusiasm aroused as warmly as was the enthusiasm of those who had the pleasurable job of writing and producing it.

James Fisher
Editorial Director of Aldus Books

Introduction

There are many books that include the word "art" or "artist" in their titles, but in almost every case, these words are used with specific, limited meanings—to refer to paintings and painters, for example, or sculpture and sculptors. But in this book, "art" and "artist" are used in the widest possible sense—the sense that the great Dutch painter Vincent Van Gogh had in mind when he wrote to his brother that "there is something of Rembrandt in Shakespeare . . . and of Delacroix in Victor Hugo."

Van Gogh's words imply two truths about art : that it is a many-sided activity, and that beneath this many-sidedness lies a unity. It is often difficult for us—and for artists as well—to understand that the arts have this dual nature. It is all too easy to discuss an individual art—architecture, say, or the ballet—as an isolated activity. It is also quite easy to overlook the second truth that however much the arts *do* differ, they all spring from the same source : man's need to seek meaningful ways to express and communicate his thoughts and emotions, to create satisfying symbols for his ideas and beliefs, and to give form and substance to the world of his imagination.

The editors have therefore arranged *Man the Artist* to emphasize both the unity and the diversity of the arts. The opening chapter shows how the complex and specialized art forms of today can be traced back to prehistoric origins that are closely associated with primitive impulses toward magic and ritual. It is fascinating to realize that each human being, as he grows from childhood to maturity, relives in one way or another this progression. As a child, he is likely to make free, uninhibited use of pebbles, mud, bits of wood or paper, as well as more sophisticated materials such as paint and crayons, to make —with a belief in their having a kind of magical effectiveness—shapes that express intensely personal and private feelings about people close to him and about his immediate experiences. Later, as his awareness broadens, he makes shapes, tells stories, or acts out dramas with a wider significance that others can share. This change from private self-expression to ordered, meaningful communication of experience probably parallels the way mankind developed artistic expression in all its variety.

The central chapters of *Man the Artist* indicate how the individual arts developed, and outline some of the creative problems that artists face. It is no more than a matter of convenience that these arts are treated separately, for as we shall see, they share many features in common. Today, for example, there is hardly an art form that does not contribute to—and in turn, reflect in its own contemporary character—that newcomer among the arts, and special phenomenon of a technical age, the cinema.

Another important aspect of the arts is the way they can give significance and value to ordinary objects and to everyday activities. A chair or a table may be well made and practical, but we value such things even more if their design, shapes, and textures are satisfying to the eye and touch. Similarly, a story may be interesting simply for the facts it contains; but we respond to it with greater delight if it is told so artfully that it possesses our imagination as effectively as if the experiences it relates were our own.

This latter quality of art—its ability to awaken in us a sense of personal involvement—explains its enduring value to human communities. A society *without* art is unknown. In a simply organized community where people differ little in outlook, the arts directly and simply express common attitudes and beliefs. Neither the people nor their artists isolate the arts from one another as we who live in complex societies tend to do. Today, men differ a great deal in the ways they conduct their lives; each of us lives by exchanging the products of his particular skill for those of other men. Often we understand little or nothing of how others work or think.

In such circumstances it is not surprising that the arts have undergone a similar differentiation. That is why it is so important to consider the unity of the arts at which Van Gogh hinted. It is useful, too, to be able to evaluate works of art—as the final chapter shows—and to have standards by which we can accept or reject them as truly expressive and meaningful.

Men have always made judgments about what makes good or bad art, and to some extent the choice of examples in this book reflects the opinions of artists and others who have seriously thought and written about art throughout the centuries, as well as what many people today feel to be true about the arts.

Looking at the works of artists through the eyes of others is one good way to help us to form our own judgments. Most of us will discover that we can agree to a great extent with the opinions shared by most experts about what constitutes great art. Yet so that the arts can remain alive, and artists create works relevant to contemporary life, new ideas are important, too. If *Man the Artist* helps you to discover *how* there can be "something of Rembrandt in Shakespeare," and leads you into libraries, museums, theatres, concert halls, public buildings, shops, homes—in short, into the great world about you—with a new awareness of the meaning and relevance of all today's arts, you will take from this book what the editors and contributors hope they have put into it.

Gerald Barry
J. Bronowski
James Fisher
Julian Huxley

Advisers

Donald Berwick

Pierre Lavayssière

Editor
Colin Sorensen

Associate Editor
Charles Bricker

Editorial Assistants
Ken Coton
Dorothy Williams

Art Editor
Malcolm Booker

Associate Art Editor
John Wood

Art Assistants
André Boszin
David Girling

Research
Elaine Barr
Enid Moore
Sarah Waters
Beryl de Haan

Index
G. Norman Knight
Anthony Walker

Contributors

Kenneth Adams
pages 26-29

Alan Houghton Brodrick
pages 22-25

Mary Clarke
pages 170-191

Ormerod Greenwood
pages 252-277

John Kershaw
pages 192-221

Bernard Myers
pages 30-35, 122-141, 304-319

Joseph Rykwert
pages 88-121

Mary Sullivan
pages 222-251

Basil Wright
pages 278-303

Historical Survey
Text: Peter Fitzgerald
Design: Bruce Robertson

Contents

Contents—continued

To evoke in oneself a feeling one has experienced, and having evoked it in oneself, then by means of movement, lines, colors, sounds, or forms expressed in words, so to transmit that feeling that others experience the same feeling—this is the activity of art.

Count Leo Nikolaevich Tolstoi (1828-1910)

In this picture I have tried to express the qualities of rhythm, proportion, harmony, and balance that are common to all the different forms of creative expression that we call the arts—Hans Erni

Chapter 1

The Creative Spirit

Most of us, living as we do in scientifically minded societies, tend to want more or less exact definitions of anything that we discuss. Throughout history, great thinkers have tried to produce such a definition of art. Each has added something to our knowledge, but none has said the last word. In fact, the only thing we can be certain of is that for as long as artists exist and work men will discuss and seek to define art.

But though we cannot give a single all-embracing definition of art, we can begin to see how important it is in our lives if we try to imagine a world without it : no singing or music, no dancing, no plays or stories or operas, no movies, no sculpture, no architecture, no paintings or drawings, and no design or decoration in the things we use in everyday life.

From that list you will get some idea of the scope of this book. Naturally, we cannot in the space of a single chapter trace the development of each of those different art forms—that is something we leave to later chapters. But here we try to lay the groundwork by examining the creative impulses underlying all artistic activity.

We show that when art first began, its functions were connected with magic and ritual—and that such functions are still with us in one way or another. Next we look at man as an artist, and show how his urge to create can be trained. We study a number of ways in which trained artists choose to work. Finally we look in detail at three important roles that artists can fill in different types of community : the role of the folk artist in primitive and unsophisticated societies; that of the so-called fine artist in highly civilized cultures; and that of the artist who works in the field of mass communications.

When early man stenciled an impression of his outstretched hand on the dark wall of a cave, he was deliberately making his own mark on the world around him. The story of art has been largely the story of man's continuing search for meaningful marks—for the shapes, sounds, words, pictures, and dance movements that can most eloquently express his experiences of the inner and outer worlds, and so enlarge and perpetuate them.

The first artists

We shall probably never know when it was that men first began to sing and dance, or to relate and re-enact events that excited them. The first men to do these things—the first musicians, dancers, storytellers, and actors—died long before our earliest written records begin. We do know, however, that men were singing, dancing, and so on at least 15,000 years ago. We know this because cave paintings of around that period show men dancing and chanting. What purpose lay behind such pictures?

When men first began to draw pictures and carve stones to represent the shapes of animals and other men, their primary purpose was almost certainly to make *magic*. They believed, or so we think, that the objects they created contained secret powers that could be used to control natural events. According to this belief, a hunter who drew, say, a deer thereby gained some kind of power over a real deer.

Around these early paintings, drawings, and sculptures there probably developed set patterns of words and gestures that were repeated at special times. Such repeated actions and gestures were the beginnings of *ritual*. Together, magic and ritual gave man the first stimulus toward perfecting those skillful uses of voice, body, and hand that we call "the arts."

Prehistoric men probably had no such word as "art."

Pictures found in the Trois-Frères cavern, southern France, include a flute-playing bison man (above, left); he may resemble masked dancers who took part in Stone Age hunting rituals. Early men probably believed that figurines, like this one (above, right) found in Austria, ensured fertility and that paintings of horses pierced with arrows (example from Lascaux, below) brought success in hunting.

To them, carvings and drawings were chiefly the materials of their magic, although some of them must have taken artistic pleasure in what they were making. Probably among the earliest forms of this art-magic (perhaps as many as 90,000 years ago) was the attempt to capture shadows permanently by tracing their outlines on rock walls. Another kind of early "picture" is the tracing of hands (p. 21). Some experts believe that these early mechanical attempts at drawing might have been magical guarantees that something of their makers' personalities would live on—an impulse that still manifests itself in modern man's desire to have his photograph taken or his portrait painted. But even if we do not fully understand the motives behind the things primitive men produced, we can derive a great deal of enjoyment and interest from looking at them, and we can even make some reasonable guesses at why they were made.

Some of the most impressive and exciting specimens of Stone Age art are in the caves of southern France and northern Spain. There, certain caves were magic or holy places; and deep inside them, where no daylight ever penetrated, men painted and engraved pictures. It must have been an awe-inspiring journey deep into the caves, lit by flickering torches, to paint natural-looking bison, deer, and other animals. These may have been painted to guarantee success in hunting. Alongside the paintings of beasts are mysterious signs and symbols, which may have been in part magical devices designed to ensure that enough children would be born to the tribe to allow it to survive.

Pictures found in the Trois-Frères cavern of southern France show that rituals were probably performed in connection with the making of the paintings. There are paintings of men dressed in skins and wearing animal masks, apparently dancing, chanting, and playing a kind of musical instrument. These suggest that our ancestors possessed a complex culture and many of the skills that were later to develop as separate arts.

Presiding over all the pictures of animals and dancing men is the so-called "wizard" of Trois-Frères, clad in animal skins and wearing stag's antlers. Someone like him probably presided over ceremonies designed either to initiate boys of the tribe into manhood or to assure that the food supply and the reproduction of children would be safeguarded. Such rites undoubtedly did achieve a certain success by making men more confident, brave, and enterprising than they might otherwise have been. The arts that derived from these early chants and dances often have a somewhat similar encouraging and inspirational effect on men today.

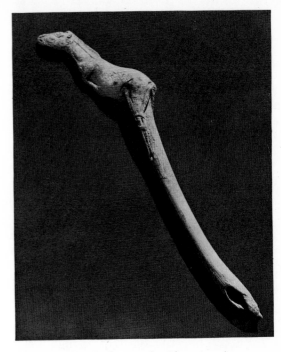

Stone Age tool, decorated with a jumping horse. The carving follows the curve of the reindeer antler from which it is made.

Animal drawings on this 5000-year-old Persian cup are as stylized as geometric symbols. Design at rim is a row of long-necked water birds; at center, a circle of galloping dogs; at base, an ibex with huge horns.

Ritual and magic

When we imagine prehistoric men performing rituals as they painted on the walls of caves, it is difficult for us to connect such activities with anything we or our artists do today. Actually, the connections are stronger than we might imagine. We saw (p. 22) that two of the main elements in prehistoric art are magic and ritual. We can find both these elements, in one form or another, in the arts of our own century.

Although magic has little connection with the arts in our highly industrialized societies, it still provides the main function for the arts among modern primitive peoples. The Sepik people in New Guinea, the Bakuba of the Congo, the many tribes of the Amazon forest, the Australian aborigines—these are but a few of the hundreds of primitive peoples who practice art-magic in their dancing, chanting, drama, sculpture, or painting. Consider, for example, the Australian aboriginals, many of whom still have little contact with the outside world. They live, without fixed dwellings or domestic animals, by hunting and food gathering.

One common theme in aboriginal painting is that of the so-called *wondjina* figures. Vaguely human in shape, with blobs for eyes and nose—but never a sign of a mouth —these figures are painted and repainted again and again. Why? "To bring rain," say the aborigines, for they believe that only the act of painting the *wondjina* can ensure that the rains will come; rain is the most sought-after blessing in the parched areas of Australia. And why have the *wondjina* no mouths? Because, the explanation runs, if they did, the rain would gush forth and cause floods.

Magic, then, as a reason for making art objects, survives in the 20th-century arts chiefly among primitive peoples. But the other element in prehistoric art—ritual —is found in all the arts in every kind of society. In some of the following chapters in this book we shall study the ways in which rituals of one kind or another have determined different art forms. To take some examples at random: Dionysiac rituals in Greece gave impetus to

Tribal artists today often make "X-ray" drawings rather like those of early men, for they also believe that by picturing the vital organs of a human or an animal, they may gain magical control over its life or death. Above: late Stone Age elephant (northwest Spain). Right: emu (Australian aborigine, western Arnhem Land). Far right: wolf swallowing a human figure (Kwakiutl Indian, western Canada).

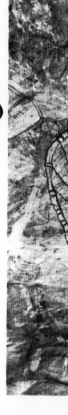

Eyes can be seen in the stylized geometric patterns on both the objects below—the Chinese ritual caldron, made between 1776 and 1122 B.C. (left), and the North American Indian box. Such traditional patterns based on the human face may owe their survival largely to the magical belief that painted eyes will ward off evil.

the development of drama (p. 254); the conventions of kabuki theatre in Japan can be traced back to their origins in Japanese religious dances (p. 254); many religious rituals more or less dictate the form of the building in which they are performed; and public celebrations such as processions and carnivals have imposed a certain form on the layout of towns where they are held (p. 96).

Even in modern times ritual has played an enormous part in people's lives and in their arts. Religious worship, state processions and formal occasions, traditional parades, political rallies, sports meetings, carnivals—each of these occasions involves some kind of ritual, and each ritual, in turn, demands art of some kind. For carnivals and rallies people make masks and tableaux; for political and other conventions they decorate halls with banners, colored streamers, balloons, and so on; and for many state occasions, composers, painters, sculptors, and other artists are commissioned to produce works especially to mark the event.

To give some examples: The khedive of Egypt marked the opening of the Suez Canal both by the building of a new opera house in Cairo, and by commissioning Giuseppe Verdi (p. 156) to write a new opera with an Egyptian setting. This was *Aïda*, first performed in 1871. In the 1950s, Pablo Picasso (p. 56) drew a symbolic dove which was used in many places in the world on banners and posters at peace rallies. Just before his death in 1954, Picasso's contemporary, Henri Matisse (p. 44), designed colorful, largely abstract decorations and vestments to be used in the chapel of a convent in Vence, France.

Ritual, then, has been an important spur to the arts today, just as it was to our cave-men forebears. But it is often an *external* spur; that is, rituals may demand art products for social or religious reasons that do not conform to the artist's own personal beliefs. Let us now look at the demands that spring from *inside* the artist: the internal power that we call *creativity*.

At the Shrovetide carnival in Binche, Belgium, an ancient ritual, of unknown origin, is still respected. The men who wear these feathered headdresses are forbidden by tradition to leave the town or to dance at any other time of year.

Creativity in the artist

A child's painting, My Garden. *Children express their interest and excitement in the world around them spontaneously, uninfluenced by conventional artistic techniques.*

The great Renaissance artist Michelangelo (p. 40) took four years of single-handed effort to complete his paintings on the ceiling of the Sistine Chapel. Much of the time he had to work lying on his back, which caused him great discomfort and permanently injured his health. Heroic persistence such as Michelangelo's shows how strong is the artist's urge to create. Nearly always a powerful impulse to create is necessary to the artist, if he is to make use of whatever abilities he has.

People often ask whether those abilities are inborn or learned. Obviously no one is born an artist in the sense that he can forgo all training in the skills of his particular art. But neither will training alone make any man into an artist. In short, for every artist both training and inborn ability are essential. The 18th-century Austrian composer Wolfgang Amadeus Mozart (p. 148), for example, started to compose at the age of five and gave concerts all over Europe at the age of seven. Clearly, such unusual talent was mainly due to his inborn abilities; but even such

A shopping game helps a group of six-year-old schoolchildren to learn writing and arithmetic. Such play activities help children to develop their personalities while teaching them something about the adult world.

precocious abilities needed a certain amount of training before the young Mozart could perform in public.

An important part of an artist's training consists of finding out the limits and possibilities of his particular art. Long before his special abilities become obvious, the child who is going to be an artist may develop his talents through playing games. For everyone, potential artist or not, games are a vital part of the growing-up process. Games like "mothers and fathers," for instance, teach children something of the ways of the adult world. In this sense, much of the pleasure children get from such make-believe games comes unconsciously from their discovery of the limitations and capabilities of their personalities. And it is in this sense that the artist is a man who never stops playing. His work is a serious attempt to probe the limits and explore the possibilities of his particular art.

Among the factors that may limit art at a particular time are sets of rules devised to discipline its ideas and methods. In the past, many artists have preferred to work according to a fixed set of rules. The 17th-century French painter Nicolas Poussin (p. 56) built up his compositions according to carefully thought-out rules that he derived from his study of the great painters of the Renaissance. In Poussin's day, a large number of art academies (p. 46) were founded in the belief that painting could be learned simply by following those rules. But in fact the creative impulse is not so easily satisfied. The truly creative artist needs freedom of choice. For *any* experience and *any* idea may turn out to be useful to him. That is why the creative urge cannot always find an outlet simply by following a set of rules.

Because there are no safe rules in creative art, the artist takes a new risk every time he breaks fresh ground. The work of a great artist, therefore, is marked not only by the successes that lead us to recognize his greatness, but also by failures. For instance, Beethoven (p. 148) wrote a so-called Battle Symphony (a collection of patriotic tunes arranged in a symphonic form) that is generally thought to fall far below the standards set by his other works.

Successful creative work usually demands great technical skill, and few artists achieve such skill without years of experiment. That is why, as history shows, most artists produce their finest work between the ages of 30 and 40. There are, however, many exceptions to this generalization. The French painter Paul Gauguin (p. 42) did not devote himself seriously to painting until he was 35; and some artists reach the peak of their creative activity in their old age.

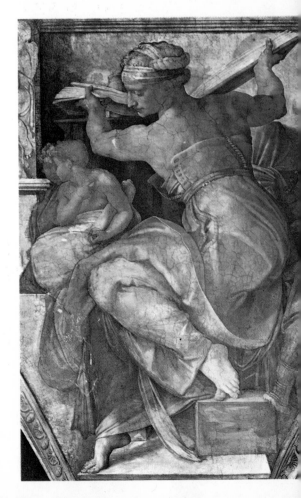

The 15th-century Italian artist Michelangelo made this sketch (top) for the figure of the Libyan Sibyl on the ceiling of the Sistine Chapel (right). Most artists make such detailed studies before beginning work.

The artist at work

Because art is such a varied activity, it is impossible for us to say in a few words: "This is how and why artists work." In general terms, however, we can at least make the following statements: (1) Behind all art lies the experience and imagination of the artist; (2) artists work by a combination of planning and improvisation. Let us look at these in more detail.

Experience and imagination: Many artists seem to rely heavily on their experience. In words or pictures (and sometimes even in music), they recapture something that they have lived through. In some cases the experience may be intense but short-lived. For example, the English poet Wordsworth (p. 196) was passionately excited by nature; and he crystallized particular experiences into vivid poems. In other cases, the experience may be that of years. The life-long concern of Émile Zola (p. 248) with the condition of the poor in mid-19th-century France can be felt in almost every line of his novel *Germinal*. He painted a grimly realistic picture of poverty, and argued that it was the cause (not, as many people then believed, the result) of laziness, drunkenness, and vice. Thus Zola's work, like that of many great artists, shows an intensity not only of feeling but of thought as well.

Intense thought and feeling does not necessarily lead to realistic art, however. Many artists choose strange and

American vibraphone-player Lionel Hampton takes an impromptu turn on the drums. Such jazz musicians usually play without score or preparation, improvising variations on an agreed theme. Above, right: part of Beethoven's draft score for The Ruins of Athens *(incidental music for a play by August Kotzebue, 1812), showing numerous alterations and corrections.*

Above: drawing by Augustus John depicting the modern Irish novelist James Joyce, who found inspiration for his writings in his recollections of people and places in his native Dublin (left).

fantastic settings. Even so, we find that their work may be filled with comments on the world they live in. For example, the story "In the Penal Settlement" by the Austrian writer Franz Kafka (p. 232) describes at great length a "punishment machine" in an unnamed, un-located prison camp. When the story was published in 1919, it must have seemed the purest fantasy. Today, two decades after the Nazi concentration camps were liberated, it reads almost like a factual report.

Sometimes, the artist has no direct memory of the experience that prompts his work. One short story by the English writer Joyce Cary (1888-1957) is about a girl with a wrinkled face. Cary himself was puzzled by the fact that he could not picture the girl's face without wrinkles. Long after he had finished the story, he suddenly remembered that he had once seen such a girl. Thus the idea or event that prompts a work of art may be completely irrelevant to the final result.

To sum up: Whether his experience is consciously or unconsciously remembered, and whether he chooses a realistic or a fantastic setting for his work, the artist is almost bound to reflect and comment on his personal experience, and also on the kind of community he lives in and on the way people think, act, look, and so on.

Planning and improvisation: The 19th-century Belgian composer César Franck (1822-90) often began by making a list of the musical keys through which he intended his work to progress. Only later did he add the actual melody. Similarly, the Irish poet W. B. Yeats (1865-1939) often began by writing his ideas down in prose. By contrast, Franz Schubert (p. 152) wrote six of his *Winterreise* songs in one morning; and the Russian poet Alexander Pushkin (1799-1837) worked by writing masses of verse extremely quickly and then selecting carefully from this outpouring.

In these four examples the first pair illustrates an unusual degree of planning; the second, an unusual intensity of creative activity, an intensity that is sometimes called "inspiration." Artists who work only when "inspired" have often believed that they are possessed by some kind of supernatural force that works through them. Such a belief can be helpful if it gives the artist courage to work despite doubt and hardship. But it is harmful if it prevents the artist from criticizing his own work.

Our own century has seen the birth of new art forms, such as the motion picture. Making a film depends on a high degree of co-operation between artists and technicians—co-operation that would be impossible without an enormous amount of planning in advance. On pages 278 to 303 we show how such plans are made.

Modern industrial buildings—like this aircraft hangar in San Francisco—are the products of teams of skilled architects and technicians. Such simplicity of design and delicate engineering are achieved only by months of preliminary discussion and research.

Peruvian clay vessel (4th-6th century A.D.), made by a Nazca craftsman, is decorated with an animal holding a twig of pepper pods, who represents the god of vegetation.

Folk art

The folk artist may be a potter or a weaver, carver or furniture maker, musician or singer. Although he is skilled, he has no formal training, but follows the traditions of his community. When he is a painter, for example, he is likely to be a decorator of useful objects rather than a painter of pictures. But even when he does paint pictures (such as icons or devotional images), he is making things that are used for specific purposes rather than things that express his personal vision.

Folk songs and rhythms, for example, often play an important part in daily work routines. Weavers in North Africa and the Middle East make carpets according to rhythmic directions chanted aloud. Master weavers travel from place to place holding patterns in their memories in the form of such chants. Most folk music is strongly rhythmic; it makes you want to sing, move, or dance to it—not think about it. When folk songs tell stories—about traditional heroes, or everyday happenings and emotions—they rarely make personal or individual comments on them.

Folk art is not self-analyzing. But that does not mean that it is naïve. The level of some folk arts is very sophisticated—as in the high quality of furniture and fabrics made by the Shakers, people belonging to an American religious sect. Here, skill and the ability to create is thought to be God-given. As a result, the act of making something should be in itself an act of worship, and nothing but the best is considered good enough.

Wherever people still practice folk art, we find that they all recognize this sense of power that lies in the act of creation. In many cases this recognition is coupled with the belief that, because only God can make creation perfect, the folk artist ought to leave a deliberate flaw in his work. If he does not, it might be thought that he was trying to "copy" God. To avoid such blasphemy, a village cabinetmaker, for example, will include a "mistake" in his work or leave part of it unfinished. A decorative painter will leave an open end to his pattern, or paint in some variation that slightly upsets the symmetry. And for similar reasons, both Oriental and Finnish weavers will leave a "tail" or flaw in their work. If they did not, they believe, their souls would be woven into the work and so be trapped.

Though the folk artist usually has no formal training, he does learn from the traditional work of the past. He copies highly stylized forms from previous artists, and, in so doing, he often takes the simplification or stylization a stage further. In this way, the folk painter does not learn how to draw a flower, but how to mix the paint, how much paint to load onto the brush, how to hold the brush,

Part of an 18th-century skirt border from Crete, embroidered with figure of a crowned woman holding carnations—an example of the stylized patterns followed by folk artists.

and, finally, how to make the actual stroke that will make one petal. In short, he learns an *action*. And it is the sum of those actions that will determine the shape and appearance of the flower.

Much folk music, too, is determined by the technique that the musicians use. Folk musicians tend to use stringed instruments that can be plucked (guitars, mandolins, zithers, etc.), because such instruments are ideal for playing strongly rhythmic melodies. All over the world, folk music makes use of complicated off-beat rhythms. These result largely from the technique of playing: On the up stroke the thumb sweeps the open strings; on the down stroke, the fingers play the melody and harmonies—often with quite complex fingering. It is this technique that gives Spanish folk music, for instance, its distinctive character.

The spiritual, a deeply felt type of North American Negro folk song, has spread right around the world in various forms. Along with it came jazz (p. 166). Unlike the spiritual, however, jazz is a typical city art form. It is more complicated, more sophisticated than the spiritual, which grew up among the Negroes on the farms and cotton plantations in the American South. For that reason, jazz has become not so much a folk art as a "mass" art—a kind of art that we study on page 34.

In Sicily, carts are still carved and painted with colorful geometric designs—legacy of 11th-century Arab invaders. Pictured on panels are scenes from medieval Sicilian history.

Tin coffeepot, made in Pennsylvania in the mid-19th century, is painted with a traditional fruit design that was carried to the New World by emigrant Dutch craftsmen.

This 13th-century Italian painting portrays the crucified Christ with stylized features according to a traditional pattern. Compare it with the 14th-century painting below by Florentine artist Giotto, who breaks with tradition and brings the same subject to life by infusing it with his own creative vision.

Fine art

The phrase "fine art" is used to single out the kind of music, poetry, prose, painting, sculpture, architecture, and so on that makes us feel that the artist's personal vision has played a major part in its making. For example, it distinguishes literature from journalism, a symphony from a hit song, a masterpiece of painting from a poster, and a piece of sculpture from a waxwork figure.

Of course, these distinctions are true only in the most general terms. The *quality* of the artist's vision and of its realization in the form of a work of art is what justifies the use of the word "fine" to describe it. For example, a man who works in an accepted fine-art medium such as water color, but whose work is lifeless and routine, is less a "fine" artist than the designer of a first-rate advertising poster. A really good poster artist can produce something as personal and technically accomplished as any work of fine art—and yet perfectly suited to publicity purposes.

The word "purpose" gives us a further clue to the meaning of the phrase "fine art." Fine art is, in fact, the kind of art which need have no immediate and easily defined purpose. A good piece of cabinetmaking is a piece of furniture. It has an obvious purpose. But many good paintings—except for a certain limited, decorative purpose—are free from any such immediate and obvious function.

The fine artist uses this freedom in order to try out new ideas, to find new forms with which to express his own personal vision. In this sense, the artist's studio is like a scientist's laboratory: Just as the scientist constantly seeks to extend the frontiers of knowledge by making new discoveries, so, too, the artist in his work is constantly trying to find new or better ways of expressing himself. And also, just as the scientist's discoveries are made use of by technologists and by industry, so does the artist's work fertilize new developments in the field of the mass arts (p. 34).

Because fine artists are so often experimental in their work, much of it is difficult to understand at first. This is particularly true of the arts in the 20th century. The works of the Renaissance, on the other hand, contained elements that were immediately understood combined with elements that were both deep and subtle. This is not the kind of fact that can be illustrated with a few words. To understand it properly you would have to spend a long time in, say, a gallery filled with Renaissance paintings. After a while, you would find that you had progressed from a stage where you saw the paintings merely as illustrations of certain events to a stage where you

Italian sculptor Lorenzo Ghiberti (p. 82) showed individuality characteristic of Renaissance artists when he included this self-portrait in his bronze door for the Florence Baptistery.

began to glimpse a new outlook on the world—an outlook that is somehow expressed by the paintings.

To appreciate the work of a fine artist, then, is not a matter of making snap judgments. It is something that takes both time and patience. This is especially true today, for, like people in many other professions, the artist has become a specialist. Five hundred years ago, any educated man could keep in touch with almost all the fields of knowledge of his time. Today few business men, for example, even expect to understand what their own scientist-employees are doing. The same kind of thing is true of the artist. We ought not to expect to understand his work at first sight or hearing.

Because it is often difficult to explain in simple terms what is happening in the fine arts, many art critics fall back on the idea that one must be born with a special kind of "sympathy" if he is to understand an artist's work. But understanding does not come so simply. It calls for a great deal of patience. It needs a willingness to be taught by the work of art itself—to listen hard, to read and re-read, and to spend far more time looking at works of visual art than we usually do.

The Villa Capra, Vicenza, designed by 16th-century Italian architect Andrea Palladio (1518-80). Such villas, with their slender porticoes and broad wings blending harmoniously into the landscape, appealed to the educated patrons of the period because they combined the stately symmetry of Roman architecture with a new lightness and grace.

Modern artists claim the freedom to express intense personal emotions in a highly individual way—as in portrait of a weeping woman, left, by Spanish-born artist Pablo Picasso (p. 56). Style of Picasso's ceramics (below) is equally personal, although it has associations with such traditional pottery as the Peruvian example pictured on page 30.

33

Art for a mass audience

The development during the last century or so of mass-production techniques in industry, as well as of mass-communications media such as journals, films, and television, has in turn brought into being a new kind of artist—one whom it is difficult to classify as either a folk (p. 30) or a fine (p. 32) artist. Typical of these new artists are movie makers, designers of all kinds, dance-band musicians, poster artists, and the writers of television serials. All these people have one thing in common : They work to satisfy the demands of a mass audience composed chiefly of city dwellers. In a way, this mass-audience art is the "folk" art of the cities, but there are great differences between mass art and true folk art.

In the first place, mass art is more sophisticated. Whereas the folk artist is generally content to work within a tradition, the mass artist constantly seeks to give his work a novel and up-to-the-minute look. To achieve this modernity, he often borrows from an artistic language created by the fine artist. The American band leader Stan Kenton, for example, has borrowed many of his strange-sounding harmonies from the composer Stravinsky (p. 158). Once-experimental techniques like those of the Impressionists (p. 44) and of various non-representational painters of the early 20th century (p. 66) have become commonplace in such fields as textile and wallpaper design, advertising art, window display, and set design for the theatre and films.

Secondly, mass art is highly mechanized. It is geared to the techniques of mass production. The industrial designer, for example, is not a craftsman in the way that most folk artists are craftsmen; he is a skilled man who has an advanced technical education. When people attack mass art on the grounds that it is slick and shallow, defenders point to this technical excellence as one of its major virtues. For instance, as much thought and care goes into the making of a "pop" record as goes into any operatic or symphonic recording. And the trumpet and trombone players in a big dance band must have as great a technical command of their instruments as do their fellows in symphony orchestras.

Why do the mass arts have such high technical standards? The answer lies partly in the fact that these arts fulfill a double purpose. Firstly, as we saw, they serve city-dwelling men as folk art serves country people, and it is natural for the artists to want to perform as well as possible. But more important is the fact that all the mass arts are trying to sell something in a highly competitive market. The would-be hit song competes with a hundred other hit songs; TV networks compete with one another and with the theatre and movies; and so on.

olivetti ———— *Elettrosumma 22*

In the 1860s, the use of Sir John Millais's painting Bubbles *(top) as a poster to advertise soap scandalized art critics. Today, poster designs (center) are often the work of specialist artists; an automobile's looks (right) may show the influence both of production techniques and the work of sculptors like Brancusi or Gabo.*

One result of fierce commercial competition is that the mass arts try to make an immediate impact on their audience. Thus the chorus of a hit song usually lasts no longer than 16 bars, and the main theme is sometimes only eight bars long. The package on the supermarket shelf must shout down its neighbors. The newspaper headline, the press photograph, the advertising poster (which is often seen from a fast-moving car)—all these are designed to get their point over to us in a second or so.

The way in which the mass arts strive for an immediate impact has important effects on our ability to appreciate the fine arts. As we saw on page 32, understanding of the fine arts does not come easily. It is something that takes both time and patience to cultivate. If we want to appreciate a poem or a symphony or a painting, we must fight back a desire for immediate understanding. There is no "instant" fine art.

This action shot from a newspaper sports page (top) shows influence of fine arts in its exciting composition. Attention-getting typography and layout of popular magazines and newspapers (center) is the work of trained artists. Some is sophisticated, but designers aim to make all of it as immediately easy to grasp as cartoon-art—like this example by England's Gerard Hoffnung.

35

Chapter 2

Painting

Modern photography, whether still or moving, has made us so used to seeing the world reproduced in pictures that we may find it hard to understand why paintings were once regarded as powerful—even mysterious or magical —objects. But, until a little over a hundred years ago, only painters could create flat-surfaced images whose colors and shapes seemed to mirror the real world. A very old story is told about a Greek artist who painted a bunch of grapes so realistically that birds came and pecked at the fruit. Whether true or not, such a story illustrates one of the earliest aims of painters : to create lifelike images.

The great Italian artist Leonardo da Vinci once said that "painting is poetry that is seen." This gives us a clue to a second and perhaps more important aim of painting : to arouse our emotions. A good painting, whether lifelike or not, must please our eyes and must in some way move us. That is why many of the world's greatest artists have painted pictures that are not at all "realistic." A good painting exists as something that *itself* has meaning, something that can be experienced for its own sake by anyone who sees it—not just as a reminder, like a photograph, of something else.

Knowing something about the techniques painters use to achieve their desired effects adds to our appreciation of what they are trying to say in their paintings. For no matter how sensitive an artist may be to the world around him, he cannot communicate what he feels unless he has trained himself to control his hands and such tools of his trade as paints and brushes. He makes things just as any craftsman does; and often the effect of his paintings depends on how well he has suited his materials and methods to the meanings he wants to express.

Like all paintings, this self-portrait by 18th-century English artist William Hogarth could be described simply as a plane surface covered with lines and colors. But —since early man began to cover the walls of caves with magic symbols and lifelike images of the animals he hunted—the art of painting has been one of the chief ways through which men have recorded their interest and pleasure in the appearances of the natural world, and symbolized their deepest feelings and emotions.

Three dimensions into two

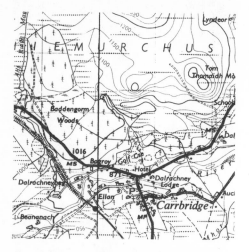

Detail from British Ordnance Survey map (of Inverness, Scotland). Appearance of map itself does not immediately convey a feeling of space; but once we have learned to understand mapmakers' conventional signs we can judge exact distances with great accuracy.

The Flagellation of Christ (*below*), *painted by Piero della Francesca* (*Italian, about 1420-92*), *is based upon a strict use of central perspective. Lines of building and pavement converge to make a framework that gives a powerful illusion of depth and spaciousness.*

Almost the first things we notice about any object are its height, its width, and its depth. When a painter wants to reproduce these three dimensions on a flat surface, he finds it easy to show how high or wide the object is, but difficult to suggest its depth—that is, how solid it is and how far separated from other objects.

Long ago, Oriental painters solved this problem by placing objects according to arrangements that act as *symbols* of distances or depths. When we have learned to recognize and accept such symbols, we are prepared to interpret them as representations of true distance or depth. Ever since the 15th century, however, most European painters have tried to give the illusion of real depth. Their method, called "central perspective," is based on the fact that objects far away from a fixed viewpoint seem to be smaller than ones nearby. Thus they make painted objects seem to exist at different distances by varying their sizes in relation to one another.

Our Western painters can also trick the eye by blurring the edges of "distant" objects and shading their tones lighter than those of "nearby" ones. And artists can take advantage of the illusion that warm colors (reds, yellows) seem to advance toward the viewer, while cool ones (blues, greens) retreat. But whatever the method of achieving depth, its success depends in large part on how accustomed viewers are to seeing it used.

In A Game of Polo (*from a 16th-century Persian miniature*) *relative distances are suggested by placing horsemen at various heights in the design without reducing sizes. Another way of creating a sense of space was used by 17th-century Flemish artist Peter Paul Rubens: The eye is led along a line of receding figures in sketch* (left) *for* Madonna Adored by Saints.

For exact indication of distances, architects use so-called isometric perspective (above). *Unlike central perspective, this allows parallel lines to be shown as equidistant. Georges Braque* (French, 1882-1963), *in Cubist painting* Still Life with Playing Cards (left), *depicts the same objects from many viewpoints.*

39

By virtue of its size and setting, the 12th-century mosaic figure of Christ dominates the sanctuary of the cathedral at Monreale, Sicily.

Setting and size

We cannot look at a painting without being aware of its surroundings, for no painting exists without some kind of setting. The impression a painting makes is affected by the character of its surroundings, and by its size in relation to those surroundings. Until recently, artists gave a great deal of thought to relating a painting to the particular place for which it was intended. Today, exhibitions in galleries and museums show great numbers of paintings—sometimes by one artist, sometimes by many—collected together, and many modern painters work with only this kind of variable and temporary setting in mind.

The settings for which artists have traditionally designed their works may be classified into two important kinds: public and private. In ancient times, for example, most painters were directly employed by their public—by the group or community in which they lived. They painted directly onto the walls of public buildings or on natural rock surfaces. Prehistoric examples can be found throughout the world, and many wall paintings have survived from ancient Egyptian and Roman times. After the fall of the Roman Empire, Christians in the Byzantine period continued the tradition of large public paintings by putting gigantic mosaic figures of Christ and the saints in their churches. Later, in the Renaissance, men filled entire walls and ceilings with religious paintings, as Michelangelo (1475-1564) did in the Sistine Chapel in Rome. Such paintings were meant to dominate their settings, and in this way to fill the people who saw them with religious awe and a sense of God's majesty.

Many early "private" paintings were wall paintings, too. We can see some still in their original settings among the ruins of first-century Pompeii, where they decorated the private houses of wealthy Romans. In the Middle

Picture gallery of Archduke Leopold Wilhelm, 17th-century Regent of the Netherlands, depicted by David Teniers II (1610-90). In large collections of paintings hung together, as here, individual works tend to lose their separate identities.

Small-scale works of art such as prints are generally intended for private rather than public enjoyment. 19th-century French artist Honoré Daumier illustrates this in The Print Collector (above).

Ages, Bibles, psalters, and other books were made the settings for small pictures meant to be seen by one or two people at a time. During the 16th and 17th centuries, painters made larger pictures with religious themes for the private chapels of noblemen and monasteries. Then, during the Renaissance, when the newly prosperous middle classes began to commission painters to do portraits and other non-religious works, artists made more paintings on wood panels or canvas—separate, movable objects that could be hung anywhere their owners chose.

Paintings like these, and even many paintings intended for public use in monasteries or churches, can lose some of their effect when removed from their original settings and placed in brightly lighted museums, where they are hung in large groups. The viewer should never forget that many of them were meant to be seen in specialized and isolated settings, sometimes dimly lit only by candles or stained-glass windows.

This matter of size and setting may be important *within* a painting as well as outside its frame : The character of a given picture can be determined by the relationship of the painted setting to the human figures in it. Western painters often emphasize the importance of people by making them dominate their backgrounds. Or, if they are more interested in scenery than people, they can add human figures simply to point up the size or grandeur of the surroundings. On the other hand, Oriental painters usually show people about the same size in relation to the objects around them as they would be in real life. One effect of this is to stress the Eastern idea that man is closely related to the rest of nature.

In Boating by Moonlight, *a Chinese painting of the 13th century, the towering mountains and broad expanse of sea reduce human figures to comparative insignificance.*

Human figures dominate design of The Expulsion of Adam and Eve, *by the Florentine artist Michelangelo Buonarroti (1475-1564). Here, in contrast with the Chinese picture above, the artist's interest is centered on humanity, not nature.*

Drawing

Most painters use drawings as the starting point for all the work they do, no matter how large their pictures or what materials they use. They learn to draw well so that they can arrange the marks they make—with pencil, pen, or brush—into intelligently organized forms. These drawings should reflect what the artists feel about the shapes they see in nature—and even shapes that they have only imagined. The French painter Edgar Degas (1834-1917) pointed out that "the artist does not draw what he sees, but what he must make others see." He meant that anyone who draws selects and arranges in an effective way what he feels are the most illuminating features of whatever he sees or imagines.

Before an artist begins his actual work on a painting, he will often make preliminary drawings. Sometimes he may make dozens of such preliminary sketches for one painting. In this way he can see beforehand how certain parts of his painting might best be organized. For example, he can experiment with the best position for a head, a hand, or the fold of a dress. Many artists keep their drawings as a record of the progress of the finished painting, or as ideas for possible future use. The Dutch painter Rembrandt van Rijn (1606-69) not only kept his own drawings but collected examples of other artists' work, including Indian and Persian drawings. Since the 16th century, many lovers of art have made collections of drawings that often have value as works of art complete in themselves, rather than as mere "studies."

The extensive sketchbooks of Leonardo da Vinci (1452-1519) show vividly how great artists can use their own drawings as a means of study. His books are full of drawings that analyze the construction of the human body and its movements, and the ways light and changes of

Leonardo da Vinci's pen study (above) reveals his interest in the structure of natural forms. The strokes of pen and brush with which Giovanni Tiepolo (Italian, 1696-1770) captured the impression of a figure in sunlight (below, left) contrast with the network of tiny lines used by Isaac Fuller (English, 1606-72) in his self-portrait (detail, below right).

Bamboo in the Mist (18th century) shows relationship of brush-drawing techniques to Chinese handwriting (at right).

The bold strokes in the above drawing by Rembrandt van Rijn suggest the forms of the body rather than trace its contours.

position influence the appearances of objects. These remarkable sketches are outstanding examples of how the artist teaches himself to see clearly by copying nature.

Most drawings are made with tools that are also used for writing, because these make direct and spontaneous lines very quickly. Thus the Chinese sketch with brushes because they are used to writing with them. Most Western artists have used pencils or charcoal. Da Vinci liked to use a pointed quill pen to make thin lines, because he felt that the most important aim of a drawing was to show the contours—or outlines—of shapes. On the other hand, Rembrandt preferred to draw with broad reed pens, brushes, or chalk so that he could easily indicate shadows and the solidity of objects.

The French artist Paul Gauguin (1848-1903) realized that drawings can have a quality as personal as handwriting. Thus, though he used them as preparations for his paintings, he refused to show them to anybody. "My drawings?" he said. "Never! They are my secrets."

Some artists may outline the form of the body at every point. Italy's Raffaello Santi (known as Raphael) made above drawing of a kneeling girl between 1511 and 1514 for his dramatic Vatican fresco The Miracle of the Mass at Bolsena, *commissioned by Pope Julius II.*

La Montagne Sainte Victoire, *sketched by Paul Cézanne about 1890. Unpainted areas combine with brush marks to convey forms of the mountain and slope in foreground.*

In the diagram-like They're Biting!, *the Swiss painter and etcher Paul Klee (1879-1940) made witty use of signs and symbols.*

Color

Nearly all painters have used color, but not all of them in just the same way. Some who were especially interested in the shapes of things simply used color to help define the natural forms of whatever they painted. Michelangelo (p. 40) is an outstanding example; in his paintings, form was far more important than color.

But during the 16th century, Venetian painters—notably Titian (Tiziano Vecellio, about 1477-1576)—introduced more sophisticated color variations and harmonies into their work. They made these a principal means of expressing emotional atmosphere as well as the physical reality of objects. In northern Europe, the Flemish painter Peter Paul Rubens (1577-1640) was one of the first artists to employ color in this evocative manner.

Toward the end of the 19th century many painters became interested in the researches scientists were conducting into color's physical nature. One group, the

In Figure with an Ornamental Background (*above*), *Henri Matisse (French, 1869-1954) created decorative effect with color patterns.*

Glowing harmonies of color convey a sensuous richness of surfaces and emphasize pagan mood of Titian's mythological subject in his Bacchus *and* Ariadne. *Setting is the Greek island of Naxos.*

Impressionists, said that our most immediate visual apprehension of the world is through an awareness of color. They wanted their paintings to reproduce the first split-second color impression the eye receives when it looks at anything. For them, actual three-dimensional forms were recognizable only through color experiences.

Another way to use color is symbolically. For example, Christian artists nearly always made the robes of the Virgin Mary blue to signify purity. Other painters have chosen colors that they felt were appropriate symbols of *personal* feelings. In his letters, the Dutch painter Vincent van Gogh (1853-90) has described how he assigned particular colors to a painting because they matched his emotional reaction to the subject. Many artists today, although they paint without any reference at all to actual objects, still rely on the contrasting and combining of colors in order to achieve emotional and symbolic effects.

Apples and Pomegranates, *by Pierre Auguste Renoir (French, 1841-1919). In this typical Impressionist painting, touches of pure color are used to suggest both the actual coloring of objects and the radiance of the light reflected from their surfaces.*

Throughout the centuries artists have used color symbolically. In The Virgin and Child with Saints *(above), Duccio di Buoninsegna (Italian, about 1255-1319) followed the Christian tradition of painting the Madonna's robe blue to symbolize purity. Vincent van Gogh made a more personal choice of "meaningful" colors. In* Sidewalk Café at Night *(right), he contrasted the hot, sulfurous yellow of the cafe's gaslight with the cool, natural blues of the starry night sky.*

Composition

Before beginning to work on a full-size painting, most artists work out final composition in sketches. In this sketch for The Raising of Lazarus, *Dutch artist Rembrandt van Rijn indicated grouping of figures, arrangement of background, with rough strokes of the pen.*

Below: The Last Supper, *by Leonardo da Vinci. In this famous picture, perspective lines of room and gestures of disciples focus attention on the head of Christ. Each group of figures is composed to give the picture a harmonious unity of design.*

No matter how skillful a painter may be at drawing, or how clever at using color, he will not produce a good picture if he cannot combine—or *compose*—shapes and colors into satisfying, harmonious relationships. In other words, the good artist is one who can fuse the various elements in a picture into a unified whole. To do this is so important that many painters like to paint *still lifes*—arrangements of a number of different objects, as in Renoir's painting on page 45—as exercises in the art of composition. Similarly, modern painters seem constantly fascinated by the problem of arranging apparently random shapes and colors into nevertheless carefully composed forms.

The way some modern non-representational painters compose their pictures has a good deal in common with the methods of the French Impressionists (p. 44). For example, Claude Monet (1840-1926) was particularly interested in how light fell on a given object—a church or a haystack, perhaps. To show this he developed his paintings carefully, but he worked according to an instinctive *feeling* for composition, rather than in obedience to a set of academic rules. Such rules had been drawn up by the academies of art that influenced painting from the 17th to the 19th centuries. They laid down ideal proportions and relationships of line and form that were meant to be observed exactly. When Monet and some of his followers ignored these rules, many people ridiculed their paintings as formless. At the same time other groups of 19th-century artists consciously worked out independent theories of composition, sometimes with a mathematical or scientific basis, and followed them exactly. Still other painters, such as Edgar Degas, combined the new spontaneity of the Impressionist vision with a reliance on the formal academic principles of composition.

Young Woman Standing at a Virginal, *by Jan Vermeer of Delft (Dutch, 1632-75), is composed of a sequence of perfectly balanced rectangles. With his talent for unifying and ordering subtle harmonies of light and color, Vermeer transformed everyday domestic scenes into masterpieces of artistic composition.*

Although as apparently casual in composition as a snapshot, the design of Jockeys before the Race *(above) by Edgar Degas (French, 1834-1917) is, in fact, held together by the vertical line of the winning post that divides the canvas according to a centuries-old system of proportion called the Golden Section (p. 308).*

Below: detail from study of water lilies by Claude Monet (French, 1840-1926). Areas of tone, almost devoid of form, seem to anticipate abstract art. Unity in the picture depends upon the way in which Monet has harmonized tone areas and bathed them in an all-enveloping light, characteristic of much Impressionist painting.

Light

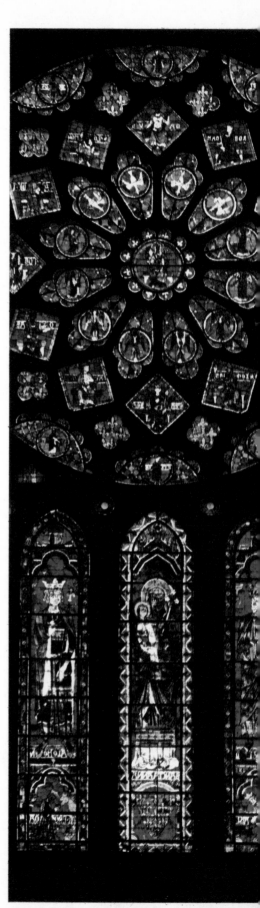

Since most painters are primarily concerned with visual experience, they have explored the effects of light on the world around them. Light influences the color of the things artists paint and the materials they use. The way light falls on objects helps us to recognize their shapes and forms. In order to reveal them and to give them an apparent three-dimensional solidity, painters try to imitate the effects of light by varying the *tones*—that is, the lightness or darkness—of their colors.

Besides telling us about the forms of objects, light can often tell us how surfaces will feel, even before we touch them. For example, a smooth sheet of glass throws back shiny reflections, while a piece of velvet absorbs and softens light. Painters try to show us not only the colors of such things as glass or velvet, but the way each reflects or absorbs light. This is one of the painter's methods of suggesting the textures of surfaces. Certain painters—particularly those specializing in flower studies and so-called still life (p. 46)—have achieved such a high degree of realism that their work is sometimes described as "illusionist," or by the French term *trompe l'œil*, which means "fool the eye."

There are also artists—the Impressionists (p. 44), for example—who have been less interested in reproducing the effects of light on forms than in showing the way it constantly changes the appearance and atmosphere of the world around us. They try to capture one of the constant variations in light so as to suggest a precise moment in

The mosaics on ceiling of fifth-century mausoleum of Galla Placidia (top) at Ravenna, Italy, rely for effect on light reflected from the walls and floor. But the 13th-century window (right) in Chartres cathedral, France, depends on exterior light to illuminate its rich coloring and complex design.

time. Landscapes are especially good subjects for such paintings. The time of day, the weather, and the season of the year all affect the quality of daylight—which, as it changes, constantly alters the appearance of an outdoor scene.

Like color, light and darkness may affect mood and feeling. By carefully contrasting areas of light and shade —a technique known as *chiaroscuro*—the painter can suggest such emotions as hope and energy (often connected with light) or fear and misery (often associated with darkness).

There are two picture-making techniques that do not reproduce light's effects but actually use light itself as a vital part of the picture. These are *mosaic* and *stained glass*. In mosaics, like those in the Italian mausoleum shown on the facing page, artists make images by embedding small pieces of colored or gilded glass and tile, called *tesserae*, in cement. When they place tesserae on walls and ceilings, artists set them at slightly varying angles so that they reflect a lively, flickering light down toward the viewers. In stained glass, artists make use of light that passes through the picture instead of being reflected from it. The best examples of stained glass are in the medieval churches and cathedrals of northern Europe, where the tall windows of such buildings are filled with representations of religious subjects. Viewed from the comparative darkness of church interiors, the whole character of these stained-glass images alters with every change of light.

Artists may use light and shade for a number of different purposes. In Annunciation *(above, left), a church fresco by Fra Angelico (Italian, 1387-1455), light illuminates equally every detail of the figures and buildings. But the Italian artist Michelangelo da Caravaggio (about 1565-1609) used light primarily for dramatic emphasis, contrasting deep background shadows with violent light effects, as in his painting of the legendary* Narcissus *(above). Three centuries later, French Impressionist painters sought to capture the shimmering of light reflected from surfaces of different color and texture. In a typical Impressionist painting,* La Grenouillère *(below) by Pierre Auguste Renoir (p. 44), even the darkest shadows contain areas of reflected light.*

Materials and methods

Painters can choose one of several methods to apply color, each of which gives a different effect. The best method is the one most clearly suited to a given painter's artistic aims and his way of working. Each technique is based on a particular *medium*—a combination of powdered colors called *pigments* with a liquid that fixes them to the painting surface as it dries.

Until the 15th century, *tempera* was the most widely used medium. It is made by mixing pigments with egg yolk thinned with water, which dries within minutes into a tough and opaque film of luminous, pure color, built up by short overlapping brush strokes. To enrich tempera colors, artists sometimes used transparent glazes made of pigments mixed with *oil*. But by the end of the 15th century, painters were using pigments in oil alone. They found that oil—which takes longer to dry—can be scraped away and reworked, can be laid on with broad strokes in textures varying from thin glazes to thick plaster-like mounds, and generally has an expressive flexibility that tempera lacks. Oil's adaptability and richness have caused it to remain the most widely popular of painters' media.

Among quick-drying media, *water color* is a favorite. English artists in particular have used it to capture delicate variations in landscape. Pigments are mixed with glue-like plant gums into dry cakes. Using water-moistened brushes, painters apply water color in thin, transparent "washes." They work quickly and spontaneously, for water colors cannot be altered easily and become dull and muddy if overworked. A large-scale variation of water color is *fresco* (Italian for "fresh"), in which colors mixed in water are painted directly on wet plaster, becoming a permanent part of the wall surface. Fresco painters must work quickly, too; they paint only one section at a time, guided by carefully planned preliminary drawings.

Pigments may also be compressed, with just enough gum to hold them together, into sticks called *pastels*, which are rubbed over paper to produce soft, bright tones with qualities suggestive of either painting or drawing, depending on how artists use them. Early in this century some painters began to stick pieces of paper, leather, cloth, wood, and other materials on their paintings in a new technique called *collage*—an attempt to add textures and meanings to paintings that none of the traditional media could give.

Effects entirely different from any of the usual painting media are obtained when artists want to make pictures that exist in more than one copy. The most important of these media are described on the opposite page.

Detail from The Tribute Money, *fresco by early 15th-century Italian painter Masaccio. Note how the flat technique of fresco painting makes it difficult for the artist to depict more than a limited variety of textures.*

This detail from Peace and War, *an allegoric painting by Flemish artist Peter Paul Rubens (1577-1640), shows how oil paint can be used to convey a wide range of textures and materials that "feel" different to the eye.*

Above: Earliest technique of printing pictures was from softwood blocks, such as those used in Cologne Bible (1478, left). Hardwood, adopted in the 18th century, made possible a wider range of tone and texture, as in engraving (right) by England's Thomas Bewick.

Left: study by John Constable (English, 1776-1837), whose water colors often depict the appearance of landscape under the influence of changing skies. Rapidly applied washes of semi-transparent water color give delicately expressive variations of tone.

ie etching technique allows artists to create de range of tonal effects, as in The Bullfight › Francisco de Goya (Spanish, 1746-1828). chers draw with a needle point on a wax-ated metal plate, then dip plate in acid that es into exposed metal. Resulting grooves e filled with ink that marks paper.

La Pâtisserie, *lithograph by Édouard Vuillard (French, 1868-1940). In lithography, design is drawn in greasy chalk on porous surface that is then wetted, so that when surface is inked over with roller only the chalked image holds the ink. Prints are made by pressing paper onto surface, then re-wetting and re-inking.*

The religious image

One of the earliest and most widespread motives for painting was to express religious ideas. People wanted artists to make pictures of events in the lives of their gods and holy men, and of scenes that symbolized religious teachings. Christianity, for example, inspired a great variety of themes and styles in Western painting until the 19th century, when changing attitudes toward religion caused painters to look elsewhere for ideas.

Most early Christian art was full of symbols. Because, for example, the Jews commonly used a lamb as a sacrificial animal, Christians used it as a symbol for Jesus Christ, whom they believed had sacrificed himself for their sins. Symbols were useful in religious art because they formed a pictorial language easily understood by believers; and they were also useful shortcuts for instructing converts.

Later, when Christianity became the chief religion of Europe, painters were often monks. As they tirelessly copied books by hand, they illustrated—or "illuminated"—them with small paintings. These contained symbols, but also showed the faces and figures of people. On the walls of churches, other artists made paintings and mosaics filled with figures that were stiff and two-dimensional, but still easily recognizable—and designed according to old traditions that were meaningful to everybody. Greek and Russian Christians made similar stylized pictures called *ikons*, but on small panels that could be carried about; they are still being made today and still being used by Orthodox Christians.

In most of Europe, however, artists gradually began to make paintings look more like "real" three-dimensional people and scenes. The first great painter in this more natural style was Giotto (about 1276-1337). He and other Italian painters of the time tried to give their figures life-like postures and facial expressions. By the 15th century, painters had begun to add background details drawn from everyday life. When anything was used as a symbol—for example, a lily, to represent purity—it was now painted realistically. This attention to life as it really was persisted most strongly in countries that revolted against the influence of the Roman Church. During the 16th and 17th centuries, artists in the newly Protestant northern European countries painted religious subjects in the same way that they painted scenes from contemporary life.

In Spain and Italy, where the people remained staunchly Roman Catholic, painters reacted against Protestantism by emphasizing the mystical aspects of faith. Through realistic pictures of martyrdom and physical suffering, they tried to portray the joy and spiritual exaltation that may result from sacrifice.

This early 15th-century icon, Our Lady of Vladimir, *by Russian monk Andrei Rublyov (1370-1430), creates an effect of deep serenity from stylized shapes.*

Scenes from the life of Buddha, such as that shown at the left, form a recurrent theme in much Indian art. This fresco is from a group dating back to 200 B.C. that lines the walls of cave monasteries in Ajanta, central India.

These three paintings show how widely Christian art has varied according to particular religious attitudes and national traditions. Typical of late medieval religious painting is the Crucifixion (*left*) by Matthias Grünewald (German, about 1470-1530). The agonized faces and gestures of onlookers are distorted to emphasize Christ's physical suffering. Grünewald's work—like medieval church drama—makes a direct assault both on the viewer's conscience and on his fear of death. The gentle character of the Crucifixion (*below left*), centerpiece of a church fresco by Italian painter Il Perugino (1446-1523), reflects the restraining influences of classical art. Here the crucifixion is seen as a symbol of reconciliation and hope for the future of mankind. The Martyrdom of St. Bartholomew (*below*), by Spanish-born José Ribera (1588-1652), makes its impact in a third—and very different—way. Ribera presents the scene realistically or as it might have been managed by an inventive stage director determined to emphasize every aspect of the saint's agony. He demands the devotion of the viewer by appealing not only to his religious feelings but also to his human experience of suffering.

Events and ideas

The emphasis that medieval artists used to place on religious themes was one instance of an important role that painting plays in every society: It expresses the important ideas and traditions of the society and records significant historical events. Thus Roman artists took their mythology as a subject, as Indian artists took Hindu or Buddhist mythology.

Painters have also been required to portray battle scenes or scenes of the discoveries of new lands. The people who commissioned such paintings wanted to celebrate the glory of powerful rulers and nations. As a result, the painter needed to be more than merely expert in the techniques of painting; he needed to know about history, literature, the classical art of Greece and Rome, and contemporary politics. In Italy in 1563 the first *academy of art* was founded by Giorgio Vasari (1511-74) so that painters could meet to study these matters and everything else that related to the creation of works of art.

Academies modeled on Vasari's were eventually established throughout Europe. They exercised a great degree of control over the work of artists until quite recently. But in the 19th century many painters began to rebel against what they considered the rigid and restrictive academy conventions. Today fewer artists than in the past tackle large social themes. Those who do so usually express personal feelings rather than attitudes that represent an official ideological or patriotic point of view. In fact, the camera has largely taken over historical and political documentation of this kind.

In Raft of the Medusa (below), *the 19th-century French painter Théodore Géricault depicted a recent shipwreck that had roused great public feeling, boldly treating it on a scale previously reserved for scenes from myth and history. Spanish-born Pablo Picasso commemorated the mass slaughter of civilians during Spanish Civil War in* Guernica (1937). *Distorted figures (as in detail, right) create an effect of suffering and overwhelming horror.*

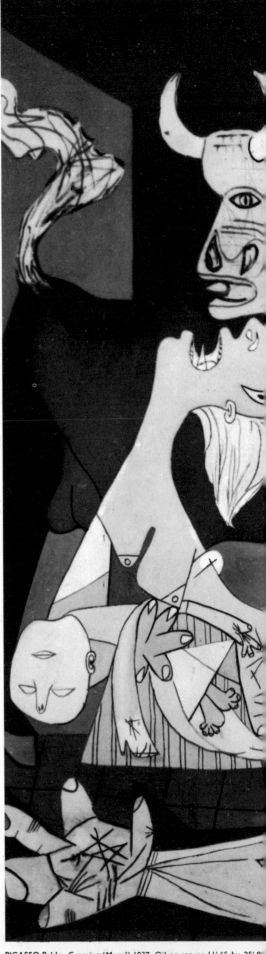

PICASSO Pablo. *Guernica* (Mural) 1937. Oil on canvas 11' 6" by 25' 8", extended loan from the artist to The Museum of Modern Art, New Y

In The School of Athens (*detail, above*), *one of the frescoes painted in the Vatican between 1509 and 1512 by Raphael, the great philosophers of antiquity are assembled to suggest the range of human intellect.*

By the way in which Spanish painter Diego Velázquez (1599-1660) recorded an event of his own day, the surrender at Breda in 1625 of the Dutch forces to the victorious Spaniards, he created a lasting symbol of peacemaking.

The nude

In the 15th century, Renaissance respect for the cultures of ancient Greece and Rome reawakened interest in the nude human figure as a subject for painting. For the next 400 years the nude inspired nearly all artists, and the study of human anatomy and practice in drawing the nude model were basic to every painter's training. Artists regarded the body as central to any study of natural forms, for its endless variety of gesture, movement, bearing and facial expression reflect all possible subtleties of thought and feeling.

But the Greeks—and the Romans who copied them—represented the body as something more than a mirror of human emotion and intelligence; in their art the body was *idealized*. Each part of the body was arranged in an ideally perfect harmony with every other. The Greeks made physical beauty a symbol of moral and spiritual perfection. They gave concrete expression in their art to a view summed up by the philosopher Aristotle: "Art completes what nature cannot bring to a finish. The artist gives us knowledge of nature's unrealized ends." This idea motivated the greatest Renaissance painters, notably, in Italy, Raphael (Raffaello Santi, 1483-1520), Leonardo da Vinci (p. 42), and Michelangelo (p. 40). They instinctively grasped the true meanings behind classic form. Lesser artists tried to achieve classic perfection by using standardized proportions based on what they considered the "perfect" geometric forms of the square and the circle, or on proportions derived from the dimensions of the head in relation to the whole body.

Interest in the classic nude extended beyond the Renaissance through the 17th century, when such painters as France's Nicolas Poussin (1594-1665) incorporated unclothed or partly draped figures into the composition of pictures—usually mythological or biblical in subject—as exercises in pure classic form. Later the French painter Jean Dominique Ingres (1780-1867) made careful studies of the classic nude—as most 19th-century artists did—but he was also influenced by another way of painting that

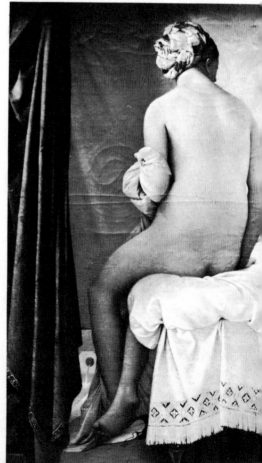

Artists have had many different attitudes toward the subject of the unclothed human figure. In Susannah and the Elders *(detail above), 17th-century Dutch painter Rembrandt van Rijn sought to fix the likeness of a particular woman, and created a figure alive with the qualities of a real human being. Inspired by the classical art of Greece and Rome, Ingres aimed to transform nude into an image of ideal beauty, as in* La Grande Baigneuse *(right).*

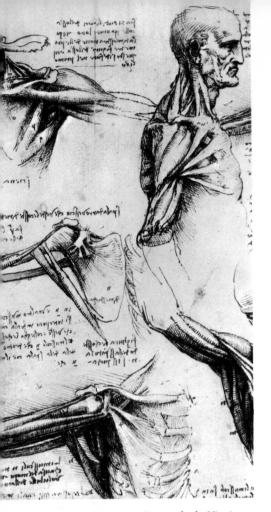

...fteenth-century Italian artist Leonardo da Vinci con-...ibuted greatly to scientific research of Renaissance ...holars into the structure of the human body as well ... of the natural world. The sketches in Leonardo's ...otebooks display meticulous accuracy of observation. ...mong Leonardo's hundreds of anatomical drawings ... the above study of the positions of the neck and ...oulder muscles in the human body.

The Young Ladies of Avignon, by Picasso. Many 20th-century painters give little importance to scientific accuracy in portraying the human body. Instead, they often use it as a symbol for mankind. In this painting (1907) Picasso treats nudes neither as embodiments of ideal beauty nor as individuals. Twisted figures and mask-like faces serve as starting point for a design with violent emotional impact. Painting was partly inspired by primitive African art.

had arisen in the 16th century among Venetian painters. Titian (p. 44) and others subordinated the cool, sculptural qualities of ideal form to the appeal of flesh textures and color. Closer to our own times, France's Auguste Renoir (1841-1919) painted nudes in this sensuous fashion. By Renoir's time, painters seldom felt the need to rely on traditional myths and love stories to justify the nude as a subject.

Since the 17th century, many painters, in fact, had been interested in portraying the body as forthrightly as possible. They wanted to show the qualities that make human bodies individual. Rembrandt (p. 42) shocked contemporary opinion in 1631 with an etching, supposedly of the goddess Diana, but clearly based on an unidealized, shapeless female model. Rembrandt's way of portraying the nude was in some respects related to northern attitudes to the body. Medieval art in the north had included only a few naked figures, generally in scenes of the Fall of Adam and Eve or of the Last Judgment; and often these nudes seemed clearly ashamed of their bodies. The tardy acceptance by northern Europe of Renaissance thought isolated many artists from the classic tradition of the idealized nude, though Rubens (p. 44) introduced the sensuous qualities derived from Venetian painting into Flemish art in the 17th century.

In the 17th-century art of Italy and Spain, painters distorted the body not to indicate realistic human suffering but rather to suggest intense emotional and spiritual conflict. In some paintings of the Spanish artist Domenico Teotocopulo (about 1548-about 1614), born in Crete and called El Greco, human figures are elongated almost as if they were flames licking up toward heaven. In the 20th century another Spanish painter, Pablo Picasso (born 1881), has sometimes distorted the body to underline the suffering men have gone through in modern times. Both painters were less concerned with showing individuals than, like the Greeks, with using the human body to symbolize universal values.

The portrait

People have always considered a man's face to be the most valuable guide to his character. From our earliest childhood we learn to "read" the meanings that lie behind the constantly changing facial expressions of those around us. It is perhaps surprising, therefore, that portraiture—the pictorial representation of individuals—should have taken so long to become an accepted branch of Western painting.

Portrait making flourished in ancient Egypt and in Roman times, chiefly in the form of sculpture, or in painted funeral portraits placed in tombs. The heads of kings and other great figures were often reproduced on coins and medals. In post-Roman Europe, however, it was not until the middle of the 15th century that painted portraits of living people began to appear in any number. Like biography and autobiography (pp. 244, 246), portrait painting was a characteristic art of the Renaissance—for it was a period during which people became increasingly aware that everyone is an individual being with a distinct appearance and personality. By the 17th century many artists had taken to portrait painting as a full-time profession.

It has remained a profitable one throughout the succeeding centuries—but less profitable for most painters ever since the development of photography in the middle of the 19th century made it possible to obtain satisfactory

Above: Jean le Bon of France, painted about 1360 by an unknown Burgundian artist. Profiles give us a less intimate view of the sitter, but they offer the simplest means of capturing an individual likeness. Flemish painter Jan van Eyck (about 1370-1440) created a much closer contact between subject and spectator in A Man with a Turban (below). *In his idealized portrait of Napoleon crossing the Alps (below, right), Jacques Louis David (French, 1748-1825) aimed chiefly to suggest the courage and heroism of a national leader.*

portraits cheaply. For this reason, the demand for painted portraits has decreased, and many artists have never undertaken professional portraiture at all. By 1900, in fact, the great period of portrait painting was virtually over.

Before then, artists had approached the problems of this type of painting in many different ways. Some, such as Germany's Hans Holbein (about 1497-1543), painted objective and carefully observed studies of people's physical features. Others sought to suggest something more about their subjects' temperaments and characters. They did so by emphasizing or distorting certain postures or facial expressions. Or they showed the subject dressed in characteristic clothing, surrounded by other possessions that indicated his profession or special interests.

Sometimes painters wanted—or were hired—to show people simply as private individuals, in ordinary situations and attitudes. Such domestic portraiture, as typified by the paintings of Gerard Ter Borch (1617-81), was especially popular in Holland during the 17th century. In the next century in England, where such pictures were known as "conversation pieces," German-born Johann Zoffany (1733-1810) was one of the leading exponents of this type of group portrait.

More frequently, however, portraits were required to commemorate a person's public, rather than his private, personality—that is, to display his social rank and importance. Such pictures often dignified and flattered the subjects by showing them in the costumes of famous historical or legendary figures. Portraits were also used to mark notable occasions in people's lives. There are many marriage portraits, for instance, such as the *Arnolfini Marriage Group*, painted by the Flemish artist Jan van Eyck (about 1370-about 1440).

Most artists at some time or other have painted portraits of themselves. Some painters—Rembrandt (p. 42), van Gogh (p. 44), and France's Paul Cézanne (1839-1906), for instance—did so many times. These painters found in their own faces a ready and inexhaustible subject for the penetrating analysis of character that they and others tried to reveal in the faces of all their subjects.

In his portrait of Ferdinand VII (detail above), Spanish painter Goya (1746-1828) revealed the ordinary man beneath the trappings of royalty. Flemish artist Frans Hals (about 1580-1666) captured the fleeting expression of his sitter Hille Bobbe (below, left) with rapid brush strokes. Portrait of Émile Zola (detail below, center) by French Impressionist Édouard Manet (1832-83) seems to catch the novelist unaware in a moment of relaxation. Like many self-portraits, that (below, right) by Austria's Oskar Kokoschka (born 1886) possesses extraordinary force and concentration.

The painter and everyday life

Between the 15th and 17th centuries artists habitually portrayed traditional religious subjects in contemporary clothes and surroundings (p. 54). We have seen, too, how Rembrandt (p. 56) treated the nude figure and a mythological subject in this everyday manner—and both in the same painting. By the 17th century, when middle-class people began commissioning artists to paint pictures for them, painters began simply to show scenes from daily life without any religious or historical significance. It was in Holland especially that this kind of painting—sometimes called *genre* painting—flourished. The middle classes there were prosperous, and the Protestant Churches no longer employed artists to the extent that the Church and nobility of Catholic countries did. In Spain and Italy, for example, genre painting did not become widely popular for another century. Genre paintings usually included figures; but sometimes artists portrayed only objects or the interiors of rooms.

While Dutch painters showed scenes of daily life in a straightforward manner, some English painters of the 18th century, such as William Hogarth (1697-1764) and Thomas Rowlandson (1756-1827), ridiculed the behavior of society by exaggerating its faults. In the 19th century the French Impressionist painters again painted ordinary people, but they did not attempt to make fun of them. Renoir (p. 56), for example, painted scenes of Parisians in their gardens, in restaurants, public parks, or at home. Today many painters, such as Ben Shahn (born 1898) in the United States, or Diego Rivera (1886-1957) in Mexico, have shown a continuing interest in painting scenes that suggest the particular quality of daily life in their countries.

A Woman and her Maid in a Courtyard, by 17th-century Dutch painter Pieter de Hooch. Such small domestic pictures were painted for a prosperous middle class that preferred scenes from everyday life to the grandeurs of historical or mythological themes.

Gustave Courbet (French, 1819-77) invested scenes from peasant life with the grandeur and nobility of religious or historical subjects. His Burial at Ornans *(1850), a huge painting with over forty life-size figures, caused a sensation when it was first exhibited publicly.*

With biting satire, England's William Hogarth attacked the evils of 18th-century society and of human behavior in general. Shortly after the Marriage (*left*) is second in the series Marriage à la Mode, *in which Hogarth condemns practice of arranging marriages solely on basis of rank and wealth. The idea of moralizing on a contemporary theme in such picture stories was entirely new. Hogarth's series pictures—particularly* The Rake's Progress—*won great popularity in the form of engravings.*

White Rain at Shono, *a print by Ando Hiroshige (Japanese, 1797-1858). Japanese artists began to establish a tradition of social realism in art in the early 18th century. Many adopted the medium of the colored woodcut; and they chose for their subjects portraits of popular actors and actresses, events from Japan's history, and scenes from peasant life. Such prints won a wide audience, and those that reached Europe had a marked influence on late 19th-century painting, especially in France.*

Fernand Léger (*French, 1881-1955*) *was one of the few outstanding painters of recent times to have found his themes in the daily life of ordinary people, both at work and at play (as in* The Leisure Pastimes, *left*). *Léger's work was strongly influenced by the geometric forms and metallic surfaces of machinery. Because he was also interested in the effects of industry upon society, Léger depicted people in a generalized way—as robot-like figures rather than as individual human beings.*

Landscape

When painters in the 17th century began to find their subjects in the world about them, many took to painting landscapes. The changing seasons with their variations in weather and light could all be drawn on for an expression of the painter's own ideas and emotions. For centuries, painters in China and Japan had been sensitive to the beauty of landscape, which always dominated their pictures; but, as with genre painting (p. 60), it was in Holland that European painters first began to devote much attention to landscapes for their own sake—though carefully detailed landscapes had appeared in the backgrounds of medieval book illustrations as well as in some 15th- and 16th-century religious pictures.

It was such artists as the Dutch Jacob van Ruisdael (about 1628-82) who first specialized in landscape subjects. Since his time, artists in many countries have painted landscapes—and for a variety of reasons. Some have been interested only in showing familiar picturesque places; others in painting places with historical or literary associations. Still others have wanted to show the variety of life in the countryside, and to capture the changing seasons and weather on canvas. Perhaps most importantly, many artists have found that the moods of the landscape suggest personal emotions. One of England's greatest landscape painters, John Constable (1776-1837), hinted at this when he said that "painting is another word for feeling."

By the 15th century many artists were beginning to include a detailed landscape in their religious pictures. But human figures continued to dominate the design, as in the detail (above) from Madonna with Chancellor Rollin by Flemish painter Jan van Eyck.

Flemish artist Pieter Brueghel the Elder (about 1520-69) painted a series of landscapes that portrayed the characteristics of various seasons and formed the natural setting for such richly detailed studies of peasant life as Winter, Hunters in the Snow (above).

Giorgione da Castelfranco (Italian, about 1478-1511) is often regarded as one of the founders of modern painting. The thunderous landscape of The Tempest (left) is far more than a setting for figures; it evokes a mysterious world of its own.

Seeking to recapture the spirit of classical Greece and Rome, French-born *Claude Lorrain* (1600-82) painted luminous landscapes such as Aeneas at Delos. *The design of the buildings and the costumes of the people serve to heighten the sense of the past. Through subtle gradations of tone, Claude caught the atmosphere of different times of day and seasons. So popular was his work that natural scenery was often judged by its resemblance to his art.*

England's J. M. W. Turner (1775-1851) modeled many of his early landscapes on those of Claude Lorrain. He used landscapes not only as a setting for dramatic events, but also as an indirect yet powerful means of expressing human feelings. In many of his oil paintings he matched the pale, brilliant effects of water color. Full of wind and light, his works vary in mood from benign calm to the stormy passion of The Shipwreck.

Le Lac d'Annecy, *by Paul Cézanne (French, 1839-1906). In portraying his native Provence, Cézanne sought to capture every aspect of the landscape—the mass and weight of rock, spaciousness of land and lakes, and brilliance of light and color. Unlike most other French painters of the period, Cézanne worked slowly, making deep and subtle analyses of the forms of natural objects, which he organized into a single pictorial unit.*

The painter as observer

Since most painters find their inspiration in the world around them, it is natural that they should observe it closely. In some ways they know more about nature than scientists do; through constantly looking at people and the way they act, the artist often reaches as profound an understanding of human behavior and thought as the philosopher or psychologist does. Most painters express this knowledge intuitively—that is, without reasoning it out—through paintings instead of scientific or philosophical writings. In prehistoric times, it was perhaps *only* painters who could throw much light on the workings of nature. The men who painted early cave pictures (p. 22) had a remarkably clear idea of how animals' bodies were constructed and how they moved. In the Middle Ages the accuracy with which painters showed animals and men was often closer to truth than contemporary theories about physiology.

During the Renaissance, when men began to inquire into nature with great precision and to do scientific experiments, many artists also found fascination in scientific research. They wanted to know how things worked, not just how they *appeared* to work. One aspect of mathematics that they found important concerned perspective (p. 38). They wanted to know how they could actually measure the way objects apparently receded into space and became "smaller." Only then could they convincingly produce an illusion of three dimensions. In Italy, such artists as Paolo Uccello (1397-1475) and Piero della Francesca (about 1420-92) did some pioneer work on this kind of mathematics.

Some artists of the Renaissance investigated nearly all branches of the sciences. The best known example of such a "universal man" is Leonardo da Vinci (p. 42). Some of his finest drawings were sketches he made for scientific reasons. In Germany, Albrecht Dürer (1471-1528), like da Vinci, recorded his observations in sketchbooks full of drawings that helped him analyze the workings of whatever he saw. His technical interests led him to perfect methods of wood and copper engraving (p. 50), and his artistic achievements in these media have not been surpassed.

An 18th-century artist whose scientific observations influenced his painting was England's George Stubbs (1724-1806). His researches in anatomy resulted in detailed and accurate paintings of animals. Another Englishman, John Constable (p. 62), studied clouds and weather as extensively as any meteorologist, with the result that the skies in his landscape paintings are impressively true to nature. In the 19th century, Impressionist painters were much influenced by contemporary

Tall Grasses, *by Albrecht Dürer. Its botanically accurate detail combines scientific observation with powerful artistic vision.*

Noted for his meticulously accurate paintings of animals, English painter George Stubbs was a skilled anatomist. Drawing here is from his book The Anatomy of the Horse.

researches into the physical nature of light and color.

Today, painters are seldom scientists; but they remain aware of scientific advances, and especially of the effect the machine has on daily life. As far back as 1907, influenced by Cézanne's advice to artists to look for geometrical structures in nature, painters calling themselves *Cubists*—among whom were Pablo Picasso (p. 56) and France's Georges Braque (1882-1963)—painted several simplified views of an object superimposed on top of one another (p. 38). These paintings experimented with analyzing and recording the basic structures of objects. At about the same time, the short-lived *Futurist* school of painting tried to show the actual movements of machinery. Prominent among painters who continued to observe the machine and incorporate its forms into their paintings was Fernand Léger (1881-1955). He combined geometrical Cubist effects with such machine shapes as cogwheels and pistons (p. 61).

Painters have also been influenced by psychologists' researches into the unconscious mind. This is most obvious in the work of *Surrealist* painters—such as Spain's Joan Miró (born 1893) and Salvador Dali (born 1904) and Italy's Giorgio di Chirico (born 1888)—who tend to place familiar objects in fantastic, dreamlike relationships. In later styles, like so-called *Action* painting (exemplified by the spattering and dribbling techniques of the American Jackson Pollock [1912-56]), artists have deliberately given free rein to the subconscious mind and have created paintings almost automatically.

Nineteenth-century French artist Théodore Géricault painted a penetrating and sympathetic study of a mad woman in a Parisian mental hospital (above). When his English contemporary John Constable made studies of changing cloud forms such as that below, he noted wind direction and time of day.

Painting without an object

The free arrangements of form and color that we see in many galleries and museums today are often vaguely called *abstract*, but they are perhaps better classified as *non-figurative* or *non-objective* paintings. Their creators do not "abstract" forms from nature; non-objective artists such as Jackson Pollock and other Action painters (p. 64) create colored splashes on canvas for their own beauty and emotional impact; they paint without reference to natural forms. Other artists may select forms, colors, and textures from the things they observe and arrange them in paintings that do not represent recognizable objects. This latter kind of painting can rightly be called "abstract," and it has been done since men first decorated pottery with simplified designs derived originally from human and animal forms. Today many artists paint abstractions not as decoration but as a way of bypassing representational and storytelling subject-matter in order to deal directly with color and form.

Modernists of both the above types can be called *non-representational* painters. Whatever their style, it is probably a logical outgrowth of late 19th-century Impressionist experiments with pure color. As we have seen, Cézanne was influenced by the Impressionists but added an emphasis on essential geometrical forms, which in turn inspired the Cubists (p. 64). Cubist art influenced a group of artists in Germany known as *Der Blaue Reiter*. Most important among them was Russian-born Vasili Kandinski (1866-1944), many of whose paintings were much like later non-objective experiments.

In Russia just before the 1917 revolution, artists such as Kazimir Malevich (1878-1935) and Vladimir Tatlin (1885-1956) initiated movements called *Suprematism* and *Constructivism*, which relied almost entirely on geometric forms, simple colors, and scientific technology. (Constructivist works actually included wire, plastics, metal, and even moving parts.) In Holland at about the same time certain Dutch artists, called the *De Stijl* group after a magazine that promoted their theories, restricted painted forms to disciplined geometrical shapes and the primary colors. Their influence spread to architecture and to advertising art. The best-known member of this group was Pieter Mondriaan (1872-1944).

The originators of most modern schools of painting often had personal, political, or social aims that they thought their painting styles symbolized. The Constructivists, for example, were concerned with the planning of a new society along scientific lines. The De Stijl group wanted to harmonize all the arts and thereby advance social harmony. The intuitive Action painters wanted to free the artist from the dictates of conscious reason.

Pieter Mondriaan evolved a disciplined geometric style by using only rectangular shapes and a restricted range of colors. Such self-imposed limitations were intended as a means of evoking mood and creating effect solely by means of the simplest pictorial elements—as in Victory Boogie Woogie (above).

The French painter Robert Delaunay (1885-1941) sought to express the energy and vitality of life and nature through a dramatic pictorial "language" of contrasting pure colors, often arranged in circles and radiating forms, as in Simultaneous Composition, the Sun Disks, *shown below.*

Collection, The Museum of Modern Art, New York; Mrs. Simon Guggenheim Fund.

Composition 8, No. 260, *by one of* Der Blaue Reiter *group, Vasili Kandinski. He believed art should express man's spiritual insight rather than his knowledge of the physical world. He aimed to discard all subject matter from his paintings, and to evolve a new language of form and color that should be almost as abstract as the language of music. Kandinski trained in Munich and taught in Germany from 1922 to 1933. His ideas, explained in the pamphlet* The Art of Spiritual Harmony, *have greatly influenced modern art.*

Outstanding among European artists of our own time is Joan Miró (Spanish, born 1893), who took part in the first Surrealist exhibition in Paris (1925). Influenced by Freud's theories of psychoanalysis, Surrealist painters aimed to grasp elements in the unconscious mind and to express them in terms of form and color. Only distantly related to natural objects, the forms in Miró's Morning Dew in the Moonlight *are symbols that make a strange, dreamlike impact. Such symbolism has been the chosen means of expression of many modern artists.*

Among the most controversial works of recent years are the "action paintings" of America's Jackson Pollock (1912-56). Pollock and other artists of the so-called New York school sought to bypass all previous techniques of pictorial composition. Works like No. 23, 1948 *were produced by throwing and dribbling paint from cans onto a panel or canvas laid on the floor. This method continues to attract artists who want to dispense with traditional painting techniques and to express their emotions in a direct and spontaneous way.*

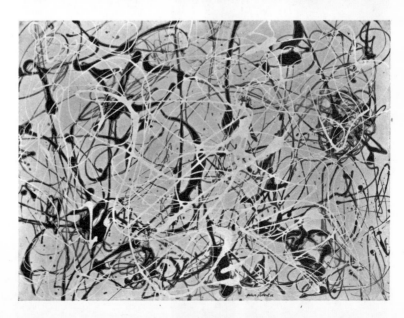

The painter and his patrons

Today most successful creative artists are self-employed; that is, they seldom work on direct commissions from either public or private *patrons*—such as town councils, religious bodies, or wealthy individuals—who used to support, or *patronize*, a large share of a painter's work. Some modern painters do get commissions from state or religious groups, or from large business corporations; but the bulk of their earnings comes from private buyers who purchase finished works exhibited for sale.

The change in the make-up of the artist's patronage has had an effect on his methods. Until the middle of the 19th century, painters were supported by important patrons and what they painted conformed to the ideas of society at large, since such works were made to order. Successful painters were thus much more integrated in their societies than they are today.

In the earliest, prehistoric periods of art, people probably regarded picture makers as men with no unusual social status or responsibility, but simply as men possessing socially useful skills. In historic times, until the end of the Middle Ages, painters were regarded as a special group responsible for preserving their skills and passing them carefully on to succeeding generations. They were craftsmen, in much the same way as weavers or carpenters. Medieval painters belonged to associations of artisans hired to work in groups on such projects as the decoration of cathedrals. By the 14th century, former members of these groups—or *lodges*—were joining the freer *guilds*, where they banded together to protect their own interests but took individual commissions for paintings from the nobility and newly rich middle classes. They were free now to work by themselves instead of in teams, and many gained great reputations both in their own countries and

Left: view of frescoes in the Scrovegni Chapel, Padua, painted by the early Renaissance artist Giotto (about 1276-1337). Before the 19th century the work of most painters was commissioned for a specific social—òften religious—purpose. In our own time, an artist is more likely to have his work shown to the public in an art gallery, or in an exhibition such as that below.

Corner of the Artist's Studio, *by Eugène Delacroix (French, 1798-1863), one of the leaders of the Romantic school. Since the early 19th century, the natural center of a painter's activity has been his own studio. And his work is usually the expression of a private, rather than a public, purpose.*

internationally. Such widespread fame enabled many artists to have more say in their choice of subject matter and to demand high prices for their work.

By the middle of the 16th century, when the Renaissance was well advanced, artists no longer were content to remain in the guilds merely to acquire technical skills as apprentices in a master's workshop. The professional usefulness of the guilds declined as painters began to study at the new academies of art (p. 54). There they obtained the wide-ranging knowledge of history, literature, and philosophy that put them on an equal intellectual footing with their Renaissance patrons. The independent and highly personal attitudes that we today find almost synonymous with the profession of the artist began to appear at this time. For example, in the 16th century the almost superhuman artistic achievements of Michelangelo (p. 40), who was notably independent of the people who hired him, helped to establish the popular idea that artists were somehow different from ordinary men. A century later, the young Rembrandt (p. 42) accepted scores of commissions from town councils and private citizens. But as he grew older he became increasingly independent of his patrons—and increasingly unwilling to paint or to live as they wanted him to.

During the 18th and early 19th centuries ideas about the purpose of art and the role of the artist were deeply affected by romanticism. According to the romantic theory, personal instinct and feeling should guide the artist to original ways of expressing himself. Since painters were no longer responsible to Church or state patrons, many of them eagerly adopted the romantic ideal. Near the end of the 19th century, van Gogh (p. 44), Cézanne (p. 58), and Gauguin (p. 42) typified the new popular conception of the struggling, eccentric, isolated painter.

Artists remained at a distance from their public, for people seldom saw their work except in exhibitions organized by art dealers to help painters sell their pictures. The new profession of the art critic came into existence. In books and newspapers, critics interpreted painting and artists' ideas to the public, who were often uncertain or hostile to artists cut off from society. Art criticism, the organization of exhibitions in museums as well as in dealers' galleries, the offering of prizes for outstanding paintings, and the financial support of both government and private foundations have lately been of much assistance to struggling painters. For the most part, though, they remain isolated from the rest of society. They pursue new styles, experiment with new methods, and formulate personal artistic aims that often seem utterly out of step with accepted conventions.

Self-portrait by 17th-century Flemish painter Peter Paul Rubens. In a period when an outstanding artist was accorded great honor and international respect, he became influential in diplomacy and public affairs.

69

Chapter 3

Sculpture

Exercising what men regarded for centuries as an almost divine creative power, the sculptor turns his materials into objects that seem to have lives of their own. From earliest times, that living quality has made sculpture the target of conquering armies and enthusiastic followers of new religions who wanted to destroy or deface the statues of old leaders and gods.

But now we tend to think of sculptures as art objects rather than living presences. The realistic colors, the gilt, precious stones, and even clothes that embellished statues until the 16th century have disappeared. Nevertheless, the durability of the materials underneath has helped preserve for us one of the fullest visual records of past ages. We have, for example, sculptures of the Greeks and Romans in comparative abundance, though their paintings have mostly disappeared.

In modern times, sculptors have emphasized the textures of wood, clay, stone, and metal. This stress on essentials has helped underline another important aspect of sculpture's fascination. Auguste Rodin, one of the greatest of modern sculptors, put it accurately if somewhat inelegantly when he defined sculpture as the art of the "hole and the lump."

What he meant was that sculpture more than any art except architecture is concerned with solid form (the "lump") and its relationship to space (the "hole"). Sculpture may not only be looked at, touched, and experienced in a variety of lights and environments; it also "inhabits" space as we do; in brief, we could say that it lives with us. This chapter shows how the aliveness of sculpture has determined both the sculptor's use of his materials and the uses he has made of sculpture.

Since ancient times, sculpture has provided man with a means of giving form and substance to his beliefs and ideas. From a variety of materials—wood, clay, metal, and stone—he has created images of gods, human figures, and abstract forms. In this detail from The Battle of the Centaurs *(1492) by Italian sculptor Michelangelo, a whole range of human experience and emotion is expressed through the features, gestures, and grouping of the figures; the work seems to possess a personality of its own.*

Images in space

A power that belongs uniquely to the sculptor is his ability to make a work of art that seems to possess a personality, an identity—even a separate life—of its own. A statue inhabits the three-dimensional world in a way that paintings or films or photographs cannot. This special quality of free-standing sculptured figures helps explain the Greek legend of the sculptor Pygmalion, who made a statue of a woman so beautiful that he fell in love with her. His love moved Venus to bring the statue to life.

The feeling that sculptured images have some kind of powerful vitality probably inspired prehistoric men to carve the first examples of free-standing sculpture we know of: amulets or talismans—portable charms with magical powers. Men believed—as many primitive peoples do today—that such charms could give them protection or special powers, or could make sure that they would have children.

In more recent times, small free-standing sculptures continue to play "protective" roles. The portable crucifix is a familiar Christian example, and small figures of Buddha are carried by many Chinese and Indians. Christians point out carefully that the crucifix is a *reminder* of a person (Jesus Christ), an event (the crucifixion), and an idea (the redemption), and has no magical power of its own. But such small-scale sculptures do have a kind of power derived from their significance as representations of certain ideas or gods. Their three-dimensional independence of other objects and their small size enable people to live in intimate contact with them.

The vital quality of sculpture has inspired sculptors to make images to protect the souls of the dead. The most famous examples are the figures found in Egyptian tombs. Sculpture has also been used to commemorate great men and heroes. Symbolic poses, clothing, and other objects suggest personal attributes. One symbol, used since the time of the ancient Greeks and Romans, is the horse. The figures in such equestrian statues receive added dignity from their commanding position astride horses.

Two famous Renaissance equestrian statues, sources of inspiration to sculptors ever since, are the memorial to the

This 5000-year-old marble statuette from the Greek islands (above, left) was probably believed to possess the power of granting fertility. The limestone Mayan figure above, found in the city of Chichén-Itzá (between 948 and 1697 A.D.), represents the rain spirit Chac Mool, who holds a cup ready to receive the hearts of sacrificial victims.

Left: the dominating statue of Bartolommeo Colleoni—general in chief of the Venetian armies, and a popular hero—that was set up in 1496 in a public open space. Modeled by Florentine sculptor Andrea del Verrocchio, it was cast by Alessandro Leopardi of Venice.

soldier Gattamelata in Padua, made around 1446 by Donato Bardi, called Donatello (about 1386-1466), and the Colleoni statue in Venice, of about fifty years later, by Andrea del Verrocchio (1435-88). These famous free-standing sculptures form the focal points for the buildings and squares that surround them. Before the 17th century, free-standing sculptures were usually designed to face the spectator from a single viewpoint, most often from a niche or pedestal so situated that one had to approach the statue on its own terms. This kind of siting kept viewers at an emotional as well as physical distance, and despite the impression of vitality and life, a certain detached impressiveness—what we often call a monumental quality—was conveyed.

But with the coming of the Baroque period in the 17th century, the portrayal of realism and strong emotion became important, the spectator was no longer kept at a distance, and sculpture was placed as a unifying center of interest in public squares, parks, and gardens, where the spectator could walk around statues, viewing them from all angles. An outstanding modern example of such free-standing realism is *The Burghers of Calais*, by the Frenchman Auguste Rodin (1840-1917). Each of the six figures —representing hostages delivered up to English invaders in 1347—faces a different direction. We feel as we look that we could move among them; we feel caught up in the drama of these men. Rodin has arranged their posture, their gestures, and especially their spatial relationships to one another so as to emphasize their tragic heroism.

Most modern sculptors have preferred to make free-standing works because in them they can employ to the full the three-dimensional character of sculpture. Standing free, clear, each with its personal identity, they symbolize the freedom and independence the modern artist claims for himself.

Right: This bust of the 18th-century French writer Voltaire, by French sculptor Jean Antoine Houdon (1741-1828), captures all the famous satirist's keen observation and mordant wit. Such portrait sculptures seem to perpetuate much of the personality of the subject.

Carving

When an artist *carves*, he cuts away the parts of his raw material that are not to form the finished work and, gradually, the sculptured image emerges. Wood is especially suited to the carver's methods—but it is perishable; prehistoric wood sculptures have not survived. We do, however, have carvings made of easily worked bone and ivory. There are prehistoric limestone carvings, too.

The sculptors of the great Assyrian and Egyptian civilizations used relatively soft sandstone or extremely hard granite and basalt. In Greece, in about the sixth century B.C., sculptors began to exploit marble, perhaps the most familiar of all carving materials. It is strong, and not too difficult to work, and has a beautiful color and texture.

We sometimes forget, however, that in ancient times, as well as in the Middle Ages, carvings were almost always painted—and even decorated with metal ornaments and precious stones. The visual quality of the sculptor's basic raw material was considered of little importance. What was important was the effective bringing to life of a person or story, which realistic decoration served to strengthen. It is only in relatively recent times that Western sculptors have tried to emphasize such natural qualities as the "stoniness" of stone, or the color and grain of a particular wood.

How do sculptors work when they carve? In much the

This 19th-century figure from Hawaii, carved from a cylindrical tree trunk, represents the war god Kukailimoku ("Ku the Man-eater"). Softness of wood allowed the carving of elaborate details. The head of an Egyptian prince (below), made in Giza about 2840-2680 B.C., was carved out of hard limestone. Although subtle in form, projecting details are simplified and reduced to a minimum.

Tilman Riemenschneider (about 1460-1531)—greatest of German woodcarvers— made this figure of an angel for an altar in Munich. Details of such figures were often carved from separate pieces of wood and joined together with wooden pegs.

same manner now as sculptors did thousands of years ago. The earliest techniques involved chipping away at a material with sharp-edged stones that were a little harder than the surfaces they cut. After the Greeks, metal chisels and files were common, but the technique of cutting away material to "liberate" the form was still the same.

Sculptors often make wood carvings of separate pieces glued together or jointed with metal fastenings. Stone and marble carvings are usually made from single blocks of material. Their forms tend to be simpler and more compact than wood carvings because unsupported projections like arms or fingers are brittle and liable to break off. But this did not prevent many Roman and Renaissance sculptors from attempting immensely complicated forms. A notable example from the Baroque period is the emotional work of Giovanni Lorenzo Bernini (1598-1680).

Despite achievements like Bernini's, carving as a technique is particularly associated with monumental sculpture—Egyptian, Greek, Gothic, Aztec, for instance—for the carver's hard and inflexible materials limit the spontaneous expression of emotion. Michelangelo felt carving *was* sculpture, and said that modeling (p. 76) —as used by sculptors interested in expressing emotional and physical energy—was more like painting because it evoked the moods and actions of a moment.

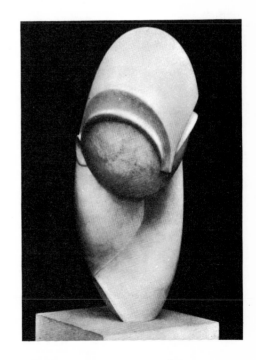

Modern Romanian sculptor Constantin Brancusi (1876-1957) created simplified forms that revealed the basic qualities of his material—as in this marble, one of his studies of Mlle. Pogany.

Modeling

Michelangelo likened modeling to painting because a
sculptor *builds* an image somewhat as a painter does, by
adding layer after layer of a material such as clay or wax.
Taking advantage of modeling's special quality of flexibility, the sculptor can rework and manipulate his
materials to get just the effect he wants.

Modeling is a technique especially suited to expressing
personal feelings and physical movement. The soft and
pliable nature of modeling materials allows sculptors to
create shapes much more directly and spontaneously
than is possible in carving. Modeling enables a sculptor
to construct forms of nearly any dimensions he chooses.
To do this, however, he needs a framework. Usually, this
is of wood or metal; sculptors call it an *armature*. They
press clay or wax onto this armature, building outward
from it until they have produced forms that satisfy them.

Although they are easily handled, most modeling
materials have the disadvantage of not being durable:
Clay crumbles, wax melts, and both are fragile. One way
of giving a modeled form permanence is to make a replica
of it in some durable material, such as bronze or lead.
But making molds and *casting* metal (as the replica-
making process is called) demands a high degree of
technical skill. That is why casting was rarely used by
primitive peoples. One important exception is the highly
sophisticated method of casting that was once used in
western and central Africa—notably in the kingdom of
Benin on the Ivory Coast during the 16th and 17th
centuries.

Briefly, metal casting has almost always been done like
this: First, a mold of damp sand, plaster, or fire-hardened

*The Greek god Perseus holding the head of the
Gorgon Medusa—a masterpiece of metal
casting by the Italian sculptor Benvenuto
Cellini (1500-71), who described how it was
made in his famous autobiography (p. 244).*

clay is made over the original model. Usually, a wax coating is given to the model if it is not already made of wax. When molten metal is poured into the mold, it melts and displaces the wax, giving, after it hardens, an exact reproduction of the forms and textures of the original model. Metal's strength means that the sculptured image usually needs no internal support.

Another method of producing durable modeled forms is by baking clay images in the sun or in a furnace called a kiln. The Italian phrase *terra cotta*, used to describe an unglazed clay figure of this kind, actually means "baked earth." This is an ancient form of sculpture—as ancient as the art of making heat-hardened pottery or bricks. Such figures can be simply modeled, from naturally soft clay, like much Japanese and South American sculpture and ancient Sumerian statuettes. Or they can be handled in a more sophisticated way: Clay—often mixed with stone, glass, or bone ash—is ground into a fine powder. Enough water is added to make a paste thick enough to model or thin enough to pour into a mold. After objects made like this have been baked, they can be colored with glazes, just as pottery can. These melt under intense heat, giving a hard, shiny surface.

Some of the most famous terra-cotta sculptures are the Greek Tanagra figurines (made in the town of Tanagra about 350-200 B.C.). While metal casting is usually used for large, monumental sculptures, terra cotta is especially suitable for subjects like those the Tanagra figures portray: actors, peasants, townspeople, and, in general, decorative subjects of an amiably everyday character that tell us much about daily life, costume, work, and recreation in ancient Greece.

After the decline of the Roman Empire, terra cotta was not much used, but there was a great revival of it during the Renaissance, especially for architectural decoration. In the 18th century, a special form of heat-fired pottery sculpture became popular in Europe (though the Chinese and Japanese had used it for centuries). This was *porcelain*, which is made by hardening a very fine clay paste like that described above in a kiln until it is glass-hard and translucent.

The most famous European porcelain modeling was done in the 18th century in Meissen, near Dresden, in Germany. Somewhat like the Tanagra figures of 2000 years before, the Meissen figurines represented little anecdotes, often of shepherds and shepherdesses, or actors dressed as characters from the Italian *commedia dell'arte* (p. 254) such as Harlequin and Columbine. Although miniature, such masterpieces are full of movement and vitality.

Terra-cotta figure of a horse, made in China between 265 and 589 A.D.

This delicately balanced statuette of a dancer was modeled by 19th-century French sculptor Auguste Rodin (p. 72), and cast in metal in the manner described in the text.

Sculpture and architecture

Sculpture and architecture have this in common: They both exist in three-dimensional space. And, in fact, for thousands of years sculpture was often carved from stones that made up the surfaces of buildings. Sometimes, as we shall see, this sculpture served a definite purpose; at other times, it was little more than applied decoration.

Much of the finest sculpture created in connection with buildings has been religious in character. In every age and civilization, men have incorporated sculpture into the designs of their temples and churches. In many Indian temples, for example, the sculptural and architectural elements are so closely linked as to be indistinguishable from each other in the final effect. Some of these temples are virtually huge pieces of sculpture themselves, cut entirely out of solid rock. The highlights, shadows, curves, and rhythms of the carved people and animals follow the building surfaces as closely as some natural growth like moss or lichen. The west front of the Gothic cathedral at Chartres in France is a good example of this kind of sculpture in Europe. The figures of saints have the same rigid, vertical forms as the columns that frame them.

In other buildings, architectural surfaces have served as a backdrop against which figures play out a kind of sculptural drama. In these, the sculpture is usually fastened to the building after it is built. A famous example is the sculpture that once filled the triangular roof ends (called *pediments*) of the Parthenon (p. 93). In the 19th century they were taken from Greece to the British Museum. Even removed from their original setting, they still make a powerful effect. Similarly, in many late

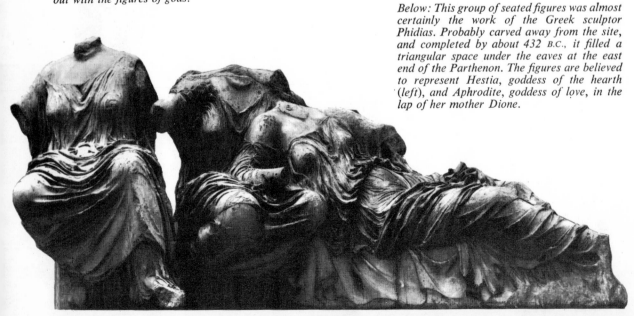

Sculpture and architecture have always been closely associated. The architecture of such Indian buildings as Rajrani Temple, Bhuvaneshvara (above), is inseparable from the sculptured figures. Built from blocks of sandstone around A.D. 1100, it is carved inside and out with the figures of gods.

Below: This group of seated figures was almost certainly the work of the Greek sculptor Phidias. Probably carved away from the site, and completed by about 432 B.C., it filled a triangular space under the eaves at the east end of the Parthenon. The figures are believed to represent Hestia, goddess of the hearth (left), and Aphrodite, goddess of love, in the lap of her mother Dione.

Gothic churches figures occupied ledges or niches like actors on a stage.

Were these sculptures then mere decorations? No, for at least until the Renaissance, sculpture generally had a religious purpose. By symbolizing gods, saints, or rituals, and illustrating religious stories, the sculptures served to intensify a building's spiritual power and meaning. On the Parthenon, for example, there was a long *frieze*—a horizontal band of sculpture. It showed the religious procession that ascended the Acropolis every four years to pay homage to Athena. The sculpture ran along the temple walls so high up under the eaves of the roof that it was difficult to see. The chief importance of the frieze was not that it was a wonderful piece of work in its own right—like the pediments, it was carved according to designs by Phidias (fifth century B.C.), the greatest sculptor of Greece's "Golden Age"—but that it added to the meaning and significance of the building. Many of the carvings in medieval churches, such as those on altars and baptismal fonts, had a similar role.

Toward the end of the Middle Ages, the character of European art became more and more secular. Though sculptors continued to provide works to be used in and on buildings, their purpose was more and more to provide images of political or patriotic significance. This type of sculpture, especially during the 19th century, was incorporated into the design of many public buildings.

The 20th-century emphasis on glass, metal, and reinforced concrete as building materials, and on plain surfaces and clearly defined angles has meant that little sculpture appears in buildings now, even as decoration. When artists decorate a modern building, they are more likely to use murals or mosaics.

Left: two of the elongated figures—possibly representing ancestors of Christ—on the west front of Chartres Cathedral, France (about 1150). Below: view of the modern theatre at Gelsenkirchen, Germany, showing how the bold forms of the foreground sculpture stand out against the metal and glass façade.

The body

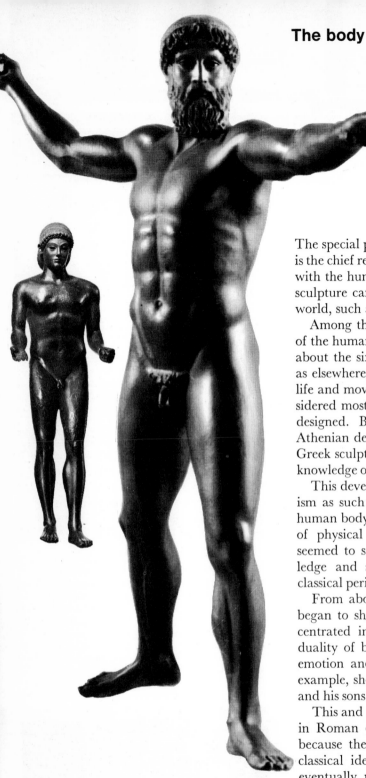

The special power of sculpture to suggest living presences is the chief reason sculptors have always been preoccupied with the human figure. Another reason is that a piece of sculpture cannot easily show other aspects of the visible world, such as the sea, sky, and landscape.

Among the most impressive and influential sculptures of the human figure were those made by the Greeks from about the sixth century B.C. Before this time, in Greece as elsewhere, sculptured figures for the most part lacked life and movement. The front view of the body was considered most important, and it was usually rather stiffly designed. But during the fifth century B.C.—when Athenian democracy and civilization was at its height—Greek sculpture showed a new naturalism and an expert knowledge of the body's structure.

This development was not due to a search for naturalism as such; it arose out of the Greeks' belief that the human body was the most perfect symbol for their ideals of physical and spiritual beauty. Man, these statues seemed to say, is capable of perfection through knowledge and self-discipline. This was Greek sculpture's classical period.

From about the fourth century B.C., Greek sculptors began to show less concern with ideal forms, and concentrated instead on emphasizing the physical individuality of bodies in a realistic way. They also stressed emotion and drama. The famous *Laocoön* group, for example, shows the agony of the Trojan priest Laocoön and his sons as they are destroyed by serpents (p. 82).

This and many other Greek sculptures exist for us only in Roman copies. The Romans copied such sculpture because they preferred its emotional realism to earlier classical idealism. Many of these Roman copies were eventually rediscovered during the Renaissance. They were a revelation to artists of the time. Sculptors such as Michelangelo used them as models for their attempts to express dramatic emotional conflict in stone and marble.

But the eventual unearthing of earlier Greek art meant that sculptors could draw inspiration from ideal classical

Both the Greek figures above—the Apollo (left) and the bearded god (seen in cast, right) date from the fifth century B.C. The Apollo, like earlier figures, is naturalistic yet lacking in movement; but the bearded figure (known as the Zeus of Artemision) has the vigor and idealized beauty of classic Greek sculpture.

forms, too. Until the end of the 19th century, Greco-Roman sculpture provided a unique source of inspiration to Western sculptors. After the Baroque borrowings from later Greek art, the neo-classical sculptors of the 18th and early 19th centuries harked back to classical purity in their own somewhat coldly correct works. Men like Antonio Canova (1757-1822) in Italy, and John Flaxman (1755-1826) in England, worked in this style.

In the later 19th century Auguste Rodin (p. 72), perhaps the greatest modern European sculptor, displayed the continuing influence of the Greeks. But he began to experiment with the surfaces of his statues, giving them a texture that reflected light in a way that resembled the play of light in Impressionist paintings. Then, as the 20th century opened, sculptors began to turn to sources hitherto unknown or ignored, especially tribal sculpture from Africa and the Pacific islands. And as the century grew older, some sculptors even began to show that there are analogies between the human body and machine-made and industrial shapes (p. 86).

The figure of Evening, carved by the great Italian artist Michelangelo (p. 40) for the tomb of Florentine statesman Lorenzo de Medici. Like the three other symbolic figures in the chapel (Dawn, Day, and Night), it shows the influence of late Greek sculpture in its powerful expression of mood.

A reclining figure carved in wood by the modern English sculptor Henry Moore, who has created many works that resemble both human figures and the forms of such natural objects as weatherworn rock formations.

Sculpture that tells a story

Detail from an Assyrian frieze (between 727 and 745 B.C.), telling how King Tilgiath-Pileser III stormed a city, probably in Babylonia. On the right stand his wooden siege engine and two archers; on the left are soldiers scaling the walls; near the city are the impaled bodies of slaughtered prisoners.

This famous group of figures (Greek, about 25 B.C.) illustrates the legend of the Trojan priest Laocoön and his sons, who were crushed to death by two serpents that came out of the sea at the command of Athena.

For thousands of years men have told stories in sculpture. Most of these stories have recorded military and political achievements, or shown scenes from the life of a god or a religious leader. For this sort of storytelling, sculptors have favored certain special sculptural techniques.

The technique used most often is called *relief*. Instead of carving or modeling free-standing images, the sculptor works on a flat surface—a wall, perhaps, or a door panel, or even a tall column. He cuts away part of the surface so that the figures he has conceived stand a little forward from the background. The effect is somewhat like that of a picture, but instead of painting in the shadows and highlights, he creates them by the depth of his carving.

In countries where the sun is strong and bright, sculptors need make only shallow cuts into the stone to create deep shadows. Egyptian wall carvings with their rows of hieroglyphs are an example; we say that they are *incised*, or cut into the surface, for they do not stand away from it. Sculptors use the shadow lines of the cuts to outline shapes as in a drawing.

Friezes showing hunting and battle scenes on the walls of Assyrian palaces of about the seventh century B.C. are carved in very shallow relief. Sculptures that project a little farther from the background (though no part of any figure actually is entirely detached from it) are called *low relief* or *bas-relief*. Some relief sculptures are so deeply carved that features like arms, legs, flowers, spears project in completely three-dimensional form. We say that the sculptor has carved them in *high relief*.

Relief sculpture bears a resemblance to painting other than in its use of light and shade to suggest three dimensions. Since the Renaissance, sculptors have often used the painter's device of central perspective (p. 38). In the doors of the baptistery of the cathedral in Florence, for example, which took Lorenzo Ghiberti (1378-1455) 21 years to make, suggestions of distant landscape in low relief are combined with foreground figures in high relief. The panels, telling the story of the fall of man and Christ's redemption, show a mastery of what was then the new science of perspective. Donatello (p. 72) also used perspective skilfully in the bronze low-relief panels (telling Biblical stories) that he cast for the sacristy doors of the church of San Lorenzo in Florence.

To show movement—an important element in narrative sculpture—sculptors can *imply* it. An arm drawn back, for example, indicates that a blow is to follow; a leg raised from the ground suggests running or dancing depending on the attitudes the sculptor has given his figures. Another method of suggesting movement is to repeat shapes with a rhythm that produces an almost cinematic effect as the eye moves along them. Long processions of soldiers or captives, for example, in Assyrian and Roman reliefs look almost as though they are really marching; horses seem to gallop.

By the 17th century, sculptors found in the dramatic realism of Baroque art a good way of telling a story. The use of free-standing sculpture for narrative purposes was not a brand new idea, of course; we saw how the emotional qualities of late Greek sculpture helped to portray the story of Laocoön and his sons. Baroque art carried realism even further. The works of Bernini (p. 74), for instance, involve the spectator in the event taking place —as it seems—in front of him. The figures of saints in ecstasy look as though they are really ascending toward heaven. As a spectator moves about sculptures like these, each new viewpoint reveals a little more of the story.

Since this period, little advance has been made in developing narrative sculpture. During the 18th and 19th centuries, most sculptors used relief or free-standing sculpture, but they added hardly anything to the techniques we have been discussing. Today, sculptors in general are more concerned with producing works that are interesting chiefly for their shapes and the way they inhabit the space around them; stories, most sculptors feel, are unnecessary.

The carving above, from the head of a column in Autun Cathedral (1120-30) in France, shows an angel awakening the three Magi and pointing to the star that will lead them back to their homes. A more sophisticated treatment of a Bible story—that of Joseph and his brethren—is seen in the bronze panel below. Covered in gold leaf, it is part of one of Ghiberti's doors for Florence's baptistery (1452). He combines high- and low-relief forms, and uses perspective like a painter.

A group of stone figures set up on Easter Island in the mid-Pacific by the Polynesians who lived there three or four centuries ago. These giant statues, sited on hillsides and burial grounds, may represent ancestors who were worshiped as guardians of the community.

Religious sculpture

More than any other art, sculpture has been the means of providing effective and satisfying images and symbols for religious worship. Sculptures have often formed the emotional center of religious buildings. In fact, many churches and temples were specifically designed to house such images.

This was so, for example, in the case of the temples of ancient Egypt, some of which enshrined monumental carvings of enormous size. The Parthenon was also a "god-house," sheltering a figure, over 30 feet high, of Pallas Athena, the patron goddess of Athens, made by Phidias (p. 78). By their stillness and lack of expression, statues like these seemed to stand supernaturally aloof from the everyday world of men.

The materials from which religious sculptures are made also play a part in creating an emotional impression on the worshiper. Hard stones like granite, comparatively unaffected by weathering, are particularly suitable materials from which to carve figures that will suggest ageless durability and bring a feeling of security to the spectator. The mysterious stone heads that stare out into the Pacific from Easter Island, for instance, must have given their makers a vivid sense of continuing life.

Also important in religious sculpture, with the notable exception of Christianity, has been the maintenance of unchanging tradition. The sculptor's task was not to carve *his* idea of a particular god, but to maintain the continuity of religious teaching by reproducing traditional forms. Thus, for example, Japanese and Chinese images of the Buddha (whether old or new) are similar in almost every detail. In most tribal societies, the shapes given to effigies of gods and demons have remained basically unchanged for centuries. The religious sculptor showed his skill and imagination not by inventing new forms, but in perfecting and enriching traditional ones.

This has not always been the case with Christian sculpture. Since the early days of the Church, it has undergone a number of distinct changes of style. These have been caused both by changes in the Church's teaching and by the influence of new "purely" artistic ideas. Although most of the sculpture produced for the early Church retained some of the look of Roman sculpture, all sense of three-dimensional solidity vanished. Byzantine and Romanesque Christian sculpture was, in general, confined to relief carvings on walls, caskets, and so on. Stiff, spiritual, and austere in character, it lacked the human warmth of classical art.

By the end of the 13th century, a more naturalistic treatment had begun to appear. Both figures and decorative details, such as plant forms and leaves, were shown

Statuette of the Buddha preaching his first sermon, from Sarnath, India (between 318 and 566 A.D.). As in many religious images, the position and gestures of the teacher have a specific meaning for believers.

with greater realism and more fully "in the round," though they were still part of essentially flat surfaces.

During the 15th century, especially in Italy, Christian sculpture was strongly affected by Renaissance interest in the art of the classical past. Notably in the work of Donatello (p. 72), sculpture was released from a long connection with architecture. The free-standing human figure, designed to be looked at from every angle, became, as it had been in the classical past, the subject through which many sculptors expressed their deepest feelings.

The 16th-century Reformation had an immediate and powerful effect on sculpture, as it did on all forms of art. In the newly Protestant countries, religious sculpture was discouraged, and the art fell into decline. But in Roman Catholic countries it became, like the painting of the period (p. 52), increasingly emotional and dramatically realistic in its treatment of religious subjects. At this time, too, especially in southern Germany and Spain, artists combined sculpture with architecture and painting to produce churches designed to overwhelm worshipers with a visual illusion of heaven made real on earth.

Two contrasting Christian sculptures. Above: The Adoration of the Magi—*an austere relief on whalebone (English, early 12th century).* Below: Madonna and Child with Saints, a *glazed terra-cotta relief by Luca della Robbia (Italian, about 1400-82).*

Modern sculpture

Speed, space, technological advance—these are among the aspects of 20th-century life that have excited the imagination of sculptors as well as scientists. As early as 1909, the Italian Futurist movement, typified by one of its leading members, Umberto Boccioni (1882-1916), tried to relate the forms of the human body to those of the machine—the 20th-century symbol of movement.

Of course, sculptors as far back in time as the ancient Assyrians and Greeks tried to give an illusion of movement in sculpture. Their repetitive, rhythmic designs and figures caught on the brink of a gesture anticipated the interest of 20th-century artists in moving forms.

Cubist painters, for example, had learned from Cézanne (p. 64) to look for the simplified geometric foundation to every form. Sculpture, in which many aspects of any image can be seen by a spectator moving around it, was ideally suited to the new emphasis on simplified forms. This emphasis was further intensified by the fact that men were beginning to see beauty in the

Pablo Picasso (p. 56) drew a startling comparison between machine-made and natural forms in making this bull's head (above) out of a bicycle saddle and handle bars. A number of Picasso's sculptures incorporate such everyday objects, which are given a new meaning by the bold, imaginative way in which they are combined. Russian-born Naum Gabo makes use of materials like plastic, steel, and aluminum to create such transparent sculptures as Linear Construction (*below.*)

In this characteristic work by the American sculptor Alexander Calder, the wrought-iron tripod supports carefully balanced "mobile" shapes that move with every breath of air, creating constantly changing patterns in space.

clean shapes of machines. Futurist sculptors and other artists tried to include such ideas in their works.

The new interest in machines and the materials and techniques involved in their making and functioning resulted in the 1920s in another movement, far-reaching in its influence: Constructivism. Using transparent plastics, welded or polished metals, wire, and glass, such sculptors as Naum Gabo (born in Russia in 1890) and Antoine Pevsner (1884-1962) made non-representational objects with names like *Kinetic* (moving) *Sculpture* and *Dancer*, which, through reflected light and rhythmic shapes, gave the impression of machine-like movement. Other sculptors have made works that actually moved, being driven by small motors.

They did not try to make their sculpture represent anything recognizably human or mechanical, however. What emerged as important was what had always been important in all sculpture : the lively relationship of mass to space (p. 70). It was, however, the special achievement of the 20th century to invent sculpture in which the spaces themselves changed shape, and new patterns evolved and replaced one another constantly. The American sculptor Alexander Calder (born 1898), one of the originators of such sculpture, gave the name *mobile* to these forms. In Calder's works delicately balanced shapes made of metal and plastic hung on wires circle and weave among one another at every breath of air.

Other modern sculptors created works that contain space within skeleton-like frameworks, such as some of the welded metalwork of Reg Butler (born 1913) in England, or the complicated gold-wire constructions of the American Richard Lippold (born 1915). Still other sculptors have used the cast-off materials of 20th-century manufacturing and industry in a way that often startlingly reveals similarities between man-made objects and those of the natural world.

But not all sculptors have abandoned old materials and techniques. England's Henry Moore (born 1898), for instance, while always conscious of modern experiments with space, has used stone and wood—carefully shaping their volumes and spaces—to express his highly personal feelings about the oldest of the sculptor's subjects, the human body (p. 81).

The human figure remains one of the sculptor's major themes. This bronze statuette of a dancer—one of the many figures made in metal, wood, or colored terra cotta by the Italian sculptor Marino Marini (born 1901)—captures in modern idiom the mysterious living quality that is the essence of sculpture.

Chapter 4

Architecture

Both animals and men need shelter from the weather and the physical hazards of the world around them, but men want another kind of shelter, too. They need protection from threats to their spiritual and emotional well-being. Awareness of this need is what makes our houses and towns something more than just places in which to work, eat, and sleep. Wherever men have planned buildings and settlements, they have tried to give them some kind of *order*—an order that would provide a stable background for day-to-day activities and that would also suggest that there is a meaning and purpose to human life.

Architecture is the art of planning buildings that will satisfy human needs for physical and psychological security and men's desire for perfection. During classical Greek and Roman times, and in modern times since the Renaissance, the planners—or *architects*—have therefore been men educated in many branches of knowledge. At other times, the construction of buildings was supervised by men who were actually involved in the work of building, as the Greek roots of the word "architect" indicate : *archos* (chief) and *tekton* (builder).

Today the architect seldom works with his own hands upon a building he has designed. He must understand construction and the technology of building, of course; but it is even more important for him to know about people and society as expressed in religion, politics, education, and other activities for which he may be called on to build. In this chapter we shall see how the modern architect (guided by his study of man's past and present needs) and his forerunner, the master builder (guided by tradition), have tried to meet the special need of men to find order and purpose in their buildings.

All over the world, architects seek ways to house expanding populations. Some problems—providing large-scale, low-cost residential quarters, as well as ready-made shopping, social, and service facilities—are new. Yet architects must also supply what men have always wanted in their buildings and towns: visual order and interest, a sense of community, and a generally satisfying environment. Typical of architects' solutions to such problems is Roehampton Estate in suburban London, built 1956-57.

The forms of the shelter

Contemporary life is so complex and varied that we have a special kind of building to shelter each one of nearly all the activities in which we are involved. And individual buildings are often grouped into the larger, more complicated organisms we call the town and city. Yet all these building forms derive from the simple shelters and settlements of our earliest ancestors.

Knowing a little about the forms men chose for their first shelters can help us to understand some of the factors that have influenced the planning of buildings through the ages. First of all, men wanted shelters that gave them protection and warmth; fire could provide both. When human beings had learned how to control fire, they were well on the way toward putting some useful order into their surroundings, and a fireplace quite naturally became both the focus of early shelters and a center of worship—an altar.

Early man also found sanctuary from real and imaginary dangers in such places as natural caves, as well as inside the protective circle of a fire. The famous painted caves at Lascaux in southern France (p. 22), for example, were almost certainly used for religious or magical rituals. But early men were often nomadic—that is, they wandered as the seasons changed, looking for fresh supplies of food. Since they could not always find caves, they had to build artificial shelters—the first huts. These were often made, like the American Indian wigwams and tepees, of branches arranged in a circle and bound together at the top. Such a cone was the most practical shape for supporting the weight of covering thatch or skins.

Circular forms persisted in later, more permanent mud-and-brick buildings—but for other reasons. Because fires cast their light and heat in a roughly circular area, people could use the fire best by gathering around it in a circle. Moreover, when men learned to dig artificial caves in the form of holes or pits—which, roofed over, made good shelters—they probably dug in the instinctive round shape a child uses when digging in the sand. Round hut foundations nearly 8000 years old have been unearthed in Cyprus and at Jericho, in modern Jordan. Of course, many early buildings were built in shapes that were not round, but all were built around a focal point, generally the hearth.

Even from earliest times, men grouped their buildings into settlements, both for protection and for easier transaction of day-to-day affairs. Like individual dwellings,

Prehistoric family life centered around fire's warmth and protection. Men's earliest shelters reinforced fire's usefulness by conserving its heat, keeping out weather and animals.

At first, men sheltered themselves like the animals in trees and caves. Earliest man-made shelters probably were branches leaned against steep banks (1), trees (2). Eventually men dug holes, covered them (3). Better protection (easy to build anywhere) came later: dome-shaped frames (4) covered by woven twigs; tent-like tepee frames (5) covered with skins.

1

2

3

4

5

In present-day Greece (above), wandering peasants still build circular huts. Domed construction, a technique natural with pliable, freshly cut branches, is also a traditional building shape in Africa, Asia, the Americas.

About 1000 mud-walled, thatched-roof huts make up this village in Northern Rhodesia. Protected inside circle are penned cattle—tribe's most precious possessions. In central circle are chief's own house, his wives' huts.

each settlement had a central place of activity—for work, or perhaps for the religious ceremonies that were so closely tied to daily life in early times. We can see similar settlements today among such primitive tribes as the Bororo Indians in Brazil's Mato Grosso. Their settlements—and those of primitive peoples in places as scattered as Malaya, Africa, and Australia—are also influenced by the social patterns of the tribe. The care taken in the placing of such important buildings as the house reserved for the men of the tribe helps preserve the order of society. People feel reassured about what to expect from life when their surroundings are not likely to change.

We cannot be sure, of course, that such sophisticated aims as achieving psychological security were in the minds of men when they began building huts and villages. But it is interesting—and significant for understanding later developments in architecture—that early men did connect building forms with religious ideas about the formal order their gods had willed for the universe. Builders in ancient India, for instance, followed explicit instructions for planned settlements defined in a book called the *Mansara*, which also contained religious rituals meant to accompany the building process. In Rome, as in most ancient towns, ceremonies were performed both at the center of the town and around the boundaries, to mark the laying of the original foundations.

We shall see how such ancient concerns with the maintenance of tradition are closely connected to the role the architect plays today. For even in modern societies we celebrate the traditional importance of building with ceremonies to mark the laying of cornerstones or the raising of roof beams into place.

Technique and tradition

New ways of building do not always bring about quick changes in the looks of buildings, for people generally dislike living in unfamiliar surroundings. Today, for example, builders have a wider choice of new techniques and new materials than men have ever had before. Yet we can look almost anywhere and find "new" buildings with imitation 18th-century exteriors. And those 18th-century building styles were in many respects adapted from building forms as old as those of ancient Greece. Civilizations with established traditions—religious, political, social—change the way their buildings look very slowly; yet advances in building are possible only in such stable societies.

Our prehistoric ancestors—wandering hunters and food-gatherers like some of the peoples that live in tropical or arid parts of the world today—needed only temporary shelters. They could not be burdened with anything more permanent than simple windbreaks or lean-tos, like those that African Bushmen still make. But in temperate lands, where farming and animal raising were practical, people established communities, settled down, and looked for ways to build more durable shelters.

One of the first advances came when men realized that their lean-tos—made to cover cave entrances and pits, or propped against convenient tree trunks—could be propped against each other so as to form a tent-like structure. Such structures doubled the shelter given by the old lean-tos and could be erected anywhere. Much later, by putting this peaked shed on top of upright posts rammed into the ground, early men found they could make even larger buildings, such as the rectangular timber houses found at Lindenthal, near Cologne. These are typical of houses built around 3000 B.C. over a large area of Europe. In other places, such as Asia Minor, where there was little timber, men bound together bundles of reeds to make supporting columns. They used woven-reed mats, straw, or thatch to make walls and roofs. They often plastered mud over the walls to close the chinks.

Other building techniques developed from locally available materials were the use of mud bricks (p. 102) and of stone. But however much they advanced technically, most ancient builders were reluctant to change the actual appearance of their buildings. For instance, in the huge Egyptian temples, such as that of Ammon at Karnak (one of the largest religious buildings ever made), the columns were modeled after the bundles of bound lotus stalks like those that had been used in much earlier buildings. The ropes that bound the reeds were imitated at the top of the stone columns in the form of engraved

In Iraq, huts like the mudhif—*a kind of inn— shown above have been built the same way for centuries. Bundles of thin cane are bound together to form arched framework. Moslem tradition demands that entrance face Mecca.*

Painting of hypostyle (columned) hall of Temple of Ammon at Karnak. Design of shafts, capitals, suggests primitive use of bound plant stalks to support roofs. Stone columns are 69 feet high, 11 feet 9 inches in diameter.

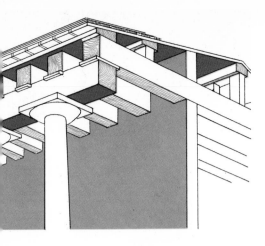

Probable origin of Greek Doric order or style: Wood posts, each cushioned by a flat block called an abacus, support roof beams.

The three Greek orders (below). Earliest is the Doric with its simple capital (left). The slender Ionic (center) has a scrolled capital; the later Corinthian (right), favored by the Romans, has elaborate acanthus-leaf carving.

The Parthenon is best known of Greek temples. Doric columns support the entablature: *a long flat* architrave; *a* frieze, *divided into panels by grooved projections (like wooden beams); and on top, a projecting* cornice.

bands. The carved tops—which we call *capitals*—represented lotus blossoms. Karnak was built about 1350 B.C.; as late as 237 B.C. the same kind of column was still being used in buildings such as the temple of Horus at Edfu.

Direct imitation of primitive construction can also be seen in many Egyptian tombs that were carved out of rocky hillsides, as at Beni Hasan (about 2500 B.C.). The tombs show such details as the ends of projecting wooden roof beams. The first Egyptian buildings of mud-daubed reeds and mud bricks had walls made by piling the material up: thick at the base and narrower at the top. Even though stone walls do not need to be built this way, Egyptian builders retained slanting walls in nearly all their stone buildings—even those they carved, rather than built, out of solid rock.

When you look at Greek temples—like the most famous of all ancient buildings, the Parthenon (built about 490 B.C.)—you can see other examples of ways in which builders preserved details of primitive timber construction when they built with stone. Among surviving details were marble versions of wooden pegs, once used to fasten roof beams; and, just as at Beni Hasan, the ends of the roof beams were reproduced in the new material. Still keeping to traditional ways, the Greeks put a thin layer of plaster—painted in vivid yellows, reds, and blues—over their stone temples, just as they had plastered the walls of early wooden buildings. Today, of course, we see only the bare stone and marble.

When men revived classical styles during the Renaissance, the idea of painting buildings brightly did not occur to them. But they copied ancient architectural features as they believed them to have existed, and since the 15th century architects have used Greco-Roman details—so meaningful because of their associations—in nearly every kind of building.

House into town

1

Early Iron Age British farm defended by wooden palings.

2

Peaked-roof "long house" typical of Neolithic Europe.

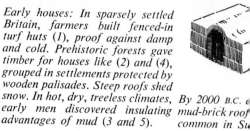

3

Early houses: In sparsely settled Britain, farmers built fenced-in turf huts (1), proof against damp and cold. Prehistoric forests gave timber for houses like (2) and (4), grouped in settlements protected by wooden palisades. Steep roofs shed snow. In hot, dry, treeless climates, early men discovered insulating advantages of mud (3 and 5). By 2000 B.C. mud-brick roof common in Su

Whether or not new building ideas are better than old ones, people in general tend to prefer traditional patterns. In the planning of houses and towns, familiar patterns help to maintain the stability of family and community life. One basic traditional form is the building that is planned around a focus—a central point of activity or attention. What this focus becomes in a given society depends on how people live and what they believe; in any town, both the town itself and the houses in it tell us much about the people who live there.

Roman houses, for example, centered on a court called the *atrium*, from which all other rooms opened. Until about the end of the Roman republic, the atrium was the center of all household activity, for the hearth was located there. When Roman houses became so complex and luxurious that there were many rooms and courtyards, and the kitchen was a separate room, the atrium remained the symbolic center of the house, where the head of the family transacted all official business. Its plan mirrored ancient Roman religious and social traditions—especially Roman concern with the preservation of family life. Around the walls stood sculptured portraits of family ancestors, and in a corner or in a neighboring alcove stood an altar to the household gods, the *lares* and *penates*. Nearby, a flame that symbolized the continuity of family life was always kept burning.

Roman town plans paralleled many features of Roman houses. For one thing, there was the flame lit in the temple of Vesta, the goddess of fire. It derived its symbolic origin from the importance of the hearth in primitive times. In fact the Romans believed that a great disaster would overtake any city in which the flame was allowed to die. The temple of Vesta was near the *forum*, a central square in which the townspeople met to conduct their daily business affairs. The gods who protected the community—like the domestic lares and penates—were honored in the city's chief temple, located near one end of the forum. Around the forum were statues of important heroes and statesmen, just as ancestral portraits were placed in the atrium of each private house.

Aerial view of Pompeii (above), destroyed by eruption of Vesuvius in A.D. 79, shows typical Roman city plan. Town layout reflects emphasis on focal points in Roman house, whose floor plan and exterior are shown below. Daily life centered in forum (large open square at left center). At north end, city's chief temple honored Apollo. In private houses, open court called atrium (1), flanked by shrine (2) to household gods, was the center of family life.

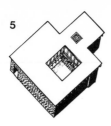

*...e Bronze Age
...r farmhouse in
...tral Europe.*

*Brick house in Indus
Valley (2500 B.C.)
had flat mud roof.*

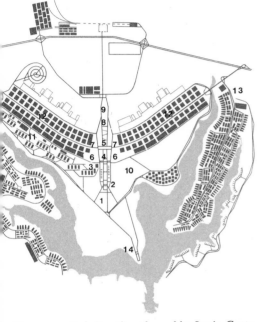

*...azil's new capital, Brasilia, planned by Lucio Costa
...d Oscar Niemeyer, focuses on Plaza of Three
...wers (1), government buildings (2). Other important
...es: cathedral (3), cultural area (4), recreation area
..., business center (6), shops (7), stadium (8), muni-
...al square (9), university (10), embassies (11),
...artment houses (12), detached houses (13), presi-
...nt's palace (14), airport (15). Artificial lake (pale
...e) is part of plan. City is 600 miles inland.*

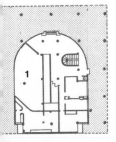

Other early civilizations, both before and after the Romans, had a similar concern with traditional focal points. In ancient Sumer, for example, the city focused on a mountain-shaped temple (p. 102) on the top of which lived a god—considered the "landlord" of the town and owner of the temple grounds. There is evidence that Sumerian temples like the one at Ur (about 2300 B.C.) were built as houses for each city's god and included quarters for the king, who was the god's high priest, as well as his "tenant farmer." No matter how complicated the maze of rooms in these temples, each had a central room or court, as did the houses of ordinary citizens. In the northern countries there was no central court, but there were great halls built around a central hearth. And here lived, ate, and slept the master of the house, his family, his servants, and even his dogs. Another example of focal planning is the typical cathedral town of Europe's Middle Ages. These towns clustered about cathedrals and the large squares—often also market places—in front of them.

But in modern cities of, say, the Americas or Australia, it is immediately apparent that few of them are actually centered about some kind of forum or square. Since the early 19th century, rapid expansion of population, the use of machines, and the development of rapid transport has meant that single communities often sprawl across vast distances. In many cities, such as Los Angeles in the United States, roads seem to take up more space than people and buildings. City planners nowadays have to deal with the whole region surrounding a city, as well as its central districts. In older cities, highways reaching out to new suburbs show how much we rely on cars today. Plans for new cities—Brasilia, for example—take into account the need for broad, efficient roads.

Modern houses, too, often mirror our 20th-century preoccupation with machines and cars. For instance, in one famous house, whose plan has influenced much contemporary house design, a great deal of space is given to housing the family's cars. Built in 1929 by the Swiss-born architect Le Corbusier (born 1887; real name, Charles Édouard Jeanneret) in a suburb of Paris, the house is also typical of contemporary building in that improved heating and air-conditioning methods mean that the hearth need no longer be at the center of the building plan; rooms need not be a series of box-like, shut-in spaces. Modern houses, with their flexible, open plans, concentrate less on formal arrangements of rooms—like those common in 18th- and 19th-century houses—than on accommodating a variety of constantly changing activities.

"The house—a machine to live in." Le Corbusier's slogan took form in his Villa Savoie (1929). Driveway enters ground floor, ramp leads from carport (1) to living quarters: glass-walled living room (2), terrace (3), kitchen (4).

Civilization—and towns—evolved as wandering bands of hunters and shepherds settled into highly organized farming communities, symbolized by this model of a granary (above), taken from an Egyptian tomb over 2000 years old. Markets, where men could exchange things they had made for grain and other necessities, became the nucleus of countless towns. Markets like ancient ones still exist in Africa (below)—with mass-produced wares.

Market place and shrine

At the heart of most towns and cities is a center of activity much like the Roman forum (p. 94). This center may be devoted to buying and selling—in financial districts similar to Wall Street in New York—or to some kind of religious or political activity, such as the Mohammedan shrine of the Kaaba in Mecca or the government buildings in London. In the earliest towns, centers were simply market places, which often incorporated religious shrines. In every society, a time came when food-producing methods improved until it was no longer necessary for everyone to spend his time working in the fields or hunting. People with special skills—toolmakers, weavers, potters—developed their abilities and wanted to exchange their products for food others had grown. Priests and religious communities prospered in the security of large settlements, and believers were able to congregate at regular times in convenient buildings.

The best example of an important religious center and market place is the Greek *agora*. The Greek market was more than just a commercial center; indeed, wherever goods are exchanged, news and ideas are also discussed. The Greek agora was a center for culture as well as trade, and political, judicial, educational, and religious buildings grew up around it. There were long colonnades or covered porticos called *stoae*, and under them there were often rows of shops. In Athens, the agora was not arranged in any apparently orderly fashion, though the placement of the colonnade and nearby buildings probably furnished a series of pleasing views. Other Greek cities had agoras that were sometimes built on a rectangular or square plan, and occupied a central position similar to that chosen by the Romans for their forums. Under the Romans, central markets and meeting places characterized towns throughout the empire.

Towns also grew up around important shrines, such as that to Hera at Olympia in Greece, where pilgrims—and visitors to the games held in Hera's honor—needed to be fed and housed. Often there was an alliance between market and shrine like that in the forum and agora. In Venice, for example, which had grown in the 9th and 10th centuries into Europe's leading center of trade with the East, the great church of St. Mark was both the private chapel of the doge (chief magistrate) and a religious shrine. Early in the 9th century, during the reign of the 12th doge, the body of St. Mark was brought to Venice from Alexandria. The church itself was located in the Rialto district, the center of commercial activity among the islands that make up Venice. Throughout Europe in the Middle Ages towns grew up around cathedrals and abbeys. The local market was often situated in

A major use of the Piazza del Duomo (Cathedral Square) in Florence was for religious processions, as 18th-century print above shows. Even today, dome of Santa Maria del Fiore dominates skyline, and its piazza, enhanced by Giotto's tall campanile (bell tower) and the famous octagonal Baptistery, is still the center of town. Postwar rebuilding in English cathedral city of Coventry, devastated in World War II, includes "shopping precinct" designed for pedestrians and oriented toward main city square and spire of ruined cathedral.

the square in front of the cathedral. Some cities, like Cologne, flourished because of the large number of both religious and commercial interests settled there.

It is easy to point out what the "market place" of a city today consists of: Blocks of office buildings are to be found in every modern city. There are large department stores and, in many cases, shopping centers planned around squares. But what are today's "shrines"? They are usually civic or patriotic, such as the city center designed by the Finnish architect Alvar Aalto (born 1899) at Sunyatsala, Finland. And many capital cities focus around their government buildings, as do Madrid and Washington.

Persian walled city of Susa is seen in detail from relief showing its capture by Assyrians in seventh century B.C. (note chariot wheel, lower left). Susa (upper right) was protected not only by walls but by location between river and canal. Outside walls were forts, set among gardens famous throughout ancient world.

During the Middle Ages, warring feudal lords built thick-walled stone fortresses surrounded by water-filled moats. Welsh castle of Harlech, shown here, was typically situated on steep slopes of a rocky hill. Origin of the castle was the castellum—*Latin name for a primitive camp fortified by wooden palisade called a* bail; *castle court is called a* bailey.

The growth of cities

In ancient times, planned space in most large cities was conditioned by—among others—two important factors: walls for defensive purposes, and meeting places built to accommodate large crowds. Though city planners today do not surround cities by defensive walls, they still must visualize any given urban area as a unit, and still have the problem of providing room for people to assemble.

Among the earliest city walls we know of are those at Jericho that may date from sometime before 7000 B.C. Jericho was sited on a plain, near the shores of the Dead Sea, but many ancient walled cities, such as Mycenae in Greece (about 1400 B.C.), were built on hilltops. Such a hilltop was called an *acropolis*. The famous Acropolis of Athens, well fortified by stone walls, sheltered that city's chief temples. Defensive walls also surrounded Rome and Roman towns throughout the empire. During the Middle Ages, not only towns but also castles—like little towns themselves—were protected from attack by water-filled moats, high walls, and towers. By the middle of the 18th century, artillery had rendered walls obsolete, and in most towns they were eventually demolished. Yet walls left their mark. When the Viennese dismantled their city walls in the 19th century, they built on the site the famous "Ring" of promenades, boulevards, and parks.

During the 19th century, rapid population growth and expanded facilities for transport caused many cities to explode beyond their original boundaries into great sprawls of uncontrolled suburban building. Both London and Paris were victims of such haphazard growth. The process has continued until the present day, when many cities spread for miles in all directions along networks of high-speed roads. Plans to avoid this gigantic formlessness have been successfully put into effect both in old towns—such as Amsterdam, where all building since

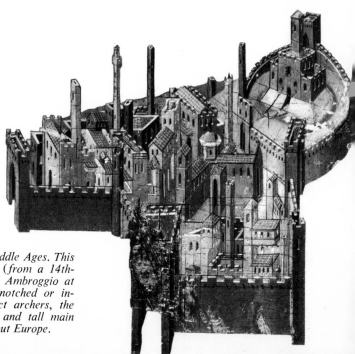

A typical walled city of the Middle Ages. This imaginary example is Italian (from a 14th-century mural by Lorenzo di Ambroggio at Siena), but the crenellated (notched or indented) battlements to protect archers, the towers, citadel (upper right), and tall main gate (left) were found throughout Europe.

Amphitheatre (upper left) and theatre (lower right) at Arles, France. Such vast buildings for public spectacles were a feature of most Roman cities. They could contain almost all of a city's population. Crowds were provided with plenty of exits; central location meant people's homes were within walking distance.

1933 has been carefully controlled—and in new ones—such as the English "garden cities" of the 1900s and their more recent counterparts, the so-called "new towns," which have been planned to preserve the advantages of urban living without destroying surrounding countryside.

Some of the first structures built to contain large assemblies of people in an orderly fashion were the Greek *theatres*. These generally featured semicircular rows of stone seats built into natural hillsides (p. 256). The Romans developed the multi-storied masonry *amphitheatre* which held tiers of seats arranged in a complete oval. Amphitheatres, used chiefly for elaborate shows and games, were much more complicated buildings than theatres. Some, like the famous Colosseum in Rome (p. 114), could even be flooded for naval spectacles. Theatres were not built again until the Renaissance, when many were directly inspired by Roman models. During the 18th and 19th centuries, larger theatres were built everywhere, especially for opera performances. Other large public buildings in ancient times included open-air stadiums—devoted to athletic contests—much like those of today. Perhaps the largest modern stadium is the Maracaná in Rio de Janeiro, built in 1950 to hold 200,000.

The theatre and amphitheatre at Nîmes in France, as in many Roman cities, were located near each other. Today, however, stadiums, theatres, and other types of assembly hall are seldom grouped together near the administrative and business center of a city but are spread out over a wide area, serving the populations of separate suburban localities. Nevertheless, in some cities, notably London and New York, large areas of aging buildings have recently been cleared to make way for specially planned centers that incorporate public open spaces and gardens, theatres, and concert halls.

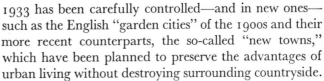

In midtown New York, Lincoln Center—whose Philharmonic Hall is shown at left—replaces slum areas. Concert halls, theatres, opera house, and library border plazas and wooded park. Nearby is good transportation.

99

England's Stonehenge is the most impressive of many stone monuments set up in Western Europe during the New Stone Age. It probably marked the center of the known world for local tribes. Like stone circles in France, it may later have been dedicated to sun worship.

Buildings as symbols

Men long ago were attracted to certain building plans and forms as especially satisfying symbols for a world they believed was divinely protected and ordered. They tried to harmonize the settings and ground plans of buildings with their notions about the plan of the universe—as did the Greeks, who sometimes situated temples so that they faced toward the rising sun. Builders have also repeatedly used forms that suggest the structure of the universe: sky-like domes, for example, or towers that "lift" men closer to their gods.

One reason for the use of the domed shape was because it resembled a mountain, a widespread symbol in ancient times for the creation of the world. Another common belief was that the sky actually *was* a great dome hanging above the earth. The famous Treasury of Atreus—really a tomb, built about 1400 B.C. at Mycenae in Greece—has a domed roof even though it is underground. Rows of bronze rivets indicate that star-like decorations may have emphasized the idea of a sky. Primitive burial mounds all over the world indicate that the rounded "tumulus" shape was regarded as an appropriate burial symbol, signifying both nearness to heaven and a return into the womb-like earth to be reborn. In India, solid brick mounds of this kind—called *stupas*—were eventually refined into large domed shrines, extravagantly decorated and carved (one in Ceylon was 400 feet high). In Christian buildings, domes have also been significant. The most important early examples were the domes of Byzantine churches, which looked almost as if they floated, and gave a sense of space comparable with the open sky.

The tower is another architectural shape that has been used throughout history as a symbol, particularly of fertility and of power. High towers visible from long distances have also been used to mark especially significant sites. Gothic church spires, for example, are landmarks all across northern Europe. Many peoples have believed that the actual center of the universe lay within the borders of their country, and have marked the site with a special building—often with a tower. Such towers also sometimes had a further symbolic role: to act as a so-called "sky tower" supporting the heavens. Chinese pagodas (which derive from stupas) are such symbols. Each of their projecting roofs represents one of the stages that Buddhists believe lie between earth and paradise.

The most famous tower of modern times was also built as a symbol. The great steel tower 985 feet high built in Paris by Gustave Eiffel (1832-1923), and subsequently named after him, was intended as a symbol of the 19th century's power and prosperity. Originally designed in 1889 as the centerpiece of an international exposition, it

Pagodas, like this one in China's Hunan province, originated in India, derived from towers built over tombs of Buddhist saints. The many levels of Chinese pagodas are said to symbolize stages of spiritual advancement.

has since become a universally recognized symbol of the city in which it stands.

During the Renaissance, European churches that combined domes with tall towers sprang up everywhere. The interiors were often made to represent a glimpse into heaven by the skillful combination of elaborate sculptures and paintings. Ingenious planning—especially during the 17th- and 18th-century Baroque period—made the walls seem to blend gradually into a vast, light-flooded heaven filled with ranks of angels and saints.

Like the tower and the dome, the ground plan of a building could also have symbolic meaning. For hundreds of years, Christians built churches that had a cross-like ground plan, representing the body of the crucified Christ. The top of the cross pointed eastward toward the holy city of Jerusalem—which appears as the center of the world on many medieval maps. The idea that a building's walls should point squarely toward each of the four corners of the earth also resulted in cruciform plans for the majority of Buddhist temples scattered throughout Java and Burma—such as the 11th-century shrine to Ananda in Pagan, Burma. Planned as a 180-foot square, it has 40-foot projections extending symbolically toward each point of the compass. The Chinese, who believed that "Heaven is round, Earth square," planned Peking as a square exactly oriented north, south, east, and west, with a gate in the center of each side of the city wall. In the same city, the perfectly circular Temple of Heaven has four stairways leading up to the central altar, one from each direction.

Today, buildings based on ancient symbolic plans retain their power to affect our emotions not only through the skill that their builders showed in their construction, but also perhaps because the ideas that their shapes and forms symbolize still call up a response in us.

Baroque church interiors such as St. John Neponuk (Munich, 1733-50) heighten religious symbolism by use of optical illusions, surging curves (above). Today, architecture often symbolizes national pride. In Le Corbusier's plan for East Punjab's new capital at Chandigarh, central plaza (below) is dominated by 50-foot-tall "Open Hand" monument, seen here as sketched by Corbusier.

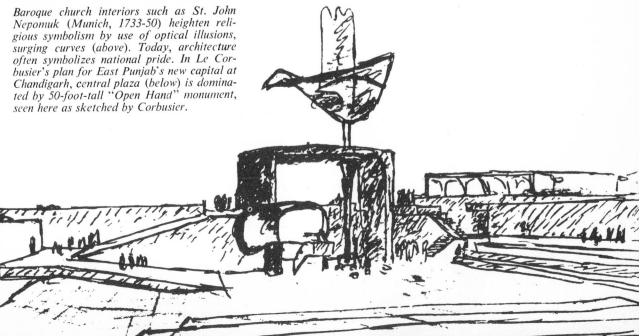

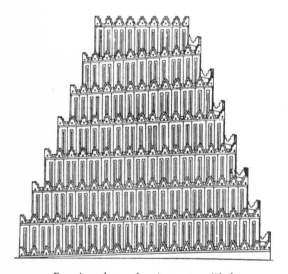

King Khefren's tomb, over 4000 years old and nearly 450 feet high, is one of three famous Egyptian pyramids at Giza. They were so massively built that they remain one of world's wonders despite time's ravages.

Drawing shows the ziggurat or "holy mountain" of Khorsabad (in what is now Iraq) as it probably looked over 2000 years ago. Base was 143 feet long. Most Babylonian and Assyrian cities had one of these temple towers.

Building for posterity

Many of the world's greatest buildings—vast monolithic tombs, splendid temples, and grandly planned palaces and public buildings—have resulted from the attempts men have made to perpetuate their achievements, honor their gods, or show off temporal power and wealth.

The desire to defeat death inspired one of the best-known of all building forms: the *pyramid*, which is a kind of artificial mountain made of stone. The most famous pyramids of all were built in Egypt before 2500 B.C. as tombs for Egyptian kings. The ground plan was perfectly square, with each triangular side facing toward one of the points of the compass. Inside there were mazes of passages and rooms designed to house the dead pharaoh and his possessions, and to keep intruders from finding their way to the central burial chamber. The passage of 4500 years has not substantially altered the pyramids, so massive is their scale (the Great Pyramid of Cheops covers 13 acres and rises 482 feet into the air) and so skillful were the techniques the Egyptians used to fit the great stone blocks together.

Cruder relatives to the pyramids were Mesopotamian *ziggurats*—immense, man-made mountains of mud brick. Since they were not built of stone, only a few (such as the ziggurat of Ur, built about 2300 B.C.) have lasted until the present day. But the sheer size of the brick ziggurats guaranteed that there would be a fair degree of permanence. Ziggurats were not smooth-sided but were built up in a series of set-back terraces, reached either by ramps or long flights of steps. They were not tombs; rather, they were substitutes for the mountains on which early civilizations often built their shrines.

Men also built artificial mountains in an entirely different part of the world—Mexico and Central America—where they were probably put to much the same use as ziggurats. These were the pyramidal *teocallis* ("god-houses") of the Mayan Indians. Those in Chichén Itzá are typical. Built of stone during the 6th through the 11th centuries A.D., each is crowned with a temple.

The Japanese had a different way of building important religious shrines so that they would last. Even though they used perishable wood, they preserved the exact appearance of Japan's holiest Shinto shrine (at Ise on the island of Honshu) by knocking the old temple buildings down every 20 years and rebuilding them on a neighboring site in exactly the same style. The Ise buildings have been renewed in this way for over 1200 years.

During the Middle Ages and the early Renaissance, Christians built great cathedrals and churches—perhaps the last buildings anywhere that were erected through the financial and physical efforts of virtually an entire

The pyramid or mountain form was found in the new world too. In Mexico, the Mayas built teocallis *("god-houses") like this 90-foot-high temple pyramid at Chichén Itzá dedicated to Kukulcan (the Aztec god Quetzalcoatl).*

society. Everybody wanted these soaring stone-and-glass buildings to stand as testaments to a universal and unquestioned faith in the Church. Then, as Europe entered an age of religious upheaval and skepticism, and new nations began to emerge from the feudal structure of medieval Europe, the palaces of kings and ruling families began to acquire a new kind of architectural splendor. Some of the most magnificent buildings of ancient times had been palaces. We know something about them today because, like tombs and temples, the most important ones were built of enduring materials: stone, marble, or—in Roman times—concrete.

The most impressive of Renaissance palaces was the one Louis XIV built at Versailles, near Paris. Louis used this palace, which was over a quarter of a mile long, not only to display his majesty as *Le Roi Soleil* (the "Sun King") but also as a means of controlling the nation and preserving the monarchy at the expense of any effective political opposition. He was able to do this because inside the great palace and its flanking buildings he had gathered most of the aristocracy and the principal government ministries, so that France was governed virtually within sight of his bedroom—the central room in the whole plan.

Today, people still want buildings that testify visibly to their power and achievements. But such buildings are more likely to be commissioned by big business concerns (the partly functional, partly monumental Lever House in New York) or by the state (the skyscraper universities and cultural centers in Moscow). The United Nations buildings in New York are perhaps the buildings that come closest to commemorating in spectacularly monumental style the ideals of contemporary civilization.

A French historian described Louis XIV in his court at Versailles as "a god in his temple, celebrating his own worship in the midst of his host of priests and faithful."

United Nations headquarters in New York, designed by an international team of architects, symbolizes postwar hopes in world cooperation for peace. Glass and marble slab is Secretariat; dome marks General Assembly.

The architect plans

When someone wants to put up a new building, he calls in an *architect* to help him decide what form it should take, and how it should be built. There have always been skilled men able to design and supervise construction. Until the Renaissance they were often professional carpenters or masons, many of whose names are now forgotten. Among those who are remembered are the 13th-century Frenchman Villard de Honnecourt and England's Henry Yevele (d. 1400). We also know some architects of ancient times—for example, Callicrates and Ictinus, the fifth-century B.C. designers of the Parthenon.

But in the modern world, the use of the word architect —to denote a man who follows the specific *profession* of architecture, who is a *designer* rather than a builder— dates only from the Renaissance, when men began to be so interested in the architecture of classical Greece and Rome that they studied building styles without actually knowing how to lay bricks or carve stones. For instance, the Italian architect Leon Battista Alberti (1404-72), designer of churches and palaces in Florence and elsewhere, had studied chiefly law and Latin, yet he wrote a famous book on architecture : *De Re Aedificatoria*.

The rediscovery in the 15th century of a book full of information about Roman building methods, written by Vitruvius, an official architect of early imperial Rome, exerted a strong influence on architects who looked back to the buildings of ancient Rome for inspiration. The architects, carpenters, and stonemasons of the Middle Ages had often combined a high degree of skill in traditional techniques with a restless eagerness to experiment. The result was that, in time, many nations developed their own distinctive building styles.

The Renaissance revival of interest in Roman architecture produced many buildings in which elements of the Gothic and classical styles were combined. The 16th-century French châteaux, such as Chambord (p. 116), show a blending of Gothic and classic details. And everywhere in the 19th century, public buildings were designed in one or another of nearly all the styles that had developed throughout history. Today, however, architects recognize that new buildings present problems that past traditions cannot solve; contemporary needs stimulate the development of new materials and techniques.

It is easy to see that the tasks of modern architects can be much more complicated than those of ancient and

Interest in planning methods of Roman architects as described by Vitruvius inspired the Florentine Leon Battista Alberti to write a similar work for use by Renaissance architects. The woodcut reproduced above from Alberti's book shows a land surveyor measuring a site.

Medieval artisans worked to plan, but with enough skill to be able to add individual touches such as decorated bosses or keystones (close-up below) on ribbed vaults of Exeter Cathedral, England (right).

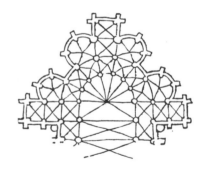

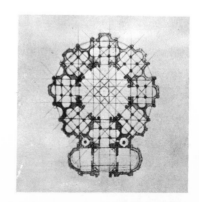

Plans by two influential architectural theorists: at upper right, a drawing from Gothic master Villard de Honnecourt's sketchbook (about 1235). Below it, Leonardo da Vinci's late 15th-century design for an octagonal church.

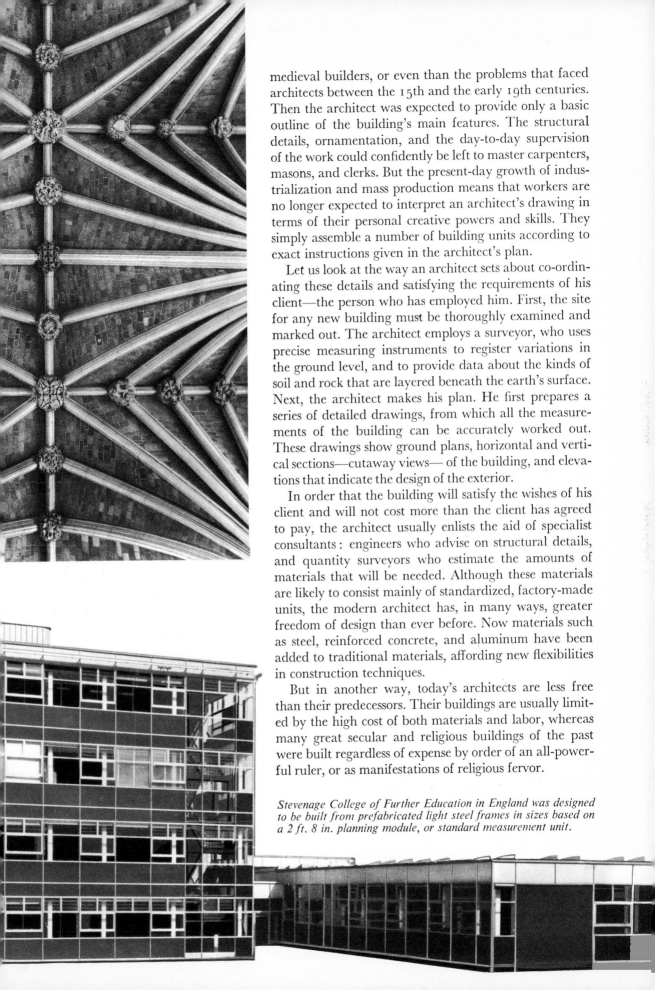

medieval builders, or even than the problems that faced architects between the 15th and the early 19th centuries. Then the architect was expected to provide only a basic outline of the building's main features. The structural details, ornamentation, and the day-to-day supervision of the work could confidently be left to master carpenters, masons, and clerks. But the present-day growth of industrialization and mass production means that workers are no longer expected to interpret an architect's drawing in terms of their personal creative powers and skills. They simply assemble a number of building units according to exact instructions given in the architect's plan.

Let us look at the way an architect sets about co-ordinating these details and satisfying the requirements of his client—the person who has employed him. First, the site for any new building must be thoroughly examined and marked out. The architect employs a surveyor, who uses precise measuring instruments to register variations in the ground level, and to provide data about the kinds of soil and rock that are layered beneath the earth's surface. Next, the architect makes his plan. He first prepares a series of detailed drawings, from which all the measurements of the building can be accurately worked out. These drawings show ground plans, horizontal and vertical sections—cutaway views— of the building, and elevations that indicate the design of the exterior.

In order that the building will satisfy the wishes of his client and will not cost more than the client has agreed to pay, the architect usually enlists the aid of specialist consultants : engineers who advise on structural details, and quantity surveyors who estimate the amounts of materials that will be needed. Although these materials are likely to consist mainly of standardized, factory-made units, the modern architect has, in many ways, greater freedom of design than ever before. Now materials such as steel, reinforced concrete, and aluminum have been added to traditional materials, affording new flexibilities in construction techniques.

But in another way, today's architects are less free than their predecessors. Their buildings are usually limited by the high cost of both materials and labor, whereas many great secular and religious buildings of the past were built regardless of expense by order of an all-powerful ruler, or as manifestations of religious fervor.

Stevenage College of Further Education in England was designed to be built from prefabricated light steel frames in sizes based on a 2 ft. 8 in. planning module, or standard measurement unit.

Rhythm, proportion, and scale

Repetition and pattern are essential in all forms of art. Great poems, paintings, and symphonies are all alike in that they are built up from patterns of repeated shapes or sounds. This kind of repetition is what we mean by *rhythm*. In any complete work of art, it is not only the individual units—the sounds, or the shapes and colors, for instance—that are grouped together rhythmically. These groups are themselves also arranged in such a way that they form the rhythms of the complete work.

We can see rhythm at work in a building when we look at its exterior, which includes many separate but similar features, such as windows, or at its interior hallways and suites of rooms. The architect tries to unite these details into rhythmical groupings. The shape and size of a series of windows or doorways is partly governed by the number and size of the shapes the architect chooses, and partly by larger rhythms with which he controls the design of the building as a whole: repeated columns, towers, or arcades, for example. All these repeated shapes and forms go to make up a rhythmical, unified design much as various steps repeated in their proper order make up a dance. But as in music or poetry, for example, constant repetition of the same rhythm can become monotonous. In order to keep the design of a building interesting and lively, architects often break up a long sequence of repeated shapes by introducing slight variations. In a row of arches, for example, every third arch might be made taller or wider than its neighbors.

If we call rhythm the "dance" of architecture, we can call proportion its "music." Just as a group of musical notes can create a harmony of sound, architectural dimensions can be "tuned" to one another to produce

Unbroken rhythms of colonnade in Ravenna's six[th] century basilica of S. Apollinare in Classe (abo[ve] focus attention on altar. In the nave, or central ais[le] of Amiens Cathedral (completed 1236), rhythms str[ess] verticality (right) yet lead the eye on to high altar.

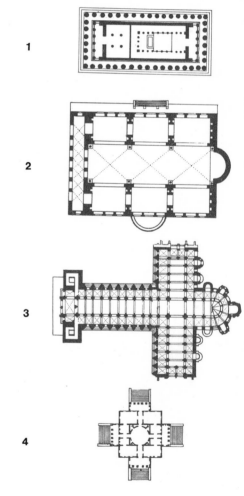

The Parthenon's colonnaded exterior (plan 1) w[as] more important than interior, rarely entered [by] worshipers. Romans designed large-scale interiors, [as] in Basilica of Maxentius (plan 2; about A.D. 320) [to] accommodate crowds. Spanish pilgrimage church [at] Santiago de Compostela (plan 3; begun 1077) w[as] suited to processions. Villa Rotonda (plan 4; desig[ned] by Palladio in 1567) is small-scale private house w[ith] four symmetrical wings. Façade of cathedral at P[isa] (left; late 12th century) has rhythmic arcades.

visual harmony. Proportion may be described as the harmonious relationship among all the heights, widths, and depths of the various parts of a building. Architects have usually accomplished this by means of standard systems of proportion. Many calculate related dimensions arithmetically; others use geometric systems. The Greeks and Romans both seem to have relied chiefly on numerical calculation whereas the ancient Egyptians drew up a network of squares and diagonal lines to work out the proportions of their pyramids and temples. In medieval Europe, the builders of the cathedrals used systems based on the angles and divisions created by placing triangles inside squares, and one square inside another.

During the period of elaborate Baroque architecture in the 17th and 18th centuries, many architects employed systems of solid geometry involving the complicated interlocking of forms such as the cone and sphere. The best-known of the architects who worked in this manner was Giovanni Lorenzo Bernini (p. 74), who provided St. Peter's in Rome with its famous piazza and colonnade. But even he was exceeded in originality and ingenuity by Francesco Borromini (1599-1667), designer of the tiny oval church of San Carlo alle Quattro Fontane, and the star-shaped chapel of San Ivo della Sapienza (both in Rome), and by Guarino Guarini (1624-83), who was responsible for such complex structures as the dome of the Chapel of the Holy Shroud in Turin.

The architect's third planning element, linked to proportion, is *scale*. When the word "scale" is applied to a finished building, it usually describes the relationship between the building's proportions and those of the human figure. For instance, people often speak of St. Peter's as being "on a huge scale," meaning that people are dwarfed in relation to its great size. This effect is one architects often try to achieve in public buildings when a sense of awe and power is appropriate. Or they may wish to give a feeling of spaciousness to buildings through which thousands of people pass, such as railway terminals.

In other kinds of buildings architects want to be sure people will not feel lost or insignificant. Le Corbusier (p. 94), for example, has carefully planned the proportions of buildings meant to be lived and worked in constantly, like his Paris Salvation Army Hostel (1929), so that they do not overwhelm people. Later he worked out a system of scaled dimensions called the "Modulor" for mass-produced building components. These proportions are designed to suit an ideal human figure, six feet high. But Le Corbusier's method is itself related to systems used by Renaissance artists and architects—which were themselves similar to those used by the Greeks (p. 308).

Many architects have studied relation between buildings and human proportions, as in Francesco di Giorgio's 15th-century church plan (far left) and Corbusier's 20th-century "Modulor" system based on ideal figure (left).

107

Building materials

The forms of architecture have always been dictated by the physical limitations of timber, stone, clay, and other building materials, much as the make-up of the human body governs the movements of a dancer. The ziggurats (p. 102) of ancient Sumerian architecture, for instance, can still be seen today because they were built in the shape of huge mountains of brick, made from the inexhaustible supply of river mud in the plains between the rivers Tigris and Euphrates. But smaller, less solidly built Sumerian buildings—houses and even palaces—have disappeared because mud bricks deteriorate easily. In all early civilizations, methods of building were naturally based on the use of available materials. In time, building forms evolved in this way became fixed by tradition.

In the case of mud-brick building, skills stayed at almost the same degree of development in North India, Persia, and Mesopotamia for about 2000 years. At first, bricks of mud and straw were dried in the sun, but eventually builders in these lands found they could make bricks stronger and more weatherproof by baking them in an oven—called a *kiln*—at extremely high temperatures. Assyrian and Persian builders discovered how to bake a hard, glass-like surface on to bricks. They used the glazed bricks as a decorative, as well as a structural, element. *Bitumen* (a form of natural tar used as an adhesive and waterproofing material) was also introduced as a long-lasting mortar to bond layers of bricks together. Bitumen was replaced in Roman times by a cement made from burned limestone mixed with hair and sand. Another product of burned limestone—plaster—had been known since prehistoric times; it was used by the Egyptians, as well as the Greeks, to cover the surfaces of buildings.

The laying of stone masonry was the greatest technical achievement of the Egyptians. At first, layers of stone were cemented together with mortar, but around 1000 B.C. the Egyptians began to use bronze clamps and jointing pieces. The Greeks later refined this method to a point where the joints between stones were nearly invisible.

The Romans developed the techniques of building with stone still further, but their most important contribution

The ancient Persians faced walls with glazed, weatherproof brick, sometimes modeled in relief, like this archer (top right) from a wall in Susa (p. 98). From the 11th to the 17th centuries, builders in Russia's northern regions used wood skillfully in the manner of the Church of St. Nicholas (center), near the seaport of Archangel. In Peru's ancient city of Cuzco, 12th-century Inca masons fitted together—without mortar—stones several feet across (bottom).

was the perfection of *concrete*. A great variety of building stone was available, but by far the most plentiful material in Italy was a sandy volcanic ash. The Romans made a cement of this, mixed it with water, and added rubble such as broken stones and crushed pottery. They poured this mixture into molds; when dry, it became rock-hard and was able to bear very heavy loads. The Romans used it to form arches, vaults, and domes that were larger than any built before.

But when the empire declined in the fifth century, Roman building methods were almost entirely transformed. After the Romanesque period (from the fall of the Roman Empire in the sixth century until about 1200) when walls were thick and windows few, Gothic builders learned how to use stone in such a way that they could build soaring, thin-walled, relatively light structures. The Roman secret of making concrete had been lost and remained so until the 18th century, when various recipes were devised, first in Holland, then in Britain and France. In the late 19th century a technique of reinforcing concrete with metal rods or girders was introduced by such engineers as France's François Hennebique (1842-1921).

Metal itself did not come into general structural use for building until the 19th century, when cheaper methods were invented to produce great quantities of iron and steel. In the late 18th century a few architects used cast iron, first as a substitute for masonry in bridge building and then as a strong and fireproof replacement for timber beams in frame buildings. Cheap manufacturing methods enabled the Englishman Joseph Paxton (1801-65) to build the great Crystal Palace for the 1851 Exhibition in London entirely of standardized cast-iron and glass units. It was one of the earliest examples of prefabricated building, and a forerunner of the modern glass and metal skyscraper.

Roman mastery of concrete made Pantheon's dome (A.D. 120) possible. Light enters 27-foot opening (above). Sectional drawing (below) of Auguste Perret's Champs-Élysées Theatre (Paris, 1911) exposes framework of reinforced concrete, a material Perret pioneered. In Paris exhibition of 1889, engineers roofed vast Halle des Machines with steel (lower right).

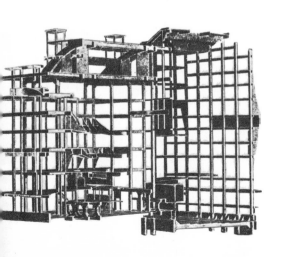

The defeat of gravity

When architects were primarily interested in expressing order and preserving a formal harmony in their buildings, styles remained the same for centuries, as in the dignified architecture of ancient Greece and Egypt. As though architects themselves were infected with the general fever for expansion during periods of great religious, colonial, commercial, and industrial enterprise and prosperity, their buildings embodied attempts to master gravity. Throughout the rise of the Roman Empire, the later Middle Ages in Europe, and during the last two centuries throughout the industrialized world, the struggle to create seemingly weightless buildings has been one of the principal themes of architecture.

The gravitational forces against which builders must fight exert themselves in three principal ways: by *compression*, *tension*, and *torsion*, which are the technical names for pushing, pulling, and twisting. Compression is the most common force. It occurs as soon as one object is placed on top of another. The object's weight pushes outward or presses down, causing whatever is beneath it to collapse if it is unable to bear the weight. That is why, in order to pull materials like earth or brick together under such a crushing pressure, some kind of reinforcing framework is generally incorporated with them. The woven reeds or branches forming the skeleton of a primitive mud hut served such a purpose, as does the latticework of metal rods that today's architects use to reinforce concrete in modern buildings (p. 108).

The history of building techniques contains many other examples of ways men have tried to counter the forces of compression. Even primitive builders had to solve the problems that arose when they formed roofs by spanning the space between walls or rows of columns with timber beams. To span wide spaces, the weight of the beams meant builders had to provide very thick supporting walls or put the columns close together; to have thin walls, only short beams could be used. Eventually it was discovered that the distance between walls could be greatly increased if horizontal beams were replaced by

Horizontal lines of buildings such as Inigo Jones's Queen's House (below; Greenwich, England, 1616) show calm compromise with force of gravity. Contrast with Ulm Cathedral's 630-foot spire (right), Europe's highest, begun in 1482, not finished until 1890.

Simplest way to roof a space is to use horizontal beams (diagram, top right). For wider distances beams may be angled, or pitched, but outward thrust tends to push walls apart (diagram, lower right). To avoid this, builders tie rafters together with beams, as shown in diagram below. Photograph shows timber roof of St. Cuthbert's parish church, Wells, England, with richly carved tie beams and braces.

Photograph of Abbey of the Trinity, Vendôme, France. Pointed arch (top diagram) increased height; stone buttresses counteracted weight thrusts (lower diagram).

Arched iron roof of St. Pancras Station (London, 1868) spans 240 feet. Diagram shows how underground tie beams counteract thrust.

pairs of beams propped together at an angle, with one end of each beam resting on the walls. However, this created a further difficulty: The beams not only exerted a downward force, but they also created an outward force—called *thrust*—that tended to push the walls over. This was overcome first by making the walls thicker and stronger, and later by adding extra supports called *buttresses*, to divert some of the roof thrust away from the walls and allow them to be thinner. One of the most interesting examples of this kind of support is the "flying" buttress of the Gothic cathedral. It is a heavy stone pier built a little distance away from the main wall, but connected to it by an arch through which the weight of the wall or the roof is channeled through the buttress into the ground.

All roof forms, whether peaked, vaulted, or domed (p. 114), exert outward thrusts that must be overcome if the building is to remain stable. In the case of angled roofs, instead of using a buttress, an architect may fix a horizontal tie beam that links or ties together the lower ends of the angled beams. In this way, a complete triangle is formed in which each beam is pulling equally hard against the other two, lessening the outward thrust. Thus the architect has conquered a second gravitational force, tension, by making it his ally. Ties are often used with arches or vaults (p. 114) and may sometimes be of cable or even rope, as well as the more usual timber or metal. Some of the world's largest steel tie beams run underneath the railway tracks at St. Pancras station in London; they link together the ends of the great steel arches that form the walls and roof.

The third force that architects must counter is torsion. If a structure is too tall or thin to support itself, the pull of gravity will cause it to twist downward about its own axis. To overcome this twisting, very tall buildings, like the skyscrapers of New York, are strengthened internally with rigid steel supports. Such supports are frequently built in a triangular shape that creates the same kind of tension that helps to counteract roof thrust.

Torsion stress, set up by strong winds, destroyed Tacoma Narrows Bridge (U.S.A.) in 1940. Gravity can affect tall buildings similarly.

Framework and structure

In a number of ways, the basic construction of many buildings is like that of the human body. Both are held together by a strong, weight-bearing skeleton and covered with an outer skin. A very close parallel to the human body may be seen in so-called "frame" buildings. In these, the structural members—horizontal beams, vertical posts, and angled braces or struts—are arranged, like the bones in a body, to form a rigid framework. In such buildings, the walls—of glass, for example, or brick or stone—serve simply as a protective skin to keep out the weather or give the occupants privacy.

Sometimes buildings constructed solely of columns and beams, such as the temples of ancient Egypt and Greece, are inaccurately called frame buildings. They are more properly described as *trabeated* (from the Latin *trabs*, a beam). The stone beams used in these buildings were usually very heavy, and thus able to span only short distances. The columns supporting them had to be of great strength and size, placed very close together. This massiveness, combined with the powerful rhythmic effect produced by rows of regularly spaced columns, is a feature common to many of the most visually impressive buildings of ancient times.

For less formidable buildings, such as houses, framing techniques were devised. One ancient and straightforward framing material has always been timber. Since it is easy to cut and shape, builders used it in most early frame buildings. Late Stone Age huts on the shores of the North Italian and Swiss lakes were made of frames of timber poles lashed or notched together and covered with a skin of reed matting and thatch. In medieval times, builders

Wood framing in 16th-century "half-timbered" English inn (above) is filled in with plaster-covered brick. In Crystal Palace (below; London, 1851) Joseph Paxton used glass to fill spaces between tubular cast-iron framing.

Japanese use careful rectangular proportions in their buildings. Exposed wood framework, screen panels, floor mats are all related, as in house exhibited in New York's Museum of Modern Art.

112

in many parts of northern Europe used wood frames, filled in with brick and plaster, to make the timbered houses we can still see in many German and English towns. In the Orient, Japanese builders brought timber-frame construction to such perfection that they still employ it in buildings today. During the past 2000 years they have developed particularly elaborate methods for jointing wood. The interior walls of Japanese timber-frame houses are made of lightweight paper screens that can easily be moved and rearranged.

Like medieval European builders, the Japanese nearly always allow posts and beams to be exposed; they are a decorative element of both interiors and exteriors. We have seen, too, how medieval architects framed cathedrals with complex stone elements such as the buttress (p. 110), a kind of exposed "bone" of the soaring Gothic skeleton, which was otherwise covered with thin glass and stone walls. Although Renaissance buildings (modeled after ancient Roman structures) appeared to be more solidly constructed, they achieved open effects through the use of load-bearing arches, vaults, and domes.

At about the end of the 18th century, Western architects began to replace wood and stone framing with cast iron, especially in factories and theatres, where strong, slender, fire-resistant iron columns were a decided advantage (p. 118). By the 1840s a few architects had begun to build frameworks entirely of prefabricated cast-iron sections. These sections were sometimes made with slots so that they could be fitted together without rivets or bolts. An example of a building made in this fashion was the London Coal Exchange, designed by James Bunsten Bunning (1802-63). Since the 1860s, when better qualities of iron and steel began to be made in large quantity, riveted or welded steel frames have been widely used, making possible such building forms as the skyscraper.

Steel and iron have also been used to give added strength to concrete (p. 108). Structures made in this way have the advantage of forming a complete unit with no jointings. Reinforced concrete may also be used to form *cantilevers*. The form of a cantilever beam resembles an outstretched human arm holding a heavy weight. The cantilever is fixed at one end to a column or wall through which the beam's weight thrusts itself downward. Some new buildings consist of a central tower or column that contains elevators and stairways; and rigid cantilever beams project from the column to hold up each floor. The weight of the building travels inward and down through the central tower. On such buildings, as on steel frames, architects can hang lightweight curtain walls, often made entirely of glass.

Simplest form of construction—column and beam—is characteristic of Egyptian temples, such as Temple of Ammon at Luxor, above (about 1400 B.C.). Massive, close-ranked columns over 50 feet tall support heavy beams.

In Johnson Wax Company's laboratory tower (Racine, Wisconsin), designed in 1947 by Frank Lloyd Wright, cantilevered square and round floors alternate around a central core. Wall is simply a skin of glass tubing and brick.

Assyrians were among earliest builders of continuous semicircular arches, or vaults. In vaulted culvert at Khorsabad (above; eighth century B.C.) each ring of bricks, strengthened by mortar, leans against its neighbor.

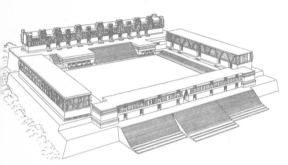

Flat concrete-covered roofs of 10th-century Maya palace at Uxmal, Mexico (above), are supported by wedge-shaped arches of stones that project from side walls in graduated rows.

Wall, column, roof, and dome

Today, architects often leave the frameworks of their buildings exposed—a logical development from modern techniques of making steel or reinforced-concrete frames from which thin walls can be hung like curtains (p. 112). But until such strong, light framing became possible, architects generally had to rely structurally on the walls themselves, and to adapt roof forms to the loads walls could bear. The alternative was to erect heavy columns close together, as in Egypt and Greece, or to use the lighter-looking, but by today's standards still massive, columns and buttresses of the Gothic builders.

One reason early builders probably constructed walls was to provide shelter for their families, and it could not have been long before they tried to find ways of roofing over such wall-enclosed areas. The most obvious method was by means of beams of stone or timber laid horizontally. This was fairly simple to do when roofing small areas, but it became a major problem as men gradually began to build walls that were higher and farther apart. The roofing beams for these larger buildings were generally very heavy—and often had to be transported from distant forests or stone quarries. For these reasons, the preparation and the raising of such beams into position is regarded as one of early man's supreme technical achievements.

The first walls must have been made from whatever materials came to hand—stones, mud, wooden stakes, interwoven branches, or stretched skins, for example. The strength and usefulness of such materials could often be increased by combining them together. Rows of stakes could be daubed with clay to fill in the cracks; mud walls reinforced with timber or reeds. In countries rich in timber, such as China or northern India, defensive walls were made entirely of wooden stakes bound tightly together. But in other lands, such as Egypt, where the chief building material was sun-dried mud, timber was used sparingly. Wooden poles were inserted into the mud walls at regular intervals simply as a reinforcement.

The two methods of using upright poles or columns—either as a basic building unit, or as a reinforcement—continued to influence architecture long after materials like mud and wooden posts had been superseded by stone. For example, whereas the Greeks surrounded the inner walls of their temples with rows of columns supporting a massive roof of stone and timber beams, Roman and, later, Renaissance architects often used columns as a form of decoration, fixing them to buildings when their brick or masonry walls were already complete.

The building forms most commonly associated with the Romans are the semicircular *arch* and *vault*, and the

Romans used rows of stone arches—their major architectural feature—to build up tiers of Colosseum in Rome (A.D. 72-80). Columns attached to outer walls have no structural function, but make façade seem less heavy.

dome. Although the arch form was known and used by the Sumerians (p. 96), it was the Romans who really explored its structural possibilities. Throughout their empire, the Romans employed the arch as the basis of almost every kind of building. It became, and has remained, a recognized symbol both of Rome's technical achievements and of her imperial power.

The name given to a continuous semicircular arch that joins together two parallel walls is a *tunnel* or *barrel* vault. By means of such vaulting, the Romans were able to roof the immense halls of their public baths (p. 116) and other large buildings. The dome (really a vault shape in the form of a sphere) had also been used by the Sumerians, and, to a limited extent, by the Greeks. But it was the Romans, with their mastery of building techniques, who first developed the dome into an architectural feature of great size and importance.

One of the first and still one of the largest of the world's important domes was that of the Pantheon at Rome, built about A.D. 112. Since then, architects in almost every age have made use of domes—from the sixth-century builders of the great Byzantine church of St. Sophia in Constantinople to the modern American engineer-architect Buckminster Fuller (born 1895), who has designed many lightweight structures that he calls "geodesic" domes, made of interlocking metal rods, and covered with translucent glass or plastic panels.

Columns lining wall at Saqqara (upper left) show how Egyptians translated forms of reed construction into stone. Similar "engaged" columns appear in 16th-century façade of Palladio's Palazzo Chiericati in Vicenza (lower left), along with functional colonnade. Central pier of the chapter house of England's Salisbury Cathedral (built about 1275) carries the weight of inward-thrusting vault ribs.

The dome is characteristic of Moslem architecture. An outstanding example is this small mosque in Isfahan built between 1600 and 1618 as private chapel for the Shah of Persia. Dome is covered with mosaic tiles set in glazed brick.

Services and facilities

The kinds of comfort people have wanted to incorporate into their buildings have varied from age to age, and from country to country. For instance, in 18th-century Europe all those who could afford it filled their houses with comfortably upholstered furniture, and lined their walls with rich fabrics or carved woodwork. But although people often spent a great deal of money on this kind of comfort, they paid almost no attention to sanitary arrangements, either public or private.

By contrast, the houses of the ancient Romans were comparatively barely furnished, but almost every city and town in the Roman Empire was provided with an elaborate system of drainage. And each town had its own public baths, supplied with heated water, and capable of accommodating large numbers of people.

Drainage and furnishings are not, of course, the only forms of services and fittings that men have developed to make their buildings more pleasant and comfortable to live in. One of the first refinements added to the design of houses was the chimney. At first, this simply took the form of a hole cut in the roof above the fireplace to let out the smoke. But later, chimneys developed a variety of shapes to suit different climates and building methods. Windows, another familiar building feature, serve a double role. They not only provide a way of looking through a wall, but also can be made to let in as much air and light as is needed.

A regular supply of fresh water has always been an essential requirement of civilization. Nowadays in most large cities, water is pumped to each building along underground pipes from special storage tanks and reservoirs. Roman cities were often supplied with water brought down from mountain springs or rivers along great arched aqueducts. But after the collapse of the Roman Empire, these aqueducts were allowed to fall to ruin. In most cases, the cities that they had once supplied with a regular flow of water did not receive comparable facilities again until the middle of the 19th century.

The 19th century also saw the development of many new sources of energy, among which were coal gas and electricity. These were quickly adapted to domestic as well as industrial use to supply various kinds of power, lighting, and heating. Electricity was also the basis of new methods of communication such as the telegraph and telephone and, later, radio and television. But although things like chimneys and windows have for centuries been treated as important architectural features, architects have tended to regard many of the newer services simply as functional necessities to be ignored as far as possible. That is why roofs of many modern buildings are cluttered

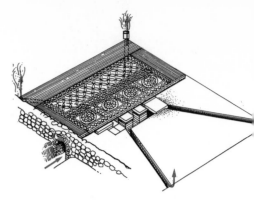

Roman underfloor heating (above). Arrows show hot-air flow from furnace to pit, trenches, flues at room corners. Servants carried water heated elsewhere to French 18th-century "sofa-bath" (below).

Chimneys and large glazed windows become part of architecture. Disappearance of necessity for fortification, and influence of spacious Italian Renaissance palaces, resulted in houses like French château of Chambord (1519).

116

up with an unorganized array of objects such as ventilators, radio and television aerials, elevator machinery, and water-storage tanks.

Certain architects have tried to give such features a visual unity by grouping them together inside walls, as the American Louis Kahn (born 1901) did in the Richards Medical Laboratories in Philadelphia (1960). In his Unité d'Habitation (1950), a Marseilles apartment house, Le Corbusier transformed rooftop apparatus into forms of architectural interest in their own right.

As well as affecting the appearance of individual buildings, the new services have also begun to change the look and character of whole towns. In most technically advanced countries today, the people who live in cities and towns tend to be much more isolated from one another than ever before. This is largely because they are now supplied in their own houses with many of the facilities that were once available only as public services. For example, most modern houses have their own supply of piped water, and a gas or electric refrigerator, as well as radio and television sets. Clearly, people living in such houses do not need to go, as their ancestors did, to a crowded public bath to wash, or pay a daily visit to the market place to buy food and to hear the latest news and gossip.

Thus in many cities the large buildings and open spaces that were originally intended as meeting places are used less frequently today; in fact, they are often demolished or built over. It is probable that people from Roman or medieval times (when the layout of towns was based on public rather than private activities), would find many of our modern cities and towns very uncivilized indeed.

Problem for 20th-century architects: how to accommodate services like lamp standards, telephone wires in modern city street (right), and other conveniences (far right) caricatured by American artist Saul Steinberg. Corbusier's solution in Marseilles: sculptural forms for rooftop ventilators, tanks, elevator housings.

New needs, new buildings

Early 19th-century manufacturing community in New Lanark, Scotland, was experimental project of mill owner and socialist Robert Owen. Layout of factory, housing, schools, stores heralded much present-day planning.

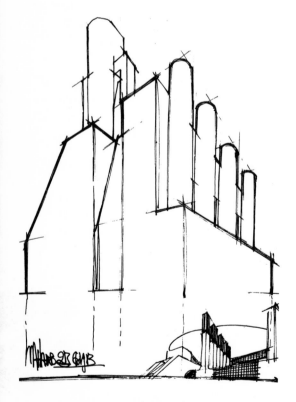

Drawings of Italian "Futurist" architect Antonio Sant'Elia (1888-1916) show remarkable insight into forms expressive of machine age. He died in World War I before any of his plans were realized, but like his 1913 power-plant design, they were to prove prophetic.

The industrial advances of the 19th century created two new building problems: the need for factories, and the need for large-scale blocks of offices or apartments. New machines needed shelter, and so did large numbers of workers and their families who were beginning to flood the industrialized cities. Quarters were also needed for the expanding army of office workers who handled planning and paper work in the emerging age of big business and concentrated city populations.

The size and weight of new machines and power plants, along with the complexity of mass-production processes, meant that sturdily built factory buildings with large areas of uncluttered floor space were necessary. The engineers and architects who designed the first factories concentrated on these two central requirements of structural strength and interior space. As a result, the exterior of the buildings received little thought. In most cases, walls were simply skins of brick, pierced by rows of identical, undecorated windows.

There was no historical precedent for such buildings; and though many of the first factories presented a rather grim appearance, others had a grandeur that resulted from their being straightforward and fresh solutions to a new problem. Such buildings, quickly copied throughout Europe and America, appeared first in England, where the earliest techniques of the Industrial Revolution—such as steam power and expanded iron production—were most extensively developed.

Large office and residential blocks were an American invention, however. The boom in industry and trade that

Skyscraper office buildings were an American innovation. Guaranty Building in Buffalo, New York (Louis Sullivan, 1890), reveals its steel structure in verticality of façade.

Two of today's solutions to architectural problems first posed in 19th century: Pirelli office building (above; Milan, 1959), by Gio Ponti and Pier Luigi Nervi; and Park Hill Estate (right), housing project supervised by J. C. Womersley in 1957 for Sheffield, England.

followed the American Civil War of 1861-65 meant that much new office space was needed in the cities. Land in the commercial centers of towns was expensive, and usually divided into evenly rectangular plots. In order to accommodate the greatest possible number of people in offices on each plot, architects began to build tall, tower-like buildings with many floors. At first they built them of masonry. But during the 1890s they experimented with steel-frame structures, like those designed by William Le Baron Jenney (1832-1907) and Louis Sullivan (1856-1924) in Chicago. The steel frame, together with the introduction of the electric elevator, made it possible for architects to design giant skyscrapers, the largest of which today have as many as 70 to 80 floors.

Though the skyscraper solved the problem of providing maximum floor space in a minimum of land space, it created another problem. When builders filled city blocks with these tall buildings, all but the upper floors of neighboring skyscrapers were in shadow. To overcome this and other problems of modern city planning, architects created so-called *slab* buildings. These, unlike most skyscraper towers, occupy only part of a rectangular site. They are built along one side of it, thus leaving enough open space between themselves and their neighbors for each floor to get as much daylight as possible. In congested New York, Skidmore, Owings, and Merrill designed separate gardens for the public and for office workers as part of Lever House. The same architects have provided a large public plaza with trees and a pool for their 60-story Chase Manhattan Bank building.

The slab form of building has also been used increasingly by modern architects when they design large-scale residential schemes. Perhaps the most notable and influential example is the block of flats at Marseilles, France, designed by Le Corbusier (p. 94). This building contains shops, restaurants, and a health center, as well as homes for over 1500 people. In fact, it is a self-contained neighborhood, but arranged vertically one street above another under one roof instead of being spread out over many acres. Building in this way leaves the surrounding countryside unspoiled.

Le Corbusier's pilgrimage church on a hilltop near Ronchamps, France. Billowing concrete forms enclose small chapel to seat 50. Plan allows for open-air congregations of up to 12,000 people.

Western civilization nowadays is not bound by a single code of accepted religious and social beliefs—as it was during the Middle Ages, for example, or at the time of the Roman Empire or the Greek city-states. In such periods, the entire community was involved in architecture; whether as free men or slaves, the people themselves were the shapers of buildings. What ideas, then, go into the making of today's buildings? What aspect of modern society decides how they will look?

In the 19th century, buildings often indicated only the confusion that resulted from a sudden demand for new kinds of buildings coupled with a bewildering choice of new materials. People were not sure how these materials ought to be used. At first, new buildings such as banks, railway stations, and offices—symbols of industrial and social change—were hidden behind assorted Greek, Roman, Gothic, Moorish, and Assyrian façades. And although a number of architects sought more honest and straightforward solutions, it was not until the turn of the century that a distinct new architectural style began to emerge, notably through the work of such architects as the Germans Walter Gropius (born 1883) and Ludwig Mies van der Rohe (born 1888), and the Swiss-born Le Corbusier (p. 94). They designed new buildings that made use of undisguised contemporary materials and advanced construction techniques.

But good architecture, however straightforward and

Exhibition halls need space and light. Pier Luigi Nervi's hall in Turin (1948-50) includes three great rooms daringly spanned with prefabricated reinforced-concrete framing units.

Air, rail, and road passengers transfer from one form of transport to another in a single efficient building at London's Gatwick Airport, designed in 1958 by Yorke, Rosenberg, and Mardall.

practical, cannot avoid expressing something of the beliefs of the society that produces it. Buildings in the 20th century strongly reflect our preoccupation with science and technology. Early in the century, some architects tried to create a kind of architecture that was strictly practical, and owed nothing to previous styles. But today most architects have realized that architecture of its very nature must express ideas at the same time that it satisfies functional requirements. Under the influence of Frank Lloyd Wright (1869-1959), one of America's best-known architects, many have come to believe that the wisest solution is to design each building in harmony with its particular natural environment. Building materials like wood, concrete, and glass should be combined as harmoniously as trees, rocks, and water in a natural landscape.

Another kind of recent architecture parallels nature in the organic structure of its forms. The reinforced-concrete buildings of the Frenchman Eugène Freyssinet (1879-1962), for example, and those of the Swiss Robert Maillart (p. 124) are all characterized by a unified strength and simplicity of design.

When we study the history of man as an architect, we see clearly how the structural efficiency of buildings has never been enough, in itself, to satisfy his eye and mind. For men have always felt the need to make their buildings significant as symbols of their different ideas and beliefs.

Chapter 5

Design

We often speak of "good" or "bad" design as if design were something that has its own physical existence. But it really exists only as a property or quality of an object —an object that exists because someone had ideas about how to make it, what materials to use, the best way to use them, and how the object should look. *Design* is the art of planning and clarifying such ideas so that either the planner or someone else can create the object.

The man who plans the making is the *designer*. He may work alone, like a potter (who both conceives the idea for a bowl and makes it on his potter's wheel), or he may work as part of a group to design something that others will make, such as an automobile. The thing he designs is good or bad depending on how well he solves the problems involved in planning and making it.

How can we measure the quality of his design? Is it good if the object is useful but not very attractive? Is the design bad if the object is handsome but impractical? Everything material that goes into its making can be weighed or measured, but it is harder to judge what makes it well or badly planned, beautiful or ugly.

Yet it is necessary for us to try to do this. We are the supporters, or patrons, of good design in everyday objects —much as wealthy men once were patrons of artists they favored and gave financial support to. We give similar support to designers when we choose what we shall buy from among the great variety of things manufactured for our use. To exercise this choice wisely, to choose the well-designed article and to avoid the bad, we must know some of the problems the designer faces. We must find standards by which we can measure the success of his solutions to problems in design.

Any functional object—a wrist watch, an automobile, or an ocean-going vessel like this one—may be good to look at; but we cannot say that it is well designed unless it also works efficiently. Thus, the designer's task is to strike a balance between beauty and practicality, to find the most pleasing and the most suitable shape for the job. Today, technology offers him opportunities to create exciting new designs, scientifically planned to meet the changing needs of the modern world.

Thinking about design

There are two ways in which we can think about the design of objects. We can examine, first, the way they *look,* and, second, the way they are meant to be *used.* Imagine, for example, that while out walking you come upon an elegant bridge like the one pictured on this page. Perhaps you pause only to admire its pleasant appearance. But you might also begin to wonder why the bridge was designed in just that way—why it was given just that particular form.

Your first impulse is to look at the bridge much as you might look at a piece of sculpture in a similar setting, admiring the graceful curve of the arch and the way it is mirrored in the water. But even though looking at objects in this way may give you pleasure, it will not bring you much nearer to understanding fully what makes them well or badly designed.

To do this, you must examine things a second way: from the point of view of their *use.* For example, imagine that you want to drive a car over the bridge. Your pleasure in its beauty will soon change to annoyance if, although its appearance is pleasing, the bridge does not *work* the way you want it to. What had seemed a beautiful shape you now regard as a highly impractical one. Why, then, was the bridge built like this?

If we suppose the builder to have been a sensible man, the answer must be that long ago, when the bridge was built, the water was a more important highway than the path over the bridge. A high arch was necessary so that small boats could sail through without lowering their masts and rigging. The only people who crossed the bridge would have been either on horseback or on foot; and they could have passed over the curve of the arch without difficulty.

Instead of simply *looking* at the bridge, we have now thought about its uses as well, and we have guessed at some of the problems its designer faced. The bridge exists as his solution to those problems. He probably did want to build a handsome bridge, but he had to do so in terms of what was *needed.* Whatever a man designs, he must take into account such practical requirements.

A bridge is a good example of a man-made object

This 15th-century bridge in the gardens of the Summer Palace in Peking combines beauty with practicality; the high arch is graceful, and allows tall boats to pass under it.

Good design can make any object—from a mach part to a fabric—as good to look at as it is practic While the ball bearing pictured above is stric functional, its precision and symmetry make pleasing to the eye. And although the 16th-centu Turkish velvet on the opposite page was design chiefly to be decorative, its pleasantly repetit pattern of stylized plants and flowers made it practic for curtains and furniture coverings too.

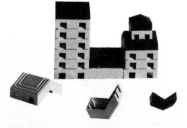

Salginatobel bridge in the Swiss Alps (1929-30, Robert Maillart) seems to soar across the mountain gorge. Reinforced-concrete arch spans distance unsuited to masonry or steel arches.

whose form is almost entirely dictated by the necessity for practical solutions. Hundreds of years after the first stone-arch bridges, bridge builders sought new solutions to cope with the heavier traffic of horse-drawn vehicles, railway trains, and, finally, cars and trucks. And they also looked for ways to span rivers, bays, and mountains that no one believed could ever be bridged.

Engineers experimented with new materials to see if they were adaptable to contemporary needs. Near Coalbrookdale, the birthplace of the English iron industry, Abraham Darby (1750-91) built the first iron bridge. It imitated the techniques of stone bridge-building in which the roadway thrusts its weight down through the ends of the arch into the earth.

Changes in materials, however, soon lead to changes in techniques and in design. In the case of bridges, engineers discovered that iron formed into thin rods or cables could easily withstand immense tensile, or pulling, forces exerted by weights hung from them. Early in the 19th century, engineers began to build such "suspension" bridges. The platform for the roadway was suspended from chains or cables supported by tall towers. Designers had given bridges a new look—a look that actually resulted from an effort to make the best use of new materials to solve new problems.

Another new material—concrete reinforced with steel rods—allowed bridges to assume useful new shapes. Designers could now build practical bridges in places where neither heavy stone arches nor the towers for suspension bridges could find secure footing. Such new solutions to design problems create new kinds of beauty. The Swiss engineer Robert Maillart (1872-1940), for example, used reinforced concrete for bridges whose sweeping curves follow the winding mountain roads they carry.

Like the bridges we have discussed, any well-designed object should be able to satisfy us in two ways : It should do the job it is intended to do, and it should be a pleasure to look at. If we think about it from these points of view —as a designer himself does—we shall be better able to judge whether a given design is good or bad.

The design of useful objects must solve several problems, as shown by examples here and on page 124. A child's toy (far left) may be designed for creative play; a camera, for precision control; a zipper, for reliability; a saw, for safety; and the printed circuit of a television set, for quick, easy manufacture.

Technique and material

More than the painter or sculptor, the designer must understand the *technological* properties of his materials —that is, the ways they may be adapted to manufacturing requirements. His understanding of raw materials and the way each can be used will influence both the usefulness and the appearance of what he designs.

The designer works, in fact, with two conditions always in mind: first, the materials available; second, the manufacturing methods suitable to those materials. The order of priority is significant, for the material the designer must work with determines what methods he will use. To make this clear, let us consider some examples.

If we look at the potter's materials and methods, we can see how they have influenced traditional pottery design. Since clay is a *plastic* material, it can easily be molded or modeled by hand. The potter takes wet clay and throws it onto a revolving platform or wheel. As it spins, the potter "designs" his pot spontaneously—pulling and pushing the clay into a shape that records the movement both of his guiding hands and of the wheel. That shape is the familiar round one we associate with most handmade pottery.

Glass, another plastic material, is too hot in its fluid state to be worked with the hands. The designer-maker can, however, blow it into bubble-like shapes that harden quickly. There are still other ways of working with glass and clay. If designers wish, they may pour either material into molds. In this way, they can contrive square bottles to save packing and storage space, or they can reproduce decorative designs in relief.

If designers use plastics, which derive their very name from their properties of being easily molded and shaped, they must plan complex machines and carefully engineered molds. For plastics in their raw state exist as chemical powders, and we can fuse them into a solid state only by using intense heat and pressure. Plastic objects reflect the processes of their manufacture: They have a molded

The designer's methods depend on the material that he uses. Vases like the Chinese example above (between 960 and 1279 A.D.) are shaped from easily worked clay on a revolving wheel. Barrels are made from strips of pliable wood; the photograph on the right shows coopers securing the strips with metal hoops.

126

5 **6**

look, with smooth, clean surfaces and rounded edges.

Even metals may be worked in a plastic state and cast into molds. But such castings are generally so heavy and expensive that the designer may prefer to use metal sheets. These can be stamped with great presses into shapes as simple as bowls, or as complex as car bodies. Since metal sheets are more easily stamped or bent into rounded shapes than into sharply angled ones, the design of metal objects shows this. We see round tin cans, round coffee pots, round pewter tankards, round storage tanks, and rounded edges on metal boxes.

When the designer works with materials derived from trees or plants, his problems are different. He can control the manufacture of metals or of plastics, but it is harder to control nature. If he wishes to make a wooden bowl all in one piece by hollowing out a block of wood, knots or cracks in the block will limit him. The waste and extravagance involved in finding blocks of wood of a workable size may inspire him to join smaller pieces, free of flaws, into kegs or barrels, held together by glue and metal straps.

The designer working with wood can choose other solutions, too. He can break the wood into fibers by grinding it or dissolving it with chemicals. Wood fibers, matted together again, make paper, which the designer may wax to make waterproof and shape into lightweight disposable cups or milk containers. And plant and animal fibers that can be woven offer the designer special flexible qualities. For instance, he may find them useful for making collapsible, easily stored canvas buckets or fabric bags.

Our examples have shown how materials influence the designer's solutions for such problems as providing various kinds of containers. But whatever the design problem, the creative designer will meet it in the same way. He will gear his design to the most suitable materials available and to the methods appropriate for working those materials.

The methods and materials used in modern automobile factories mean that car roofs can be stamped out of sheet steel in a few seconds.

How methods of manufacture influenced the design of three different kinds of containers. The elegant oil cruet above, made in Venice during the 16th or 17th century, was blown by a skilled craftsman out of a bubble of molten glass. Mass production demands simpler designs—like this machine-molded plastic bucket (far left). Spherical petroleum tank (left) is shaped from pliable steel sheets.

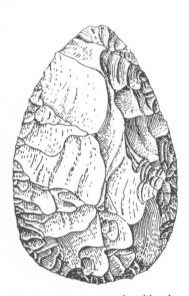

German aviation engineer Otto Lilienthal—fascinated as a child by the flight of storks—designed gliders based on a bird's wings. In experiments like the one above (1890), he discovered how a pilot might control his machine in the air by shifting the weight of his body to counteract wind resistance.

Flints with a cutting edge, like the one above, were among the first tools made by men. By the late Stone Age, bone and antler were being used to make tools for different purposes—awls, sharp arrowheads, serrated harpoons, and broad flat blades (below). Today, a special tool is designed for every job. Right: household tools—table knife, bread knife, scissors, linoleum knife, fish knife, dessert knife, cheese knife, chisel, butcher's knife.

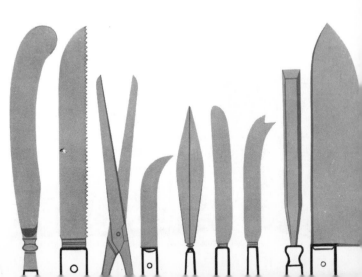

Design and function

Early in history, man discovered that the sharp edge of a broken stone could cut. As he hit upon uses for such stones—for self-defense, for hunting animals, for cutting up meat and hides—he found that each new task demanded a differently angled edge, or a different size stone. When he began to shape stones into forms appropriate to those tasks, he became a designer. He had discovered that the shapes and sizes of objects must be planned to suit various purposes.

These uses—the *functions*—for which objects are intended have an even greater influence on their design than the designer's materials and the way he uses them (p. 126). Wielding knives, for example, whether in a butcher shop or in a dining room, calls for skill. If a knife handle is so shaped that it helps you use the blade with a minimum of conscious effort, it is *functionally* designed.

A good design usually suggests its function. The shapes of the knives we have been talking about tell us a great deal about their uses. Table knives look blunt and harmless, with broad tips for spreading; a butcher's knives are large and sharp. The blade of a scythe is curved so that it will gather grass toward the mower as it is swung; the blade of a saber is curved to give it extra strength. Similarly, we might expect, even if we had never heard either instrument played, that the thin curve of a trumpet would produce high-pitched notes, and that the heftier, fuller shape of the tuba would emit deep, resonant tones.

Function has also dictated the design of objects whose looks may not reveal their uses so readily. When we compare a 19th-century European railway engine with its American counterpart, we recognize each as a locomotive, but we notice curious differences in detail. Are these differences only a matter of taste? Why is the European railway engine plain and sober looking, while the American one seems elaborate and complicated?

If we investigate the conditions for which each was designed, we realize that the European locomotive, with

its rigid frame, long wheel base, and partially concealed wheels and machinery, was generally intended to travel relatively short distances along well-laid track. Plenty of skilled help was available in case of breakdowns. The American locomotive was designed for roughly laid track that followed the curves and bends of the mountains through which it passed after crossing vast prairies. The locomotive's frame was necessarily lighter and more flexible. The designer placed most of its simple machinery externally, where partly skilled workmen far from well-equipped workshops could easily repair or replace it. To avoid prairie fires, he provided a large trap to catch sparks from the wood used as fuel. A huge oil headlight and a "cowcatcher" were necessary for journeys across unfenced prairie wilderness. All this apparatus and exposed machinery was useful; it was only *apparently* flamboyant and complex.

In recent times, many designers have thought that because function and the form of an object are so closely related, the most efficient solution to a design problem— that is, the design that best enables an object to accomplish its purpose—is naturally the most beautiful one. But this is not always so. For example, cups are made so that people can drink from them. Within the limits of depth and breadth convenient for this purpose, many shapes are possible. Each may accomplish a cup's functions, but not all of them strike us as equally good-looking.

Having met functional requirements, the designer often has no other limitations to dictate his final design. The way the designer uses this freedom is what gives us variety in the appearance of objects otherwise alike. We may decide that one design satisfies our feelings about what is beautiful more than another that is equally useful. This power to satisfy is as important a part of good design as is practical usefulness. One of the functions of any object should be to give pleasure to those who see it.

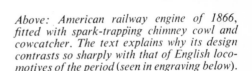

Above: American railway engine of 1866, fitted with spark-trapping chimney cowl and cowcatcher. The text explains why its design contrasts so sharply with that of English locomotives of the period (seen in engraving below).

Good design does not depend solely upon function. The modern teacup on the right (manufactured in Germany) and the 1891 example (left) are by no means equally attractive, although both are convenient to drink from.

Craft design

Today most designers work at drawing boards. They tackle the problem of what to make and how to make it, but they are seldom involved in the actual making. However, before the middle of the 19th century, designers were able not only to plan the manufacture of an object but to make with their own hands the thing they had designed. Such designers were called *craftsmen*; the sets of skills they acquired through long practice were called *crafts*. Museums are full of beautiful everyday objects designed by craftsmen as different from one another as ancient Chinese potters and medieval French tapestry weavers. What these people shared in common was their participation in age-old craft traditions.

Though the art of craft design has not vanished, there are very few craftsmen-designers today. If you buy a set of dishes, it is likely that they were made almost entirely by machine. Some designers still make pottery by hand, however. They set to work at once on their materials without any obvious planning or designing beforehand. They shape the clay as they work, since practice has taught them how to *feel* their way to the final design.

But even when, as in the 18th century, craftsmen worked from patterns or drawings made by other people, each man was expected to interpret designs in the light of his own experience. A cabinetmaker working from the *Directory of Designs* by the English furniture designer Thomas Chippendale (about 1718-79) would expect to find no more than a guide in the *Directory*. He had to make his own decisions about dimensions, and he would modify details of construction to suit his own skills.

The master designers themselves, such as Chippendale, derived their ability from their understanding of craft techniques, for they were trained essentially as craftsmen. In the same way, architects were trained chiefly as masons or structural woodworkers. Significantly, one old workman has been quoted as saying that the great English machine-tool designer Henry Maudsley (1771-1831) was "a real pleasure to watch with a file in his hand."

Training in a craft took a very long time. Though the theory of working with a hand tool is soon understood, there is no way to acquire skill in using it other than through long practice, just as in learning to play a game that requires quick and deft body movements. It is only after you have reached a point at which these movements become unconscious that you can relax to concentrate on the game itself.

So it was with the craftsman-designer. After a long apprenticeship he became so much at one with his tools that he could take his skill for granted and concentrate on the actual *shaping* of the piece of work in hand. His

A 14th-century painting showing weavers preparing their wool. Their designs were improvisations based on traditional patterns.

Interior of a watch made by Claude de la Porte of Delft (1725-50). Such craftsmen combined the skills of the watchmaker, the silversmith, and the jeweller, for their watch-cases were finely chased and engraved.

designs would therefore change according to his skill. They seldom were altered because of fashion (p. 136); changes were usually evolutionary. Expert craftsmen here and there might refine certain curves or proportions, and other craftsmen, according to their abilities, copied such changes as pleased them.

These hand-crafted designs were never identical. Each of a set of dining chairs, for example, had unique qualities. It did not matter if there were slight variations in joints, because each tongue of wood was adapted to its own particular socket.

Materials were selected because of their suitability to a specific purpose; they did not need to be standardized to fit machines. Cracks or knots in wood presented no insoluble problems, for the chair maker could make what use he liked of the grain, selecting each piece by eye. He could easily modify faults in design, and he could correct on the spot any defects in workmanship. He could make improvements at any stage without interrupting production. All these sound technical advantages permit us to admire the products of craftsmen with an enthusiasm that has little to do with sentimental reverence for "antiques."

Such craftsmen-designers defy imitation. A modern designer can learn all there is to know about an 18th-century designer and his craft, but this theoretical knowledge of the past cannot make him into a craftsman. Unless he actually has had a long apprenticeship in a craft, he will be only an imitator, copying laboriously what was once made spontaneously.

In the 18th century, designers who were trained as craftsmen often published drawings for other craftsmen to work from. This sketch for part of a carved table was made by one such craftsman-designer, England's Matthias Lock. Today, most objects that are designed for domestic use are mass-produced in factories; but a few craftsmen-designers still make articles by hand—like the rug below, designed in Denmark by Irma Haajanen.

Industrial design

Right: early 20th-century assembly line. Each worker was trained to do a single unvarying task. Assembly-line methods, manufacturing aims—lower costs, increased output—brought design changes.

The designer of a 20th-century object usually belongs to a team. And his team is likely to include other designers as well as engineers, who plan and control machine processes, and sales and market experts, who give advice about what the customers want. The *industrial designer*, as the design member of any such team is called, must have theoretical knowledge of specialized techniques and materials rather than practical experience in *making* things; for the needs of industrial design are geared to the demands of the machine. He may be asked to help design metal furniture because he is a metallurgist rather than because he knows much about chairs.

Accordingly, the industrial designer's training is gained mostly in schools. He no longer spends years as an apprentice practicing and perfecting manual skills. He attends art school or a technical school, perhaps after studying mechanical engineering; there he spends most of his time at a drawing board. He differs from the few designers, still directly involved with the execution of their designs, who receive both such schooling and craft training. The scenic designer, for example, must get practical theatre experience; the interior designer must work directly with fabrics and furnishings.

Actually, learning a craft might hinder rather than help the industrial designer. The craftsman would think of furniture, for instance, in terms of handmade wooden joinery. But wood varies; and machines do not modify their workings to suit variations in materials. If a designer is trained to think in terms of precise, completely interchangeable machine-made parts, he will probably produce a better design, using materials especially suited to machine processes.

The industrial designer's responsibility is greater, too, than that of the craftsman-designer, for he knows that his design may be reproduced thousands of times before it can be changed. He searches for a language of design and for standards of industrial production that will satisfy man's desire for both useful and beautiful things, and that does not merely use machine processes in order to imitate old handicrafts.

When machines first began to replace hand tools, people thought of them chiefly as labor-saving slaves, useful for reproducing the work of craftsmen. Even the Scottish inventor James Watt (1736-1819), famous for his pioneer work with steam power, spent years trying to perfect a machine that would automatically copy

English fireplace of mid-19th century, sh... ing the swollen curves florid decoration fav... by designers of the per...

Replaceable saw te... 1852. Industrial mech... zation gradually led ... signers to produce cl... machine-made forms.

A simple, well-propor... ed street lamp creat... 1907-8 by the Ger... architect Peter Behre... a pioneer of mo... industrial design.

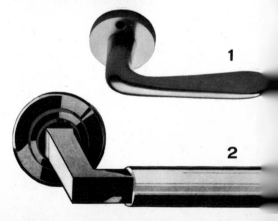

1

2

Right: Door handle designed in 1956 (1) is tailored to fit the hand, yet simple enough for mass production. Its forerunner (2) was a 1922 model designed with machine processes in mind by German-born Walter Gropius (p. 120).

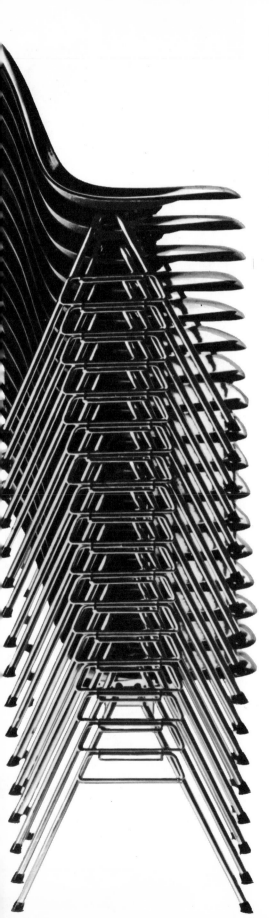

sculpture. This was an expensive attempt to do by machine something best done by hand.

Until recently, many industrial designers and manufacturers made things by machine with not too different an end in view. They sought to make such things as light fixtures or stoves in the image of traditional carved and sculptured objects. Many people felt that machine-made objects were somehow inferior to the traditionally handmade ones, and they wanted these things to *look* handmade. Designers for modern industry, however, have shown the way to new kinds of beauty and form in their modern designs for great bridges, ocean liners, railway engines, and airplanes. Their forms are clear, practical, and "scientific"-looking. And many such forms have been adopted as standards for objects to be used in the home (p. 140). Radio sets are now often designed to look like the scientific instruments they really are, rather than to be hidden in imitation Florentine cabinets. Stainless steel tableware is given the clean and smooth forms characteristic of the precision machines that manufacture it, instead of forms that imitate 18th-century handworked silver.

In fact, the products of industrial design have greatly influenced style in the arts and crafts. Sculptors such as the Romanian Constantin Brancusi (1876-1957) or France's Hans Arp (born 1887) have given their works a polished machine-turned look. Today's hand-made jewelry, too, often resembles industrial forms like propeller or turbine blades.

Today, machine-made objects are no longer disguised to look like the handwork of craftsmen; designers with a thorough knowledge of industrial techniques have given them a new beauty and efficiency of their own. The clean, smooth lines of the chairs on the left (designed by America's Charles Eames) allow them to be stacked conveniently. The businesslike appearance of the portable typewriter below—far simpler in design than early models —is borne out by its improved performance.

The language of style

The distinctive look that a culture gives to the things it makes is called *style*. Just as we speak English or Russian or French according to where we live, so designers "speak"—that is, design—in the style characteristic of the time and place in which they live. And just as the words we use express our ideas, so style indicates something about the ideas of the society that produces it. If we can learn to "read" this language of style, we can find out a great deal about what men have thought at any given time or place. For example, even if we had no written records, we should know by studying the look (or style) of the objects that the ancient Egyptians left behind them that they had achieved a culture of great sophistication.

Yet it would be foolish for a designer of today to try to reproduce the Egyptian or any other style, for styles change as ideas arise, develop, decay, and succeed one another. A style natural for one historical period often seems out of place in another. But the function (p. 128) of many objects remains the same whatever the style. A chair, for instance, meant the same thing to the Egyptians as it does to us—something one can sit upon. Because most designers keep in mind an object's basic function, style change—unlike fashion change (p. 136)—is not capricious. It is the fruit of the social and technical conditions of the age that produces it.

The Greeks, for instance, raised philosophical thought and discussion to perhaps the highest levels they ever reached in the ancient world. The style of the objects they made hints at this. Look at their chairs: Vase drawings suggest that with its elegant and rational proportions, the Greek chair was delightfully suited to conversation. In contrast, the style of much Roman furniture, while it echoed the Greek, was heavy and pompous, like the prosperous empire that produced it. The parts of a Roman chair were lavishly decorated with symbols of power, luxury, and wealth.

In the Middle Ages, men built plain box-like furniture of heavy oak or elm that could survive in the rough-and-tumble world of a castle. If it was decorated, it was carved in the current architectural style, with thin vertical lines and pointed arches. The style of early Renaissance chairs changed from the solid box to a more elegant open frame. Designers abandoned square shapes for turned, column-like legs influenced by the rebirth of interest in Greek and Roman architectural styles. Later, increased world trade made available new close-grained woods like mahogany, which allowed chair makers to modify styles again. They could curve the lines of their chairs and make them lighter-looking. In the late Renaissance, when houses were warmer, people wore clothes less thickly padded

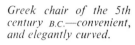

Greek chair of the 5th century B.C.—convenient, and elegantly curved.

Roman chair (1st or 2 century A.D.), decora with winged sphinxes.

Enamelled porcelain clock, made in Strasbourg about 1780. Its elaborate design, flowing curves, and brilliant colors, which typify the fantastic rococo style, tend to echo the frivolity of much of contemporary society.

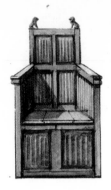

Square, box-like chair made in the Netherlands during the 15th century.

Open-frame Italian chair of the early 16th century, made of carved walnut.

English dining chair (18th century), designed by Thomas Chippendale.

Elaborately upholstered and padded French armchair (about 1780).

than medieval ones, and a new style change evolved: Designers began to upholster chairs to make them more comfortable. They also widened them to accommodate women's ample skirts and men's tailcoats and swords.

Late in the 18th century, new archaeological discoveries led to the introduction of styles that recalled the elegance of the best Egyptian, Greek, and Roman models. However, it is important to note that the new designs, whether of chairs or clothes or buildings, were adapted to contemporary craftsmanship, materials, and functional requirements. Then, in the 19th century, the versatility of mass-production methods led to copying the looks of objects from all historical periods. What resulted was less a new language of style than a babel of confused meanings and ideas, for "styles" were reproduced without reference to the social and technological conditions that originally inspired them (p. 120).

Toward the end of the century, though, designers began to discover a style that seemed to reflect modern ideas (p. 140). The Austrian Michael Thonet (1796-1871), for example, found a way to use machine processes to make bent wood furniture in a style that actually "spoke" the new technical language. The new emphasis on designing for machines and mass production led to a modern style, recently exemplified by such objects as the plywood chairs of Finland's Alvar Aalto (born 1898), the metal ones of Hungarian-born Marcel Breuer (born 1902), and the plastic chairs of America's Charles Eames (born 1907). No matter how each is made, all share a *style* in keeping with contemporary attitudes.

Any object that thus "speaks" in the idiom of the society that produces it has a *style*. It has a definite visual relationship to when and where it has been made, to the materials available to the maker-designer, and to the ideas that have dominated the life of that society.

Each of the chairs pictured above represents a designer's answer to the particular needs of his period, in terms of the materials that were available. Thus, each has its distinctive style, from the cultured elegance of the Greek and the opulence of the Roman to the sturdy serviceability of the 16th-century European example. The sculptured shape of the modern armchair below (designed 1957 by Finnish-born Eero Saarinen) solves the problem of how to make the best use of modern methods of manufacture and materials—in this case, molded plastic.

The whim of fashion

The word "fashion" suggests what is new, what is up to date; it suggests constant and sometimes whimsical change. It is sometimes confused with style, but style emerges gradually to mark technical progress and functional design changes. On the other hand, fashion (from the Latin *facere*, "to make"), which originally meant simply the way in which anything was made or "fashioned," now signifies superficial changes that are widely and temporarily popular.

Fashions in clothing, for example, are notoriously changeable. By finding out some of the reasons for this, we can see what is behind the rise and fall of other kinds of fashion. We can also see how changes in fashion differ from changes in style. When buildings were drafty and unheated, clothes consisted of heavy furs, velvets, and brocades. Anyone who invested money in an elaborate wardrobe wanted it to last a long time, and only the very rich could ever afford to discard clothes before they were completely worn out. That a man could do this was a sign of his wealth and high social position. Louis XIV of France established a custom of changing his wardrobe once a year to give the state silk monopoly a boost and increase his personal revenues. He made his courtiers follow his example. Such change simply for the sake of change (and profit) has long been a mainstay of the "fashion industry." Clothes made by leading dress designers—notably those of Paris—are still symbols that identify the rich and important.

The patronage of wealthy customers helps stimulate fashion at another level. Within a few weeks after Paris dress collections are first shown, women everywhere can buy mass-produced copies of expensive designs. Since few women expect these cheaper machine-made clothes to last a long time, and since replacement is easy and inexpensive, changes in fashion follow one another swiftly.

Unchanging climate, static social conditions mean that Arab dress (above) remains the same for centuries, unaffected by fashion. In Europe (below) style of 1780—seen in François Boucher's portrait of Madame de Pompadour (1)—is basically same as that of 1870 (2); superficial fashion changes indicate preoccupation with social elegance. Disappearance of servants, mass production of clothes, led to simple, carefree styles of 1920s (3). Style remains same today (4); fashion changes continue in fabrics, hem lengths, accessories.

1

2

3

Changes in style, on the other hand, are not subject to whim. Whether hems rise or fall, the basic style underlying each superficial fashion change is constant. Cleaner cities, improved heating and laundering methods, and new lightweight materials have caused us to adopt clothes that, whatever the fashion, are constructed in a simpler and more lightly constructed *style* than those of earlier centuries. In terms of the way we live today, they are, in a word, more *functional*.

Climate has been another factor that influences style rather than fashion. In lands where climate is constant and predictable, clothes change little; witness the Indian sari or the robes of the North African Bedouin. In less certain climates, man has had to construct more elaborate clothing whose functions vary according to the weather. Such variations make the introduction of fashion changes easy.

Other changes in fashion (whether in dress, furniture, house decoration, or cars) happen because each generation wants to lead its life in a distinctive way. Nothing appears so ludicrous to us as the fashions of our parents' youth. But those of our grandparents are far enough removed in time for us to regard them as "quaint," and we may even re-adopt some of their fashions.

Fashion change sometimes has an economic motive in addition to the ones we have mentioned. American car bodies, for example, change yearly despite the absence of important engineering improvements. Like our parents' clothes, last year's models become out of date, even though they still function efficiently, and many people replace cars as frequently as they do clothes. When such changes spur buying, industries benefit. But this dependence on fashion can be harmful and wasteful in the long run, for it too often does not relate to function (p. 128) and is a substitute for truly useful advances in design.

The exterior designs of American automobiles are changed annually to boost sales—and thousands of one-year-old models find their way to the scrap heap. Photos (above) show how the bodywork of one 1961 model was modified in the following two years. Changes in interior design are almost as frequent, for they also help to keep industry moving. The furnishings in rooms like the one below, modeled on lavish film sets, influence the design of mass-produced furnishings. People want "the latest thing," copy what they see in films.

4

The purpose of decoration

Functional decorations on the faces of playing cards convey value and suit. Suit emblems (simplified in the 14th century for easy stenciling) have not changed for over four hundred years. But all-over patterns typical of playing-card backs disguise value, constantly change according to fashion.

Painted leaves and flowers emphasize the curves of this Chinese stoneware vase (between 960 and 1279 A.D.), forming an integral part of its design. Like all successful decorations, they enhance the form of the object without disguising it or defeating its function.

Many designers in the early years of this century reacted strongly against adding any kind of ornament to the things they designed. They felt that decoration was a kind of dishonesty—that those who enriched an object by adding ornament were simply trying to cover up its defects. Yet designers as diverse as Chinese potters, medieval armorers, and 18th-century furniture makers made decoration an essential part of their designs.

Obviously, decoration did not always have a bad name. Some of the earliest man-made objects were decorated. Prehistoric weapons and tools have handles of horn or bone engraved with the figures of men and animals, or with geometric designs. Men probably decorated these tools for one of two *functional* reasons. First, a toolmaker might have wanted to distinguish his implement from others like it. Second, he might have wanted to use pictures as a kind of magic to attract the animals he was going to hunt with his weapon.

Stone Age men also covered the walls of caves, such as those at Lascaux in France, with realistic animal paintings (p. 22), but we do not call these paintings "decoration." They existed as "functional"—probably magical—objects in their own right, and the wall surfaces were far less important than the paintings themselves.

The toolmaker who engraved pictures on a handle was limited by the handle's size and shape. The object was more important than the decoration he placed on it. Today, too, when someone values what he has made, he may decorate it, either to suggest how it is going to be used, or simply to add to the pleasure that its basic shape already gives. He does not try to change or hide it; he underlines what is already there. This is why decoration is different from paintings or sculptures that exist as separate objects, each with its own meaning. When a designer uses drawing or painting or carving decoratively, he must be sure that his decorations draw attention to the qualities of the thing he has decorated. Think what we mean by a military "decoration": It is a medal or badge that is a mark of bravery. It is meant to tell us something about the man who wears it.

You can perhaps guess now why some 20th-century designers came to believe decoration was a bad thing. People in the 19th century had been more interested

Protective paint on this Portuguese fishing vessel is also highly decorative. The design follows the curves of the boat's hull.

in decoration as a sign of wealth than in the essential worth and usefulness of the decorated objects. They wanted to own things that *looked* expensive but did not cost much. Because they knew that handmade things were the product of a craftsman's valuable time and skill, they equated intricately decorated surfaces with costliness, no matter whether the decoration enhanced or impeded an object's usefulness. Cheaply and quickly, the new machines turned out extravagantly decorated objects by the thousands.

Designers were tempted to show off their skill by producing complicated decorative designs. During the 18th and 19th centuries there was a flood of pattern books produced by scholars and antiquarians. They were filled with details from antique European and Oriental buildings, furniture, handicrafts, and textiles. Designers copied any of these designs that took their fancy, but few understood the original function of such decoration. They applied it to the designs of their mass-produced objects with an effect that provokes ridicule today.

This was the kind of misused decoration against which some designers protested. They felt that decoration was a substitute for intelligent thought and planning, and too closely related to the whims of fashion (p. 136). Even today, for example, the title "decorator" is used by people who plan how the interiors of houses should look. Many do this without having planned the houses; and their decoration of a room may be superficial because, like a woman's dress, it does no more than reflect the latest vogue. However, truly creative designers plan decorations as an integral *part* of a house, such as the walls, mantelpieces, ceilings, and furnishings that the English architect Robert Adam (1728-92) planned for his houses.

To avoid decoration on the principle that it is "dishonest" is perhaps as foolish as to use it as a disguise or as an instrument of fashion. In recent years many designers have realized this. They know that if they keep in mind the functional part decoration has to play, they can incorporate it into the design of any object.

The entrance hall of Osterley Park, an English country house designed by Robert Adam. Marble floor, molded patterns of the delicate stucco work covering walls and ceiling emphasize the room's geometric design.

The decorative patterning of this pocket-size radio (made in Germany in 1960) is formed from the speaker and control panel—two essential elements in its design. Such decoration is both pleasing and practical, because it is planned with the function of the object in mind.

Modern design

When somebody says a thing is streamlined, we immediately think of something with sleek, shiny, rounded, swept-back contours, and metallic surfaces. Above all, we think of something up to date. If we consider why streamlined design is so readily associated with modern design, we can begin to understand some of the problems that designers have to solve. "Streamlined" was originally a technical word used by engineers studying the movement of a solid object through fluids like air or water. They called the lines that marked the path of the fluid around the object streamlines. By measuring them, scientists could tell how much resistance a given object would meet. This knowledge helped engineers to design speedy and efficient aircraft, ships, and automobiles.

The value of streamlining as a way of improving the performance of moving objects has been known since men shaped arrowheads and spears that would fly rapidly and penetrate animal hides cleanly. The Vikings in the north and the Greeks and Romans in the Mediterranean built ships with streamlined hulls so that rowers could propel them with an economy of effort. But the first truly modern attempts at scientific streamlining date from the latter half of the 19th century. In France, for example, engineers introduced a new "wind-splitter"

The development of modern design was greatly influenced by the work of French physiologist E.J. Marey (1830-1904), who photographed the action of wind against various shapes, and proved that a streamlined shape caused minimal disturbance in the air flow (photo above). Today, designers continue to seek methods of improving streamlining techniques. The Caravelle (below), a French jet liner designed in the late 1950s, has engine pods attached to the fuselage in front of the tail surfaces, which makes possible a sleeker, more efficient wing design.

Extravagant jukebox design (above) mimics 20th-century technology. Purpose of good industrial design: to make objects work efficiently. Here, efficient-looking fittings copy design features of spacecraft, scientific apparatus, merely to gain up-to-date appearance.

Streamlining improves the appearance and the performance of any moving object, from a ship to a steam iron. And today, sleek, efficient appliances that reflect the latest advances in scientific and technological research can be found in almost every Western home.

locomotive for the Paris-Lyons-Mediterranean line in the 1890s. Everywhere, as engineers experimented with more efficient designs for steamship hulls, and for airplane and automobile bodies, the modern streamlined style began to evolve. Eventually, streamlining became a popular symbol of modern design, for high-speed travel had caught the public's imagination.

Yet most things we use are not meant to move at high speeds. Why have designers "streamlined" so many of them? Is streamlining really a style, or is it a fashion? The answer is that it is both. Some things, such as electric irons, are logically streamlined, for they move. An iron pushes aside wrinkles and folds in cloth much as a ship pushes through water; the iron must be free of projections that might catch or tear fabrics. Because the flowing lines of functionally streamlined objects can be given to forms that do *not* move, the use of the word streamlining has been extended to such things as typewriters and telephones. These objects have smooth, compact, rounded cases that protect their enclosed mechanisms, do not waste space, and are easy to keep clean.

On the other hand, some objects—for example, coin-operated record-playing machines known as "jukeboxes" —are often extravagantly streamlined, only so that they will look fashionably up to date. Neither the function of such a machine nor the necessity for easy cleaning and upkeep can justify its missile-like forms. Other victims of merely fashionable streamlining have been objects so diverse as eyeglasses, coffee pots, and picture frames. When designers use the streamlined look in this way, it becomes a cliché—an overworked device to satisfy fashion. Thus, automobile designers, for example, have introduced changes into car bodies simply to make one year's model *look* different from the last (p. 137).

Our most creative designers today are those who, taking into account modern materials, manufacturing methods, and needs, have produced carefully designed solutions to meet these needs. In 1937, for example, American designers produced the famous "porthole" model that everywhere symbolizes the automatic washing machine. In recent years, Italian and German engineers have designed office machines that perform complicated mathematical calculations and are noted for their handsome appearance. Perhaps one day art historians will use the word "streamlined" to describe 20th-century style; perhaps not. The important thing to remember is that the best answers to modern design problems reflect contemporary advances in technology and scientific research.

Chapter 6

Music

Nobody knows just when people began to make music, but we do know that in today's world no society, no matter how primitive its way of life, is without music. This indicates that man has probably always been a music maker, for anthropologists tell us that the primitive tribes of modern Australia or Africa, for example, live much as our prehistoric ancestors did.

Primitive music evolved as a natural way of expressing such fundamental emotions as joy, sorrow, anger, love, and man's awe of the unknown. Some music formed a natural accompaniment to ritual dances and work activities. Chanting voices and rhythmic stamping or hand-clapping were probably the first "instruments," but gradually men found out how to get sounds from hollow gourds or sticks, either by beating them or blowing through them. They also found that taut strings could be plucked or scraped to give interesting sounds.

When men began to "shape" these sounds, combining notes and rhythms in various ways, the art of music was born. Yet deep beneath music as a fine art there still lie primitive emotional impulses and simple delight in musical sounds and shapes.

For nearly two thousand years, musicians have been refining the elements of music, developing and organizing them into complex sound structures with the power to dramatize and comment upon—in a subtle way denied to words—the conflicting emotions and complexities of life. Music can vastly enrich our experience, providing, as Beethoven remarked, a link to connect "the spiritual with the sensuous life." As an aid to understanding how it does this, let us now look at a few of the physical facts of music and discover something of its history.

Throughout the centuries men have found pleasure and inspiration in music. By ordering the musical sounds that their own voices make, as well as the sounds of various instruments, men have created a complex language even more vividly expressive than speech. In this detail from a painting called The Concert, *by Lorenzo Costa (Italian, about 1460-1535), friends gather to sing to a lute. On the table lie song books, a flute, and a small viol with its bow.*

The qualities of sound

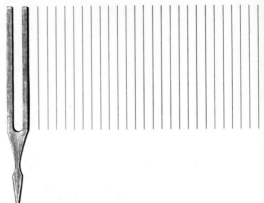

When you strike a tuning fork (above) it vibrates, disturbing the air much as a stone thrown into a pond (left) sends waves through water. Sound waves strike our ears, set up vibrations our brains receive as sounds—high or low, loud or soft, pleasant or harsh, depending on how the vibrations are controlled.

Just as painters use color as a means of communicating feelings and ideas to other people, and writers use language, composers and musicians use *sound*. Sound begins when an object—like a piano string or a set of vocal cords—starts to vibrate and sets up sound waves in the surrounding air. These waves are collected by our ears, which sort out and pass on information about sound qualities to our brains, and so we hear the sound. When composers, singers, or instrumentalists control these sounds, we call them music; uncontrolled sounds are merely noise. If properly controlled, the sounds that come from slapping an empty oil drum, blowing into a bottle, or plucking at a rubber band can all become music.

The first thing most people notice about a sound is whether it is loud or soft. This quality is called the *dynamics* of sound. When you pluck a guitar string, for instance, the sound gets fainter as the string vibrates through an ever-diminishing distance. The distance that the string travels from its normal position before it returns is called the *amplitude* of the string's movement.

We must be careful not to confuse loudness with *pitch*, the second most important quality of sound. Pitch depends on frequency, or the number of vibrations per second. A large number of vibrations produces a high-pitched sound (called a *tone* or *note*); a small number produces a low-pitched note. Frequency depends on such things as the length or size of the vibrating object. A long harp string, for instance, will give slow vibrations and a

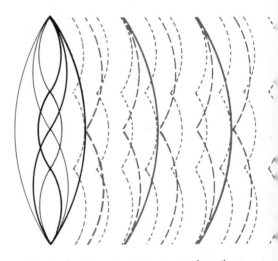

A plucked guitar string sets up complex vibrations (above). Vibrating as a whole, it emits fundamental tone (heavy curves); but it may vibrate in two parts (broken curves); three (dotted curves), or more to produce softer, higher-pitched overtones that give a guitar its characteristic tone quality, or timbre.

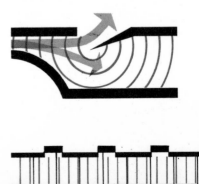

In whistle (above right), air blown through mouthpiece sets up high-pitched vibrations in tiny air column. In flute (right), stops help control air column. Vibrations are fewer, pitch lower, when holes are closed; pitch rises (color) when a hole is opened.

low note; if we shorten the string, the vibrations become more frequent and the note rises in pitch.

The third thing we notice about sounds is their *timbre* or distinctive character : whether they seem, for example, harsh or gentle. Timbre depends on how complicated vibrations are. Different sections of a piano string, for example, vibrate at several different speeds, making extra, fainter sounds called *overtones*. These accompany the basic or fundamental tone, which determines the over-all pitch. Overtones distinguish one voice or musical instrument from another. A plucked harp string may produce a sound of the same pitch and loudness as a note sounded on a trumpet, but the vibrating string and the vibrating column of air inside the trumpet produce very different sets of overtones. Musicians frequently refer to differences in timbre as *tone color*.

But a single pleasing sound or even a particularly interesting combination of tone colors does not make attractive music. It is much more exciting to hear notes arranged in a pattern : heavily and lightly stressed notes with more or less regular pauses and rests. In other words, we like *rhythm*. Very early in the history of making music people discovered how natural and satisfying it is to match chanted or sung musical tones to the rhythm of dancing and working. A sense of rhythm is so basic in most people that nearly all of us can recognize certain kinds of music simply by hearing their rhythmical patterns : the *ONE, two three, ONE, two three,* dancing rhythm of waltzes, for example, or the *ONE, two, ONE, two, ONE, two* of a march.

The speed, or *tempo*, of a rhythm is important, for it influences the music's mood. We feel differently about the same sounds and rhythms if their speed changes. It seems natural for people to associate dignity, solemnity, or even sadness with a slow tempo; a quick one, on the other hand, suggests liveliness, energy, or gaiety.

Wind (brass horn, wood flute), strings (viola da gamba), percussion (kettledrum). Woodcuts illustrate three chief ways to produce musical sounds: by blowing, scraping, striking. In the 18th century, craftsmen like those below gave many instruments—strings especially—sound quality not often surpassed since.

A 15th-century experiment in fixing the pitch of musical notes. The more water in a glass, the lower the pitch of the note it gives when struck with a rod. Lowest-pitched note is at left; highest, at far right.

Marks—called neumes—*above the words in plain-song manuscripts like this 10th-century example reminded singers of changes in pitch and rhythm. The chant melodies were traditional ones that they knew by heart.*

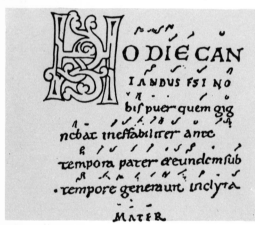

Below: By the 13th century, sets of lines called staffs *indicated rise and fall of pitch more exactly (left); refined neume shapes indicated precise time values. Even singers unfamiliar with the music could sight-read easily from books on lecterns (center). Five-line staff and the note shapes in 17th-century printed music (right) resemble today's notation.*

Scales and notation

Men long ago learned that it was useful to organize musical notes into sequences of rising or falling steps called *scales*—an easy way of locating the pitch of any single note in relation to ones above and below it. Experts think most ancient civilizations that possessed musical instruments eventually organized notes into scales, though they are not at all sure what any of this music sounded like.

In the West, almost every trace of early music disappeared with the fall of the Roman Empire in the fifth century. But Greek methods of arranging notes in a number of different scales called *modes* survived to influence early Christian religious chant—the oldest Western music still in use. For centuries, such *plainsong*, as it is called, consisted of long verses (usually Biblical texts) chanted basically on one note, like a kind of accented speech, with changes of pitch introduced chiefly to emphasize significant words. These simple rising and falling notes easily fitted into one or other of the modes. All voices sang in unison; that is, all voices sang the same note at the same time, even though deep voices might actually be singing an octave lower than higher voices.

We use the word *octave* because, like the Greek modes, traditional scales in Western music consist of groups of eight notes. (In Greek, *okto* means eight.) Each note is named after one of the first seven letters of the alphabet. We need only seven names because the top note of each group *repeats* the bottom note, but it is pitched twice as high, the frequency of its vibration being twice as great, and it begins another octave. The pitch rises from the bottom to the top note in seven steps, of which five are full steps (whole tones), and two are half-steps (*semitones*).

In the 10th century, singers began to exploit the discovery that singing two or more notes at once, separated by certain intervals of other than an octave, gave a pleasing effect. This happened whenever the notes of two or more different melodies sung at the same time came together, producing a blend of sound called a *chord*. This gave rise to the development of a musical technique called *counterpoint*, or *polyphony*.

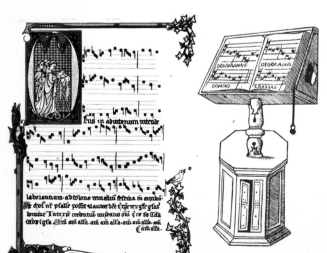

...me white keys on piano keyboard at top right are ...lored; these produce scale in key of C. Diagram ...neath, similarly colored, shows notation for such ...scale, including some notes above and below it— ...gher notes on upper staff marked by treble clef; *...wer ones on staff marked by* bass clef. *Interval ...tween any two successive keys (regardless of their ...lor) is a half step or semitone. Thus, where black ...y is missing, interval between one white key and ...xt is a semitone. Scale progresses in two whole ...eps, a half step, three more whole tones, and a ...mitone. To begin a scale on a note other than C, ...me notes are sounded by using black keys. To ...dicate this, musicians use signs shown below. Left: ... natural and C sharp (a semitone higher); right: B ...tural and B flat (a semitone lower).*

F G A B C D E F G A B C D E F G A B C D E F G

...low: major and minor scales in C. In C major (top), ...ervals between E and F, B and C are semitones. In ...rmonic minor scale of C (beneath), flatting of E and ...changes interval values. Melodic minor (not shown) ...oids step-and-a-half interval between A and B.

By the 17th century, composers had begun to take such delight in making music by using chords, or *harmonies*, that except in the churches, unison singing gradually fell into disuse. So did polyphony, with its web of interweaving melodies, whose harmonies occur almost incidentally. Composers now preferred the sound of a single melody deliberately designed to be supported by a series of chordal harmonies.

They largely abandoned the traditional modes, except for two that they found especially useful in building harmonies. One became the familiar *major* scale, which runs from C to C on the white keys of a modern piano keyboard; another, running from A to A, was modified to form our *minor* scale. The illustration at the left shows that in a minor scale the third and sixth notes are a semitone lower than those of a major scale.

Until about 1900, most composers wrote music based on these two scales. But this did not mean that they were limited to using only a few notes, for major and minor scales can be pitched to begin on any note or semitone. That note becomes the "*key*" to the scale built on it and to any piece of music that is centered about that scale. Musicians may pitch their music in any key they like, and also modulate, or change, the key within the same composition. Performers can *transpose*, or change, the music to a different key, to suit a given voice or instrument.

Composers often choose major keys because they seem to express cheerful or optimistic feelings. They generally choose minor keys for music that they want to sound melancholy or dramatic. Many 20th-century musicians have written music that departs from traditional ideas about scales and major and minor keys because they want to avoid such expressive connotations (p. 168). Yet most music you are likely to hear today dates from the three centuries in which those ideas predominated.

Shapes of notes (in color, above left) show duration: whole, half, quarter, eighth, sixteenth, and so on. Beneath: Time signatures show rhythmic pattern. Common time, $\frac{4}{4}$, has four beats of a quarter note each to a bar; $\frac{3}{4}$ is waltz time; $\frac{2}{4}$, $\frac{6}{8}$ are march rhythms.

Left: "Frère Jacques." Each bar or measure, as time signature shows, contains equivalent of two quarter-notes. Flat sign means that B is always sung as B flat. Letter notation above words is based on syllables do, re, mi, fa, sol, la, ti, do. Do, or doh, begins on F. **147**

Form in music

The development of musical forms that has gone on almost continuously since composers mastered harmony in the 17th century emphasizes the fact that people want to hear meaningful patterns in music. Patternless, aimless music would soon bore its listeners. When men began to make music for no other purpose than to please the ear and the mind, they wanted larger patterns than those derived from such activities as dancing, working, or worship. The new forms turned out to be more varied and subtle than most of those that had grown up chiefly as accompaniments to other activities. To see how this came about, we can trace the growth of certain Western musical forms that reached their highest development with the sonata and symphony.

Tunes written to be played for court dances in the 16th and 17th centuries made use of well-defined rhythms, easily recognizable contrasts of mood, and pleasant harmonies. Musicians often arranged dance tunes in *suites*, or groups, that offered plenty of contrast; fast, slow, gay, or stately dances followed one another. Among early influential composers of dance suites were the Italian Arcangelo Corelli (1653-1713) and the Frenchman François Couperin (1668-1733). England's Henry Purcell (1659-95), and Germany's George Frederick Handel (1685-1759), and Johann Sebastian Bach (1685-1750), as well as many other composers, all wrote instrumental suites of this kind.

Many dances had two melodic sections, the first based on the key, or *tonic*, note (p. 146) of the composition. The first section moved from the tonic to the *dominant* note (the fifth note up the scale from the key note). In the second section, the melody returned from the dominant, and the piece ended satisfyingly in the tonic, or home, key. Composers—notably Corelli, among early experimenters—borrowed this two-part, or *binary*, form from dance suites, modifying it to form the basis for instrumental works called *sonatas*, from the Italian *sonare* (to sound or play). Domenico Scarlatti (1685-1757), a pioneer in the technique of playing keyboard instruments (p. 154), wrote over 500 binary-form, one-movement sonatas for the harpsichord.

Later composers, especially K. P. E. Bach (1714-88), a son of J. S. Bach, expanded the early sonata into what is now known as the *first movement form*, and also added two or three contrasting movements: independent pieces in simpler forms. These sonatas were written for a soloist or a small group of players. Sonatas written for full orchestras (p. 158) came to be called *symphonies*; sonatas written for an orchestra with solo parts for an instrument

Many of today's musical forms evolved from medieval music written for special occasions, such as this 15th-century wedding celebration at the court of a French noble. Trumpeters play in gallery, far right.

Not until the 17th century was much music written in purely instrumental form. Early instruments like these, in a scene from psalter of Duke René II of Lorraine (1473-1508), most often accompanied songs or dances. Players hold trumpet, viol, tabor (drum), dulcimer, shawm (a primitive oboe), portative organ.

Early sonatas da chiesa (*church sonatas*) *were written for strings and organ; sonatas* da camera (*chamber sonatas*), *for strings and harpsichord. The 17th-century composer Arcangelo Corelli, one of the first great violin players, wrote 60, featuring two violins and a cello.*

Mozart at 13. By his time, sonata and symphony were taking form as we know them: three or four movements —either allegro-adagio-allegro (quick-slow-quick), or with Beethoven's sprightly innovation, the scherzo, inserted before the final allegro (instead of the minuet that Haydn and Mozart used).

(as for example, a piano or violin) or for a small group of instruments, are called *concertos.*

Composers borrowed a three-section, or *ternary,* form for sonatas from another kind of dance consisting of three parts: a dance such as a minuet (p. 176), followed by a contrasting section, followed by a repetition of the original dance. Most sonatas contain three or four movements; concertos generally three, and symphonies four.

In the first movement of a sonata or symphony, two dramatically contrasting *themes,* or musical ideas, are presented, "taken apart," analyzed or expanded musically—*developed,* as musicians say. Then each theme is finally returned to its original key. Back in the tonic key now, the first section is repeated, or *recapitulated,* but this time the original thematic contrasts are softened and any "conflict" is resolved. Sometimes the movement is rounded off with a *coda:* a kind of concluding passage that gives a sense of finality and completion.

The second movement is generally slower in tempo, in contrast with the drama of the first movement. Composers usually write this movement in ternary form, which allows for a completely different mood between the first section and the last. The next movement (not often found in concertos) is a short dance movement. The Austrians Franz Joseph Haydn (1732-1809) and Wolfgang Amadeus Mozart (1756-91) usually gave it the form of a minuet, for example, while Germany's Ludwig van Beethoven (1770-1827) speeded up the tempo of the minuet and called this movement a *scherzo.*

One form the final movement can take is the *rondo,* which has a recurring *subject* (a word musicians use to describe the main musical idea) separated by musical episodes less dramatically contrasted with one another than the two first-movement themes. They follow one another in an order something like this: the first theme A, followed by theme B, followed by A, then by a new theme, C; A again, followed by D, and so on, ending with the first theme.

As we consider other aspects of music in this chapter, we shall see that there are many other forms composers have given to their music. But examining the form of the sonata-concerto-symphony in detail can help us appreciate how almost all the music we hear has an underlying, carefully thought-out structure.

Design and expression

The new harmonic music of the 18th century was a method of composing in which melodies were supported by chords. This was in contrast to such music as that written by the masters of the culminating phase of polyphony, especially that of J. S. Bach (p. 148). Much of their music was built up from groups of melodies that moved along, touching and harmonizing at certain points, to form a complex "web" of sound.

K. P. E. Bach (p. 148) rejected the mathematical intricacy of forms like the fugues his father wrote in favor of the newer sonata, with its orchestral contrasts of loudness and softness, and variety of tone color. The *fugue* was an instrumental form that had developed from polyphonic choral singing (p. 152); many instrumental "voices" discussed a musical theme in contrapuntal fashion; that is, according to the rules of counterpoint (p. 146).

Haydn and Mozart (p. 148), who followed the younger Bach, widened the emotional range of music using the new resources offered by harmony and orchestral tone color. The popularity of opera (p. 156) was another spur toward more dramatic and expressive techniques. But Haydn and Mozart held their emotions gracefully in check, and the restraint, clarity, and general compactness of expression that marks their music is what musicians recognize as the *classical* style.

After 1800, in common with the other arts, music came under the spell of the *romantic* movement, with its emphasis on the expression of individual, often highly personal emotions. The music of Beethoven (p. 148)

Polyphonic composition found its fullest expression with J. S. Bach (above). His music was forerunner of restrained classical style. Beethoven (below left) introduced strong emotional content, influenced 19th-century romantics. But among them, Brahms (below right) often harked back to classical style.

formed a bridge between works of classical composers and those of the romantic period. Especially in his later works, written early in the 19th century, Beethoven made many departures from the formal structure and discipline of the classical style.

Most of Beethoven's successors, stirred by his example, concentrated on the expression of strong personal feelings. Many composers, such as the Hungarian Franz von Liszt (1811-86), drawing inspiration from romantic literature, sought ways to increase the range of orchestral sounds and color. Liszt used the device of introducing a recurrent theme to represent the changing emotions of the heroes of "tone poems" or "symphonic poems" based, for example, on poems by Victor Hugo (*Mazeppa*) and Byron (*Tasso*). Some composers invented their own *programs*, or stories, as in the *Symphonie Fantastique* of the French composer Hector Berlioz (1803-69), which described the love-sick visions of "a young musician of morbid sensibility."

Pre-romantic music had included descriptive passages such as those in Haydn's choral work *The Creation*, which describe the chaos that existed before God created the world. But while classical composers kept such music under strict formal control, romantic composers often allowed feeling to be the decisive shaping factor. Yet even some of the romantics preferred classical forms such as the symphony. The most important of these "classical-romantic" composers was Germany's Johannes Brahms (1833-97).

Patriotism was another inspiration to many 19th-century musicians. It spurred many young composers to develop styles that were distinctively national in character. One of the most important of the new national groups was in Russia. Beginning with Mikhail Ivanovich Glinka (1803-57), composers such as Aleksandr Borodin (1834-87) and Nikolai Andreevich Rimski-Korsakov (1844-1908) drew inspiration from their country's legends and history, and made extensive use of folk tunes in their music.

At the end of the 19th century, some composers in the nationalist tradition reacted against the strongly emotional qualities of romantic music. Their interest in folk music helped them find new musical forms. Béla Bartók (1881-1945), for example, derived new ideas from his study of the archaic scales on which the folk tunes of his native Hungary were based. Such composers helped bridge the gap between romantic and modern music (p. 168), with its revived interest in "pure" patterned music without deeply emotional or literary associations.

Frédéric Chopin plays the piano to a few friends in a candle-lit room. Chopin's poetic works for the piano form one of the most moving legacies of the romantic period. The personal feeling he put into such forms as the étude, nocturne, and prelude gave them a distinctive and expressive romantic cast.

As the 20th century opened, composers reacted against romanticism. Igor Stravinsky (here sketched by Picasso) experimented with stronger rhythms, less emotional harmonies. In the 1920s he returned to 18th-century forms, has since written in a variety of historical styles.

Music for voices

Religious music is basic to the development of much vocal music. The psalm melodies handed down from one generation to another by the ancient Hebrews, for example, were adapted to Christian purposes by the first converts from Judaism. Together with the Greek modes (p. 146), absorbed into the Church as it spread throughout the Mediterranean world, Hebrew chants helped form the first Christian music, plainsong (p. 146).

We saw how plainsong developed into a more complicated kind of vocal music: polyphony. Before the 17th century, when a great deal of music was written to be sung, polyphonic settings for the mass offered the most spectacular opportunities for composers. In Italy, Giovanni Pierluigi da Palestrina (about 1526-94) spent his life composing polyphonic masses that are still sung in Catholic churches everywhere. The Spaniard Tomás Luis de Victoria (about 1540-1611) was one of many composers who wrote imposing settings for the mass for the souls of the dead (called a *requiem*). In England, William Byrd (about 1540-1623) wrote masses in Latin for Catholics and in English for the Church of England, even though he remained a Catholic himself.

Another great composer for the Church was a Fleming, Orlando di Lasso (about 1532-94), but he was as well-known for worldly compositions called *madrigals* as for his masses. Madrigals were musical settings of secular lyrics—made up of as many as six melodies sung in counterpoint. They were especially popular among the Flemish and Italians. Later, people all over Europe gathered to sing madrigals. Latin had been the common language of church music, but madrigals were set to words in the language of the country. In England these were of extremely high quality, and collections of English poetry contain many madrigal texts from the 16th and 17th centuries.

At about the same time, professional composers turned their attention to the song for solo voice. One reason for this was that the polyphonic style had reached a point where the sense of the words was often obscured by the intricately interweaving music. Another was the development of harmony. Now, composers were able to enrich a single melodic line with supporting chords on instruments like the lute or the harpsichord (p. 154).

One of the early masters of the song was Henry Purcell (p. 148), who was particularly skillful at suiting his music to the rhythms of the English language. The 19th-century composer Franz Schubert (1797-1828) matched this facility in his setting of German words to music in the more than 600 songs he wrote during his brief lifetime. So important were German song composers, that

Especially popular from the 14th to the 17th centuries the canon is a composition for several voices. A sing the same melody, but begin at different places In a "circle" canon, or round, melody leads bac to the original note and may be repeated any num ber of times. The melody is designed so that t parts harmonize interestingly with one another. (T best-known English round is probably "Three Bli Mice.") The 14th-century French example shown abov by Baude Cordier, is written in actual circle form

Handel turned to the oratorio when production difficulties frustrated his attempts at opera. Oratorios such as Israel in Egypt *(1737) and the* Messiah *(1742) were dramatic religious works given in Lent when theatres were shut.*

An oratorio rehearsal in the 18th century. Then, as now, oratorios were usually given in contemporary dress. But Handel's first English oratorio, Esther, was given with scenery and costumes—like the first oratorio ever given (Rome, 1600), The Representation of Soul and Body, *by Emilio de' Cavalieri.*

their word for song, *lied*, has often been used to describe a particular kind of emotional and expressive song typical of the romantic period. The newly perfected piano (p. 154) was especially valuable to composers who wrote songs of this kind, for it was the ideal instrument to add to and enrich the mood.

But let us go back to church music. The 16th-century Reformation split Europe into two religious camps. In Germany the Lutherans began to draw on folk songs for hymn tunes, and even to write original melodies. The words for the new hymns were in the language of the people instead of Latin. In Protestant churches hymns became one of the popular parts of the service, for everyone was able to join in the singing.

The German word for hymn was *choral*. Composers made *chorales* (as they are called in English) a part of elaborate *cantatas* and *passions*. Cantatas were written for solo voices, chorus, and an orchestra. Passions were similar musical settings, but written especially for New Testament texts telling the story of Christ's suffering and death, with singers taking the part of Christ, the Evangelist, and so on. The entire congregation sang the chorale parts of a cantata or passion in unison. Some of the most impressive works of this type were written by Germans, such as Heinrich Schütz (1585-1672), and a century later, J. S. Bach (p. 148).

A related kind of music came out of Catholic Italy: the *oratorio*. Seeking, like the Protestants, to appeal to the common people, St. Philip Neri established (in the 1560s) a religious order called the Congregation of the Oratory whose priests held services made up of excerpts from miracle and morality plays (p. 264), and dramatic orations on religious subjects interspersed with popular hymns. In 1600, the Oratorians sponsored the first oratorio with soloists, chorus, and orchestra in Rome. The rest of Europe soon adopted the form, especially the Germans. The German Handel (p. 148) made the oratorio popular in England, and his *Messiah*—written in English—is one of the most famous of oratorios. All these forms—cantata, oratorio, passion—are full of dramatic feeling; out of them and along with them, a special kind of dramatic music developed: opera (p. 156).

Austrian composer Franz Schubert at the age of 30. He died only a year later (in 1828), but left an astonishing number of works, most important of which were his lovely solo songs, such as the Winterreise *cycle written in 1827.*

153

Music for instruments

During the Middle Ages, wandering troubadours and minnesingers (p. 208) plucked the strings of a lute or some other portable stringed instrument as they sang. The sung words were more important than the accompaniment. But by the 16th century, a composer like William Byrd (p. 152) could mark his music for songs as "apt for voyces or viols." He meant that his madrigal tunes could be played as effectively on instruments as they could be sung.

The viols Byrd mentions had six strings, like lutes, but they were not plucked. People played them by drawing a taut bow back and forth across the strings. Viols were made in various sizes that differed in pitch. A musical household was likely to have a set of them: a "chest" of viols. Their clear, resonant tone was just right for the small groups who liked to come together to play contrapuntal "fancies" such as those written by England's Orlando Gibbons (1583-1625).

But by the early 18th century, violins, with their flexible tone and "singing" quality, had almost entirely replaced viols. The works of Corelli (p. 148), a great violinist himself, were important in helping to establish the new instrument. The skill of Italian violin makers, who originated the violin in the 16th century, was another vital factor in its success.

Stringed instruments controlled by a *keyboard* were also being perfected at this time. They were of two kinds, those in which the strings were pressed, such as the clavichord, and those in which the strings were plucked, such as the virginal or the harpsichord. More music was written for the harpsichord than for any other of the early keyboard instruments.

But today the best known, most widely played of all keyboard instruments is the *piano*. Around 1700 the first "harpsichord with *piano* and *forte*" was built in Italy. The pianoforte (named from the Italian words for "soft" and "loud") is, like the violin, exceptionally versatile. Its tones—produced by small hammers hitting the strings—can be sustained or cut off at will; the volume of sound can be easily controlled. No other keyboard instrument has all these advantages. Though J. S. Bach saw, and disapproved of, some early models, by 1800 many composers were writing music that utilized the piano's expressive qualities. Haydn and Mozart, for example, wrote piano sonatas that were freer in technique than any that had been composed for the harpsichord. Beethoven (p. 148) extended still further the range of piano technique

The viol, a favorite instrument of the 17th centu… (from a contemporary engraving). Six-stringed a… tuned like the lute, played with a bow like the ol… rebec, viols fell principally into three groups: t… treble, tenor, and bass. A full "consort" of vio… could include as many as eight types, however.

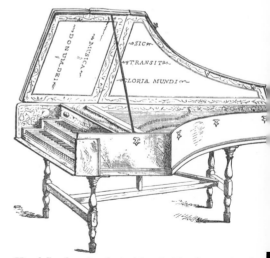

Handel's favorite harpsichord. The harpsichord w… a piano-shaped keyboard instrument popular durin… the 16th to the 18th centuries. Its keys produc… notes by plucking the strings, unlike a piano ke… board which controls small hammers that strike t… strings. Left: part of the score of "The King's Hun… written for the virginal by England's John B… (about 1563-1628). The virginal was like the har… sichord, but oblong, with its keyboard on the lo… side. A triangular version was called a spinet.

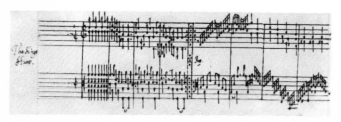

with his 32 eloquent sonatas for this instrument. In the
19th century, some composers, who were also celebrated
concert pianists, wrote for the piano almost exclusively.
Two of the most important were Liszt (p. 150) and the
Polish composer Frédéric Chopin (1810-49).

During the 16th and 17th centuries people gathered
in their houses to play music together, just as they did to
sing madrigals. Both string and keyboard instruments, in
various combinations, were used for this intimate kind of
chamber music. Haydn and Mozart were the first important composers to write music for the *string quartet*,
which consisted of two violins, a viola, and a cello (larger
and deeper-voiced versions of the violin). Mozart introduced wood-wind instruments (p. 160), such as the flute,
oboe, and clarinet. Since his time composers have written
chamber works for a variety of instruments. Usually,
however, strings form the basis of a chamber group, but
the piano and various combinations of wood winds sometimes make their appearance.

Another important keyboard instrument, known to
ancient Greek, Roman, and Jewish musicians, was the
organ. In the Middle Ages, organs were still comparatively simple affairs, used mostly to guide the singers of
plainsong. By the 17th century, especially in Germany,
the organ was capable—with the addition of a keyboard
operated by foot pedals, among other improvements—of
music as complicated as that of the Danish-born master
Dietrich Buxtehude (1637-1707), whose organ-playing
Bach walked 200 miles to hear. The organ of today,
which may include up to five keyboards, is the most
complex and versatile instrument ever devised.

*The 18th-century baroque organ in the Marienkirche,
Lübeck, Germany. The masters of baroque organ technique, Buxtehude and J. S. Bach, composed for organs
like these, which had a unique clear-cut tone and
contrast. Later, more complex romantic organs
were favored for their colorful orchestral effects.*

*Getting together to play music has
always been a favorite pastime—
whether in 17th-century consorts
of viols like that shown above or
in modern chamber groups like
England's Melos Ensemble (right).
So-called chamber music for small
groups is still popular with amateurs, but most often today it is
played by professional musicians.*

Opera

The history of opera is largely the story of how various composers tried to solve the problem of presenting what the 17th-century Italians called *dramma per musica*: drama through music. Interest in rediscovered Greek plays inspired some people in late 16th-century Florence to present plays on Greek themes in which the words were recited to musical tones in what they felt was probably the ancient Greek fashion. They called this *recitativo secco* ("dry reciting," or *recitative*, so called because there was no full orchestral accompaniment).

Among the earliest composers whose operas are still performed today is Claudio Monteverdi (1567-1643). In his *Orfeo* (1607) he introduced choruses, more complicated orchestral accompaniment, and sections of melodic recitative that carried on the action of plot between the arias. An aria is a song-like passage in which individual characters express their emotions.

Another feature of opera as we know it today is the *overture*, a purely orchestral piece of music with which an opera usually opens. Jean-Baptiste Lully (1632-87) introduced the overture into French opera with *Alcidiane* (1658). In Italy, Alessandro Scarlatti (1659-1725)—the father of Domenico (p. 146)—developed the overture and in addition refined the melodic line and rich harmonies of the opera itself to a degree that shaped the operatic taste of all Europe throughout the 18th century.

By the middle of the 18th century, French and Italian opera had become extremely formalized. Arias followed set forms and had to be carefully allotted to the various singers in such a way that each could exhibit their talents in a spectacular fashion. The German composer Christopher Willibald Gluck (1714-87) tried to change all this. In his operas *Orfeo ed Euridice* (1762) and *Alceste* (1767) he made the music follow the action of the plot. He also introduced the type of overture that carefully sets the mood for the story that is to follow.

By Gluck's time opera houses existed in every major city in Europe, and lavish opera productions were well attended by fashionable audiences. In such a favorable climate, nearly all composers tried their hand at opera. The greatest of them was Mozart (p. 148). Some of his operas are among the most frequently performed operas of all: *The Marriage of Figaro* (1786), *Don Giovanni* (1787), and *The Magic Flute* (1791). The other musical giant of the period, Beethoven, wrote only one opera, *Fidelio*, first produced in 1805.

So far, opera librettists—men who wrote the texts—had concentrated on mythological stories and plots of aristocratic intrigue. In the early 19th century, these were forsaken in favor of romantic stories, often built

Monteverdi, the first important opera composer, voices and orchestra for dramatic effects new to mu

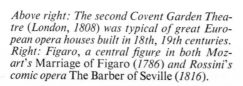

Above right: The second Covent Garden Theatre (London, 1808) was typical of great European opera houses built in 18th, 19th centuries.
Right: Figaro, a central figure in both Mozart's Marriage of Figaro (1786) *and Rossini's comic opera* The Barber of Seville (1816).

156

econd-act climax of Wagner's The Valkyrie *(1870),*
~mund withdraws the magic sword his father Wotan,
f of the Norse gods, has embedded in a huge ash
. Joyfully, Siegmund's twin Sieglinde is reunited
~ her brother. In the music, recurring themes
~esent Siegmund, Sieglinde, and the sword.

around peasant characters or historical events. *Der Freischütz* (1821), or *The Marksman*, by Karl Maria von Weber (1786-1826) is typical of early 19th-century romantic opera, with its story about a forester who makes a pact with the devil in exchange for some magic bullets.

Like Gluck in the 18th century, Richard Wagner (1813-83) tried to "reform" opera by integrating the music with the drama as closely as possible. He developed a continuous, colorfully orchestrated style that was not broken up into sections of recitative, arias, or choruses. Wagner made much use of *leitmotiv*; that is, he used special musical themes as recurring symbols for particular characters or ideas. He based many of his music-dramas, as he called them, on old German legends. Four separate operas, for example, made up the famous *Ring of the Nibelungs* (first performed as a cycle in 1876), which tells how gods and mortals struggle for possession of the magic ring of the title. In Russia, composers celebrated their nation's history in such operas as *Boris Godunov* (1874) by Modest Moussorgsky (1835-81).

Italy produced many prolific composers of operas during the 19th century. Gioacchino Rossini (1792-1868), for instance, wrote 36. His best-known work is the lively *Barber of Seville* (1816). During his long career, Giuseppe Verdi (1813-1901) produced some of the staples of every opera-house repertory, ranging from melodramatic works like *Il Trovatore* (1852) to the serenely mature *Falstaff*, written when he was 80. Giacomo Puccini (1858-1924), on the other hand, is famous for his many popular melodramatic operas full of affecting, highly emotional music. Their settings ranged from the Parisian artists' garret of *La Bohème* (1896) to Japan in *Madame Butterfly* (1900).

Opera since its "golden age" in the 19th century has tended to discard lush vocal displays and symphonic orchestrations. In France, Claude Debussy (1862-1918) wrote his *Pelléas et Mélisande* (1902) in a flowing, reticent style that achieved a complete integration of music and plot. The German composer Paul Hindemith (1895-1963) sought a similar integration in *Mathis the Painter* (1938), based on the life of Grünewald (p. 52). Other composers returned to classical forms, as Alban Berg (1885-1935) did in *Wozzeck* (1925), each of whose 15 scenes is cast in a form such as the fugue, suite, sonata and so on. But the music had a new sound, for he had to a great extent abandoned the tonal systems of the 19th century. In 1951, Russian-born Igor Stravinsky (born 1882), inspired by the paintings of Hogarth (p. 60), borrowed 18th-century musical idioms to tell the story of *The Rake's Progress*.

English contralto Kathleen Ferrier (1912-53)
as Orpheus in Gluck's Orfeo ed Euridice. *Role*
was written for male alto but is sung today by
contralto (lowest female voice). Other voice
ranges in descending order: of women, soprano,
mezzo-soprano; of men, tenor, baritone, bass.

Music for the orchestra

When opera became fashionable in late Renaissance Europe, the bands of musicians who accompanied the singers sat in front of the stage in the *orchestra*, a name borrowed from the Greek theatre (p. 256). Before long, such a band of musicians was itself called an "orchestra." But you should not imagine early orchestras as the well-organized ranks of strings, wood winds, brass, and percussion that you see in a concert hall today (p. 160).

They were, in fact, often limited to whatever players and instruments were available. The typical orchestra consisted mainly of a few viols, with some flutes, horns, and usually a harpsichord, although the one gathered together in 1607 to play for Monteverdi's *Orfeo* (p. 156) had 40 instruments—a tremendous number for that time. Theatre orchestras accompanied recitatives, arias, dances, and perhaps played a few introductory phrases before the performance began. In time, many composers became interested in the sound of the orchestra independent of singing and dancing, and they often used the overture to try out different combinations of instruments.

In France, Lully gave impetus to the growing interest in orchestral music with his opera overtures (p. 156). In Italy, an overture was called a *sinfonia*, a term that could refer to any instrumental piece; those by Alessandro Scarlatti (p. 156) helped determine the form that the symphony (p. 148) eventually took. Opera overtures are a popular feature of most concert programs today. The overtures to many Rossini operas (p. 156), for example, are more often performed than the operas themselves; the four overtures Beethoven (p. 148) wrote for *Fidelio* are also popular concert pieces. Other composers, such as the German Felix Mendelssohn (1809-47), wrote overtures that were meant to be played only in concerts.

Another kind of orchestral music, which originated in Italy, came into fashion among the private court orchestras kept by German and Austrian aristocrats during the 17th and 18th centuries. It made its effect by contrasting groups of instruments with one another. In

J. ALESSANDRO SCARLATTI MRO DI CAPP

Italians of the 17th century gave the name sinf... to the three-movement overtures with which Alessa... Scarlatti and other composers prefaced operas. ... sinfonia was an ancestor of the modern symphon...

Many European kings and nobles of the 17th and ... centuries kept resident orchestras. Seated at ... harpsichord, Joseph Haydn, musical director ... Prince Esterházy, conducts the orchestra at a c... operatic entertainment (below left). Frederick ... Great, a patron of K. P. E. Bach, liked to play ... flute with his court orchestra (below right).

...th-century performance of Handel's Messiah *in ...on's Crystal Palace typifies vogue for gigantic ...estras, whether for oratorio, opera, or symphony.*

...9th-century caricature of Hector Berlioz. It ridi-...s his experiments in increasing the range of ...estral sound by introducing new instruments.

Today, orchestra personnel must adapt themselves to rapid changes of size and make-up. The same concert, recording session, or broadcast (like the one at the left) may demand that players perform both small-scale chamber works and large romantic symphonies.

such a work, called a *concerto grosso*, passages for a small section or "concertino" of violins, for example, alternated with passages played by the concerto grosso—that is, the "whole group." Perhaps the best known concerti grossi are the six J. S. Bach (p. 148) dedicated to the Margrave of Brandenburg in 1721.

In opera houses, violins gradually assumed the strongest role in orchestras, for they approached the voices of the singers in range of tone and expressiveness. They were important in court orchestras too. In one famous 18th-century orchestra belonging to the Hungarian Prince Esterházy, over half the personnel were string players. Haydn (p. 148) was in charge of this orchestra for many years. During the 1770s composers from all over Europe came to Germany to hear Johann Stamitz (1717-57) conduct the orchestra belonging to the Elector of Mannheim. It was famous for its controlled dynamics (p. 144) and expressiveness. Orchestras like this offered new resources to composers like Mozart who were experimenting with the symphonic form. Mozart used much the same orchestral combination as Haydn (with the addition of clarinets) and brought the art of blending orchestral tone colors to a high level. Beethoven did little to change the orchestra's basic structure, but he made such enormous demands on the technique of the players that the orchestra sounded like a new thing altogether. His vigorous orchestral sound strongly influenced romantic composers (p. 150).

By the middle of the 19th century, Wagner (p. 156) in Germany and Berlioz (p. 158) in France, had revolutionized the symphony orchestra. They added great numbers of players and wrote passages for many new instruments, particularly in the brass and wood-wind sections. Yet Brahms (p. 150) wrote four symphonies for orchestras the same size Mozart and Beethoven used.

The rich sound of the romantic orchestra continued to be a favorite with composers interested in magnificent color effects. Austria's Gustav Mahler (1860-1911), for example, wrote a "Symphony of a Thousand" (his Symphony No. 8) that required several soloists, three choruses, an organ, *and* a huge orchestra. But an interesting point about Mahler's orchestrations is that different groups of instruments can be heard, each clearly distinct from the general colorful flow of sound.

A preference for clarity and economy is a feature of orchestral music of the present day. Stravinsky (p. 156), for example, perhaps the most influential composer of our time, started out by writing for large-scale orchestras, but by the 1920s he was writing music for smaller orchestral combinations.

Instruments of the orchestra

The *strings* are the most important of the four families that make up the modern orchestra: They constitute almost two thirds of its total strength. The expressive sounds of the violin, viola, violoncello, and bass rival the human voice in variety and flexibility, and composers often entrust them with the principal melodies in their compositions.

Next in importance are the *wood winds*, with their wide range of pitch and dynamics. There are the clear-voiced flute and bright, shrill piccolo; the plaintive oboe with its lower-pitched cousins the cor anglais and bassoon; and the mellow clarinet.

The *brasses*, whose powerful voices are placed at the rear of the orchestra, include the versatile, rich-sounding French horn, the brilliant trumpet, solemn trombone, and deep-voiced tuba.

Some members of the *percussion* family—the bass drum, the triangle, and the cymbals—produce sounds that composers use to accentuate rhythms or add drama. But the timpani, or kettledrums, can be tuned to a definite pitch, producing more delicate effects.

Most orchestras also use a harp, and sometimes a piano, organ, or some other instrument may be added. The size of a full orchestra is generally from 60 to 100 players, which makes it capable of ranging easily from small-scale 18th-century compositions to works in the grand romantic manner.

Top right: strings. Violins have formed orchestra's backbone since 17th century, when Louis XIV's orchestra under Lully was famous as "the King's 24 violins." Center right: wood winds. Shown are two clarinets and a bass clarinet. First important scoring for clarinet was by Handel. Below right: brass. Such instruments as trumpets, trombones, tuba are among oldest known; those in modern orchestras are improved 19th- and 20th-century versions. Below left: percussion. From left, side drum, tenor drum, triangle (all of indefinite pitch); xylophone, kettle drums (whose pitch may be fixed); and in rear, bass drum (indefinite pitch).

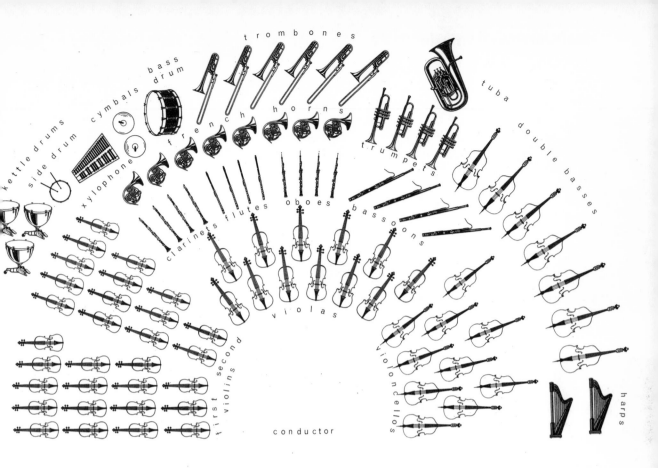

kettle drums · side drum · xylophone · cymbals · bass drum · french horns · trombones · trumpets · tuba · clarinets · flutes · oboes · bassoons · double basses · first violins · second violins · violas · violoncellos · harps · conductor

Above: a typical placing of the 20th-century symphony orchestra for best blending of sound. The strings—the heart of the orchestra—are placed in front, soft-voiced wood winds next, harsher brasses behind them. Percussion is at rear except for gentle-sounding harps.

Below: Otto Klemperer (born in Germany, 1885) conducts the London Philharmonic in a performance of Brahms' Requiem. *To suit this particular work, orchestra's size and placement are modified. Double basses are at right, harps center foreground. An organ (rear) is added, as well as a large chorus and two soloists. Percussion and brass sections are reduced in number.*

Interpretation of music

Pipers and drummers provide a gay accompaniment to peasant celebrations shown in this 17th-century French engraving. On joyful occasions, problem of interpretation hardly arises, for the players' emotions take over. In more sophisticated music, a marking such as vivace *(lively) might be used to guide players.*

Only solemn music is suitable for such occasions as funeral processions—such as the one (shown below) for the Duc de Morny, a 19th-century French statesman. Death and bereavement have inspired some of the world's most deeply felt music. A composer often marks such music largo *(slow and stately) to guide players.*

To bring a piece of music to life, anybody who sings or plays an instrument must have some clue to its mood. Often, many clues can be found outside the music itself. The words of a folk song, for example, tell you what sort of emphasis—joyful, sad, satirical—to give to the music. And you do not need much practice to know when to soften your voice for a soothing lullaby or add vigor to it for a sailor's work song, or sea chantey.

Songs such as the Negro "blues" are often pitched in a minor key (p. 146). This—especially when their lyrics are melancholy instead of ribald—helps singers interpret them instinctively, even when they cannot read music. In the same way, the rhythms of particular dances decide how the music for them should be played; most South American dances, for example, are pointless if given a slow and stately treatment.

But what about more complicated music, the music of an opera or a symphony or a concerto? For these, musicians need the extra clues provided by the composer. Musicians read a printed or written score in the same way actors study the script of a play. They try to find out what

The great Italian conductor Arturo Toscanini (1867-1957). The role of the conductor is both to co-ordinate the orchestra's performance and to interpret the score according to his idea of the composer's intentions.

the composer intended. Just as printed texts of Shakespeare's plays do not have many directions for the actor, early written music gave little indication of how it should be expressed. Performers depended largely on such clues as they got from hearing other music played according to the customs of the time. But in 17th-century Italy, composers began to add brief directions in the form of words and extra symbols to the notes of a printed score.

These gave performers some idea of how to interpret a piece. Because music printed in Italy was sold throughout Europe, and Italian musicians traveled everywhere giving concerts and lessons, Italian became the accepted language for terms used to indicate expression. You may run across music on which the composer has written directions in his native language, but you are more likely to find words like *cantabile*, which shows that the performer should use a "singing" style in the music, or *legato*, which indicates that the notes should be "bound" smoothly together. A symbol like < indicates *crescendo* (getting louder), > means *diminuendo* (getting softer).

Another problem in interpreting music is tempo (p. 144). The composer can indicate it, but each player will have slightly different ideas about just what the composer means. In an orchestra or chorus, the players and singers submit to the judgment of one man, the conductor. He controls the performance, shaping it according to what he believes the composer's intentions were.

But conductors, singers, and instrumental performers all must use their own judgment and draw upon their own feelings and emotions, for not everything in a piece of music can be written down. Technical skill can help a singer and his accompanist, for example, to follow the notes and phrasings of a score without a mistake, but if they do not have some insight into what the composer was trying to say, or some sympathy with the composer's feelings, they will not give a very interesting or exciting performance.

Above: Nicolò Paganini (Italian, 1782-1840), most widely acclaimed violinist of his time. His interpretive playing exploited violin technique to the full, and appealed to the new taste for romanticism. Below: German soprano Elizabeth Schwarzkopf (born 1915) as the Marschallin, a role she often sings, in a television production of Strauss's Der Rosenkavalier. *Frequently singers display a sympathy with certain composers that enables them to interpret their music especially satisfyingly.*

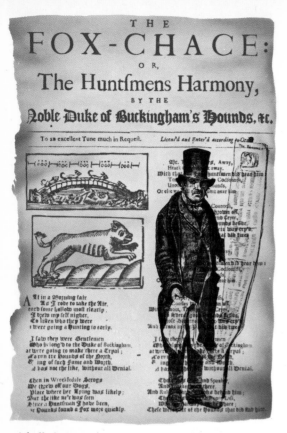

A ballad always told a story. Above (in color): a 17th-century English ballad in the form of a printed "broadside." Superimposed figure is a 19th-century ballad seller hawking his "long-song" sheets.

Light music

Some music seems especially designed to "cheer and repose in some measure the spirit"; so said the French philosopher Jean-Jacques Rousseau about a kind of popular 18th-century music. He was talking about the *intermezzo* —a musical entertainment inserted between the acts of serious operas to relieve the strain that "matters of gravity" put on the spectator. From these Italian intermezzi to Broadway musical comedies, there has always been a place for lighthearted, easy-to-take music—the kind people whistle and sing in the street.

In 1733 an intermezzo was performed in Naples for the first time as an independent work. This was *La Serva Padrona*, by Giovanni Pergolesi (1710-36). The gaiety of its score and its inconsequential story about a "servant turned mistress" scored an immediate success. At the same time in England, *ballad operas* were in vogue. The most successful of them all, *The Beggar's Opera*, with dialogue by John Gay (1685-1732), and music arranged by John Pepusch (1667-1752), opened in 1728. Its tunes —actual ballads and folk songs of the day (p. 164)—were popular with an audience bored by the foreign lyrics and high-flown themes of fashionable Italian opera, which *The Beggar's Opera* mocked.

In fact, popular musical entertainments were often adapted to satirical purposes. Since the beginning of the 18th century, French composers had supplied satirical songs for *opéra-comique* parodies of grand opera. (Later, opéra-comique lost its "comic-opera" meaning and signified any opera with spoken dialogue, whether its subject was comic or serious.) In Paris the success of *La Serva Padrona*—performed there in 1746—inspired a century and a half of French *opéra bouffe*. Probably the best-known composer of light-hearted opera of this kind was German-born Jacques Offenbach (1819-80). He mocked Parisian life during the luxurious Second Empire by putting typical high-society characters into the mythological settings of operettas like *Orpheus in the Underworld* (1858) and *La Belle Hélène* (1864).

Offenbach suggested that Johann Strauss the younger (1825-99), whose Viennese waltzes were captivating Europe, should try his hand at operetta. His waltz tunes and gay plots influenced a host of lesser composers. The Viennese tradition continued into the 20th century with Franz Lehár (1870-1948), who turned from attempts at writing grand opera to compose *The Merry Widow* (1905), one of the most popular operettas ever written and, like Strauss's, widely imitated. In England, Sir William Gilbert (p. 218) wrote satirical librettos set to music by Sir Arthur Sullivan (1842-1900). These light operas poked fun at Victorian society and grand opera.

Jacques Offenbach, shown here in a portrait by Gustave Doré, filled the scores of about a hundred light operas with such gay melodies and witty orchestrations that Rossini called him "the Mozart of the boulevards." He wrote one serious work: The Tales of Hoffman.

SOUSA
AND HIS BAND

AN ORGANIZATION OF NEARLY 100 MUSICIANS

LIEUT. COM'D'R. JOHN PHILIP SOUSA
CONDUCTOR

AN ORGANIZATION OF NEARLY 100 MUSICIANS

[Th]e entire band of America's John Philip Sousa (1854-[19]32) shown on a huge billboard poster. "The March [Ki]ng's" world tour of 1910-11 gained him an inter[na]tional reputation as a composer of stirring marches. [Th]eir exuberance and patriotic feeling did much to [ins]pire new standards of brass-band playing.

Operettas in the early 20th century were not so distinguished by originality and wit, however, and, in general, sentiment prevailed. But in the 1920s Broadway began to produce musical comedies whose music owed a good deal to jazz (p. 164), and by the 1930s elements of satire crept back into the music and plots. Since the end of World War II, America has exported its musicals to stages and motion-picture screens all over the world.

Songs often gain wide popularity independent of stage or film productions, however. Radio and television give immediate and world-wide celebrity to songs—often to songs written simply to exploit the market for phonograph records and sheet music. But the "popular song" is not a new concept. The intermezzi and ballad operas of the 18th century owed some of their success to the fact that they were frequently made up of tunes already popular in the streets. Many of these were ballads whose printed music was hawked on street corners or at fairs, much as records are sold everywhere today. In the 19th century, people could hear popular songs and ballads in music halls (p. 274), theatres, and cafés.

Today, mostly through records, songs sung by performers like the French singer Édith Piaf or the American Frank Sinatra become internationally famous. Or a song may so catch the mood of the times that it becomes popular everywhere. During World War II, for example, soldiers on both sides of the lines sang the German "Lili Marlene." Yet universal popularity does not turn a song into what we ordinarily call a folk song. No matter how closely we identify a popular song with a singer or an occasion, the song's composer himself is easily identifiable; the anonymous "composers" of folk songs are the people who sing them.

The American singer Frank Sinatra (born 1915) photographed at a late-night recording session. Sinatra, popular for over 20 years, is typical of entertainers whose way with a song can make it internationally known. His record sales have hit a fantastic 10 million a year.

165

Folk music and jazz

It is the performer rather than the composer who is important in folk music and jazz, for it is only during the performance that either kind of music is created: The performers *are* the composers. People at work or play make up folk music as they "go along," introducing little changes nearly every time a song or dance is performed.

To most people the term *folk* suggests rural music: the songs and dances of wandering Hungarian gypsies, or of Russian farmers, or American settlers. Ordinary people like these have always made songs to sing as they worked, or they have sung and danced (p. 176) as a kind of home-made entertainment. They based their songs on life as they knew it. Cowboy work songs, for example, often include cries that cowhands use when herding cattle; the rhythms are like natural riding rhythms. The songs cowboys sang around campfires or as they rode through the lonely plains of the American Far West told stories about their way of life.

In fact, many folk songs tell stories. One Scottish *ballad* (as storytelling songs are called) tells about the unhappy love of Barbara Allen and Sir John Graham. You can hear people in the hill country of the American South singing to the same tune about "Barbry Ellen" and "Sweet William." Because folk songs pass orally from one singer to the next, their words often change, though the tunes stay more or less the same.

The music of one group of people—the Negroes—has been especially influential during the last hundred years. When the Negroes were taken across the Atlantic as slaves during the 17th, 18th, and 19th centuries, they brought their own music with them. Before long, they took up the music of their owners, too, and Negro folk music, colored by English, French, and Spanish influences, flowered throughout the Americas.

Negroes in the southern part of the United States sang religious songs called *spirituals*, derived from English hymns. They heard these hymns from the Baptist and

The melodies of many folk songs were originally set to work rhythms. Turn-of-the-century photograph above shows sailors singing a "chantey" to the tune of a fiddle. Rhythm of the chantey co-ordinated the efforts of men working to raise the ship's anchor.

Majorcan peasant plays a pipe and drum (below left). Such "one-man bands" are an age-old form of folk-dance accompaniment. New Orleans marching bands (below right) syncopated or "jazzed" marches by shifting musical accents to unexpected places. On-lookers clapped or shouted to fill in missing beats.

Methodist preachers who converted them to Christianity. But they added African rhythms and the distinctively sad quality that characterizes much 19th-century Negro music. In New Orleans, French brass bands and marching music influenced the Negroes, for the Mardi Gras carnival was a time for parades and dancing.

Eventually these elements combined to produce *jazz*. When the slaves were freed, at the end of the American Civil War in 1865, they began to play European-style instruments discarded by army brass bands. Before this, their music had been mostly vocal. They clapped and shouted as they sang in much the same way their African ancestors had, improvising words and rhythms. When the Negroes played instruments, they adopted the same spontaneous, emotional style; by the end of the 19th century, it was called jazz. When jazz players formed themselves into professional groups about the time of World War I, the piano or string bass supplied the regular beat. In a kind of counterpoint technique (p. 146), each instrument of the jazz band improvised its own variations on whatever basic tune the musicians had decided to jazz.

By the 1920s, jazz had spread everywhere through the United States and Europe. In the 1930s, *swing* appeared. Swing—syncopated in jazz fashion—was written music; it was rehearsed, and though it often gave plenty of opportunity for virtuoso performance, it lacked the spontaneity and true folk quality of jazz. Such music, manufactured in great quantities for the sheet music and recording industries, put jazz into eclipse until about the end of World War II, when interest in truly improvised jazz revived. Today, jazz might well be called the urban folk music of the 20th century.

American trumpeter Dizzy Gillespie (born 1917) plays in France at the 1962 Antibes Jazz Festival. After World War II, Gillespie helped popularize "bebop," which relied on some of the harmonies developed by Stravinsky, Schönberg, and others—an example of the interaction between jazz and "serious" music.

Modern music

Modern music began to take shape late in the 19th century when the experiments of Wagner (p. 156) and the composers who followed him—people like Germany's Richard Strauss (1864-1949) and Gustav Mahler (p. 158) with their symphonic "poems"—led to the exploration of new scales of notes and new instruments. In France, Claude Debussy (p. 156) and Maurice Ravel (1875-1937), influenced by experiments in the other arts, wanted to evoke moods or impressions rather than to tell stories as many romantic composers had tended to do.

But musical impressionism was not the only way composers reacted to romantic music. Many turned to the straightforwardness of folk music. In England, for example, Ralph Vaughan Williams (1872-1958) rediscovered and arranged a great deal of early English music. In Brazil, Heitor Villa-Lobos (born 1881) combined Brazilian folk music with classical forms to produce works such as his *Bachianas Brasilieras*. The Hungarians Béla Bartók (p. 150) and Zoltán Kodály (born 1882) made serious researches into the genuine folk music of Hungary. The rhythms and scales they found and the uses they made of them influenced composers of several nations.

Other composers re-emphasized classical forms and explored the pleasing effects they could obtain from using counterpoint and small orchestral groups. Typical of such composers is England's Benjamin Britten (born 1913), who scored many of his operas for chamber-sized orchestras. In France, just after World War I, a group called *Les Six* typified composers who sought new, more economical and objective ways of writing music. Francis Poulenc (born 1899) and Darius Milhaud (born 1892), for example, wrote music—much influenced by jazz—often played by small groups and making use of musical threads in different keys (a technique called *polytonality*).

But the third and most revolutionary approach was toward an entirely new organization of music. This involved "abandoning" the major and minor scales in favor of the so-called *12-tone* system. Each of the 12 notes of the traditional scale was given equal value; the key system (p. 146) had given importance to eight notes, all related to the tonic or key note of a scale. People who heard 12-tone music for the first time were confused; no tonic note was there to unify the sounds. Such *atonal* music seemed meaningless.

The man who initiated this musical revolution was Arnold Schönberg (1874-1951), an Austrian. After an early period in which his music was strongly Wagnerian in style, he set out to find an "entirely new road in music"

Ravel (above) is linked with Debussy as an "impressionist." They tended to abandon structure of classic[al] and romantic music (Ravel less than Debussy) in fav[or] of atmospheric tone colors and harmonies.

After World War I, groups such as France's Les S[ix] reacted against impressionism as well as romanticis[m]. By 1924, when this photograph was taken, Lou[is] Durey had left; the others collaborated on music for [a] play by Jean Cocteau. But their styles, though [all] influenced by Erik Satie, were not similar. Abov[e:] Germaine Tailleferre, Francis Poulenc, Arthur Honeg[er, Darius Milhaud, Cocteau, Georges Auric.

From chaos of early-20th-century experiment emerg[ed] Schönberg's revolutionary 12-tone system. Composer[']s diagram shows one way it works. Set of 12 tone[s] (tone-row or series) may be used backward (retrograd[e] set), upside down (inversion), or both (retrograde i[n]version), but always in the same relative order.

so that he could achieve greater control of all elements of composition. One of Schönberg's pupils, Alban Berg, introduced atonal elements into his opera *Wozzeck* (p. 156), yet he did not entirely abandon late romantic harmonies. Anton von Webern (1883-1945), who studied with Berg, also took a number of pupils. The economy and discipline of his works influenced a great number of composers such as the Italian Luigi Dallapiccola (born 1904) who composed chiefly with 12-note techniques. Major composers, such as Stravinsky (p. 158) and Hindemith (p. 156), experimented too, and showed that music did not have to be straight-jacketed into one inflexible system.

Under Schönberg's influence, some composers used the 12-tone technique to form a *serial* method of composition. The composer chose a particular arrangement of 12 tones called a *row*, and predetermined the length of each note, the rhythmic patterns, and so on. The row could be used backward or even upside down, but all the notes remained in the same relative order. The advantage of such a system from the composer's viewpoint is that it gives him stricter control over the ideas contained in his themes and over their development.

One serial composer, Germany's Karlheinz Stockhausen (born 1928), experimented with ways to extend this control even further. He and others have taken electronically produced sounds and built them into electronic music in which both performers and classical notation are dispensed with. In France, a similar kind of music was developed, made up of tape-recorded natural sounds combined in new ways. It is called *musique concrète*.

Both the scientifically precise and the apparently chaotic aspects of contemporary music—together with influences like jazz—reflect aspects of contemporary life. Probably the future of music will include the coming together of the latest experimental techniques with some from the past. As Schönberg remarked, there is still "plenty of good music to be written in C major."

Using the austere resources of atonal music, Alban Berg composed one of the most effective of modern operas, Wozzeck (1925). It tells how a simple-minded soldier, Wozzeck (seen here as sung by Welsh baritone Geraint Evans), baited by his superiors, murders his unfaithful mistress and drowns himself. The music was received sensationally with either ovations or riots at each of its premières.

As well as experimental electronic music, Karlheinz Stockhausen has written "space music" in which orchestra, vocal groups, loudspeakers surround listeners. No themes are developed; Stockhausen wants such music to "contribute to inner peace." He is seen in photograph (below) at extreme right, conducting one group at 1960 broadcast in Hamburg of his Carré.

Chapter 7

Dance

In its most elementary forms, dancing springs from a natural instinct. From the moment human beings appeared on earth, they have danced to release their emotions and to communicate them to others. The urge to respond *physically* to an emotion seems to be common to all peoples and all ages. For example, at one time or another every one of us has "danced for joy" upon hearing some very exciting news. All over the world, tiny children skip gaily about long before they are old enough to have learned how to explain their happiness in words.

But such spontaneous movement, although it marks the beginnings of dance, is not yet dancing. Hops and jumps first begin to approach an artistic form when bodily movement is controlled by a definite rhythm. Rhythmic bodily movement alone, however, cannot be called dancing—at least, not the *art* of dancing.

Dancing can be said to have become an "art" when the natural impulse of early peoples was gradually harnessed to rhythm, first provided by the stamping of feet, and later by drums and other musical instruments. Then, when steps were arranged in formal patterns intended to express various ideas and beliefs, some performers began to train their bodies carefully in order to make them more supple and expressive. Eventually, dancing developed into three distinct kinds: the religious, the social, and the theatrical. In time, all three of these acquired the high degree of skill and artistry that they have today.

It may seem a far cry from primitive man's re-enacting the pursuit of his prey to the splendor of an Indian temple dancer or the virtuosity and beauty of a Russian ballerina. But all of them have this in common: They create a drama of movement through expressive use of the body.

All dancing springs from man's natural urge to translate his feelings into movement—whether it takes the form of a child's jump for joy, a tribe's ritual invocation to their gods, or a theatrical performance. Throughout the ages, and in almost every society, a dancer has been expected first to master intricate traditional movements, then to transform them into a dance as free and flowing as this one—a design for the ballet Schéhérazade *(1910), by Russian-born artist Léon Bakst.*

The dancer's body

Men have always felt the impulse to dance. In this South African cave painting, dancing Bushmen mimic the praying mantis.

For centuries, children at play have matched dance steps of their own invention to the rhythms of songs and rhymes. The London schoolgirl (above) kicks high in the air while chanting traditional counting rhyme. Children from all over the world also mimic adults. Boys and girls in the Republic of the Congo (below) re-enact a ritual dance that is usually performed by the adults of their tribe.

Dancing requires no raw material apart from the dancer's body. But discoveries about the way his body works have helped man to dance in special ways. How we train our bodies and put them to work determines the way in which we dance.

The degree of movement of which a body is capable depends on its shape, on the length of the ligaments (bone-connecting tissues), and on the flexibility and strength of the muscles. Generally speaking, women's bodies are more flexible than those of men. And the bodies of members of races living in warm climates are usually more supple and relaxed than those of people who live in colder lands.

Ligaments, unlike muscles, are not flexible—they do not, in other words, expand and contract—but they can easily be lengthened by special training at a very early age. Thus, dancers who want to acquire exceptional technical skill must start young, before their ligaments have had time to harden.

The least flexible part of the body is its bony frame—the *skeleton*. The shape of bones and joints permits only a limited amount of bodily movement. For instance, the *thoracic* region of the body (the ribs and chest) can easily be turned and bent forward and to each side, but it cannot be bent backward. The ball and socket structure of the hip and shoulder joints permits some degree of movement, but not very much. All movement from the hip is easier in a forward direction; the leg, for example, can be raised about sixty degrees forward from the vertical without effort, but less movement is possible to the side, and less still to the rear. If the leg is to be raised high, the hips have to be tilted, and this in turn affects the position of the spine (or backbone).

The human body performs such actions automatically. When you throw your leg up in a high kick or bend down

to touch your toes, you do not need to stop and think about how your muscles and ligaments are working. But a professional dancer needs to understand how to make each part of his body work in a special way, while, at the same time, making sure that *all* the parts remain in harmonious balance. In dancing, as in riding a bicycle, keeping one's balance is simply a matter of controlling the distribution of weight. The dancer has to practice until he can do this instantly and without having to think about what he is doing.

Although dancers of every type are alike in that they must learn to keep their balance, dance skills and techniques differ greatly from continent to continent. In Indian Hindu temple dancing, for example, there are at least 4000 *mudras* (picture gestures of the hands). So a Hindu dancer must develop control over the movement of each separate finger. There are also special movements for other parts of the body, including nine positions for the head, eight for the eyes, and four for the neck. The Western ballet dancer also trains his whole body, but he pays special attention to the feet. He needs to be able to leap high into the air and to do intricate movements with his feet while actually airborne, crossing and uncrossing them or beating them together. His feet are not merely used as a firm base for balancing and bearing the weight of the body, but are also a means of propulsion: They lift the body into the air, and they act as a shock absorber when it returns to the ground.

Because the trained dancer has brought his instrument of expression—the body—to the highest possible state of alertness, he is always a better dancer than an untrained individual. His body is both more beautiful and more efficient than an untrained body, and so it is more likely to achieve the harmony of posture, balance, and co-ordinated movement that is essential for the art of the dance.

To achieve suppleness and poise, a dancer must be trained. Ballet classes all over the world begin, as at the famed Bolshoi Ballet School (above, left), with exercises at the bar. A Hindu temple dancer must train even more rigorously to master picture gestures like the "lotus blooming on a stalk" (above). Equally intricate movements for every part of the body were laid down in the Natya Sastra, *the 2000-year-old manual of Hindu dance.*

Ancient Indian statuette (below) shows the Hindu god Siva setting the world in motion with a dance. Hindu temple dancers of today echo Siva's gestures; their art has changed hardly at all during the past 20 centuries.

The language of movement

In its simplest form, dancing is a natural means of expression. Through bodily movement, one person can convey his ideas and emotions to another. In the beginning, man, like many animals, used this means of communication instinctively, stamping ferociously to indicate his anger, for example. Even at that stage of its development, though, dancing was probably more often an expression of pleasure (as it is in civilized countries today) than of rage or ferocity.

As civilizations developed, the dance was also put to work; in other words, it was made to serve serious purposes. The blessings of nature—sunshine, clear skies, and rich harvests—continued to inspire dances expressing joy and happiness. But man had also to contend with such natural disasters as flood, fire, and famine. So symbolic ritual dances were devised that would, it was hoped, appease the gods, who were believed to control the forces of nature. Again, if a hunt was to take place, special dances were performed, representing the pursuit and killing of a quarry. These dances were intended to ensure the success of the hunters by means of magic. If rain was needed, the tribe would tirelessly do a rain-making dance in which the constant beating of feet upon the ground raised dust that would form (it was believed) into a rain cloud; thunder might be suggested by the beating of drums, lightning by the crackle of twigs. When a man fell

For centuries, men have devised ritual dances to invoke their gods. These Nigerian tribesmen dance with seed pods tied to their calves to ensure a good harvest. Round dances, adopted by the early Christian Church, are still performed in some places on saints' days. Fra Angelico's 15th-century painting (below) depicts angels dancing a round in heaven.

ill, the witch doctor would perform frenzied steps and gestures in order to frighten the devils out of the sick man's body.

In savage communities today, witch doctors still perform magic rites to cure the sick or to speak to the gods. In more advanced countries, too, priests have always used dance and symbolic ritual as a means of communicating with the supernatural. Priests in ancient Egypt, for example, took part in dance rites honoring the gods Isis and Osiris. The early Christian Church also encouraged ritual dances, especially "round dances" that represented circles of angels ringed about God's heavenly throne.

Dances were performed by primitive man to celebrate every phase of life. Birth, manhood, marriage, and death all became the subjects of ritual dances. Although more sophisticated in form, many of the dances found in civilized countries today have actually sprung from just such fundamental experiences of human life. For instance, friends and relatives still often celebrate a young person's "coming of age," engagement, or marriage with a special dance.

In the past, social relationships outside the family were expressed in dances of welcome to strangers, or in frenzied war dances that served both to inflame the courage of the warriors and to terrify the enemy. Gradually, however, dancing simply for pleasure became a popular activity, occurring wherever people gathered together. Such social dancing naturally varies greatly in different parts of the world. Eskimos, bundled up in warm clothing, obviously dance quite differently from the lightly clad inhabitants of the South Seas. A warlike tribe has fierce and vigorous dances; a more peaceful race develops dances that are graceful and decorative. In a country where people tend to be heavily built, the dances are sedate; more active races indulge in leaps and bounds. But whatever the national differences, the sense of group activity is the same.

The dance steps and gestures performed by the people of vanished Western civilizations, such as those of the Greeks or the Etruscans, cannot be exactly known. They can only be guessed at from the figures of dancers shown in surviving fragments of carvings and in paintings. In the East, however, the story is different. Hindu temple dancers in India and Ceylon, Chinese acrobats, and the actor-dancers of Japan still carry on dance traditions that date back thousands of years. These are still part of a way of life that has remained almost unchanged. Through wars and famines, conquest and poverty, the beliefs and culture of the Asian nations have proved remarkably strong.

Heavy clothing hampers dancing Eskimo (right), depicted by a 19th-century artist. In Spain's warm climate, light clothing allows vigorous movements like those on the left.

Ancient Egyptian painting (about 1450 B.C.) shows acrobatic dancer entertaining at court.

One of the most elaborate—and ancient—dance forms is the kathakali, *the sacred dance-drama of Kerala in south India. Masked and magnificently clad, male dancers use traditional mime to retell life stories of gods.*

13th-century temple carvings at Chidambaran, India, depict the oldest form of Hindu dance, the bharata natyam. Temple dancers of today still dedicate their lives to the god Siva.

19th-century Japanese woodcut shows an actor performing a centuries-old religious dance.

Temple, village green, dance hall

Indian temple dancing, like the other arts of India, spread in time throughout most of Southeast Asia. It was carried northward into Tibet, and eastward into China and Japan, by warriors, traders, and missionaries. Gradually, each Asian country developed its own styles. In China, performers acquired such acrobatic skill that they became tumblers rather than dancers. In Japan, dancer-actors perfected a complex mime language with which to present elaborate dance dramas. The dances that most clearly retain their Indian origin are today found in Ceylon, Malaya, Thailand, and the islands of Indonesia. In those countries, as in India, a dancer's movements are confined mainly to the upper part of his body.

The Hindu temple dances of today are still recognizably similar to those recorded in ancient statues and temple carvings. By contrast, European dances have hardly any recognizable religious tradition; instead, they have grown out of the popular dances of ordinary people.

We know little about the kind of dancing done in Europe before the 15th century. But there is no doubt that people continued to dance for pleasure throughout the so-called Dark Ages. Most European traditional dances preserve traces of an ancient pagan origin in the form of ritual steps and gestures whose symbolic significance modern dancers can no longer comprehend. Such primitive dance movements were usually retained by later peasant communities simply as a form of relaxation in a world that was often made grim by plague and famine.

Peasant, or *folk*, dancing is mainly a country pursuit, belonging to fairs and the village green. Today, the folk dance is performed spontaneously only in places where people's lives have not been affected by modern industry and city sophistication. Thus, Russia, Yugoslavia, Poland, and Spain—all of which still have large peasant populations—are rich in folk art of all kinds. Their governments wisely want to preserve this heritage; and so professional and amateur groups are encouraged to study and perform traditional dances.

In the cities, where folk dancing long ago declined as a popular pastime, its place was taken by more elegant ballroom dancing. But even there, the influence of folk dance can be seen. The origin of nearly every present-day ballroom dance can be traced to a folk dance. As early as the 15th century, one boisterous peasant dance was taken over by polite society and transformed into the stately *basse danse* (literally, "low dance," so called because the dancers hardly lifted their feet from the ground). By the end of the 16th century, this was giving way to the livelier *branle*, the *galliard*, and the graceful *pavane*.

In Siam, magnificently costumed ceremonial dancers like this one use precise, traditional picture gestures to mime such religious epics as the Ramayana, first learned from southern Indian missionaries centuries ago.

The rollicking peasant dances of medieval Europe, pictured (right) by 16th-century Flemish artist Brueghel, were refined and polished in France. In his book Orchésographie, *Thoinot Arbeau recorded both music and basic dance steps such as the* révérence *(left).*

Much of what we know about such early dances comes from a book, *Orchésographie*, written in 1588 by a Frenchman, Thoinot Arbeau. It was he who first described the way a dancer could learn to improve his balance and enlarge his range of movement by turning out his legs and feet. The five basic positions of the feet used by ballet dancers today stem from the principles defined by Arbeau. *Orchésographie* also describes many different *branles*, for each province of France had its own version. For example, the *gavotte* was a branle of Provence, the *minuet* a branle of Poitou.

The minuet was introduced into Paris, in a more polished, less boisterous form, in 1650, and it was danced in public by King Louis XIV himself. The minuet dominated the ballrooms of Europe until the end of the 18th century, when it was conquered by the *waltz*. The waltz, too, comes from a folk dance—the *laendler*, a slow, turning dance for pairs of dancers, from southern Germany and Austria. But by the 1840s the public had begun to demand new dance rhythms. From Bohemia (now Czechoslovakia) came the *polka*, and from Poland came the *mazurka*. Both of these soon found their way into ballrooms all over Europe and North America.

Although the Americans adopted many of Europe's rhythms, they also turned to folk-dance rhythms they found on their own doorstep. The *foxtrot*, based on the dances of American Negroes, was introduced at the beginning of this century; and it was soon followed by the *tango* from Argentina and the *rumba* from Cuba (p. 188).

Changes in the popularity of certain types of dancing usually come about as a result of social change. The French Revolution, for example, rapidly brought an end to the courtly dances of the 18th century. In our own century, the two world wars have helped break down class distinctions. The informal, democratic dance hall is now more suited to modern dancing habits than the fashionable ballrooms of earlier times.

The cotillion, *as it was danced in England in 1788. The cotillion, derived from peasant* branles, *reached the height of its popularity in the 19th century, and was usually danced to conclude an evening's entertainment.*

Enter the ballet-master

In the 16th and 17th centuries Italian princes planned magnificent pageants to welcome royal visitors. In the War of Beauty, *held in Florence in 1615, groups of horsemen moved in geometric patterns that foreshadowed the movements of modern* corps de ballet.

Just as folk dancing acquired elegant manners and became accepted as part of European court life, so the fashionable court dances also merged into something else: They evolved into a form of theatrical dancing known as *ballet.*

Ballet was born about five hundred years ago in Renaissance Italy, where such rich and powerful merchant-princes as the Medici of Florence and the Sforza of Milan employed professional dancing masters to supervise the production of pageants and other spectacles. These court dance displays, called *balletti,* became a regular feature of every lavish entertainment. Great pageants, with hundreds of performers, took place everywhere, both indoors and in the open air. Such displays required little technical skill from the dancers—who, in any case, were dressed so elaborately that they could manage only the simplest movements. Thus, Renaissance Italy's *choreography*—the planning of dance movements, from the Greek words *khoros* ("dancing") and *graphia* ("writing")—was as much a matter of geometry as of dancing. It consisted almost entirely of working out complicated patterns of group movement, a little like the countermarching of soldiers on parade.

State banquets were a favorite occasion for the production of balletti. For example, the marriage of the Duke of Milan to a Spanish princess was celebrated in 1489 with a lavish but typical "dinner ballet." With each course was performed a special dance based upon an appropriate theme chosen from classical mythology. The fish course was brought in by attendants who then performed a ballet about the gods of the sea; and so on.

In 1494, King Charles VIII of France marched into Italy at the head of his army and claimed the throne of Naples. While there, both the king and his courtiers were so delighted by the dance pageants given in their honor that they soon set about importing Italian dancing masters and musicians into France. Among these musicians was Baldassarino de Belgiojoso, called Beaujoyeulx in France. In 1581, he staged the *Ballet Comique de la Royne,* which told of the mythical enchantress Circe, who lured travelers to her palace. This famous ballet, designed

Typical of the spectacular ballets given at the courts of 17th-century Florentine princes was the Liberation of Tirreno *(1616). Dancers trod a stately measure on the ballroom floor, while courtiers looked on from the galleries.*

The sumptuous, slow-moving Ballet Comique de la Royne (*above*), *presented at the French court by the Italian musician Beaujoyeulx in 1591, was the first ballet to tell a story. A century later, Italy's Jean Baptiste Lully transformed French ballet with lively music, and—in* Le Triomphe de l'Amour (1681)—*introduced women dancers (above right).*

to celebrate a royal betrothal, was a mixture of music, declamation, dance, and pageantry. Beaujoyeulx himself called it "a geometrical arrangement of many persons dancing together."

Court ballets of this kind remained popular in France for over a hundred years. The whole court became obsessed with dancing; and the greatest enthusiast of all was King Louis XIV (1638-1715). He danced in his first ballet at the age of 12 and went on playing leading parts —such as Apollo, Mars, or Jupiter—until, in his early thirties, he got too fat to dance. Louis lavished immense sums of money on staging ballets, and he employed men of genius to produce them, realizing that this would bring him even greater prestige. In England, a rather different kind of court entertainment evolved: the *masque*. Although this made use of dancing, it was dominated by the poet or dramatist rather than the dancing master.

Jean Baptiste Lully (1632-87), an Italian musician and dancer in the service of Louis XIV, was among the first to compose a complete musical score especially for a ballet. Earlier ballet music had always been arranged from various pieces by a number of different composers. Declamation and songs, written by a poet, were used to tell the story. Thus, in its early days, ballet shared many of the features of what was later to become the separate and distinct art of *opera* (p. 156).

Louis XIV's greatest service to the art of ballet was the foundation, in 1661, of the *Académie Royale de Danse*: a council of 13 dancing masters that codified all the court dances and laid down rules for their execution. The academy's chief importance, however, was that it established the principle of royal or state patronage of an academy of dancing. Louis' example was soon copied by other courts, notably those of Vienna, Copenhagen, and —later, but most thoroughly—Russia.

Louis XIV of France fostered the art of ballet at Versailles, where he and his courtiers danced to the music of Lully. Louis wore this magnificent costume for the role of the Sun in the Ballet de la Nuit, *given in 1653.*

179

The beginnings of modern ballet

When Louis XIV of France gave up dancing in ballets (p. 178), his courtiers followed his example, and the demand for private ballets soon declined. Professional dancers, realizing that their palmy days at court were over, thereupon sought employment in the public theatres of France. Louis had shown foresight, for in 1669 he had granted permission for an opera house to be built in Paris; and he had thus ensured a permanent home for his beloved dancers, singers, and musicians. In 1671, Jean Baptiste Lully (p. 178) took charge of the Paris Opéra; for 16 years, until his death, he wrote every opera that was produced there.

Since Lully had himself been a fine dancer, he invariably included dancing as an important part of his operas. The opera-ballet remained popular in Paris until well into the 18th century, reaching its highest level in the works of Jean Philippe Rameau (1683-1764). His most famous opera was *Les Indes Galantes*, composed in 1735. Like other French operas of its time, it was made up of a series of scenes, magnificently staged, in which an operatic opening was followed by a suite of dances.

Until almost the end of the 17th century, only men danced in the theatres, but then women dancers began to appear at the Paris Opéra. Mademoiselle Lafontaine, who took the principal female role in Lully's *Le Triomphe de l'Amour* in 1691, may be regarded as the first true *ballerina*. She and the other women dancers wore tight bodices and long skirts, and so their movements were very much hampered. The male dancers, on the other hand, because of their less restricting costumes, were able to leap in the air and do quite athletic steps. But the men did not hold their monopoly of agility for long. By 1730, the brilliant Marie Anne de Cupis de Camargo (1710-70) had shortened her skirt and had mastered a number of steps previously performed only by men.

A loss of artistic vitality often occurs when too much interest is taken in technical skill for its own sake. Throughout the history of ballet there have been a few

Baroque setting for a ballet by Giuseppe Galli da Bibiena. Throughout the 18th century the Italian Bibiena family enriched court entertainments with ornate architectural designs.

In 18th-century France, dancer Marie Anne de Cupis de Camargo (below, left) won fame for her light vivacious style. In ballets such as Jason and Medea (below), *1781, dancer-choreographer Jean Georges Noverre began to simplify costumes and movement.*

Giselle, *perhaps the greatest of the romantic ballets, was first performed in 1841. This drawing, from a book of the period, portrays a scene in which the* wilis (ghost-maidens) *drive forester Hilarion to death by drowning.*

periods when the public seemed to care mostly for the virtuosity of its favorite dancers, allowing them to indulge their whims and "show off." It usually takes the emergence of a gifted reformer to point the way to a new, better order of things. So it was that while Camargo was thrilling Paris with her unparalleled technique, her great rival, Marie Sallé (1707-56), was trying to find a way of making dancing more expressive.

In 1734, Marie Sallé went to London, where she produced her most famous ballet, *Pygmalion*. In this, she wore a simple dress of muslin instead of the usual hooped skirts, so that her movements could be clearly seen. Another early champion of expressive dancing was an English dancing master, John Weaver (1673-1760). For the London theatres, he produced many ballet-pantomimes in which a story was told entirely by means of music, mime, and dancing. These were the closest things so far to what we now consider true ballet.

A further step forward was taken by France's Jean Georges Noverre (1727-1810), who, like Marie Sallé, left France in order to put his novel choreographic ideas into practice. In many European cities, including Stuttgart and Vienna, Noverre produced highly popular *ballets d'action* in which mime, dance, costumes, and setting were all combined to express a single theme. Noverre generally took heroic subjects for his ballets. His pupil Jean Dauberval (1742-1806) chose more homely themes. Dauberval's famous *La Fille Mal Gardée* ("the badly guarded daughter"), first produced in 1786, still holds the stage today.

In the 1820s, the growing cult of romanticism in the theatre (p. 270) coincided with the introduction of satin ballet shoes with blocked toes and stiffened backs. These enabled a ballerina to dance on her toes—*sur les pointes*, as it is called. The best of the romantic ballets *La Sylphide* (1832) and *Giselle* (1841), made subtle use of *pointe* dancing to give the ballerina an other-worldly look as she appeared to hover above the ground. The popularity of such ballets increased the importance and fame of star ballerinas. In the mid-1800s, outstanding dancers, like Italy's Marie Taglioni, Carlotta Grisi, and Fanny Cerrito, Austria's Fanny Elssler, and Denmark's Lucile Grahn were idolized by the public in every capital of Europe.

So great was the popularity of the ballerina that the male dancer almost disappeared from the stage. Inevitably, a period of artistic decadence followed, and ballet went out of favor in Western Europe. It was only in Russia that a high standard of teaching and performance endured.

Carlotta Grisi, Marie Taglioni, Lucile Grahn, and Fanny Cerrito, four star ballerinas of the 19th century, were pictured by English artist A. E. Chalon when they danced together for the first time in Le Pas de Quatre (1845).

181

Interior of Maryinsky Theatre, Leningrad. Onetime home of Russia's Imperial Ballet, the Maryinsky (now known as Kirov) Theatre was opened in 1860. It saw the first spectacular productions of Tchaikovsky's romantic ballets, and the emergence of many brilliant dancers. Russian caricature of the period (below) shows a wealthy young enthusiast of the type we would today call a "balletomane."

The Sleeping Beauty was first produced at the Maryinsky Theatre in 1890. The christening scene (below, right) featured ballerina Kulich-evskaya (below) as the Bread Crumb Fairy, with Kchesinsky as her page.

The Imperial Russian ballet

For the last hundred years, the world of ballet has been influenced chiefly by the example of Russia, especially in matters of training and organization. The first Russian state ballet school was established at St. Petersburg (now Leningrad) in 1735. This was followed by academies of dancing in Moscow and Warsaw. Profiting from French experience and employing French and Italian teachers, the Russians began to evolve the system of training that was, in time, to produce the incomparable traditions of Russian ballet.

The academies and the theatres to which qualified Russian pupils graduated were state organizations in the widest sense. Their directors were appointed personally by the tsar, and students and teachers were all imperial servants—subject to strict discipline, but supported by almost unlimited funds. Ballet pupils got their entire general education as well as their dance training in the academies. On graduating, they passed into the ballet companies of the imperial theatres, from which, after a fixed number of years of service, they retired on a pension.

The dancers dedicated themselves to their art very early in life, usually entering the academy at about nine years of age. The conditions for training were ideal. Boys and girls were given equal attention, and they were taught all the subjects necessary for a cultured dancer. For instance, they had to study music and other historical dance forms as well as ballet. The ballet schools of tsarist Russia are still the model for those of the Soviet Union, as well as for the state-run ballet schools in many other countries.

As early as 1830, the scientific basis of modern ballet teaching had been defined by Carlo Blasis (1797-1878), an Italian dancer and choreographer. His *Code of Terpsichore* laid down a rigorous system of training and daily exercises designed to develop strong and supple bodies. Blasis tended to stress strength and technique at the expense of expressiveness. But the Russians, who learned much from Blasis, also absorbed the best of French ballet through Christian Johannson, a Swede who had studied with the French-trained Danish ballet master Auguste

Bournonville (1805-79). To these different styles—one forceful, one precise—the Russian dancers added their own special grace and vitality.

Another leading European dancer who had a great influence on Russian ballet was Marie Taglioni (p. 180). Her visit to St. Petersburg in 1837 aroused great public enthusiasm and inspired Russian ballerinas to emulate her success. Nevertheless, until 1869, Russia's ballets remained mostly the work of visiting French choreographers. In that year, Marius Petipa (1822-1910), a Frenchman who had been leading male dancer in St. Petersburg for over twenty years, assumed full command there. With the aid of his gifted assistant Lev Ivanov, Petipa built up a repertory of ballets that are known as the Russian "classics." As themes for his ballets, he chose fairy tales such as *The Sleeping Beauty*, *Swan Lake*, and *The Nutcracker*, for all of which Pëtr Tchaikovsky (1840-93) wrote wonderfully suitable music. These ballets were built around brilliant solo dances and *pas de deux* (dances for two people), which displayed the technique and artistry of the principals. Nothing shows off a ballerina to better advantage than the *pas de deux* and the solo dances that Petipa invented for the role of Princess Aurora in *The Sleeping Beauty*.

Although magnificent as displays of marvelous dancing, Petipa's ballets were in many ways rather absurd. It made no difference, for example, whether the plot of the ballet was laid in Fairyland, Egypt, or Timbuctu; the ballerina always danced on *pointe* (p. 180), and always wore a *tutu* (the conventional short ballet skirt). Enthusiasts among the Russian nobility opposed any change in their beloved art. Revolutionary new ideas were necessary, however, if the ballet was not to be utterly smothered by uncritical adoration. Strangely, when the big change did come, it was started by a company of Russian dancers dancing outside Russia. For many years, St. Petersburg and Moscow remained unaffected by a movement that was to change the nature of ballet throughout the rest of the world.

Anna Pavlova and Michel Fokine in Arlequinade, *produced at the Maryinsky Theatre in 1900. Pavlova and Fokine, both trained at the Maryinsky School, became principal dancers of the Imperial Ballet. In 1909 they left Russia to join Diaghilev (p. 184).*

The original décor for two of the greatest romantic ballets, first danced at the Maryinsky Theatre to Tchaikovsky's music. Below: the ornate palace set for Swan Lake *(1895). Below, left: the "Kingdom of Sweets" for the last act of* The Nutcracker *(1892).*

Diaghilev

The ballets that were danced in Russian theatres at the end of the 19th century may have lacked originality and freshness, but they none the less contained exceptionally good dancing. Standards of teaching in Russia were higher than ever before.

Early in the 20th century, though, Michel Fokine (1880-1942), who was a brilliant dancer and a fine teacher, rebelled against the stuffy officialdom of the imperial theatres and the absurdity of their productions. "Why must the style of a dance not harmonize with that of the theme, its costume, and its period?" he demanded. "Because it is tradition," was officialdom's answer. And Fokine was given no chance to produce new ballets of his own. But his pupils were devoted to him, and many shared his ideals. For student productions and charity performances Fokine began to experiment with short ballets in which the styles of music, movement, and settings were all well integrated.

In 1909, he was appointed choreographer to a private ballet company that was being organized to show the richness of Russian dancing to audiences in Paris. The choice of Fokine was to prove particularly fortunate, for of all the members of a ballet company the choreographer is the most important. It is he who sets the dancers in motion, who creates the steps that will charm or astonish an audience and the gestures and expressions through which the theme of a ballet is communicated.

The sponsor, or *impresario*, of this new venture was Serge Diaghilev (1872-1929). Diaghilev was to guide the fortunes of his ballet company for twenty years, making it the meeting place for many of the most distinguished artists of the time. Through him, it became a major influence not only on the dance, but on all forms of art.

Early in life Diaghilev had abandoned the study of law in order to indulge his love of music and the theatre. Aware that he was not a creative artist himself, he devoted his energy to discovering and nourishing the talents of others. His first successes were with imaginatively arranged art exhibitions and with an illustrated art magazine that he ran in association with painter friends. He then worked for two years in the imperial theatres, but his originality, blunt speech, and extravagance made him enemies, and he was dismissed. Guided by his painter friend Alexandre Benois (1870-1960), Diaghilev had learned much about the possibilities of ballet as an art form. And so, since he knew that officialdom would discourage experiment in Russia, he decided to try his luck elsewhere.

His first ventures were to organize exhibitions of

Diaghilev's first production of Le Coq d'Or *(Paris, 1914), with music by Rimski-Korsakov, choreography by Michel Fokine, heralded a new era in ballet history. Folk art of Russia and Persia inspired Nathalie Gontcharova's set.*

Diaghilev employed the most gifted musicians, painters, and dancers of his day. L'Après-midi d'un Faune *(1912) was set to music by France's Debussy; Russian-born Léon Bakst designed central character's costume (right).*

Russian art and concerts of Russian music in Paris. Then he presented a season of Russian opera. Thereafter, however, he devoted his life entirely to ballet. The success of his new ballet company's first Paris seasons was phenomenal. Fokine's reforming zeal was given full scope, carefully guided by Diaghilev, who supervised the overall shape of each ballet. Fokine tried to find the *right* style of dancing for each work. *Pointe* dancing (p. 180) was used only when suited to the story or a particular character—for instance, the fairylike creatures in *Les Sylphides*. Oriental soft shoes were worn in *Schéhérazade*, an Arabian Nights entertainment; and in *Petrouchka*, set in the Winter Fair of St. Petersburg, the corps de ballet were dressed in peasant costume, moved freely about the stage, and danced boisterous peasant dances.

Among the outstanding artists who created the settings and costumes for Diaghilev's Ballets Russes company were Alexandre Benois, who designed *Petrouchka* and the 18th-century fantasy *Le Pavillon d'Armide*; Léon Bakst, who provided the Eastern splendors of *Schéhérazade* and *Thamar*; Alexandre Golovine, who made the fairy-tale setting for *The Firebird*; and Nicholas Roerich, whose décor for *Prince Igor* re-created the barren steppes of Central Asia. The music for *The Firebird*, *Petrouchka*, and *The Rite of Spring* was composed by Diaghilev's discovery Igor Stravinsky (p. 156). As for the dancers, Diaghilev began by drawing upon the cream of the imperial Russian ballet companies. And so such great artists as Tamara Karsavina, Vaslav Nijinsky, Adolph Bolm, and Anna Pavlova helped ensure the fabulous success of his early seasons.

Later, when World War I and the Russian Revolution cut off his contacts with the Russian companies, Diaghilev tended to concentrate on novelties of staging and choreography rather than on superb dancing. He had always believed that ballet should combine great dancing with the best in music and painting. He chose artists like Pablo Picasso (*The Three-Cornered Hat*), Georges Braque (*Les Facheux*), and André Derain (*La Boutique Fantasque*) to design sets and costumes; and he got his ballet scores from composers like Claude Debussy (*Jeux*), Maurice Ravel (*Daphnis et Chloé*), and Francis Poulenc (*Les Biches*).

The death of Diaghilev in 1929 marked the end of an epoch. For a time, there seemed little hope of continuing the revival of European interest in ballet. But gradually, in a number of countries, companies were formed that were to follow Diaghilev's great example by combining the three arts of dancing, music, and painting in a single form.

1918 sketch shows Diaghilev (left) with composers Stravinsky, Prokofiev; dancer Léonide Massine, and painter-designer Gontcharova.

In time, Diaghilev turned from the exotic sets and scores of his early ballets toward European décor and music. The Three-Cornered Hat *(1919) combined décor (left) by Picasso with music by Spain's Manuel de Falla.*

185

Ballet today

Probably the most famous of all ballet dancers was Anna Pavlova (1881-1931). Diaghilev (p. 184) had shown little interest in encouraging a wide general public, but Pavlova believed that her mission was to dance for the whole world.

A supremely gifted ballerina, trained in the Imperial Ballet School at St. Petersburg, Pavlova had ventured abroad even before Diaghilev. Although she danced with Diaghilev's company during its first Paris season, she had little sympathy for his ideals and preferred to form her own troupe. The choreography and staging of the ballets in which Pavlova appeared were often mediocre; but through her genius she was able to triumph over such handicaps. She danced everywhere—in the backwoods of North America, in Australia, India, Japan—and met with immediate success. Thus Pavlova did much to popularize ballet and to inspire young people in many countries to follow in her footsteps.

Outside Russia, ballet has developed along the lines laid down by Diaghilev. It is an international language, but it speaks with many accents. In Britain, where until recently no state aid was given the arts, a national company has been established through the efforts of British dancers themselves. In particular, Marie Rambert and Ninette de Valois, both of whom once worked for Diaghilev, formed companies of dancers and proved that British ballet was a possibility. A small company attached to the Sadler's Wells Theatre in London grew, under the guidance of Ninette de Valois, into today's internationally famous Royal Ballet. One of its principal choreographers, Frederick Ashton (who started his career in 1926 with the Ballet Rambert), has done much to mold its style of dancing—a style that reached its lyrical best not long ago in the work of the great Margot Fonteyn.

In France, where King Louis XIV established his Academy three hundred years ago (p. 178), ballet has had a checkered career in recent years. In the 1930s the ballet company of the Paris Opéra was given a temporary new lease of life by Russian-born Serge Lifar, Diaghilev's last great male dancer. Occasionally, too, dancers such as Roland Petit and Jean Babilée, trained in the Opéra school, have formed their own companies. These have achieved occasional seasons of great brilliance—but have been short-lived.

The French ballet Le Jeune Homme et la Mort (1946), *written by Jean Cocteau, told of a painter (Jean Babilée, right) seduced by Death (Nathalie Philippart). The Rake's Progress (1935), a British ballet based on Hogarth's paintings of 18th-century London, featured Walter Gore (below) as the young man who gambled his way to the mad-house.*

In America, the great choreographer George Balanchine has created brilliant abstract ballets such as Concerto Barocco, *three scenes from which are pictured here. First danced in 1941, it was a subtle interpretation of Bach's Double Violin Concerto in D minor.*

Famed Russian ballerina Galina Ulanova found one of her greatest roles in Prokofiev's Romeo and Juliet *(1940). Her expressive dancing bore the stamp of Leningrad's great Kirov School, cradle of Russian ballet.*

The Danish ballet Études—*first danced in 1948—dramatized the schooling of a ballet company in a series of sparkling exercises.*

The characteristics of early 19th-century French ballet have been best preserved in Denmark. One of the most important figures in the history of the Royal Danish Ballet was Auguste Bournonville (p. 182), who studied with the great Italian dancing master Auguste Vestris in Paris. The so-called "Bournonville style," characterized by its speed, accuracy, and lightness, remains a feature of Danish dancing today. Bournonville's ballets—for instance, *Napoli* (1842) and *Far from Denmark* (1860)—are still danced much as they were at the time of their first production. Danish dancers are also renowned for the excellence of their mime.

The use of mime is usually an accomplishment of the older established companies, which hand their traditions on from one generation to the next. Young companies in young countries often find it old-fashioned and artificial. Thus, pupils at the School of American Ballet (started in 1933 by the Russian dancer and choreographer George Balanchine) concentrated on strong, athletic dancing rather than on the communication of characterization or plot through gesture. As director and principal choreographer of the New York City Ballet, Balanchine has created a great variety of experimental works that explore many new ways of using classical dance techniques in the theatre. His works range from sharp, witty ballets such as Stravinsky's *Agon* to the romantic 19th-century elegance of Brahms' *Liebeslieder Walzer*.

Another U.S. company, the American Ballet Theatre, does more traditional things and includes many "story ballets" in its repertory. For the much more recently formed company known as Ballets: U.S.A., the American choreographer Jerome Robbins developed an exciting style that mixed classical ballet with jazz; this type of dancing has been seen most widely in Robbins' dances for the stage and film productions of the American musical play *West Side Story*.

In Soviet Russia, where ballet retains the popularity it had under the tsars, schools and theatres are richly endowed with state funds. The style of dancing is lyrical, yet spectacular, making much use of muscular strength and dramatic characterization. Russian choreography is less complex and experimental than that of certain other nations. Still, Russia's dancers remain unmatched in their expressive use of the whole body.

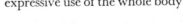

Trends in modern dance

Today, ballet is the most popular and widely studied form of theatrical dancing. But there are a number of other highly developed forms, each with its own history and technique. Tap dancing, for example, which became a real art in the hands (or, rather, feet) of America's Fred Astaire and Bill Robinson, grew out of Irish and Lancashire step dances (in which an intricate rhythm was tapped out by wooden shoes, or *clogs*). These dances were carried to North America by immigrants and quickly became popular among the American Negroes. At first "tapping" was just part of the Negro entertainer's song-and-dance routine. But, in time, the dancers learned to create their musical accompaniment with the sound of their own feet, and songs were no longer needed.

Tap dancing was one of the first skills to be acquired by white Americans from the Negroes in their midst. As a world-wide understanding and appreciation of the American Negro's rich storehouse of folk art has grown, its influence has been felt in many other ways. Jazz in particular has become a major element in 20th-century music. And social dances of Negro origin, like the *charleston*, have become increasingly popular all over Europe and America.

How did the distinctive forms of the American Negro dance come into being? For 300 years the tribes of West Africa had been raided continuously to provide slave labor for the plantations of the New World. In Africa, each tribe had jealously guarded its own customs and dances. In America, these became mixed together, and they also absorbed influences from the European culture of the slave owners. In the Portuguese and Spanish colonies of Latin America, moreover, there was a good deal of intermarriage; and so there naturally came about a kind of wedding of African tribal and Spanish rhythms. Even so, many of the West African rhythms survived in the New World virtually unchanged. The Cuban *rumba*, for example, takes some of its movements directly from a

Negro jazz band, pictured in 1910. From Negro rhythms sprang the jazz dances of the 20th century, brought to sophisticated perfection by America's Fred Astaire (below).

Choreography and décor often echo Negro themes. Below: Fernand Léger's design (1925) for La Création du Monde. *Below left: Katherine Dunham dances* L'Ag'ya (1948).

Kurt Jooss's satire The Green Table, *first danced in Paris in 1932, showed grotesque politicians deciding the fate of mankind.*

America's Isadora Duncan (pictured by French artist Dunoyer de Segonzac) pioneered modern dance by rejecting formal movements.

One of the most original of modern choreographers is America's Martha Graham, who retold a Greek myth in Night Journey (1947), *using chorus (below) to heighten the drama.*

complicated dance rhythm of a southern Nigerian tribe.

In the 1930s, Katherine Dunham, an American Negro dancer who is also an anthropologist, began studying the social dances and religious rituals of the Caribbean islands. She has since translated many of these into forms suitable for the stage; and, with her own company of dancers, she has presented them in theatres throughout the world. Such other American choreographers as Alvin Ailey and Donald McKayle are also blending African dance and American modern dance into stirring dance dramas for the stage.

The term "modern dance" is often used to describe any form of expressive dancing other than classical ballet. The principal exponent of the so-called Central European school of modern dance was Rudolf von Laban (1879-1958), a German dancer and writer. Von Laban developed a philosophy of the dance that attracted many disciples, notably Mary Wigman and Kurt Jooss. Together, von Laban and his pupils tried to free dancing from what they believed were the restrictions and artificialities of ballet, and to allow each dancer a greater freedom of personal creative expression.

An American, Isadora Duncan (1878-1927), had already proclaimed similar ideas. Dressed in flowing draperies, she danced barefoot, expressing themes and moods through free, improvised movements. She traveled widely and greatly influenced European theatrical dancing. In America, Ruth St. Denis (born 1877) and Ted Shawn (born 1891) pioneered their own form of "free dance," and in 1915 they founded the influential Denishawn School. Among the most notable of their pupils was Martha Graham. American modern dance, as developed by Martha Graham and her colleagues and successors, may *seem* less technically demanding than ballet, but it requires great skill and arduous training. In a modified, popular form, modern dance has appeared in many recent American musical plays and films.

Recording the dance

Until recent times, there was no completely satisfactory way in which to make a permanent record of the steps and gestures of a dance. Thus, all forms of dancing had to rely mainly upon the creative ability and memory of the dancers themselves to keep the particular traditions alive. Because folk dances, for example, were a regular feature of village life, there was always some older person who could demonstrate the traditional steps to the younger dancers.

In the 16th century, dancers taking part in the court balletti (p. 178) did no more than follow through the geometric diagrams drawn up by the ballet master. When, later on, ballet dancers were required to express a wide range of dramatic themes, the function of the choreographer changed. No system of diagrams and notation, however elaborate, can indicate the subtle changes in emotion that the dancer must communicate to his audience. And so the only way for a choreographer to teach a new ballet has always been for him to do it in person : to explain and then perform the particular movements he wants, after which the dancers must practice in front of him until he feels that they have fully understood and mastered their roles. When an older ballet is revived, dancers who appeared in one of its earlier stagings may be asked for their help in remembering its patterns. Or it may have to be created afresh by a new choreographer.

Many people have attempted to devise methods of writing down dances so that they can be "read" as accurately as music is read. The first successful system that we know of was that invented by the Frenchman Raoul Feuillet (1675-1730). He used curved lines to show the pattern of the dancers' movements across the stage, and indicated by small diagrams the steps they performed. This method was used at the Paris Opéra, and Feuillet's book *Choréographie* (1699) was translated into English by John Weaver (p. 180) in 1706. In the late 19th century, Vladimir Stepanov, a teacher at Russia's Maryinsky Theatre (p. 182), actually adapted music notation to record dance movements. But although these systems indicated the steps that were performed to each section of the music, they could not convey the style or character of the dancers' roles.

Recently, though, the motion picture and television have opened up new ways of recording all forms of dancing, so that not only can vast audiences watch performances by the world's greatest dancers, but such performances also remain available for future study.

Early ballets were planned as series of geometric patterns, as recorded in 17th-century French drawing (top). Later records, like the above depiction of a minuet in a 1735 dance manual, included actual steps. Modern systems like Labanotation *can record complex movements such as a somersault (shown in diagram below).*

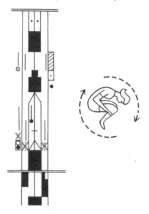

Dances of Rockettes (below), at New York's Radio City, depend on patterns of group movement

Used in conjunction with one of the more precise notation systems—such as *Labanotation*, invented by Rudolf von Laban (p. 188)—a movie can provide a full documentation of almost any dance or ballet.

Apart from its value to the choreographer as a recording and teaching medium, the film has greatly enlarged his creative scope. In fact, a number of today's leading choreographers have done much of their work for the movies, where they can try many techniques and effects that are simply not possible in the live theatre. For instance, because each section of a long dance sequence can be filmed separately and then joined together, the choreographer can ignore the limitations of a dancer's physical endurance and can plan energetic dance routines that will last for many minutes on the screen. And by using the flexible movements of the camera, altering the lenses, and editing the film (p. 284), he can design dances that will show a lone dancer at one moment, a whole company spread out over a vast area at the next. Dances for the screen are planned in a totally different way from those designed for the stage, where dancers and audience remain at a fixed distance from one another.

Trick photography, too, can produce all kinds of fantastic and comic effects. In one American film, *Cover Girl* (1944), the dancer Gene Kelly was shown dancing down a city street tormented by his "conscience"—a distorted image of himself reflected in shop windows as he passed. In the films in which Fred Astaire appeared, he created all his own dance routines, making skilful use of movie-camera techniques to heighten the perfectly groomed brilliance of his performance. He had many famous partners, but none was his equal; only when trick photography allowed him to dance with himself did he meet his match.

The cinema, then, has added to the dancer's expressive range. And the ancient art of dancing has once more shown how adaptable it is to new times, new places, new moods. No matter how it changes, however, the dance remains essentially the art of creative expression by means of the human body.

Today's choreographer may use film to record his work. Britain's Frederick Ashton was filmed as he rehearsed scenes from Symphonic Variations *(first produced in 1946) with members of the then Sadler's Wells Company (above, left). America's Martha Graham chose to demonstrate the training—and dedication—of the dancer in* The Dancer's World *(above), a documentary film made in 1957.*

With its close-ups and angle shots, the camera creates a new world for choreography. Among leaders of modern dance who have explored film possibilities is America's Jerome Robbins, who directed West Side Story *(right) in 1960.*

Chapter 8

Poetry

At various times in history, the poet has been worshiped, honored, feared, despised, or ignored. Yet at all times men have continued to write and to read poems. Why does poetry have this universal attraction?

Poetry is, of course, one form of literature; and literature is, to put it simply, the expression and communication of human experience in meaningful language. In this chapter we shall look at some of the specific qualities that distinguish poetry from literature in general—qualities that help to explain its special appeal, not only to readers, but also to those writers who find in the poetic form opportunities for a greater intensity of expression than is possible in other forms of writing.

First of all, poetry has a structure all of its own. Words are the poet's bricks, with which he "builds" a poem. Like all writers, he must be concerned with the meaning of each word; but the poet uses words for more than their generally accepted meanings. He chooses them for the special meanings they can have, and also for the way they look and sound. Above all, he arranges them into effective patterns.

The subject matter of poetry also sets it apart. It is always possible to write an exact description of an object —a car, say, or a house—but a poem can do much more: It tries to express the inner nature of an object or an experience. And the more important and meaningful the experience—for example, a deeply felt experience of beauty or love—the more it becomes the food of poetry.

Such themes are so basic that the expression of them in poetry has an enormous appeal for humanity in general. In this chapter we shall consider some of the ways in which the poet practices his art.

Poetry is the language of emotion; its musical rhythms and patterns of sound can make a deeper, more direct impact on the reader than the ordinary language of prose. Thus, writers may use it to express a moment of joy or sorrow, to tell a story, or to make ideas more memorable. The ancient Greeks explained the poet's power to intensify language as the gift of a goddess—an idea echoed in 19th-century artist Théodore Rousseau's painting of poet and muse.

Language: sense and feeling

Literature can be divided into two general categories: poetry and prose. These forms differ in many ways, but one of the main differences lies in their use of language.

Ever since prose was developed in ancient Greece, such writers as scientists and philosophers have used it to express their ideas and theories. These writers need a clear, logical language—a language that will be understood by most people (in the way that mathematical signs like 4, +, −, and so on are understood by everyone who has learned the language of mathematics). And the same kind of understanding is needed in the prose of everyday conversation.

If a scientific writer uses the word "sea," for instance, he will probably intend it to mean nothing more than "a large expanse of salt water." This is the word's most basic and familiar meaning. But words are not like signs; they can change their meanings. For example, they can be given "extra" meanings by the reader. One person reading the word "sea" might think of the blue Mediterranean; another might think of the stormy North Atlantic. In the same way, the most common words (like "house" or "man") can mean different things to different people.

Extra meanings can be given to words by the writer as well. This is the way that poets use words—not only for their usual meanings, but for the special meanings the poet can give them, and for the special effects he can cause them to have on the reader's mind and emotions. The 19th-century English poet Alfred, Lord Tennyson, for example, in a poem of mourning, used the word "sea" like this:

> *Break, break, break,*
> *On thy cold gray stones, O Sea!*

In these lines, the sea is not just an "expanse of salt water." The poet has tried to convey to his readers the feeling given by a particular aspect of the sea—its bleakness and cruelty. And in the following words from a poem by John Masefield, the poet has tried to convey the sea's beauty and mystery by saying that he has heard "the sea's spirit spoken by a bird."

The language of poetry is especially different from the logical language of expository prose, where the writer

Fishermen are used to views like this one of a storm-tossed sea—usually thought of as their means of livelihood rather than as a subject for poetry. But such a scene might make an emotional impact on another observer. In the print on the opposite page, the Japanese artist Katsushika Hokusai (1760-1849) visualizes the waves as clutching hands, thus emphasizing the sea's destructive power.

Writers who wish to record facts usually seek precise terms that carry no extra meanings. The Babylonians who recorded factual details of their fields, crops, and commodities on this clay tablet (about 3100 B.C.) used straightforward, unemotional prose.

does his best to *avoid* emotional meanings. It is sometimes much harder to distinguish poetic language from that of "imaginative" prose (like the storyteller's). The words of such writers as France's Marcel Proust (1871-1922) or England's D. H. Lawrence (1885-1930) often have a similar "poetic" or emotional effect. For example :

> *The days go by, through the brief silence of winter, when the sunshine is so still and pure, like iced wine, and the dead leaves gleam brown, and water sounds hoarse in the ravines. It is so still and transcendent, the cypress trees poise like flames of forgotten darkness, that should have been blown out at the end of the summer.*

That passage, from Lawrence's *Twilight in Italy*, conveys the feeling of winter in descriptive language as vivid and expressive as any poem.

But a writer does not make his language into poetry merely by giving words emotional meaning. The total effect of poetry is gained in ways that would be impossible in prose—even in imaginative prose. For one thing, a poet can usually make his point more briefly than a prose writer. And, for another, the poet makes a special use of rhythm.

A fifth-century illustration to the Georgics *by the Roman poet Vergil (70-19 B.C.). In this poem, facts about farming are conveyed in emotional language; the first part, which deals with the cultivation of cereal crops, opens with a description of spring. In this way, Vergil communicates the reverent devotion felt by the ordinary farmers of his day toward the patron gods of agriculture.*

Rhythm and meter

Rhythm is simply regular movement, like that of ocean waves or the human heart. It is found in all the arts, but especially in music, dancing, and poetry. In ancient Greece—which the poet Pindar (522-443 B.C.) called the "land of lovely dancing"—these three were often united. Dancers were accompanied by music and by recited or sung poetry.

Poets use rhythm partly for the enjoyment it can give, but also because it can add to the meaning or the mood of a poem. John Milton (1608-74) wrote his gay poem "L'Allegro" in a rhythm like this:

> *Come, and trip it as ye go*
> *On the light fantastic toe!*

But he gave his mournful elegy "Lycidas" longer lines and a slower movement, like this:

> *But, O the heavy change, now thou art gone,*
> *Now thou art gone, and never must return!*

Until the modern experiments in poetic technique began (p. 204), most poetry was written in "fixed" rhythms, called *meter* (or "measure"). That is, each line of a poem written in a specific meter follows more or less the same arrangement of rhythms as every other line. A metrical line can be divided into units called *feet*; each of the many kinds of feet has a specific number of syllables, arranged in a specific order.

Ancient Greek and Latin poetry was measured according to the length of the syllables (i.e., according to the time

Rhythmic movement and chanting, often to music, were part of drama in its earliest beginnings. The dancing figures in this ancient Greek vase painting are costumed like the bird chorus in Aristophanes' The Birds (414 B.C.).

To measure verse rhythms, students of poetry often use symbols shown below. Curve indicates an unaccented syllable; straight line, an accented one. (In classical Greek and Latin verse, these signs mark "short" or "long" syllables.) Syllable groups—like bars of music (p. 147)—repeat themselves throughout a line. Groups—or "feet"—that occur most often include the (1) iamb, (2) trochee, (3) spondee, (4) dactyl.

1 ⏑ —

2 — ⏑

3 — —

4 — ⏑ ⏑

Roman poet Catullus (about 84-54 B.C.) used quick iambic rhythms to describe a ship cutting through the water (5). Each line contains six feet; such hexameters were common in Greek and Latin verse. Note that short and long marks do not indicate stress but show relative time lengths required to pronounce each syllable.

Phase| lus il| le, quem| vide| tis, hos| pites,

5

ait| fuis| se na| vium| celer| rimus

‾◡◡|‾◡◡|‾‾|‾‾|‾◡◡|‾◡
Daedalus|intere a|l Cre|ten Ion|gumque per|osus

‾◡◡|‾‾|‾‾|◡◡|‾‾|‾◡◡|‾◡
exsili|um, tac|tusque ||lo|ci na|talis a|more

‾‾|‾‾|‾‾|◡◡|‾◡◡|‾◡◡|‾‾
ὦ ξεῖν,'|ἀγγέλ|λειν Λακε|δαιμονί|οις ὅτι|τῇδε

‾◡◡|‾‾|‾‾|‾◡◡|‾◡◡|‾‾
κείμεθα,|τοῖς κεί|νων ||ῥήμασι|πείθομε|νοι.

Il|n'est|point|de|ser|pent,|ni|de|mon|stre o|di|eux,

Qui,|par|l'art|i|mi|té,|ne|puisse|plai|re à|nos|yeux :

◡|‾◡|‾◡|‾|◡|‾◡|‾|◡|‾|◡|‾
Doch re|de sacht! |denn un|ter dies |em Dach

◡|‾|◡|‾|◡|‾|◡|‾◡|‾
Ruht all|mein Wohl|und all|mein Un|gemach:

In his Metamorphoses, *Ovid (43 B.C.–about A.D.17) used hexameters to tell of exiled Daedalus's longing for home (6). Trochees and spondees vary basic dactylic meter. Greek poetry (7) is similar, as in the epitaph for Spartan dead at Thermopylae by Simonides of Ceos (6th-5th century B.C.) Double vertical lines mark a caesura, or pause. Important element in French verse is number of syllables; in most poetry since the 1500s, 12-syllable alexandrines have been used. Example is from Nicolas Boileau's* The Poetic Art, 1674 (8). *German and English verse is measured by stress. Pentameter lines from Goethe's* Ilmenau (9) *each contain five iambs.*

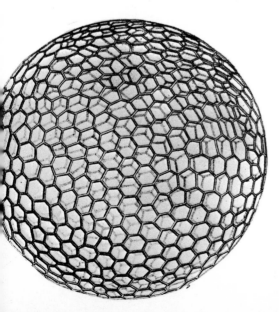

required to pronounce them). In French and other Romance languages, the meter of poetry is determined by the number of syllables in a line. But English and German poetry came to be measured according to accented or *stressed* syllables. In Greek poetry, the foot called an *iamb* consisted of one short syllable followed by a long one. But an English or German iamb is a foot with an unstressed syllable followed by a stressed one (like the word "delíght").

Some other kinds of feet are the *trochee* (a stressed syllable followed by an unstressed, like "wónder"); the *anapaest* (two unstressed syllables followed by a stressed, like "introdúce"); and the *dactyl* (one stressed syllable followed by two unstressed, like "térrible").

Different kinds of meter are named according to the number of feet within a single line. Much Greek and Latin poetry was written in *hexameter* lines, each containing six feet. Common meters in later European poetry include the *pentameter* (five feet) and the *tetrameter* (four feet). These meters are quite often written in iambic feet; for example, here is an "iambic pentameter" line, taken from "The Eve of Saint Agnes" by John Keats (1795-1821):

She dánced alóng with vágue regárdless éyes.

In spite of the regularity of meter, the lines of a metrical poem are rarely all exactly alike. Poets have different ways of adding variety to the rhythm, in order to hold the reader's interest. Sometimes two or more kinds of feet will be used in the same line. "Desert Places," by the modern American poet Robert Frost (1874-1963), begins with two lines composed of remarkably varied feet:

Snow falling and night falling fast, oh, fast
In a field I looked into going past, . . .

Or, instead of ending each line with the end of a phrase or sentence, the poet can use "run-on" lines, as Tennyson did in his "In Memoriam":

O yet we trust that somehow good
Will be the final goal of ill.

Or he can vary the placing of the *caesura* (which is a break or pause in either the grammar or the sound of most lines of regular poetry) as William Wordsworth (1770-1850) does in these lines:

The world is too much with us;/late and soon,
Getting and spending,/we lay waste our powers;

With these techniques, poets avoid monotony without losing the pleasure and effect of their rhythms.

Verse rhythms may vary in detail, yet still display a distinct over-all pattern. In much the same way, this skeleton of a single-cell creature (magnified, left) looks like a regular pattern of six-sided shapes although it contains some five-sided figures.

197

The sound of words

One of the many ways in which poets can add to the meaning and effect of their language is by a careful choice of words for their sounds. For example, they may use *onomatopoeia*—words that imitate sounds, like "bang" or "rattle." In the following lines by Edgar Allan Poe (1809-49), the words not only describe the pealing of bells but give a general impression of their sound:

> *Oh, the bells, bells, bells!*
> *What a tale their terror tells*
> > *Of Despair!*
> *How they clang, and clash, and roar! ...*
> *Yet the ear it fully knows,*
> > *By the twanging,*
> > *And the clanging,*
> *How the danger ebbs and flows:*

A more common way of using the sounds of words is in *rhyme*. Words rhyme when they end with the same sound (like "hair" and "fair"). A poet can use rhyme to add pleasure to his poetry and to make it more easily remembered. It was probably originally introduced as an aid to memorization and recitation. Rhyme can also help to underline a point. The reader becomes aware of a pattern and will expect a rhyme at a certain place. When it

In The Cry (1895), *Norwegian artist Edvard Munch used wave-like shapes to suggest echoing sound. Poets create such effects by using onomatopeia—words that imitate sounds.*

Below: eight proverbs in the form of rhyming couplets, illustrated by 16th-century Flemish artist Pieter Brueghel. Rhyme gives such ideas emphasis and makes them easier to remember.

comes, the word gains emphasis. Notice the power of the last word in these lines, from "Elegy in a Country Churchyard," by the 18th-century English poet Thomas Gray:

The boast of heraldry, the pomp of pow'r,
And all that beauty, all that wealth e'er gave,
Awaits alike the inevitable hour,
The paths of glory lead but to the grave.

The use of rhyme within single lines of poetry can add a pleasing balance and give the rhythm a stronger "swing," as in these lines from "The Rime of the Ancient Mariner," by Samuel Taylor Coleridge (1772-1834):

The fair breeze blew, the white foam flew,
The furrow follow'd free.

In rhyming words like "hair" and "fair," both the vowel sounds and the final consonant sounds are matched. But the technique called *assonance* is based on the use of similar, but not necessarily matching, sounds. Assonance is especially important in Spanish poetry; but poets of all countries use it to create variety.

Another way to match sounds is called *alliteration* (or "head rhyme"), in which several words in a line begin with the same letter. In the above quotation from Coleridge, for example, several words begin with the letter *f*. Alliteration was the main technique used in early English and German poetry, until rhyme became popular during the Middle Ages. But its value was not forgotten by later poets—a value that is illustrated in these lines by the modern Welsh poet Dylan Thomas (1914-53):

Though lovers be lost love shall not;
And death shall have no dominion.

By making the most important words stand out from the rest, alliteration can not only vary the sound of a poem but can (like rhyme) strengthen its meaning.

Part of an early manuscript of Beowulf *(about A.D. 1000). In this epic (as in all Anglo-Saxon poetry) the melodic effects are created by alliteration; in each line the poet uses several words that begin with the same letter.*

France's 12th-century epic the Song of Roland *tells how Charlemagne's nephew Roland died fighting against the Saracens. Here, he is seen as a 14th-century illustrator of the* Grand Chronicles of France *imagined him; as a battle rages, he binds a prisoner. The best-known version of the poem is rhymed, but owes its melody and majestic rhythms largely to assonance derived from an earlier, unrhymed version. Unlike end rhyme—the repetition of identical sounds—assonance depends on the correspondence of vowel sounds, not consonants.*

Patterns of sound

Poems are sometimes divided into separate groups of lines, called *stanzas*, which have identical patterns of rhyme. One value of these forms lies in the pleasing effect of balance and wholeness that they give to a poem. And because each stanza can contain a complete thought, the technique also helps the poet to develop and extend the poem's meaning.

One of the most common stanza forms is the *couplet*, which is simply a pair of rhyming lines. This form is generally written in two different ways. One is called a "closed" couplet, and is a single sentence containing a complete idea. It was widely used in the satiric or didactic poetry of the 18th century (where ideas were of primary importance), by poets like Alexander Pope (1688-1744), who wrote:

> *True ease in writing comes from art, not chance,*
> *As those move easiest who have learned to dance.*

The "open" couplet is a freer, more relaxed form, where the thought runs on to the next line, as in "Endymion" by Keats (p. 196):

> *A thing of beauty is a joy for ever:*
> *Its loveliness increases; it will never*
> *Pass into nothingness;*

The *quatrain* is a four-line stanza that can have many different rhyme patterns. For instance, it might be formed by one couplet joined to another, or by one couplet sandwiched inside another. But the most common form of quatrain is in "alternate" rhyme, like this stanza by A. E. Housman (1859-1936):

> *Give me a land of boughs in leaf,*
> *A land of trees that stand;*
> *Where trees are fallen, there is grief;*
> *I love no leafless land.*

Because the quatrain is both brief and very flexible, it is one of the most widely used forms in poetry. The minstrels of medieval Europe used it for their rollicking ballads; it has been used in melancholy, elegiac poetry

Musical rhythm of quatrains was used both by this medieval minstrel and by 19th-century French poet Théophile Gautier (above, right).

The opening couplets of Alexander Pope's satirical poem The Dunciad, *from a 1735 edition of the poet's collected works.*

OOKS and the MAN I sing,
the first who brings
The Smithfield Muses to the
Ear of Kings.
Say great Patricians! since your
selves inspire
These wond'rous Works (so Jove and Fate require)
Say from what cause, in vain decry'd and curst,
Still Dunce the second reigns like Dunce the first?

SONETTO SOPRA LE SACRE CENERI
DEL PETRARCHA E DI LAVRA.

Laura, ch'un Sol fu tra le Donne in terra,
Hor tien del cielo il piu sublime honore:
Merce di quella penna; il cui valore,
Fa, che mai non fara spenta o sotterra
Mentre facendo al tempo illustre guerra,
Con dolce foco di celeste amore
Accende e infiamma ogni gelato core;
Le sue reliquie il piccol marmo serra.
Et le ceneri elette accoglie anchora
Di lui; che feco ne i stellanti seggi
Fra Dante et Bice il terzo ciel congiunfe.
Tu, che l'un miri; e i bassi accenti leggi;
A lor t'inchina; e 'l facro Vaso honora,
Che le sante reliquie insieme aggiunfe.

Above: on the frontispiece to a 1544 edition of the works of Petrarch, appears his sonnet "On the sacred ashes of Petrarch and Laura."

(p. 208) by England's Thomas Gray (p. 198), and in bitter satires (p. 218) by France's Théophile Gautier (1811-72).

Among many less commonly used stanzas are the Italian forms, *terza rima* and *ottava rima*. Terza rima is a three-line form used by the great Italian poet Dante Alighieri (1265-1321) in his *Divine Comedy*. The first and third lines of each stanza rhyme; the middle line rhymes with the first and third lines of the stanza following; and so on. Ottava rima is an eight-line stanza in which the first six lines rhyme alternately, and the last two form a couplet. Lord Byron (1788-1824) used this stanza form in his long poem *Don Juan*:

> *"There is a tide in the affairs of men*
> *   Which taken at the flood,"—you know the rest,*
> *And most of us have found it now and then;*
> *   At least we think so, though but few have*
> *   guess'd*
> *The moment, till too late to come again.*
> *   But no doubt everything is for the best—*
> *Of which the surest sign is in the end:*
> *   When things are at the worst they sometimes*
> *   mend.*

Sometimes entire poems will be formed in the same way as stanzas—with a fixed number of lines and patterns of rhymes. The *sonnet*, for example, must always have 14 lines. Usually it is divided into two sections of eight and six lines, called the "octave" and the "sestet." In a form developed by William Shakespeare (p. 260), the 14 lines are divided into three quatrains and a couplet.

The sonnet was probably invented in 13th-century Italy; its use became widespread through the influence of the Italian poet Francesco Petrarch (1304-74). The value of the form lies in its set length: A sonnet will usually contain only one idea, but it can allow the poet to elaborate that idea within a complete and balanced form. Many sonnets have been love poems, usually written in sequences, with each individual sonnet expressing one aspect of the poet's love. An example is the sequence *Sonnets to Helen*, by the French poet Pierre de Ronsard (1524-85).

Other kinds of poems with established patterns include two French forms: the *villanelle* (five three-line stanzas followed by one four-line stanza) and the *rondeau* (15 lines arranged in three stanzas of five, four, and six lines), both of which are written with only two rhymes. Generally, however, poets seem to have preferred to let the meaning of the poem dictate its overall form, and to use fixed patterns only in the stanzas.

Terza rima was chosen by the Italian poet Dante for his three-part allegory The Divine Comedy. *Left:* The Sky of Mercury, *scene from the poem illustrated by Sandro Botticelli.*

Visible patterns

V *olpone*, childleſſe, rich, faines ſick, deſpaires,
O ffers his ſtate to hopes of ſeuerall heyres,
L ies languiſhing; His *Paraſite* receaues
P reſents of all, aſſures, deludes : Then weaues
O ther croſſe-plots, which ope 'themſelues, are told.
N ew tricks for ſafety, are ſought; They thrņue: When, bold,
E ach tempt's th'other againe, and all are ſold.

Sometimes poets arrange their words into patterns that can be seen as well as heard. For example, poems have been written in *shapes*—usually the shapes of things that represent the subject or theme of the poetry. The 17th-century English poet Robert Herrick, for instance, wrote shaped poetry; his "Pillar of Fame" looks like its subject :

Fame's pillar here, at last, we set,
Out-during *Marble, Brass,* or *Jet,*
Charm'd and enchanted so,
As to withstand the blow
Of overthrow :
Nor shall the seas
Or OUTRAGES
Of storms o'erbear
What we uprear
Tho Kingdoms fall,
This pillar never shall
Decline or waste at all;
But stand for ever by his own
Firm and well fixed foundation.

Similarly, Dylan Thomas (p. 199) wrote a long poem called "Vision and Prayer," divided into 12 parts, of which six were shaped like diamonds and six like hour-glasses.

The *acrostic* is another technique that poets use to pattern a poem's appearance. The first letter (or letters) of each line make up a word or phrase that is related to the poem's subject. In his *Life of Constantine*, Bishop Eusebius (third century A.D.) quoted a Greek poem in which the initial letters of the lines formed the words "Jesus Christ, the Son of God, the Savior." And in the 119th Psalm of the Old Testament, the first letters of the 22 sections make up the Hebrew alphabet. Sometimes the initial letters of an acrostic form the title of the poem; the Roman writer Plautus (p. 262) and the 16th-century English writer Ben Jonson (p. 260) used this device in prefaces to their plays.

Shaped poetry and the acrostic are most often used as decoration, or to show off the poet's skill. But sometimes a poem's appearance can have a more valuable use. Many modern writers of free verse (p. 204) have used visual techniques to add to their poetry's meaning. One of the simplest techniques is that in which one word is allowed to stand alone, as a line in itself. In this way, the word gains added importance and impact. For instance, in the following lines by the modern American poet William Carlos Williams, the effect of the isolated word

How two writers used visual patterns to add to the impact of their verse: Ben Jonson's 1606 preface to his play Volpone *(top picture) takes the form of an acrostic (explained in text). Poem in bottle—a satirical ode to wine—appears in a 1605 edition of* Pantagruel, *by French writer François Rabelais.*

Left: "Tavola parolibera," a Futurist poem written in a mixture of French and nonsense language by Italian-born poet and musician Filippo Marinetti (1876-1944). Marinetti (who coined the maxim that beauty has nothing to do with art) did not compose— he performed. His poems, like his musical works, combined spontaneous cries and commands with sudden actions.

would be ruined if it were tacked onto any other line:

*There were never satyrs
never maenads
never eagle-headed gods—
These were men
from whose hands sprung
love
bursting the wood—*

Other poets have experimented with more complicated techniques: breaking the rules of grammar, punctuation, and spelling; joining words together to make strange compounds; scattering words across the page. Methods like these have been used by the French poet Guillaume Apollinaire (1880-1918), the German poet Arno Holz (1863-1929), and the American poet E. E. Cummings (1894-1962), among others.

Such poems can sometimes be effective and exciting because of their originality. At other times, however, because of the complete lack of any kind of order or pattern, they can be almost unreadable. Here are a few lines from one of the less complicated poems of E. E. Cummings:

*when
            sunbeams loot
furnished rooms through whose foul windows absurd
clouds cruise nobly ridiculous skies
(the;mselve;s a;nd scr;a;tch-ing lousy full. of. rain
beggars yaw:nstretchy:awn)
            then,
                o my love
                    , then*

It's Spring

Il pleut des voix de femmes comme si elles étaient mortes même dans le souvenir

c'est vous aussi qu'il pleut merveilleuses rencontres de ma vie ô gouttelettes

et ces nuages cabrés se prennent à hennir tout un univers de villes auriculaires

écoute s'il pleut tandis que le regret et le dédain pleurent une ancienne musique

écoute tomber les liens qui te retiennent en haut et en bas

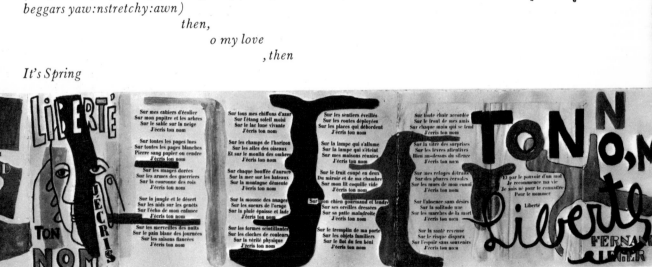

LIBERTÉ
D'ÉCRIS
TON NOM

Sur mes cahiers d'écolier
Sur mon pupitre et les arbres
Sur le sable sur la neige
J'écris ton nom

Sur toutes les pages lues
Sur toutes les pages blanches
Pierre sang papier ou cendre
J'écris ton nom

Sur les images dorées
Sur les armes des guerriers
Sur la couronne des rois
J'écris ton nom

Sur la jungle et le désert
Sur les nids sur les genêts
Sur l'écho de mon enfance
J'écris ton nom

Sur les merveilles des nuits
Sur le pain blanc des journées
Sur les saisons fiancées
J'écris ton nom

Sur tous mes chiffons d'azur
Sur l'étang soleil moisi
Sur le lac lune vivante
J'écris ton nom

Sur les champs de l'horizon
Sur les ailes des oiseaux
Et sur le moulin des ombres
J'écris ton nom

Sur chaque bouffée d'aurore
Sur la mer sur les bateaux
Sur la montagne démente
J'écris ton nom

Sur la mousse des nuages
Sur les sueurs de l'orage
Sur la pluie épaisse et fade
J'écris ton nom

Sur les formes scintillantes
Sur les cloches de couleurs
Sur la vérité physique
J'écris ton nom

Sur les sentiers éveillés
Sur les routes déployées
Sur les places qui débordent
J'écris ton nom

Sur la lampe qui s'allume
Sur la lampe qui s'éteint
Sur mes maisons réunies
J'écris ton nom

Sur le fruit coupé en deux
Du miroir et de ma chambre
Sur mon lit coquille vide
J'écris ton nom

Sur mon chien gourmand et tendre
Sur ses oreilles dressées
Sur sa patte maladroite
J'écris ton nom

Sur le tremplin de ma porte
Sur les objets familiers
Sur le flot du feu béni
J'écris ton nom

Sur toute chair accordée
Sur le front de mes amis
Sur chaque main qui se tend
J'écris ton nom

Sur la vitre des surprises
Sur les lèvres attentives
Bien au-dessus du silence
J'écris ton nom

Sur mes refuges détruits
Sur mes phares écroulés
Sur les murs de mon ennui
J'écris ton nom

Sur l'absence sans désirs
Sur la solitude nue
Sur les marches de la mort
J'écris ton nom

Sur la santé revenue
Sur le risque disparu
Sur l'espoir sans souvenirs
J'écris ton nom

Et par le pouvoir d'un mot
Je recommence ma vie
Je suis né pour te connaître
Pour te nommer

Liberté

TON NOM
Liberté
FERNAND LÉGER

Modern poets have continued to explore the possibilities of making visual patterns in their verse. At the beginning of this century, French poet Guillaume Apollinaire wrote many verses that looked like their subject, including "Rain" (top of page). Paul Éluard (1895-1952), working in German-occupied France, collaborated with painter Fernand Léger to create the poem above, "Liberty." Shaped verses were used by Welsh poet Dylan Thomas in his poem "Vision and Prayer," right.

In
The spin
Of the sun
In the spuming
Cyclone of his wing
For I was lost who am
Crying at the man drenched throne
In the first fury of his stream
And the lightnings of adoration
Back to black silence melt and mourn
For I was lost who have come
To dumbfounding haven
And the finding one
And the high noon
Of his wound
Blinds my
Cry.

I turn the corner of prayer and burn
In a blessing of the sudden
Sun. In the name of the damned
I would turn back and run
To the hidden land
But the loud sun
Christens down
The sky.
I
Am found.
O let him
Scald me and drown
Me in his world's wound.
His lightning answers my
Cry. My voice burns in his hand.
Now I am lost in the blinding
One. The sun roars at the prayer's end.

The break from patterns

Poets often need more variety than is possible within patterns of both meter and rhyme; for instance, in long poems where the thought and mood are constantly changing. In this case, they may turn to one of several more free forms of poetry.

One technique a poet might use is called *irregular rhyme*. Poetry in this form is rhymed, but has no recurring meter; sometimes even the rhymes come at irregular intervals. The French poet Jules Laforgue (1860-87) used it frequently, and it appears in the early poetry of the American-born poet T. S. Eliot (born 1888).

Another form has a definite meter but no rhyme, and is therefore called *blank verse*. It was first developed in Italy by the poet Trissino (1478-1550), and was introduced into English poetry in the 16th century by the Earl of Surrey (1518-47). It had its greatest use later in that century in the poetic dramas of William Shakespeare, and in the 17th century in the epic *Paradise Lost*, by John Milton (p. 196).

Some poets, however, have objected to the restrictions even of these forms, and have written *free verse* (with neither rhyme nor meter). Free verse is not a 20th-century invention, though it is widely used in poetry today. Ancient Greek poets like Euripides (p. 256) used it; and it appears in the work of the Italian poet Torquato Tasso (1544-95), the French poet Jean de la Fontaine (1621-95), and the English poet John Milton. Here is an example from Milton's "Samson Agonistes":

> *Just are the ways of God,*
> *And justifiable to men;*
> *Unless there be who think not God at all,*
> *If any be, they walk obscure;*

Writers of free verse are more concerned with phrases or lines than with syllables and feet. The rhythms of their poems are dictated largely by the emotional effects intended: One word isolated in a line, as has been said, has a strong effect. In the same way, short, jerky lines can often give a feeling of great excitement or emotion; the impression is of a man spitting out his words with passion.

Many modern poets use it in just that way in attacks on modern society; for instance, the Russian poet Vladimir Mayakovski (1893-1930) wrote many poems in this form celebrating communism and attacking its enemies. One of his poems was called "At the top of my voice."

But other poets have written short lines that contain slower rhythms, which give the poetry quite the opposite effect—like the feeling of melancholy in these lines by T. S. Eliot from "The Hollow Men" (1925):

Like much of the poetry that was written in the 1920s, The Poet *(1921), by Russian-born painter Marc Chagall, marks a break with conventional patterns and depends largely on evocative, abstract images for its effect.*

Above: two writers who broke away from the poetic conventions of their times. 19th-century French poet Jules Laforgue (caricature, left) rejected meter, and used irregular rhyme; 16th-century Italian poet Trissino (seen in engraving, right) pioneered the use of blank verse.

Is it like this
In death's other kingdom
Waking alone
At the hour when we are
Trembling with tenderness

At the other extreme from the free verse of short lines is the kind of poetry written by America's Walt Whitman (1819-92), whose work has been an important influence on modern poetry. Whitman generally used long lines and loose rhythms; but his poems avoid sounding like prose by their formal language and such other techniques as repetition. These methods give his work a "chanting" effect, similar to parts of the King James version of the Bible (for instance, some of the Psalms, which are also free verse). Here are some lines by Whitman:

I have heard what the talkers were talking, the talk of
*   the beginning and the end,*
But I do not talk of the beginning or the end.

There was never any more inception than there is now,
Nor any more youth or age than there is now,
And will never be any more perfection than there is
*   now,*
Nor any more heaven or hell than there is now.

Just because free verse does not obey strict rules of meter, we should not assume that it has no rhythm. The form of the best free verse is determined in much the same way that composers pattern their music—avoiding the "tick-tock" repetition of a regular beat. According to the modern American poet Ezra Pound (born 1885), a good poem should be composed "in the sequence of the musical phrase, not in the sequence of the metronome." To put it more simply: rhythm is necessary in both poetry and music, but a *fixed* rhythm is not.

In Paradise Lost *(1667), England's John Milton used blank verse to give his own interpretation of the Biblical story of Creation. The poem told of the fall of Satan and the rebel angels, illustrated here by 19th-century artist J. M. W. Turner (p. 144). 17th-century French poet Jean de la Fontaine wrote fables like "The Council of the Rats" (below) in free verse that was more direct than the conventional rhyming couplet. Modern Russian poet Vladimir Mayakovski (below, right) used free verse to give an explosive effect to his poems attacking non-communist societies.*

Conseil tenu par les Rats.

ꟲN Chat nommé Rodilardus
Faifoit de Rats telle déconfiture,

The poet's world

Much poetry is descriptive—of nature, of people, of the poet's feelings, and so on. When the poet wants to express an idea or describe an object that might be unfamiliar to his readers (or to describe something familiar in a new way), he will often compare it to something else. Such a comparison is called an *analogy*. But in poetry the more usual term for it is an *image*—because it is a brief, clear, and colorful statement that helps the reader to "see" the thing described, and to grasp the poet's meaning. Here is a famous image (from Shakespeare's *Macbeth*) for the shortness of man's life :

> *Life's but a walking shadow, a poor player*
> *That struts and frets his hour upon the stage,*
> *And then is heard no more;*

By substituting the image of an actor's "hour upon the stage" for "life," Shakespeare suggests an analogy between life's relative brevity and the evanescence of a theatrical performance. Such an implied comparison is a *metaphor*. Poets can also use "like" or "as" to make an explicit comparison called a *simile*. Here is a simile from a poem by Robert Graves (born 1895) :

> *Your tread like blossom drifting from a bough*

Generally poets make use of a variety of images throughout a poem, either to express different thoughts or to elaborate a single thought. For example, Percy Bysshe Shelley (1792-1822), in his poem "To a Skylark," conveys the beauty of the bird's singing in a flow of images; he compares the lark to a rainbow cloud, a star, a rose, a poet, and the moon (among other things), as in this stanza :

Villon

Se iayme et sers la belle de bon hait
Men deuez bous tenir a bil ne sot
Elle a en sop des biens a son souhait
pour elle seings le boucler et passot
Quât biennêt gêsie co's et happe dy pot

Woodcut above portrays François Villon, 15th-century French poet famed for his forceful imagery, with lines from one of his ballads.
Below: a woodcut by Ando Hiroshige (1797-1858) illustrates a Japanese haiku, *a verse form limited to 17 syllables. Each haiku evokes a single image. This reads: "When the peony leaves are hidden, the peony flowers look forlorn."*

William Blake (1757-1827) enriched "Infant Joy" by adding a pictorial image that compares a baby to a budding flower.

Infant Joy

I have no name
I am but two days old.—
What shall I call thee?
I happy am
Joy is my name,—
Sweet joy befall thee!

This portrait of William Wordsworth (p. 196) by English artist Benjamin Haydon includes the kind of solitary natural scene that the poet evoked in his work. Wordsworth drew his inspiration direct from nature; by abandoning the formal poetic language of the 18th century, he revitalized English poetry.

> All the earth and air
>   With thy voice is loud,
> As, when night is bare,
>   From one lonely cloud
> The moon rains out her beams, and heaven is over-
>   flow'd.

Imagery like this can be much more effective than general abstract description. One of the reasons for its effectiveness is that the comparisons are often strange and unexpected: They can shock the reader into seeing clearly and understanding suddenly. Here are a few examples of such startling imagery:

> *Like a skein of loose silk blown against a wall*
> *She walks by the railing of a path* (Ezra Pound)

> *Wandering the cold streets tangled like old string*
>   (W. H. Auden)

> *The burnt-out ends of smoky days* (T. S. Eliot)

> *Like a long-legged fly upon the stream*
> *His mind moves upon silence* (W. B. Yeats)

Another way that a poet keeps his meaning both brief and clear is by the use of *symbols.* Some poets—like France's Paul Valéry (1871-1945) or Ireland's W. B. Yeats (1865-1939)—often used symbolism to express the entire meaning of their poems. But other poets have used it only occasionally, to extend an emotional effect or to express a difficult point in a short space.

A symbolic word brings a number of meanings to the reader's mind—meanings that are not directly stated. The word "cross," for example, simply means a particular geometric shape. But it can make the average reader in Western society think of the Christian Church, the agony of Christ, the love of God, the Christian way of life, martyrdom, sacrifice, and so on. The American poet Hart Crane (1899-1932), in his poem "To Brooklyn Bridge," gives the bridge much of the sacredness and mystery of a church by the use of symbolic words—like "altar"—in these lines:

> *O harp and altar, of the fury fused,*
> *(How could mere toil align thy choiring strings!)*

The poet can add all these extra meanings to his poem by using just one word. And many words can be used in this way (like "serpent" or "crown"), as long as the symbolic meanings associated with them are familiar.

The lithograph on the left (drawn in 1875 by French artist Édouard Manet, p. 59), illustrates "The Raven," a poem in which 19th-century American writer Edgar Allan Poe used the macabre bird as a symbol of despair.

Poetry and song

In ancient times, the poet was not a writer. He was a singer, and his poems (for example, the Psalms of David) were made to be accompanied by music. Greek poets like Sappho (sixth century B.C.) sang their poems to the accompaniment of a lyre, an instrument rather like a small harp. As a result, poetry that was neither epic (p. 210) nor dramatic (that, in other words, expressed the feelings of the poet himself) came to be called *lyric*.

In Rome, poets like Horace (p. 262) and Catullus (84-54 B.C.) followed the Greek example. And in the Middle Ages, the *troubadours*, playing guitar-like instruments called lutes, wandered through southern Europe singing poems about the love they felt for the high-born ladies of the courts. *Minnesingers* extended the "wandering minstrel" tradition to Germany and northern Europe.

But with the coming of the Renaissance and the invention of printing (in the 15th century), European poets no longer combined their poetry with music. (Some of today's younger poets, especially in America, have tried to reunite the arts by experimenting with poetry and jazz. But their efforts have had only a limited influence.) The word "lyric," which had once meant a specific form of song, came to be a more inclusive term. It is now used to describe any poetry that expresses the poet's personal, private emotions and experiences.

In spite of this change, lyric poetry has retained a definite musical quality, carried over from the old tradition of the poet as singer. This quality, combined with a statement of deep personal emotion, is almost perfectly illustrated in this song from a play by the English poet Thomas Nashe (1567-1601). Here are a few lines:

> *Brightness falls from the air;*
> *Queens have died young and fair,*
> *Dust hath closed Helen's eye.*
> *I am sick, I must die:*
> *Lord have mercy on us.*

Top picture: ancient Greek figure of a poet playing a harp. Lower: two famous German minnesingers of the early 13th century: Tannhäuser (left), and Wolfram von Eschenbach. Below: American Negro plantation workers, from whose traditional songs sprang such song-verse forms as the "blues."

Within the lyric form, the poet has a broad choice of subject or theme. Love, as with the troubadours, has perhaps been the most common inspiration for such poetry, but religion would run a close second. Even within the limits of these subjects, the poems differ widely. Religious lyrics, for instance, might be as simple as many hymns or as complex and difficult as those of the modern poet T. S. Eliot (p. 204).

Aside from the themes of love and religion, the lyric can range from the rich nature poetry of Germany's Friedrich Hölderlin (1770-1843) to the disturbing, visionary poems of France's Arthur Rimbaud (1854–91); from the contemplative poems of America's Robert Frost (p. 196) to the fervently political poems of Italy's Gabriele D'Annunzio (1863-1938); from the exuberance of the Scottish poet Robert Burns (1759-96) to the melancholy of the French poet François Villon (1431-about 1462).

As well as poets like these, whose output was almost wholly lyric, there are the great figures who turned from other forms to the lyric expression: the dramatists like Shakespeare or Germany's Wolfgang von Goethe (1749-1832); or the narrative poets, like the Roman Vergil (70-19 B.C.) or the Italian Dante (p. 200). And this is just a sampling of the lyric's immense variety.

Several different poetic forms are included in the general category of the lyric; for instance, the *sonnet* (p. 200), the *ode*, or the *elegy*. The word "ode" comes from a Greek word meaning "song"; it was the name given to many poems of ancient Greece, especially those of Pindar (p. 196). But most later odes have not been imitations of the complex pattern of Pindar's odes. The elegy has also been handed down from Greek and Latin poetry; and though some elegies use a meter called the "elegiac measure"—a hexameter line followed by a pentameter (p. 196)—many elegies disobey this "rule." Instead, both odes and elegies can usually be identified partly by their purposes and partly by their moods.

Odes are long, dignified poems (sometimes written for public occasions), usually addressed to persons or things of rare beauty and importance: poems like "Ode to Joy," by the German poet Friedrich von Schiller (1759-1805) or "Ode on a Grecian Urn," by John Keats (p. 196). Elegies, which usually convey a mood of melancholy, can be poems of mourning or simply of meditation. Among the most important modern elegies is the collection called *Elegies from the Castle of Duino* by the Austrian poet Rainer Maria Rilke (1875-1926).

Hans Sachs (1494-1576), most famous German Meistersinger (member of a minstrels' guild).

The 18th-century Scottish poet Robert Burns, who wrote many poems to fit traditional tunes.

Many experiments in verse-writing have recently been made by the so-called "Beat" poets in America. Here, the influential San Francisco poet Kenneth Patchen is seen reading his verse to a jazz accompaniment.

Storytelling in poetry

A poem that tells a story is called a *narrative* poem. In the past (as with lyric poetry), such poems were not written down; they were recited and passed from person to person orally. Though they were usually told as entertainments, many narratives were based on actual events —events like great battles, or the deaths of famous men. (An example of the latter would be the 13th-century English ballad "Sir Patrick Spens.")

Narrative poetry has taken many forms; ballads, sagas of legendary heroes, and folk songs are just a few of them. Out of this traditional material, handed down from generation to generation, grew one of the greatest poetic forms: the *epic*.

Perhaps the earliest example of this form is the *Epic of Gilgamesh*, an ancient Babylonian poem that is believed to be over four thousand years old. It has many of the features of the epic that were later to become conventions; for instance, a strong element of mythology, a heroic central figure, mighty battles, and so on.

The best-known epics of all are the *Iliad* and the *Odyssey*, by the Greek poet Homer (who probably lived about the eighth century B.C.). The *Iliad* tells the story of the siege of Troy by the Greeks, and their final victory; the *Odyssey* describes the wanderings of one of the Greek heroes, Odysseus, after the Trojan war.

In later centuries, these two great poems became the accepted models for the epic form. For example, the

Greek vase painting (about 480 B.C.) depicts a rhapsodist, a professional reciter of epic poems —especially those of Homer.

Below: 16th-century map showing parts of Africa, Asia, and India explored by Vasco da Gama, hero of Camões's epic The Lusiads.

Aeneid, by the Roman poet Vergil, and the *Lusiads*, by the Portuguese poet Vaz de Camões (1524-80), both closely follow the pattern set by Homer.

Not all long narrative poems, however, obey the detailed classical "rules" for the epic—rules that insist on 12 (or 24) divisions of the poem, on an initial invocation of the muse of poetry, on lengthy lists of the characters and their possessions, and so on. But many of these long poems are still great works, in spite of their disobedience: for instance, the medieval Germanic *Nibelungenlied*—which was turned into a series of operas called the *Ring of the Nibelungs* by the 19th-century composer Richard Wagner (p. 156); or the *Divine Comedy* by the Italian poet Dante (p. 200). And, on the other hand, many poems that have tried to imitate the Homeric models were failures and have been forgotten.

Because epic poems deal with the adventures of great men, they are often called *heroic*. But the finest epics are more than just exciting stories. From the example of the hero, a great epic can also point a powerful and universal moral (without losing any of its excitement). In the seventh-century Anglo-Saxon epic *Beowulf*, for instance, such virtues as courage, honesty, and loyalty are illustrated in the actions of the hero (Beowulf) and his followers.

Also, an epic can reveal a great deal about a particular period of history. (Camões's *Lusiads* deals in part with the discovery of the sea route to India by the Portuguese explorer Vasco da Gama.)

The narrative or epic form was widely used in medieval and Renaissance Europe; for instance, in *El Cantar de Mio Cid* (The Song of the Cid), written by an unknown Spanish author in 1140; in the *Canterbury Tales* by England's Geoffrey Chaucer (1340-1400), and in *Jerusalem Delivered* by Italy's Torquato Tasso (p. 204).

Narratives are seldom written today. Many modern poets still write long poems, like the *Cantos* of the American Ezra Pound (p. 204), but they seldom tell stories.

Top picture (an 11th-century Swedish carving) shows scenes from the life of Siegfried, hero of an ancient Germanic saga, including the killing of the dragon Fafnir. Lower: woodcut depicting the pilgrims whose stories make up The Canterbury Tales, *a series of 24 narrative poems by England's Geoffrey Chaucer.*

This 17th-century illustration to the ancient Indian epic poem the Mahabharata *shows the hero, Arjuna, riding behind the god Krishna.*

The poet in the theatre

A great many poets have written their poetry in *dramatic* form, as plays. The theatre's attraction for the poet can be explained by the fact that, in a play, he can present human experience directly. Thus, his poetry (backed up by all the visual trappings of the stage) can have a powerful and immediate impact on its audience—an impact quite different from that given by poetry made to be read in private.

Poetic drama was first written in ancient Greece by poets like Aeschylus (p. 256). During the Renaissance in Europe, and afterward, the form became widely used by such great poet-dramatists as Spain's Lope de Vega (p. 260); the 16th-century English dramatists, especially William Shakespeare; the 17th-century French writers Pierre Corneille (p. 268) and Jean Racine (p. 260); and the German poet Wolfgang von Goethe (p. 208).

But many of the poetic dramas of the past that were intended for the stage are not suited to full theatrical presentation. This may not be because they are badly written; for example, Lord Byron's *Manfred* is generally considered to be great poetry. But it, and plays like it, are better read than performed, for all the effect and interest is in the words. (For this reason, such plays are sometimes called "closet drama"—that is, plays to be read in private.) In the theatre, words are only one

Poetic drama flourished in Europe during the Renaissance, particularly in the works of Spain's Lope de Vega (above) and England's William Shakespeare (below). After their time prose plays gradually became more popular, and few poetic dramas were written until the latter half of the 18th century.

PROLOGO, LELIO.

Benche fiat'uſ̃ ò Spettatori Illuſtri,
Solo di rimirar Tragici aſpetti,
O Comici apparati
In varie guiſe ornati,
I'oi però nonſdegnate
Queſta Comedia noſtra,
Se non di ricca, e vaga Scena adorna,
Almen di dopia nouità compoſta,
E la città doue ſi rappreſenta

Queſt'opra, è'l gran Theatro
Del mondo, perch'ognun deſia d'udirla:
Ma voi ſappiat'in tanto,
Che queſto di cui parlo
Spettacolo, ſi mira con la mente,
Dou'entra per l'orecchie, e non per gl'occhi
Però ſilentio fate,
E'n vece di vedere hora aſcoltate.

Left: the speaker of the prologue, from a 1597 editi__ of L'Amfiparnasso, a "commedia harmonica" writt__ by the Italian poet and musician Orazio Vecc__ (about 1550-1605). Such compositions consist of __ series of madrigals arranged in dramatic form.

of many different means through which a play can gain its effect.

Words, however, cannot be ignored. The poet writing for the theatre is not bound by the need to write in the way that people actually talk. He can use vivid, unfamiliar words (and images) that add to the atmosphere and meaning of his play. For example, in William Shakespeare's *Macbeth* (which is a story of murderous ambition, horror, and evil), the dialogue is filled with images of darkness:

> *Light thickens, and the crow*
> *Makes wing to th' rooky wood.*

But in the last act of another play by Shakespeare, *The Merchant of Venice*, the mood is one of happiness and peace, as conveyed in these lines:

> *How sweet the moonlight sleeps upon this bank!*
> *Here will we sit, and let the sounds of music*
> *Creep in our ears:*

It is partly by means of just such poetic effects that plays hundreds of years old can still come alive on a 20th-century stage.

Though some modern poets have written poetic dramas (for instance, England's Christopher Fry, or Spain's Federico García Lorca), most modern plays are in prose. But the value of vivid language has not been forgotten by many modern prose dramatists, like Germany's Bertolt Brecht (p. 274) or America's Eugene O'Neill (p. 276). This passage from O'Neill's *The Great God Brown* illustrates the kind of effects created even in a prose play:

"She was stainless and imperishable . . . so I shrank away, back into life, with naked nerves jumping like fleas, and in due course of nature another girl called me her boy in the moon and married me. . . ."

This kind of language is obviously not just a transcription of ordinary speech. It is far more expressive and colorful —in a word, more poetic.

The poet in love

Among the emotions and ideals that have always inspired poets, love probably takes first place. But in ancient civilizations like those of the Hebrews, Greeks, or Romans, the love of a man for a woman was less frequently the subject for poetry than it was, say, in medieval Europe. More usual was the comradeship that existed between warriors (as between the Greek heroes Achilles and Patroclus in Homer's *Iliad*); or an abstract love for a philosophic ideal. Women were generally considered inferior. In Hebrew literature, for instance, it is Eve who brings sin into the world, and Delilah who betrays the hero Samson.

In Europe sometime around the 11th century, attitudes toward women began to change. The change was partly due to the growing veneration for the Virgin Mary; it was believed that she had redeemed the sin of Eve. Thus, women became more and more the inspiration for such poetry as the love songs of the troubadours (p. 208).

The troubadours' poems were generally to or about actual women (the ladies of the courts). But these women were described as perfect beings, whose beauty and goodness inspired not only poems but the great deeds of knights and heroes. Later poets of the Middle Ages continued this tendency to idealize women and the emotion of love. The women they love are beautiful but very often unattainable; the love they feel is usually spiritual and pure. Love is "perfection's source" to the 13th-century Italian poet Guido Cavalcanti. And Dante (p. 200) addressed many love poems to his Beatrice in which she appears as his conception of ideal woman.

Gradually, this attitude toward women and love was replaced with a more realistic one. In the poetry of 16th-century England, conventional idealism had a longer life, partly because of the adulation of Queen Elizabeth by poets of that time. But toward the end of the century, women began to appear even in English poetry as human

Greek vase painting above (fifth century B.C.) shows Achilles, hero of Homer's Iliad, *dressing Patroclus' wounds. Right: illustration to* Romance of the Rose, *13th-century French poem in which medieval idealization of women reaches its height.*

As a love token, Nicholas Hilliard's miniature portrait of a young man includes roses—a favored love symbol in Elizabethan English poetry. In 1900, Pierre Bonnard made appropriate lithographs for verses by Paul Verlaine (1844-96).

beings rather than as ideals. William Shakespeare, for instance, described the woman he loved in this way :

> *My mistress' eyes are nothing like the sun;*
> *Coral is far more red than her lips' red: . . .*
> *I grant I never saw a goddess go,*
> *My mistress, when she walks, treads on the ground:*

Poets in the following centuries continued to write poems of love, praising their ladies' beauty, regretting their fickleness, or describing the symptoms of love. Many of these women seem impossibly beautiful or good, as in the beginning of a poem by Robert Burns (p. 208) :

> *O, my Luve's like a red, red rose,*
> *   That's newly sprung in June:*
> *O, my Luve's like the melodie*
> *   That's sweetly play'd in tune.*

But the sheer exuberance and charm of Burns's song more than make up for its possible deviations from truth.

In the 20th century, it is the reality of human love—and especially sexual love—that most poets are concerned with. The inhibitions and taboos of previous generations have largely been broken down, and the modern poet tries to explore (fully and specifically) the nature of his feelings toward the woman he loves. Some 20th-century love poetry has still been romantic and sentimental—for instance, many of the poems of America's E. E. Cummings (p. 202); but in recent years it has tended to be more realistic, personal, and factual, like the love poems of the young English poet Thom Gunn or of the American poet Kenneth Rexroth.

> *Toujours est-il, regret ou non,*
> *Que je ne sais pourquoi mon âme*
> *Par ces froids pense à vous, Madame*
> *De qui je ne sais plus le nom.*

The poet as teacher

One of the arguments most often used to defend the value of poetry (as, for instance, by the 16th-century English writer Philip Sidney, in his essay "Apology for Poetry"), is that it can be both pleasurable and instructive. The best poetry, obviously, should have both these qualities. But there is some poetry that is intended only to teach —and sometimes to preach. Its beauty is less important to the poet than the clarity and effect of his "message."

The ancient Greeks called such poetry *didactic*. One of the oldest didactic Greek poems is called *Works and Days*, by the poet Hesiod (eighth century B.C.). It is simply a practical treatise on farming.

But the purposes of most didactic poets are not usually so straightforward. Some poets have tried to instruct their readers in scientific or philosophical theory—like the huge, all-inclusive poem called *On the Nature of Things* by the Roman poet Lucretius (first century B.C.). The 17th-century English poet John Milton (p. 196) wrote his epic *Paradise Lost* for an equally broad purpose: to "justify the ways of God to man."

Other didactic poets have set out to give their readers specific moral guidance. That was part of the purpose of

This engraving, from a 1751 edition of Edmund Spenser's allegory The Faerie Queene, *shows Satan driving the seven deadly sins. In the poem the ideals of the chivalric age are embodied in characters like the Red Cross knight (who represents holiness), Sir Guyon (temperance), and the Lady Britomart (chastity).*

Ziet, kindren lief, deez' trouwe hond, | Regardez, chers enfants, ce chien vous apprend
Wacht zeker, tot zijn meester komt. | D'être toujours et partout bien à temps.

Verse is sometimes used simply as a memory-aid—particularly in teaching children. The 19th-century maker of this Flemish woodcut and the author of the verses below it—"This dog, dear children, that you see/Teaches you how to wait patiently"—were more concerned with pointing a moral than creating art.

the English poet Alexander Pope (p. 200) in his "An Essay on Man," as in these lines:

> *Know, all the good that individuals find,*
> *Or God and Nature meant to mere mankind,*
> *Reason's whole pleasure, all the joys of sense,*
> *Lie in three words—health, peace, and competence.*

Sometimes the didactic poet makes his point indirectly. His poem will be an "image" of morality (much like the parables of Jesus). The English poet Edmund Spenser (1552-99) used *allegory* for his moral purposes: Each character in his long poem *The Faerie Queene* represents a particular aspect of human nature—such as purity, sensuality, courage, or cowardice—in action. And the part of Dante's *Divine Comedy* called the "Inferno" teaches a moral lesson in the opposite way: by showing the terrible fate of sinners in hell.

Aside from moral and religious subjects, didactic poetry is often intended to sway readers toward some political doctrine, like the modern socialist poetry of Germany's Bertolt Brecht (p. 272) or England's W. H. Auden (born 1907). In 1939, for instance, Auden wrote:

> *Each language pours its vain*
> *Competitive excuse:*
> *But who can live for long*
> *In an euphoric dream;*
> *Out of the mirror they stare,*
> *Imperialism's face*
> *And the international wrong.*

More usually, however, it is some social evil—prejudice, injustice, poverty, or war—that sparks the poet's rage and inspires a didactic poem.

For example, many poets who fought in World War I wrote poems describing and preaching against the horror of modern war. One of the best of these "war poets" was the English poet Robert Graves (p. 206), who wrote:

> *War was return of earth to ugly earth,*
> *War was foundering of sublimities,*
> *Extinction of each happy art and faith*
> *By which the world had still kept head in air.*

Strictly speaking, poems of direct instruction, like those of Lucretius or Pope, are seldom written today. Prose, as in journalism and the essay form, has now become the accepted place for direct teaching and opinion. Modern poets usually convey their "messages" indirectly, through social criticism; they present an example of good or evil (often drawn from personal experience, as Graves's poem was), and let the reader draw the lesson for himself.

Below: drawing by American artist Ben Shahn, illustrating an anti-war poem by England's Wilfred Owen (1893-1918). Owen's poetry—a deeply felt protest against the horrors of war—was the crystallization of his own experiences; he fought in World War I, and was killed in action on the Western front.

The poet's laughter

Illustration from a medieval English psalter includes a familiar figure from popular verse —Reynard, the cunning fox. Reynard's tricks were the subject of a satirical French poem written by Pierre de Saint Cloud about 1175 and translated into many European languages.

Woodcut above, from a late 15th-century edition of Chaucer's Canterbury Tales, *depicts the Wife of Bath—one of the most humorous characters in English poetry. Her story, prefaced by descriptions of her five husbands, gives Chaucer an opportunity for hearty satire on the subject of women and marriage.*

In the same way that didactic poetry is written mainly to instruct, there is a kind of poetry that is written mainly for pleasure, to make the reader laugh. It is called *light* verse, or *comic* verse.

Successful comic poems will usually be short, in simple language with obvious rhyme patterns and marked "catchy" rhythms. This might also be a description of a popular song; and in fact there has always been a close link between comic verse and song—from the humorous ballads sung by medieval minstrels to "comic operas" like those of the 19th-century English collaborators W. S. Gilbert and Arthur Sullivan (whose work is still widely popular today).

The following lines, from *The Gondoliers*, are typical of the verse of W. S. Gilbert (1836-1911) and of the nature of light verse in general:

> *In enterprise of martial kind,*
> *When there was any fighting,*
> *He led his regiment from behind—*
> *He found it less exciting.*
> *But when away his regiment ran*
> *His place was at the fore, O,*
> *That celebrated,*
> *Cultivated,*
> *Underrated*
> *Nobleman,*
> *The Duke of Plaza-Toro!*

Even lighter than light verse (because less apparently "sensible") is a kind of poetry called *nonsense* verse, in which the poet also uses simple rhymes and rhythms, but includes made-up words, ridiculous characters and situations, and generally as much absurdity as his imagination can provide. The English writer Lewis Carroll (1832-98) began his typical nonsense poem "Jabberwocky" in this way:

> *'Twas brillig, and the slithy toves*
> *Did gyre and gimble in the wabe;*
> *All mimsy were the borogoves,*
> *And the mome raths outgrabe.*

Left: woodcut from the first edition of The Ship of Fools *(1494), written by Sebastian Brant of Alsace. The poet satirizes Church and state by describing how people from every social class—lawyers, priests, princes, and peasants—set sail for the Land of Fools.*

Nonsense verse is often written for children, but much of the best of it—like the verse of England's Edward Lear (1812-88)—has always appealed just as much to adults.

Some humorous poetry is intended not only to make the reader laugh, but to serve a serious purpose as well. This kind of poetry, called *satire*, combines comic and didactic poetry. It uses humor to attack the wrongs that the poet sees in his society.

Satire has sometimes been used for trivial reasons; for instance, in spiteful attacks on individuals. The poets of the late 17th and 18th centuries, like England's John Dryden (1631-1700), often used satire as a form of literary in-fighting, to mock their rivals. But the best satires usually follow the example set by the great Roman poets Horace (p. 208) and Juvenal (first century A.D.). They wrote their poems against dangerous social evils, and the positive, corrective purpose was made very clear.

In 12th-century France, the Church used satires on men's sins and faults to teach the ideals of Christian behavior. One of the best of these, the *Book of Manners*, was written by the Bishop of Rennes, Étienne Fougère. And many individual satirists have had a similar high moral purpose—for instance, the satires against religious intolerance by Germany's Gotthold Lessing (1729–81).

The satirical poet who feels a violent hatred for the evils he is attacking can sometimes emphasize social criticism at the expense of humor. Juvenal, for instance, was more often venomous than humorous; and there is little laughter in the bitter satires of the German poet Heinrich Heine (1797-1856). But there is a milder form of satire, called *parody*, which succeeds or fails only by its humor.

A verse parody imitates and ridicules a style of writing. If it is well done, it can be an effective form of criticism, revealing the weaknesses of the parodied work. Here, for example, is the first stanza of a poem called "The Old Man's Comforts, and how he gained them," by the English poet Robert Southey (1774-1843):

> *"You are old, Father William," the young man cried,*
> *"The few locks which are left you are grey;*
> *You are hale, Father William, a hearty old man,*
> *Now tell me the reason, I pray."*

And here is the opening of a parody of that poem (now far more famous than the original) by Lewis Carroll:

> *"You are old, Father William," the young man said,*
> *"And your hair has become very white;*
> *And yet you incessantly stand on your head—*
> *Do you think, at your age, it is right?"*

Top: "great Agrippa," character in Heinrich Hoffmann's comical German poem Struwwelpeter *(1847), dips disrespectful boys into his giant inkwell. Center: Illustration by Sir John Tenniel shows the antics of Father William in Lewis Carroll's verse parody. Right: the Jellicle cats, from* Old Possum's Book of Practical Cats, *by American-born poet, dramatist, and critic T. S. Eliot.*

219

Poetry today

In the early years of the 20th century, enormous changes were beginning to take place in the world and in men's lives. New ideas of every sort were appearing—in politics, economics, psychology, science, and technology—and many of the poets of the time were caught up in this mood of change. They were beginning to rebel against the traditions and conventions of earlier poetry.

Their rebellion was principally concerned with poetic techniques. The rejection of rhyme and meter in free verse was one of the less startling innovations produced by experimental writers. Many poets seemed also to reject any meaningful pattern; their lines and words were arranged with apparently little regard for the accepted "rules" of grammar and logic. For instance, the American writer Gertrude Stein (1874-1946), one of the leading experimentalists of the time, wrote lines like these :

> *How many acts are there in it.*
> *Ring around a rosey.*
> *How many acts are there in it.*
> *Wedded and weeded.*
> *Please be coming to see me.*
> *When this you see you are all to me.*
> *Me which is you you who are true true to be you.*
> *How many how many saints are there in it.*
> *One two three all out but me.*

To many poets (or groups of poets, like the "Imagists" in England), conventional meaning was of less importance than unique effect. Technical novelty was combined with scholarly references to ancient mythology or modern

Late 19th-century poetry hinted at the future. French symbolists such as Verlaine sought to make it as mysteriously subtle as music. About 1890, Alfred Jarry wrote (and illustrated, top) a parody-play in symbolist free verse: King Ubu. *By 1916, Dadaists like Tristan Tzara attacked all meaning in art: 1920 edition of his chaotic verse had Hans Arp's frontispiece (above). Unrest of the '30s—typified by Spain's civil war (below)—caused many poets to reject meaninglessness in favor of social awareness.*

science, lines in other languages, unfamiliar quotations from literature, wildly imaginative analogies, and so on—all of which added to the strangeness of modern poetry. In France, the group of poets called the "Surrealists"—which included André Breton, Paul Éluard, and Henri Michaux—discarded any aspects of rational or conventional meaning, and found the source and material of their poetry in the uncontrolled, irrational world of fantasy and dreams.

Usually, at that time, if the meaning of a poem became clear at all, it generally seemed to be a statement of the poet's isolation, or a radical attack on the spiritual and cultural emptiness of the world (like T. S. Eliot's widely influential poem "The Waste Land").

Because of these and other tendencies much early 20th-century poetry was attacked for its obscurity. Many critics felt that poetry's audience was dwindling because the poets had withdrawn from any contact with the actual world of men. It seemed to many people that poets like America's Ezra Pound were writing only for other poets, not for the general public.

In the years between the wars, however, poetry began to change again. Poets became more concerned with human problems and with political and social questions. In the work of poets like England's Stephen Spender, France's Jacques Prévert, or Germany's Bertolt Brecht, the emphasis was on the meaning or "message." Although such poets often used many of the new techniques, they drew their subjects, imagery, and inspiration from the world around them.

Since World War II, the concern with humanity and reality has persisted. Young poets today—like England's Christopher Logue or America's Gregory Corso—seem deeply aware of the problems that face men in the modern world. They find much of the material for their poems in everyday life. And they try to avoid needless obscurities, whether of style or content. Thus, the mood of rebellion has died down. Some of the techniques that startled and alienated readers in the 1920s are now accepted "conventions." Many of the wilder innovations have been discarded. Such younger poets as England's Philip Larkin and America's Robert Lowell have returned to the use of traditional forms—such as rhyme, meter, the sonnet, and the quatrain, among others.

Generally, poets today try to express 20th-century ideas in 20th-century language. And the number of books and magazines of poetry being produced in every country indicates that there is still an audience for poetry today —an audience that accepts it as an essential part of modern life.

Today, public poetry readings have a wide appeal. In America, large numbers of young people are attracted to readings of Beat poetry like those advertised above. Young Russians flock to hear the controversial poems of Evgeny Evtushenko (below), passionate enemy of social injustice and an international celebrity.

Chapter 9

Storytelling

From earliest times men have told stories and listened to them, for storytelling is one of the ways in which men share their experiences. By describing an event we have witnessed, we can re-create in the imagination of others something that happened in another time or place.

But reporting events is not the whole of storytelling. A list of the conquests of Alexander the Great, for instance, would have nothing of the magic of a story. But when we are told that his teacher was the famous philosopher Aristotle, and that Alexander won his first battle before he was 19, our curiosity is aroused and we want to know "what happened next." Whether our interest is held until we finally hear how Alexander became master of the whole of the Eastern world depends on the art of the storyteller. It is his skill in choosing and presenting events and characters that makes Alexander's story—or any story—real for us. The materials the narrator uses are drawn from human emotions and experiences we all recognize: joy and sorrow, love and hate, good and evil. These can form the basis of imaginary stories or serve to bring the past to life again.

Because a story above all gives pleasure to its hearers, it can be used with great effect for many purposes. From simple beginnings it has grown into a most versatile instrument. Men have used it to teach, persuade, and moralize; to express opinions, to ridicule, and to foretell the future. The many forms of the story have developed patterns of their own—patterns that are still changing. In this chapter we shall examine some of the different aspects of storytelling, particularly such written forms as the novel and the short story, and say something about biography and autobiography.

Good stories have captured men's imaginations since ancient times. Brought to life by the skill of the storyteller—who may combine the roles of historian, critic, and prophet—they have always provided a unique source of entertainment and instruction. Today, the art of the storyteller remains essentially the same. Like the great 19th-century Russian novelist Leo Tolstoi, who is seen here telling a story to his grandchildren, he must be able to hold his audience spellbound from beginning to end.

What is a story?

If someone said to you, "A man found a wallet in the road," you would immediately want to know how it came to be there and what the man did with it. In other words, you would not be satisfied until you had heard the "full story." This natural curiosity lies at the root of all stories. The art of the storyteller consists in unfolding a narrative with such skill that he holds the interest of his audience from beginning to end.

To do this, the storyteller usually chooses a central character—called the *hero* or *heroine*—to play the leading part in the events he narrates. He follows his hero's progress through a series of incidents until a final outcome is reached. The way in which the incidents are connected, and other characters related to one another and to the hero, makes up the story's framework or *plot*.

This framework gives every story its shape. The basic story *pattern* may well begin with the introduction of the leading character. We may also be told something about him and about other characters who will play a part in the story. For example, at the beginning of the fairy tale *Cinderella*, in the famous French version by Charles Perrault (1628-1703), we meet Cinderella and learn about the cruel stepsisters who ill-treat her. All is now set for the story proper—the series of events that will lead the heroine toward the story's most dramatic point. (You remember that Cinderella's fairy godmother appears and sends her to a ball where a prince falls in love with her, but in her hurry to leave at the stroke of midnight she loses a slipper.) The dramatic high point—or climax—of the story occurs after the ball, when Cinderella tries on the slipper that identifies her as the girl the prince fell in love with. To the rage of her stepsisters, it fits her perfectly. The story's outcome—sometimes called its *dénouement*—follows; all ends well for Cinderella and she marries the prince.

Within this basic pattern of introduction, climax, and dénouement the storyteller carefully arranges various incidents in a particular order so that they have a meaning for the story as a whole and draw us on toward the end. He also selects descriptive details that will help to fill out the story and add color and emphasis to it. When we are told that Cinderella's sisters are ugly, it helps to increase their hatefulness, while a description of Cinderella's ragged clothes gives us a fuller picture of the wretched life she leads. Although these details are not

The illustrations above (from a 15th-century Venetian Bible) form part of a series that tells the story of Creation. They show (top) God separating the void into day and night; (center) making the moon and stars; (lower) creating Eve from Adam's rib. The 19th-century Flemish woodcuts at the foot of these pages illustrate one version of a fairy tale told all over the world—the story of Cinderella, the kitchen maid transformed into a princess by her fairy godmother.

essential to the *action* of the story, they help us to visualize the events and so make them more real to us.

All that has been said about this story applies equally to all stories, whether fact or fiction. In both, the object of the storyteller is to make the characters stand out as real, living people. To achieve this the storyteller will have to invent credible thoughts, gestures, and dialogue for historical figures where no record of these has come down to us. And he will base the behavior of his fictional characters—however improbable—on his knowledge of how real people behave. So potent is a skilful storyteller's magic in creating character that he can often add to historical fact a gloss (or a tarnish) that influences everyone's ideas about a person—whether he did or did not act just as the storyteller says he did.

It is an historical fact, for example, that in the 17th century, Cardinal Richelieu, as adviser to Louis XIII, virtually ruled France for 18 years. But the picture that has come down to us of Richelieu is colored by stories written about this period of French history by Alexandre Dumas (1802-70). The political intrigues of Richelieu form the background to the adventures of Dumas's swashbuckling heroes in *The Three Musketeers*.

The storyteller who creates his own imaginary characters and situations is able to invent details to create any effect he wishes. We see this clearly in the surrealistic world of *Alice's Adventures in Wonderland* by the English writer Lewis Carroll (1832-98). From the moment Alice sees the White Rabbit hurrying past, watch in hand, until the final scene when the fantasy collapses like a house of cards, the storyteller fills our imagination with a succession of dreamlike figures, characters, and incidents that nevertheless have a curious resemblance to real life.

Some of the oldest stories that have come down to us are a mixture of fact and fiction. These *legends*, as they are called, were passed on from one generation to the next, historical events and characters becoming clothed in fictitious detail. It is almost impossible, for instance, to discover the true facts about the real King Arthur—a hero of British and French legend—from the many stories that he has inspired.

Both true and fictional stories must observe the basic rules of narrative. A good storyteller presents to us a purposefully shaped and ordered sequence of ideas and incidents that satisfies our instinctive curiosity.

The 15th-century French painting (top) depicts Joan of Arc, the devout peasant girl who turned soldier and inspired the French army to rally against the invading English in 1429-30 —a story retold by many famous writers. Beneath: Arthur, legendary British king, and his knights; from a woodcut contemporary with Thomas Malory's 15th-century version of the Arthurian story, Morte d'Arthur.

We do not know just what forms early stories took. One possibility is that they were often spontaneous accounts of a personal act of bravery or feat of skill that a man wanted to impress upon his fellow tribesmen. Then, as time went on, men who found they had a gift for storytelling probably began to include other people and events in their stories to make them more interesting. At religious festivals they would be called upon to recite the tales of great leaders and the achievements of heroes, and to chant the praises of the local gods and spirits.

As these first stories were direct expressions of emotion, they probably took a songlike form closely connected with music and dancing. The storyteller would perhaps accompany himself on a stringed instrument, moving his body in rhythm with his words. He discovered that certain gestures and facial expressions made a tale more vivid, while particular phrases became expected signals, just as "once upon a time" is still the signal for the fairy tale that is to follow. The storyteller would plan his story so that it

An African tribesman holds his audience spellbound with a story. Such tribal storytellers—who are expected to be well versed in the history and legends of their communities—are skilled in the art of bringing events to life by acting them out with vivid gestures.

Illuminated page from the Lindisfarne Gospels (English, eighth century) showing St. Luke recording the life of Christ. Such accounts were copied out in order to preserve them from distortion—not for the benefit of ordinary people, who were mostly unable to read.

revealed its surprises by degrees, and by careful timing kept his audience in suspense. In this way the storyteller became a conscious artist, using all his skill to hold the attention of his hearers.

Though most early stories probably started as true reports, it was natural for men to exaggerate and idealize facts to make a stronger impact on their audiences, and their inventive powers often carried the story far beyond the bounds of reality. Thus the art of storytelling developed from simple historical accounts into richly varied poetry and prose. The Greek epic of the *Iliad* (p. 210), the Hindu *Ramayana* (which was composed about 500 B.C. and describes the wanderings of the Indian prince Rama), and the Anglo-Saxon *Beowulf* (p. 210), each celebrate a great hero in a long narrative poem. The 13th-century Norse sagas *Laxdaela* and *Njala* tell their stories in terse, direct prose to convey more forcefully the passion and violence they depict.

All these different kinds of story were passed on by word of mouth, often in the form of verse ballads and romances (pp. 208, 210). Professional storytellers repeated them as they traveled from place to place. In Scandinavia, such touring storytellers were called *scalds*; in England and Ireland, *minstrels*; in Germany, *minnesingers*. The French were entertained by *troubadours* and *trouvères* who made their stories from legends of the time of Charlemagne (A.D. 768-814).

Wherever soldiers, pilgrims, merchants, and wandering peoples traveled they took their stories with them. In the process the stories changed. Some details would be left out and others added; unfamiliar "foreign" elements were replaced by local and familiar ones. The presence in the Spanish-speaking West Indies of African folk stories is an example of the way migrating peoples—in this case Negro slaves—take their stories with them.

Some story themes, such as Cinderella (p. 224), have counterparts in almost every language, though the name and details vary from place to place. Among North American Indians, the prince who marries Cinderella appears as the son of a chief. In Finnish, Celtic, and Portuguese versions of the story, Cinderella's dead mother returns to life as a goat or cow and helps her.

The oral storytelling tradition survives in Europe and America in country places, and in city music halls, cabarets, and wherever men gather to talk and tell jokes. In recent years radio and television have helped to revive interest in oral storytelling. In Asia and the Near East, however, the popularity of the professional storyteller, traveling from village to village, remains unchallenged.

Top: The 19th-century English author Charles Dickens giving a dramatic reading from one of his novels. Right: England's Max Miller (1894-1963), one of the popular music hall and radio entertainers who helped story-telling's oral traditions survive into the 20th century.

227

The uses of storytelling

The pleasure, interest, and curiosity that stories arouse in people everywhere have led men to use the story to convey all kinds of ideas that might be much less persuasive if they were presented without narrative appeal.

One of the most popular forms of story used by religious teachers is the *parable*, meaning "a placing side by side," a comparison. The parable usually takes some incident from everyday life and uses it to illustrate some spiritual or moral truth. One example is Christ's parable of the Prodigal Son. Christ meant the great celebrations arranged by the father in the story to welcome back his remorseful son to represent God's forgiveness to sinners. We also find parables in the Chinese religion of Taoism and in the Koran, the holy book of the Moslems.

A story in the form of an *allegory* (p. 216) serves much the same purpose as a parable but is longer and more complex. The Hebrew scriptures use allegory frequently, as does the classical literature of Greece and Rome. One of the most famous examples of allegory in English literature is *The Pilgrim's Progress* by John Bunyan (1628-88), in which the hero, Christian, represents the soul, and his difficult journey the soul's passage through this world to the next. The dangers and pleasant resting places that Christian meets with on the way stand for spiritual temptations and consolations.

As in poetry, the prose storyteller's use of allegory is linked to *symbolism* (p. 206). An example of this is found in *The Trial*, published in 1925 by the Austrian writer Franz Kafka (1883-1924). Some readers take the courtroom procedures as a symbol of bureaucratic red tape.

The *fable* is a brief story intended to teach a lesson in behavior or morals, or to make some comment on them. It is usually meant to teach some lesson in down-to-earth worldly wisdom, and is generally rather ironical in tone.

John Bunyan wrote his allegory The Pilgrim's Progress *in 1678. The frontispiece to the 14th edition (1695) shows the author asleep. Behind him, his "dream": Christian (the Pilgrim) sets out along the narrow path from the City of Destruction to the Shining Gate.*

Below: drawing by Paul Klee for Candide, *Voltaire's attack against 18th-century philosophical optimism in the face of human suffering. Right: illustration by Marc Chagall for Gogol's* Dead Souls, *a protest against 19th-century Russian serfdom.*

Often the characters are animals who think and speak like human beings. Probably the most famous teller of such fables was Aesop, a Greek of the sixth century B.C. A characteristic theme of Aesop's fables is the folly of yielding to flattery, as in the story of the fox who persuaded the crow that it could sing like a lark. When the foolish crow opened its beak to sing, it dropped the piece of cheese it had been holding and the fox stole it.

Stories—short or long—are also one of the most powerful ways of focusing our attention on social evils. The American writer Harriet Beecher Stowe (1811-96) did this with her novel *Uncle Tom's Cabin*. It did more than arouse sympathy for wrongs committed against Negro slaves in the American southern states; it helped create the political climate that eventually led to the Civil War.

In order to ridicule the complacent philosophical theories of his day, the French author Voltaire (1694-1778) wrote the story of a young student, *Candide*. Candide endures a series of absurdly harrowing adventures, accompanied by his tutor, the ever-optimistic Dr. Pangloss, who continues to claim that everything is for the best.

One of the main purposes of storytelling, however, has always been entertainment. Tales told simply to give pleasure abound in every language. One of the earliest collections of such tales is the *Decameron*, a group of realistic, witty stories by the Italian Giovanni Boccaccio (1313-75), who wrote them when European prose literature was otherwise dominated by moralizing stories.

Every age has had its fund of stories written both to delight men and to increase their knowledge and understanding. The present day is no exception. Enjoyment of the story for the story's sake, however, is something that does not alter, and is the essential requirement of a story whatever else its author may intend.

Above: a poster advertising a traveling stage adaptation of Uncle Tom's Cabin, *Harriet Beecher Stowe's pre-Civil War novel about slavery. It called American attention to abuses; after the war, it was internationally popular as a novel and melodrama. Below: a scene from 1940 film version of Steinbeck's* The Grapes of Wrath *(1939). It portrayed the sufferings of depression-era farmers who fled drought-ridden Oklahoma "dust bowl" in search of work.*

George Orwell's political satire Animal Farm. *Eric Fraser's drawing shows the pig Napoleon inciting farmyard to revolt.*

Ancient Egyptian painting depicting the rising sun sailing over the horizon in a boat.

Scene from an 11th-century Japanese picture story (attributed to Toba Sojo) shows a chase: frog and rabbit pursue a straw-hatted monkey. Many folk stories ridicule human failings by transferring them to such animal characters.

Mythology, folk, and fairy tales

Early men continually came across things they could not understand: Where did men and beasts come from? What caused the sun and moon to appear and disappear? Having only the crudest notions of cause and effect, they found it easy to believe that other animals, and even the wind, rivers, trees, and mountains were endowed with motives and reactions like their own. With these beliefs in mind men set out to put their answers into words, and these answers took the form of stories—the first myths.

The ancient Greeks, for example, explained the rising and the setting of the sun by imagining that a charioteer drove his team of fiery horses across the sky every day from east to west. In Scandinavian mythology, the god Thor drove a goat-drawn chariot, and men believed that thunder was the sound made by the rolling of its wheels. Other myths derive from half-forgotten historical events, however. The "deluge" stories, for example, common to many Near Eastern civilizations, may refer to some prehistoric flooding of the Mediterranean valley. Some recorders of myths even went so far as to provide genealogical trees linking actual historical rulers with their legendary ancestors. The Roman poet Vergil (p. 210) traces in his *Aeneid* the origins of the Roman state and its people to the Trojan prince Aeneas.

Many modern writers have "rediscovered" the old myths and have used them as a source of storytelling ideas for the novel, the theatre, and the film. The story of Theseus, for example, was re-created in *The King Must Die* by the English author Mary Renault (born 1905). Orpheus becomes a ballet dancer in the modern-dress stage and film version of the Orpheus and Euridice myth, *Orphée*, by the French writer Jean Cocteau (1891-1963).

As Christianity spread through the Greco-Roman world after the first century A.D. a change came over many of the ancient myths. The Greek nymphs of woods, mountains, lakes, and rivers became harmless fairies; the host of local deities gave way to witches, sprites, goblins, and animals who could talk. Men really believed in this magical world; stories were told of flying witches who cast

Two fabulous beasts that appear in many European folk stories: (left) the unicorn, an animal like a horse with one horn; (below) the griffin, a monster who was half lion and half eagle.

spells, of fairies who could grant wishes, and of men who had been changed into strange beasts.

During the 17th, 18th, and 19th centuries many of these tales were collected and published—by Perrault in France (p. 224), by Jacob Grimm (1785-1863) and his brother Wilhelm (1786-1859) in Germany, and by Jörgen Moe (1813-82) and Peter Asbjörnsen (1812-85) in Norway. Typical of the stories they collected is Perrault's *Sleeping Beauty*, in which a princess, cursed by a wicked fairy, pricks her finger and falls asleep for a hundred years. She is awakened at the end by a young prince.

Stories that enshrine customs, traditions, and superstitions are generally known as *folk* stories. Such tales belong essentially to an oral tradition of storytelling and have their origins in the tales of legendary heroes. In 1812, the famous collection of German folk tales by the Grimm brothers was published. Soon folklore scholars in many lands published collections of stories gathered from Norway to Greece, from Zululand to Scotland. Tales of incredible feats of strength, of heroic giants—like the American lumberjack Paul Bunyan—of virtue rewarded and evil punished, and the adventures of clever animals, are common to nearly all nations. Some stories were imitated or adapted, like the "Uncle Remus" tales of the American writer Joel Chandler Harris (1848-1908), based on Negro folk stories about animals like Brer Rabbit. In Denmark, Hans Christian Andersen (1805-75) wrote over 150 original tales in the traditional vein, often inspired by old folk-story themes.

In one way, myths, fairy tales, and folklore are an early attempt to explain psychological fears of whose origins we are only half aware: fears of the dark and the unknown, and of the forces and creatures that inhabit it. From these fears arose the ghost stories and tales of the supernatural common to most countries. Writers of this type of story include the German author E. T. A. Hoffmann (1776-1822), Edgar Allan Poe (1809-49) of America, and the English writers M. R. James (1862-1936) and Walter de la Mare (1873-1956).

Above: The Giant, *by the Spanish painter Goya (p. 51). Giants figure in stories as diverse as the Greek myths and English folk tales. Ghosts, as in George Cruikshank's 19th-century illustration to a good-natured English ghost story, occur again and again, too.*

Novels and short stories

Perhaps the two most important forms of story that have been developed during the past two and a half centuries are the novel and the short story. Although there are many kinds of novel they all have one thing in common: They set out to present an illusion of real life as experienced by actual men and women. The novelist's conclusions about life (whether his theme is comic or tragic, or has a wider, social content) are expressed through the characters he invents, the situations in which he places them, and the way he describes them.

It is this wish to describe a real world that distinguishes the novel, and the modern short story also, from the earlier forms of storytelling. In fact, the novelist sees himself as the enemy of that type of fiction which is *clearly* "made up." The Spaniard Miguel Cervantes (1547-1616) was the first novelist of this kind. In the story of *Don Quixote* (1605) he satirized the romantic tales of the Middle Ages by setting them against the realities of life in his time. Since then many changes in the form of the novel have been prompted by a desire to achieve an ever greater degree of truthfulness and credibility. The underlying purpose of the novelist's work is to discover and express the truth about how men and women think and feel, as well as how they behave. To do this the novel must be broadly realistic; truth to life is essential.

The approach of some novelists has been to follow storytelling patterns developed by dramatists. England's Jane Austen (1775-1817) did this in her stylish comedies of manners, for example, and Thomas Hardy (p. 248) and William Faulkner (p. 250) in their tragedies. Other novelists have evolved forms based on the age-old techniques of the oral storyteller. One of the earliest was the *picaresque* novel which describes the adventures of its hero as he travels from place to place. *Don Quixote* was constructed on a picaresque framework. Later picaresque novels include *Tom Jones* (1749), by the English writer Henry Fielding (1707-54); *The Adventures of Huckleberry Finn* (1885), by the American author Mark Twain—the pen name for Samuel Clemens (1835-1910)—and *Felix Krull* (1954), by the German novelist Thomas Mann (1875-1955).

On the other hand, some novels give a panoramic picture of a whole society, showing its contrasts of riches and poverty, and describing its social, political, and commercial activities. Among the most famous of these are the 16 novels that make up *The Human Comedy* (1829-49), by the French novelist Honoré de Balzac (1799-1850); *War and Peace* (1869), by the Russian novelist Leo Tolstoi (1828-1910); *Middlemarch* (1872), by the English writer George Eliot (whose real name was Mary Ann

Two great Russian writers, Anton Chekhov (this page) and Maxim Gorki, whose short stories reveal contrasting aspects of 19th-century Russian society. Chekhov depicts the life of the leisured classes; Gorki realistically portrays the sufferings of social outcasts.

Left: "Boule de Suif" ("Ball of Fat"), the victimized heroine of Guy de Maupassant's first short story (1880). In this, as in many of his tales, Maupassant exposes the cruelty caused by social prejudice.

Below: harpooners hunting a whale, after a painting (by 19th-century American artist James Garneray) that was much admired by novelist Herman Melville. Melville sought to re-create dramatic scenes of this kind in Moby Dick, *the story of a sea-captain's fanatical pursuit of a white killer whale.*

Evans, 1819-80); and the three novels that make up *U.S.A.* (1930-36), by the American writer John dos Passos (born 1896).

The theme of another type of novel is the growth to maturity and initiation into adulthood of a young man or woman. Such novels are often, though not necessarily, autobiographical in origin; among them are *David Copperfield* (1850), by the English author Charles Dickens (1812-70); *Sons and Lovers* (1913), by D. H. Lawrence (p. 194); and *A Portrait of the Artist as a Young Man* (1916), by the Irish writer James Joyce (1882-1941). A variation of this kind of novel is the type that relates the adventures of a humbly born young man, perhaps from the provinces, who comes to the great city and attempts to force his way to the top of society; examples are the French novels *The Red and the Black* (1830), by Marie Henri Beyle, known as Stendhal (1783-1842); and *A Sentimental Education* (1869), by Gustave Flaubert (1821-80); and *The Great Gatsby* (1925), by the American novelist F. Scott Fitzgerald (1896-1940).

Another group of novels, such as *Buddenbrooks* (1901), by Thomas Mann; and *The Forsyte Saga* (1921), by the English writer John Galsworthy (1867-1933), deals with the rise and fall of a family. One of the most serious and thoughtful types of novel is that concerned with man in his relation to God or destiny—such as *Wuthering Heights* (1848), by the English novelist Emily Brontë (1818-48); *Moby Dick* (1851), by the American Herman Melville (1819-91); and *The Brothers Karamazov* (1880), by the Russian Fëdor Dostoevski (1821-81). Many novels—*The Immoralist* (1902) by France's André Gide (1869-1951) for one—reflect their author's personal struggles toward self-realization.

The modern short story differs from earlier forms of the story in much the same way that the novel does. The chief difference between short stories and novels is not their length—for some short stories are as long as short novels. The difference is in the short story's greater emotional intensity. The modern short story is, to borrow a cinematic term, the close-up of a single event, an account of a single crisis in a person's life or thought, and its consequences. In fact it may not be a story at all in the old sense, but simply a reminiscence or the evocation of a particular mood. It proceeds by suggestion rather than direct description. The great master of the modern short story is the Russian Anton Chekhov (1860-1904). Other outstanding exponents of the form are the Frenchman Guy de Maupassant (1850-93), the Englishman Rudyard Kipling (1865-1936), D. H. Lawrence, James Joyce, and the American Ernest Hemingway (1898-1961).

Kinds of plot

As we saw earlier (p. 224), the events that occur in a story are organized into an orderly sequence called the *plot*. Whether the plot of a novel or short story is simple or complex, its basis is usually some kind of conflict: The characters may be opposed to each other or to the circumstances in which they find themselves, or they may have inner conflicts to resolve. It is the development of whatever conflict that preoccupies them that moves the characters forward from one incident to the next and determines the part they play in the story.

The simplest kind of plot presents events in the order in which they occur. For example, both the French novel *Gil Blas*, by René Lesage (1668-1747), and *Robinson Crusoe*, by the English writer Daniel Defoe (about 1659-1731), have episodic plots of this kind; they outline a series of adventures encountered by one central character.

The idea of cause and effect is the foundation of more complicated plots: Because one thing happens, another is brought about, rather than one thing happening and then another. In *Anna Karenina* (1876) by Tolstoi (p. 232), the married heroine's philandering brother invites her to Moscow to help reconcile his wife to him. Anna's visit ironically precipitates her own tragic love affair.

Instances of very complex story structures are provided in stories with a main plot and one or more subplots, all contributing to the outcome of the story. For example, in *Vanity Fair* (1848) by the English writer William Makepeace Thackeray (1811-63), the life of the heroine Becky

In this typical comic episode from the Decameron, *by Giovanni Boccaccio (p. 228), an errant wife outwits her husband, who has locked her out of the house, by dropping a stone into a well. The splash makes him think she has jumped in. The* Decameron *consists of 100 tales (many based on folk stories) which vary from high tragedy to broad satire. They are set in a narrative framework: Seven Florentine ladies and three men, fleeing the plague of 1348, retire to the country and pass the time by telling stories. Similar devices link tales in such collections as the* Arabian Nights.

Below: map from the first edition of Daniel Defoe's Robinson Crusoe (1719). *It shows some of the most important episodes in the plot—how Crusoe is shipwrecked on the desert island, clashes with cannibals and is rescued after being marooned for 28 years.*

Photograph of 19th-century French writer Honoré de Balzac, whose series of 95 novels, known collectively [as] La Comédie Humaine, was planned as a comprehensive picture of French society. It included sections [on] private, provincial, political, and military life.

The cover of one 1864 installment of Charles Dickens's famous novel Oliver Twist. *The hero's adventures are traced from his release from the workhouse to the downfall of the various criminals who exploited him.*

Sharp becomes bound up with the fortunes of Amelia Sedley and her family.

During the 19th century, when novelists often wrote for serial publication in magazines, they had to shape their stories into separate installments. Each had to be complete in itself, and preferably end with the kind of climax that hints at further excitement to come in the next chapter. English novelists like Dickens (p. 232), Wilkie Collins (1824-89), and Charles Reade (1814-84) published many novels in this way; the rambling, involved plot of Dickens's *Bleak House* (1852-53), for instance, shows clear signs of this.

Short-story plots (p. 232) usually differ from those of novels in that they have only one main point of interest. The plot must therefore relate everything in the story to this point. In his famous short story *The Queen of Spades,* the Russian author Alexander Pushkin (1799-1837) tells of a desperate gambler who tries to obtain the secret of success at cards from an old countess. Although the story covers a long period of time, the whole tale is contained within a tight framework, because the plot focuses only on the gambler's obsession and excludes all irrelevant action.

Modern novelists have often found the constructing of a plot irksome, since its requirements may lead to a distortion of character and destroy the illusion of reality. Some of the most thorough attempts yet made to dispense with traditional plot forms are to be found in *Ulysses* (1922), by James Joyce (p. 232); and in *Mrs. Dalloway* (1925), by the English writer Virginia Woolf (1882-1941). Both deal with the lives of a very small number of characters during a single day. But though the "normal" plot has largely disappeared and the "stream-of-consciousness" flow of characters' thoughts, moods, and emotions is often the most important element, structure and pattern remain. Joyce, for example, creates the structure of his novel by basing, however remotely, every single episode on a similar episode in Homer's *Odyssey* (p. 210). Virginia Woolf establishes a sort of pattern by making her characters share common experiences, such as watching the same airplane in the sky, or hearing a city clock chiming.

But there is still much to be said for the traditional plot as used in 18th- and 19th-century novels, artificial and cumbersome though it often was. We can see, in the works of Fielding (p. 232), Scott (p. 236), Balzac (p. 232), and Dickens (p. 232) how such plots—sometimes farfetched when examined closely—allowed the novelist to show in a single story wide contrasts of scene, of social class, and ways of living.

Character

Perhaps the most interesting feature of any novel is its cast of characters. If an author creates sharply defined and vivid personalities, he makes us want to follow what happens to them. The main character, the hero (or heroine), is usually the person on whom our attention is focused because the action of the story is centered on him. He will generally be shown "in the round"—in greater detail than other characters.

On the other hand, through the emphasis of one or two particular traits, less important characters can be made very lively and memorable, even though they are "flat" in that we know only a limited amount about them. The hero encounters a tremendous variety of people in *David Copperfield* (p. 232), but because of the skill with which Dickens draws them, each one stands out as a distinct person; for example, the mercurial Mr. Micawber, who is always waiting for "something to turn up"; the fawning clerk Uriah Heep, always rubbing his hands; and David's eccentric aunt Betsy Trotwood.

As we can never actually *see* the characters of a story, the storyteller must try to create them in our imaginations. If he tells us something of their physical appearance and temperament, we begin to form pictures of them. Sometimes the storyteller succeeds so well in describing characters that they stand out in our memory quite independently of the story. Such a character is the detective Sherlock Holmes, with his deerstalker hat and curved pipe, invented by the English writer Arthur Conan Doyle (1859-1930); or the thin, eccentric Don Quixote on his old horse (p. 232).

To see a character is not enough, however; in order to

This woodcut from Pantagruel—*the great burlesque novel by French writer François Rabelais (about 1494-1553)—depicts the giant Panurge, a roistering student and vagabond. The painting below, by the French artist Honoré Daumier, shows Cervantes's aging Don Quixote riding off in search of further adventures, to the dismay of his servant Sancho Panza.*

Alice in Wonderland (1865) was one of the first books to feature a
child as the central character. This drawing by John Tenniel shows
Alice meeting the Dodo—a scene in which Carroll seems to poke
fun at Charles Darwin's Origin of Species (published 1859).

understand him as a person and to follow his story, we
must be told of the passions, thoughts, and motives that
lead him to behave as he does. The storyteller can do this
in several ways. He can, as did the Scottish novelist
Walter Scott (1771-1832) in his historical novels, assume
the role of an outside observer, giving his own explana-
tions, comments, and judgments about the characters.

Or the storyteller can let the characters in his story
reveal themselves through their own actions and
thoughts, as the American novelist Henry James (1843-
1916) does in *The Ambassadors* (1903). Alternatively,
one character may comment on the motives and behavior
of another in the form of conversation, perhaps, or as
private thoughts that only the reader can "overhear."
A storyteller need not, of course, confine himself to only
one of these methods of presenting his character but may
use a mixture of them to achieve the effect he desires.

The vividness of a character can often be heightened
by contrasting one type of person with another, so as
to bring out significant differences. For instance, in
Fathers and Sons (1862), by the Russian writer Ivan
Turgenev (1818-83), the brash, offensive Bazarov is set
against his mild-mannered friend Kirsanov.

In inventing characters, the novelist naturally draws
on his own knowledge and experience of actual people.
But to hold the reader's interest, he must ensure that his
characters conform, to some extent at least, with the
reader's own experience of people. In a story, we expect
a person to do and say only what such a person *would* do
and say, even though he may act—as real people sometimes do—completely "out of character." Apart from
this one restriction, the novelist can draw on all the rich
possibilities of human nature.

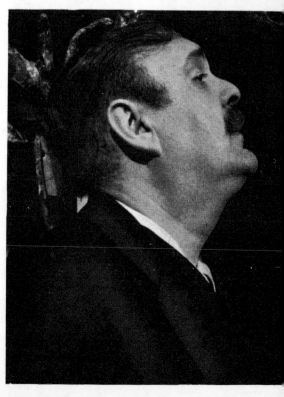

Top right: Nana, the bohemian singer and actress—heroine of the
boldly realistic novel (by Émile Zola) that bears her name. Right:
American actor Zero Mostel as Leopold Bloom—one of the most
fully described characters in modern fiction—in a stage version of
James Joyce's stream-of-consciousness novel Ulysses.

Point of view

A storyteller may narrate a story as though he were personally involved, or invent a character through whose words the story is unfolded. The question of viewpoint—who tells the story—is usually decided by the artistic effect each point of view can serve.

The hero who tells his own story in the first person singular gives the impression of a person drawing on his own memory of past events. In *Robinson Crusoe* (p. 234) Crusoe speaks not only as an eyewitness but as an active participant in events: "I was born in the year 1632, in the city of York, of good family, though not of that country, my father being a foreigner of Bremen, who settled first at Hull."

The selection of events appears to be the character's choice rather than that of the author. Jane Eyre, in the novel of the same name by Charlotte Brontë (1816-55), the sister of Emily Brontë (p. 232), tells us that nothing of importance happened to her in the nine years between her first year at school and her departure from it to become a governess. We accept the statement since we suppose that Jane is the best judge of what is important to the story.

The device of making the major character use the first-

English novelist Oliver Goldsmith (1728-74) narrated The Vicar of Wakefield *from the viewpoint of the central character, the benevolent, puritanical clergyman Dr. Primrose (above). In the self-portrait at the left, Belgian artist James Ensor (1860-1949), a face in a sea of masks, has a role like authors who adopt an omniscient point of view. They can tell us everything about their creations.*

Paddleboats like the one below were a familiar feature of Mississippi river life in the boyhood of American author Mark Twain (p. 232). Twain re-created such scenes in Huckleberry Finn, *told from a boy's viewpoint as he flees down river with his friend Jim, a runaway slave.*

person voice limits the author to describing the experiences and perceptions of that one character. But by making the narrator a secondary character who is a witness rather than an actor in the main events of the story, he creates opportunities for descriptions of scenes, events, and characters that form the background to the main events. Marlowe, in *The Heart of Darkness*, by the Polish-born author Joseph Conrad (1857-1924), is such a narrator; Nick Carraway in *The Great Gatsby*, by Scott Fitzgerald (p. 232), is another. In *Wuthering Heights*, Emily Brontë uses two narrators, Ellen Dean, the housekeeper, and Mr. Lockwood, the tenant of a neighboring farm. Their interlocking narratives are used to bind together past and present.

By standing apparently aloof from the events described and acting as an anonymous narrator an author can tell us more about characters and events than he could if he were limited to the point of view of one person. This is the method English writer Graham Greene (born 1904) chose in *Brighton Rock*: "Hale knew they meant to murder him before he had been in Brighton three hours." The author is omniscient; he sees all and knows all. He tells the reader about his characters' thoughts without having to explain where he gets his information.

Occasionally an author interrupts the flow of his story to make an observation of his own. Thus, in the opening pages of *Tom Jones*, Fielding (p. 232) suddenly stops and says, "Reader, I think proper, before we proceed any further together, to acquaint thee, that I intend to digress, through this whole history, as often as I see occasion; of which I am myself a better judge than any pitiful critic whatever." There are limitations to this technique, however, as the intrusion of the author into the story may tend to destroy the illusion of reality the novelist is seeking to create. The characters are shown to be puppets controlled by the author instead of creatures of flesh and blood with minds of their own.

Toward the middle of the 19th century, writers were experimenting with methods whereby the figure of the novelist could, as far as possible, be hidden altogether so that the events of his story can be seen entirely through the eyes of one of the characters. The reader shares the character's feelings and reactions to what is happening to him. We are taken right into the character's mind as the action proceeds so that we seem to take part in it. A pioneer author of this type of novel was Flaubert (p. 232), in *Madame Bovary* (1857), but perhaps the most extreme and complete examples of stories told in this way are the stream-of-consciousness novels *Ulysses* (p. 234) and *Finnegans Wake*, by James Joyce.

A child gazes in on the adult world. Children often see people and events around them with penetrating clarity. Many authors have chosen to narrate from a child's viewpoint in order to revaluate or satirize adult behavior.

Time and place

In reality, events affecting someone's life often happen simultaneously. But language imposes a single-file order of events upon the storyteller who sets out to describe them. To overcome this limitation, the storyteller can treat time in other ways than as an evenly flowing stream.

The events in a story can be placed in several kinds of time schemes. For example, a man going to keep an appointment at a certain hour might be shown as doing so *chronologically*, or according to clock time, which is always the same for everybody. *Psychological time*, on the other hand, varies according to individual mood. A young man eagerly awaiting his fiancée would measure the passing of clock time less by his watch than by the excitement and anticipation filling each moment. Someone looking back over a period of years might recollect according to *emotional time*. He would not relive every event in his life, but selecting only those most important to him, he would interpret time through his emotions.

The storyteller can also range backward and forward in time, either using past events to illuminate the present, or interpreting the past in the light of the present. This is done amusingly by the English novelist Laurence Sterne (1713-68) in his *The Life and Opinions of Tristram Shandy* (1759-67). The book is supposed to be written in the first person by Shandy himself. As he writes one thing continually reminds him of another with no apparent connection between them. Sterne exploits this to show how the mind works. It is not ruled by clock-time at all but is at the mercy of the past: Shandy is not "born" until halfway through the novel. He notes: "I am this month one whole year older than I was this time twelve-month; and having got, as you may perceive, almost into the middle of my fourth volume—and no farther than my first day's life—'tis demonstrative that I have three hundred and sixty-four days more life to write just now, than when I set out. . . . It must follow, an' please your worships, that the more I write—and consequently, the more your worships read, the more your worships will have to read."

Here Sterne is exploiting the difference between clock time and time as it exists in the memory. Although he does this chiefly for a comic purpose, he is a forerunner of 20th-century novelists like Proust (p. 194), James Joyce (p. 232), and Virginia Woolf (p. 234), who have tried to recapture past time in their novels in the same erratic way peculiar to memory.

Sometimes the action of a story takes place within a stated period of clock time, though the storyteller may refer to events outside that period either directly or through the thoughts of his characters. The span of action

Illustration from Victor Hugo's historical novel Notre Dame de Paris *(p. 242), showing the gipsy Esmeralda being led past the cathedral to the gallows. In such macabre scenes, we see medieval Paris through Hugo's eyes.*

in *The Sun Also Rises* (1926), by Ernest Hemingway, takes two months; Virginia Woolf's *Mrs. Dalloway* (p. 234) takes only 24 hours, whereas her *Orlando* (1928) covers several centuries. It is common for the action of the story to cover only a vaguely defined period. At the beginning of *Middlemarch* (p. 232), two of the chief characters are young and unmarried. At the end, they are married and have resolved all their earlier difficulties. How long this has taken is not important. An approximate indication of time passing is enough.

Occasionally the storyteller dispenses with time altogether. In *The Castle* (1926), by Franz Kafka (p. 228), "K," the chief character, is subjected to bewildering frustrations in his attempts to communicate with the anonymous master of the castle, and in the same author's *The Trial* (p. 228), the central character is on trial but cannot find out why. Sequences and incidents in both novels are suspended in non-time. Events are unfolded in a nightmarish way, without any indication of their duration—or location.

Novelists often use exotic, strange, and foreign settings for their work, sometimes to show their readers scenes and events likely to be outside their experience. But more important, good novelists often choose such backgrounds in order to show their characters subjected to stresses that could scarcely operate in familiar scenes. A master of this use of the exotic is Joseph Conrad (p. 238). In his long short story *Typhoon* (1902) he describes a steamship at the mercy of a tropical storm. The storm is described with the utmost dramatic vividness. But that is not the main point of the story. Conrad's real interest is in showing us how men behave in unpredictable situations.

English author Emily Brontë had in mind a place she knew intimately—Withiu's Farm on the wild Yorkshire moors—when she chose the setting for her novel Wuthering Heights *(1848), a story of ill-fated love and revenge.*

Above: illustration from The Lord of The Flies *(1954), in which England's Louis Golding tells how schoolboys, marooned on a desert island, revert to brutal savagery. Below: Napoleon's retreat from Moscow, 1812. In* War and Peace *(p. 232), Leo Tolstoi emphasizes the futility of war by showing the effect of this campaign on his characters' lives.*

Past and future

When a storyteller begins his story we assume that the events it deals with are over and therefore lie at least some distance back in time. Even when the story is set in the future, the storyteller usually tells it as though he were looking back so that he can present a completed picture of what has happened.

We have an interest in the past for its own sake, however. The outstanding events and personalities of history attract our attention. We are also curious about the details of daily life, of custom, dress, speech, thought, and behavior in times and places different from our own. In the historical novel the storyteller can use the attributes of the real past as the setting for an invented story. Walter Scott (p. 236) was one of the first novelists to set out to re-create the past as it really was. By doing so, he was largely responsible for the sense of authenticity that we now expect in historical novels. And by drawing portraits of men set against a detailed picture of the times in which they were supposed to have lived, Scott showed later novelists—Balzac (p. 232) especially—how to describe the society of their own times.

The historical novelist, then, reconstructs the life and atmosphere of another age and clothes the facts with his own imagination. He may, of course, use both actual historical characters as well as invented ones. Richard I of England appears in Scott's *Ivanhoe* (1820), and Louis XI of France in *Notre Dame de Paris* (1831), by Victor Hugo (1802-85); the Roman emperor Nero appears in *Quo Vadis?* (1896), by the Polish novelist Henryk Sienkiewicz (1846-1916); while Charles VIII of France, Machiavelli, and Savonarola all appear in *Romola* (1863) by George Eliot (p. 232). Interest in historical novels continues today with such books as *The Man on the Donkey* (1952), by H. F. M. Prescott (born 1896), in which the English author describes the effect on 16th-century England of Henry VIII's break with the papacy; and *The Cornerstone* (1954), by the French author Zoë

Above: the prophet Solomon Eagle, from A Journal of the Plague Year, *Daniel Defoe's vivid, fictitious 18th-century tale of London's 1665 plague. Below: French writer Marcel Proust (p. 248), who sought to re-create the past in his seven major novels. Cartoon: David Low caricatures H. G. Wells juggling the world like a medicine ball—a way of emphasizing his habit of reshaping society in his prophetic novels.*

Oldenbourg (born 1916), set in 13th-century France during the time of the crusades. In the United States, novelists often choose the Civil War as a background, as Margaret Mitchell (1900-49) did in her internationally successful *Gone with the Wind* (1936).

The future as a setting gives a different kind of scope to the storyteller's imagination. He is free to invent settings and situations that range far beyond present human experience. Yet, like all storytellers, he must make them credible. *The Illustrated Man* and *Fahrenheit 451*, by the American writer Ray Bradbury (born 1920), are, in common with many other of what are called *science-fiction* stories, ingenious tales frequently set in a future when interplanetary travel has become an accomplished fact. In fact, such writers can sometimes be prophets. England's H. G. Wells (1866-1946), for example, foresaw aerial warfare, tanks, and the atom bomb in *The Shape of Things to Come* and *War in the Air*.

The novelist sometimes uses the future as a convenient setting for social and political criticism; in this sense, many novels set in the future are really *about* the present. England's William Morris (1834-96) set *News from Nowhere* in the year 2003. It is the story of an ideal state, and a kind of propaganda for socialism. Morris describes a society from which law and politics have almost disappeared, and where pain, sorrow, love, and hate are all in harmony with nature. *Brave New World*, by the English novelist and critic Aldous Huxley (1894-1963), satirized modern society by showing it so far developed along technological lines that the need for personal initiative and moral standards had been eliminated. *Nineteen Eighty-Four* (1949), by the English writer George Orwell (1903-50), is as much a warning against the possibility of men being conditioned by unscrupulous use of the media of mass communication as it is about how sinister and soulless the totalitarian state may become when developed to its extreme limit.

Above: English writer George Orwell, who drew a grim picture of future society in his political novel Nineteen Eighty Four. Below: flying machine described by French writer Jules Verne in Master of the World *(1904). Right: a rocket ship featured in a science-fiction story by modern American writer Ray Bradbury. Most science-fiction writers today draw ideas from current research in nuclear physics and astronautics.*

Biography

When a person is famous for some achievement or talent, or for some position he has held, we are naturally curious about his whole life. We want to know about his family and background, and the outside influences on his life, as well as about his development as a person and his career. The biographer satisfies this curiosity.

One of the earliest biographers was Plutarch (about A.D. 46-120), a native of Boeotia, in what is now Greece. He drew a parallel between the lives of famous Greek and Roman men, taking, for example, Theseus and Romulus as founders of states; Alexander and Julius Caesar, as leaders of armies; and two great orators, Demosthenes and Cicero. Plutarch's purpose was to present his subjects as examples of virtue and vice, but he was also interested in them as human beings. By the use of character-revealing anecdotes and the description of identifying physical traits, he made these people live.

Many lives of the saints were written in the Middle Ages, but the writers were concerned more with glorifying God than with revealing human personality. Nevertheless, the nature of saintliness is itself something very distinct, and Adam of Eynsham's life of Hugh of Lincoln in the 15th century brings out some of its quality. Modern biographers of saints and martyrs, such as the English writer Evelyn Waugh (born 1903), in his *Edmund Campion*, are more concerned with the kind of people their subjects were, and are thus able to give a more balanced and convincing account of such lives.

The Italian artist-historian Giorgio Vasari (1511-74) wrote *Lives of the Most Excellent Architects, Painters and Sculptors*, which includes 161 lives of major and minor artists of the Renaissance. His information was gathered from casual acquaintance, rumor, and the conversation of both friends and enemies of the people concerned. Although material collected in this way cannot be considered wholly reliable, the *Lives* (published in 1550) gives us vivid portraits of such artists as Giotto,

Above: Chinese woodcut (1486) from a book of stori about Buddha. Below: Jean Fouquet's contempora miniature shows Louis XI of France on a state o casion. Pierre Champion's modern biography brin such scenes to life again.

Below: memorial painting of English diplomat Si Henry Unton (1557-86), by an unknown artist. Like a written biography, the painting traces Unton's life from infancy (lower right) to death (top center). I also depicts his travels, his home, and his tomb.

*ortrait of English writer, critic, and conversationalist
amuel Johnson, from the Journal of the Tour to the
ebrides (1786) by his biographer James Boswell.

Leonardo da Vinci, Raphael, Titian, and Vasari himself.

But biography—and autobiography (p. 246)—as we normally think of it, came into existence at about the same time as the novel, at the beginning of the 18th century. The reason for this, as with the novel, was the sudden curiosity about human beings for their own sake when men had ceased to be largely God-oriented and became self-oriented instead.

It was in 1781 that the English writer Samuel Johnson (1709-84) completed his *Lives of the English Poets*, which presented the lives of Addison, Cowley, Milton, Congreve and others not merely as an account of facts but as an illumination of the poets' works, and an aid to the appreciation of them. Johnson was himself the subject of one of the most famous biographies ever written : *The Life of Samuel Johnson*, by the Scot James Boswell (1740–95). Boswell amassed every kind of information about his subject. He took notes of actual conversations; he used letters, diaries, and anecdotes, and all his memories of Johnson over many years.

People portrayed in relation to the events of their times are the subjects of biographies by such writers as Philip Guedalla (1889-1944) of England, who wrote about the English prime minister Palmerston, and Emil Ludwig (1881-1948) of Switzerland, who wrote the stories of Napoleon and Abraham Lincoln. As well as giving us a clear picture of these figures, such biographies present the historical background as an integral part of the story.

Biographies have sometimes been written which, though adhering scrupulously to the truth, have been presented more like a fictional story. The French writers André Maurois (born 1885), on Shelley; Émile Legouis (1861-1937), on Wordsworth; and the English biographer Lytton Strachey (1880-1932), on Queen Victoria, have presented the facts with considerable skill, reflecting on them dramatically as well as historically.

There must, of course, be some element of personal judgment in any biography, however objective it is intended to be. We never, in fact, know enough about any human being to make a final judgment on him possible. For this reason it is at times necessary to re-assess a character in a new biography. Not only may we take a different view of things in the perspective of time but sometimes new evidence is discovered. By marshaling all available evidence, choosing carefully both small traits and major characteristics, and following events as they happened, the biographer tries to construct a picture of what his subject has done and what sort of person he was. Even so, the subject of a biography is—like any great character in fiction—largely his author's creation.

*Left: Marie Antoinette (1755-93), queen of France
during the Revolution of 1789-99. Pierre de Nolhac
(1859-1936), among other biographers, describes in
his* Marie Antoinette *her life of luxury at court and
her later courage in face of the Revolutionary mobs.*

245

Autobiography

An autobiography is someone's account of his own life. Not only can it tell us everything about the events of a life that a biographer would relate, but it can go further. In addition to describing what its author has done, an autobiography also describes the author's thoughts and feelings at the time and afterward. The autobiographer can draw upon his memory to tell about those parts of his life, such as childhood, which are not usually well documented, and about which the biographer can only guess.

An eventful life, or one in which something of great interest and importance has happened, is always likely to interest us. The American Benjamin Franklin (1706-90) wrote an autobiography about his beginnings as a printer and about his self-education, which is particularly interesting because he became a diplomat, inventor, and statesman. *The Story of My Life*, by the American Helen Keller (born 1880), is an account of how she overcame the appalling difficulties of being blind, deaf, and dumb.

Autobiography may reveal much not only about the author but also about a period and about people of interest whom he knew. The Russian Sergei Aksakov (1791-1859) drew a picture of Russia before the liberation of the serfs and included some excellent character studies in his *Years of Childhood* (1858). Benvenuto Cellini (1500-71), Italian goldsmith and sculptor, wrote an autobiography which, with its enthusiasm and intimacy, gives a sharp impression of the vitality of his personality, and a lively, though occasionally exaggerated, picture of the rivalry among the Florentine artists of the time; while the *Mémoires* of the Duc de Saint-Simon (1675-1755) contain vivid accounts of the courts of Louis XIV and the Régent d'Orléans. *Goodbye to All That* (1929), the autobiography of Robert Graves (p. 206), deals chiefly with his experiences as an officer during World War I.

The writer of autobiography may limit himself to a

The 16th-century Italian artist Benvenuto Cellini, famed both for his sculpture and for his autobiography.

Samuel Pepys gave a vivid description of the Fire of London (above, right) in his Diary. *Right: 17th-century English playwright Colley Cibber, whose autobiography portrayed theatrical life of his time.*

Left: early Renaissance woodcut showing the Italian traveler Marco Polo, whose memoirs (1298) describe his remarkable journey to China and the years he spent in the service of the emperor Kublai Khan.

single historical event, for example, or to recording literary or war memoirs, concerning himself only with the specific period involving his own life. The British soldier and writer T. E. Lawrence (1888-1935) was sent in World War I to help the sherif of Mecca in his revolt against the Turks. Leading the Arab forces, he performed many daring exploits, which he wrote about in *The Seven Pillars of Wisdom*.

An autobiography may be restricted to the story of one aspect of the author's beliefs or philosophy. The *Confessions* of St. Augustine (A.D. 354-430) deals with his spiritual experiences after his conversion to Christianity. The *Confessions* of the French political philosopher Jean-Jacques Rousseau (1712-78) cover his life from childhood to the year 1765. It is one of the most profoundly candid autobiographies ever written. In reply to an attack on his religious views, the English Cardinal Newman (1801-90) wrote *Apologia Pro Vita Sua*, a history and examination of his spiritual life.

The story of a life can be told other than in a straightforward autobiography. The writer may set scenes and reconstruct dialogue in the manner of the novelist. In his three-part autobiography, *My Childhood, In the World,* and *Reminiscences*, the Russian author Maxim Gorki (1868-1936) uses this method.

Diaries and letters, too, are a form of autobiography. Usually they are not meant for publication and have a spontaneous intimacy rarely to be found in other kinds of writing, for the writer is unconscious of any audience. The 15th-century *Diary of a Paris Bourgeois*, by an unknown writer, was kept from 1409-31, and was intended only as a private and personal document; yet it has become a record of medieval life of immense interest. The diary of Samuel Pepys (1633-1703) is a marvelously rich and candid portrayal of his own life, and also of mid-17th-century London, including an eyewitness account of the destruction of the city by fire in 1666. *The Diary of Anne Frank* is the touching account of the thoughts and feelings of a young Jewish girl concealed from the Nazis with her family during World War II.

Letters, which can also be candid and therefore extremely self-revealing, excite interest in a personality in much the same way as diaries. *The Paston Letters* of the 15th century inform us about the lives and affairs of a family of English landowners. Madame de Sévigné (1626-96) wrote many hundreds of letters to her relatives: a spirited running commentary on both private and public events in 17th-century France. Nearer our own time, the letters of D. H. Lawrence (p. 232) give many glimpses into the personality of that gifted, but unhappy writer.

Dutch painter Vincent van Gogh (p. 44) included this sketch and description of a garden in Daubigny in a letter to his brother Theo (1890). Private documents, not meant for publication, are often the most revealing records of their writer's life and personality.

This caricature by Eric Kennington depicts T. E. Lawrence, the British soldier and writer who won fame as Lawrence of Arabia. Lawrence is pictured pinning down and preserving like beetles the people he had described in his monumental autobiography The Seven Pillars of Wisdom *(see text).*

The diaries and notebooks kept by the young Jewish girl Anne Frank while she was in hiding in Holland during World War II. They were discovered after her death in Belsen concentration camp, and published after the war.

The novel changes

Novels are shaped by the pressures—religious, scientific, political, social—of the times in which they are written. During the years bridging the 19th and 20th centuries, for instance, the novel was dominated by the artistic theory of *naturalism*. It emphasized the part played by heredity and environment in limiting man's freedom of will and his moral responsibility.

This, for example, was the theme of the "Rougon-Macquart" novels by the French author Émile Zola (1840-1902), in which the effects of environment and heredity were shown working on the members of a single family. In England, Thomas Hardy (1840-1928)—in novels like *The Mayor of Casterbridge* (1886), *Tess of the D'Urbervilles* (1891), and *Jude the Obscure* (1896)— depicted his characters as the tragic victims of impersonal natural forces. In the United States, Theodore Dreiser (1871-1945) in *The Financier* (1912) and *An American Tragedy* (1925) portrayed society as a jungle in which the ruthless and strong preyed on the weak and helpless.

Following the breakdown of traditional religious beliefs in the late 19th century, many novelists turned to socialism. Notable among these was H. G. Wells (p. 242), who wrote many novels that criticized contemporary society and offered views into the future.

Certain other novelists saw art itself as the substitute for religion: the one thing that gave life meaning and dignity. The first champion of this view of the novel was Gustave Flaubert (p. 232) in *Madame Bovary* (p. 238). The earliest writer to express a similar point of view in English was Henry James (p. 236). *Portrait of a Lady* (1881), *The Wings of the Dove* (1902), and *The Ambassadors* (p. 236) were designed by James as "fictive pictures," a phrase that implies composition in the painter's sense (p. 36). At the same time, he developed an extraordinarily complex prose style of great richness.

During the first 20 years of this century, the French novelist Marcel Proust (p. 194) wrote his long novel *Remembrance of Things Past*, in which his hero seeks to recover his whole past in memory and enshrine in art what time has killed. Like James, Proust had to rely on what traditionally is the language of poetry—image and metaphor—in order to capture the complex movements of the mind in thought and feeling. So, too, did James Joyce in *Ulysses* (p. 234).

In James, Proust, and Joyce, naturalism has been enriched by *symbolism*. This is true also of Thomas Mann. In his *The Magic Mountain* (1924), the story of a young man caught in the morbid environment of a tuberculosis sanatorium symbolizes the nature of Western civilization before World War I.

Franz Kafka was an exponent of expressionism in the novel. Expressionists distorted actuality to hint at deeper truths. "Metamorphosis" (1916), illustrated above, is a short story, but its fantastic theme (a man becomes an insect) is typical of Kafka's novels in its picture of human frustration.

This illustration from Thomas Mann's brief political novel Mario and the Magician *depicts Cipolla, the sinister and repulsive showman who symbolizes fascism, giving a terrifying display of his hypnotic powers.*

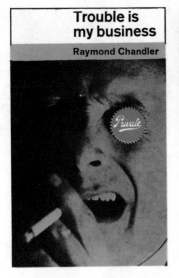

Trouble is my business

Raymond Chandler

Above: Stories by such skilled writers as America's Raymond Chandler, and France's Georges Simenon (right), have made the detective story one of the most popular forms of modern fiction.

Joyce attempted to depict characters through the uninhibited flow of thoughts and sensations (p. 234). There is an obvious relation between this device and the free-association technique used in psychoanalysis by Sigmund Freud at the turn of the century. Even more strongly in line with Freud's psychology of the unconscious was D. H. Lawrence (p. 232) in novels like *The Rainbow* (1915) and *Women in Love* (1920), works of great poetic quality that sought to delineate the real feelings of men and women in their sexual life.

During the 1930s, overshadowed as that period was by mass unemployment and the threat of fascism, the main influences on the novel were political and economic theories. Characteristic novels of the time are John dos Passos's *U.S.A.* (p. 232), and *The Grapes of Wrath*, by John Steinbeck (born 1902), both of which criticized aspects of the American political and social scene, and *The Human Condition*, by the French writer André Malraux (born 1901), a tragic novel of the Chinese Communist rising of 1924. Much influenced by Conrad (p. 238), Malraux, in his vivid rendering of the story's action, was greatly influenced by film techniques (p. 278), as the English novelist Graham Greene (p. 238) has been in such "entertainments" as *Brighton Rock* and more serious works such as *The Power and the Glory* (1940).

The philosophy of *existentialism*, a protest against the naturalism of the late 19th century, claimed that man was the master of his own fate and that by his own will could achieve anything. It was prominent in Western Europe immediately after World War II, and was given vigorous expression in France in the novels of Albert Camus (1913-60) and Jean-Paul Sartre (born 1905).

Russian writer Boris Pasternak (1890-1960). In his novel Dr. Zhivago (*proscribed in Russia and published in Italy in 1957*) *Pasternak came to grips with the problems of life in Russia in a period before and after the Revolution. Through the central character, Yuri Zhivago, he asserted his faith in spiritual values, showing that human life cannot be measured merely in terms of materialist dogma.*

American author Ernest Hemingway (1898-1961) expressed his love of action both in his life and in his powerful novels and short stories. Many unfold in wartime or in such violent settings as big-game hunts and bull-fights.

The changing audience

The public demand for stories at all levels of seriousness, whatever the medium through which they are presented, is insatiable. The audience for written stories has increased with ever-accelerating rapidity since the invention of movable type in the mid-15th century. It has increased even more during the past hundred years, with the growth of general literacy that has gone hand in hand with industrialization. Public libraries, which date from the middle of the 19th century, make the reading of books possible and normal for millions who cannot afford to buy them. Since about 1935, new methods of book production have brought into existence a world-wide reading public and taught people en masse to buy books—in the form of paperbacks—with the same freedom with which they buy magazines. It is not unusual now for a book to be read by millions of people throughout the world within a very few years of its initial publication.

Until little more than a century ago, writers of stories addressed themselves to an educated public that was numerically only a small section of the population. And in this century, novelists like Henry James, Thomas Mann, Joyce, Proust, and Lawrence, were writing for an audience that was necessarily small at first. What they wrote demanded capacities of understanding and appreciation far beyond those normally demanded by novelists.

One view of great art is that it is incapable of being appreciated by any except a small elite because of the high standards of intelligence, sensitivity, and education demanded of its audience. Those who hold this view fear the constant increase of inferior works that require no great qualities of judgment and taste for their enjoyment. They believe that there will be a lowering of standards of artistic excellence and a decrease in the power to recognize them.

Left: Noah's Ark, from The Psalter of St. Lo[uis] *(French, about 1260). Such richly decorated bo[oks] were made only for wealthy patrons. Until as [late] as 1715, when the English library above was open[ed,] books in most libraries were chained to the shelves*

The reading audience expanded rapidly after the invention of movable type (attributed to Johann Gutenberg of Mainz). Above, right: a 15th-century woodcut showing an early printing press. Right: the "Constance" Missal, one of Gutenberg's first productions.

In this cartoon (Tales of Wonder, *1802*) *English artist James Gillray ridicules devotees of such sensational novels of the period as Matthew Lewis's horrific medieval romance* The Monk.

Whether this will really be so we cannot tell, because the problem is entirely new. The possibility of its happening must be recognized, however; it would be absurd to pretend that individual human beings do not differ greatly from one another in intelligence and sensitivity, to say nothing of education. For though we have almost universal literacy in the Western world, there is as yet nothing like the same proportion of higher education.

But statistics suggest that advances in higher education continue to narrow the gap. The novels of James and Proust and the rest are now part of the heritage of our civilization; they help to provide the standards by which we judge what is written at this moment. If the cheap and sensational in literature multiply, so too do the good and even the best. There has been no more "difficult" novelist in our time than the American writer William Faulkner (1897-1962), but his readership in paperbacks in the United States runs into millions.

A work of art endures because it speaks to men from generation to generation. If the sales of books are to be taken as a test of literary merit, then by now Tolstoi, Dickens, Dostoevski, Balzac, Melville, Jane Austen and Chekhov have proved themselves more successful than even the most successful bestsellers of our times.

We should not be too frightened of the mere size of the modern audience. It is not an audience for one book alone or for a few; it is an audience for thousands of books. The mass audience, indeed, is made up of many smaller audiences; and the smallest among them may be the most important, since it is still the judgment and enthusiasm of the few that determine which books are to be read in the years to come. What really matters is that all the audiences that exist—and they are as many as the kinds of stories that exist—should be given the best.

Modern book production techniques make the world's classics available to millions in cheap but well-designed pocket editions—like the range of paperbacks shown on the right, which includes examples from Germany, Spain, Sweden, China, America, and England.

Above: an episode from Tintin, *a Belgian comic strip followed by some 15 million readers. Such comic strips reach a world-wide audience because they tell a story through pictures and a minimum of text.*

Chapter 10

Drama

When we hear the name of a great dramatist like Shakespeare or Sophocles, our first thought may be of lines of printed text or books of critical writing by learned authors; but such things do not give a true picture of the dramatist. Take Sophocles, for example: He not only wrote plays, he was also a dancer and musician, a general, a financier, and a diplomat—a many-sided man. And, of course, plays are not made by the playwright alone. The text of a "drama" is only what is written down of a performance staged by actors before an audience. A drama may be beautiful poetry or prose in its own right; but that is incidental. The written record is merely what remains from a number of activities.

The plays of the past that we know and study today are the accidental survival of such activity. For instance, we have only seven plays by Sophocles out of more than a hundred that he wrote. And we have none by most of his contemporaries, who were once equally well known. Many kinds of dramatic activity leave no written records in the form of texts.

To stage a drama often involves many skills—those of the architect, musician, dancer, acrobat, carpenter, machinist, and scene designer, as well as of the writer, actors, producers, and directors who organize the skills. Is any one of these indispensable to the drama? One, indeed, is—but not the writer's. There have been plays without words, and plays in which the actors make up their own words, like the Italian improvised comedy of the Renaissance (p. 254). Not the dancer's or musician's, either; there can be plays without dancing or music. What *is* essential is the actor—alone or in a troupe. He remains indispensable. So let us begin with him.

Drama is essentially the art of the actor. Throughout history, he has filled the double role of priest and entertainer. Hiding behind the mask of classical Greek and Roman drama, or behind the greasepaint of the modern theatre, he may raise his audience to the heights of tragedy, or simply set out to make them laugh. Honoré Daumier's picture of Crispin and Scapin, figures of French comedy, captures the magic of make-believe that is the essence of theatre.

Mask and face

Simple dramatic activity is found in various forms among all peoples. When it becomes complex and elaborate, it is usually as a result of social and political changes. These are often associated with the coming of a new religion that disturbs or destroys old ideas and thus sets men free to think afresh. The cult of the wine god Dionysus had this effect in ancient Greece. Similar results accompanied the growth of Christianity in Europe and the coming of Buddhism to Japan.

When the cult of Dionysus reached Greece from the kingdoms on the shores of the Black Sea, some people opposed it strongly; but it eventually made many converts—particularly in the northern city of Icaria. The citizens of Athens remained hostile until, worried by an outbreak of plague, they consulted the oracle of the god Apollo at Delphi, which advised them to accept the new faith.

The characteristic form of worship of Dionysus was a procession of wine-excited revelers, bearing an image of the god. Men dressed in animal skins and wearing animal heads and horns danced in the procession, impersonating centaurs (half horse, half man) and satyrs (half man, half goat). There are similar man-animal creatures in the folk-lore of every race; for pre-Christian peoples did not think of animals as inferior beings. On the contrary, men thought they had animal ancestors, and they expected the gods sometimes to take animal as well as human shape.

The goat-men in the Dionysiac procession also took part in "satyr plays" performed during the festivals (the word tragedy means "goat song"). *Comus*, the name of the procession of revelers, gives us the word "comedy." The dancing was called *mimesis*, which is often translated as "imitation" and gives us the words "mimic" and "mime." It originally meant the state of mind of the dancer who was "inspired" (breathed into) by the spirit of his god. The sign of being inspired was the mask; when he put this on, the dancer was "taken over" by the god.

Eventually, these dance-dramas were performed in a special theatre dedicated to Dionysus. As part of the play, a "chorus" of men danced and sang. This chorus grew out of the old revel-procession, but was eventually limited in numbers to only 15 men. Women took no part, because this was an activity of citizens—and Athenian women could not be citizens.

The Greek word for an actor was *hypocrites* ("the answerer") because he answered the chorus. Thespis, an actor from Icaria (the early stronghold of Dionysus), was the first performer to do this, and actors are still some-

A chorus like these processional "horses" and riders (from an Attic vase; about 550 B.C.), figured in Aristophanes' Knights, one of the oldest Greek comedies. Early Greek drama derived from popular revels held in honor of the wine god Dionysus.

This terra-cotta mask, Greek in design, was worn by a third-century Roman actor.

Ancient Lion Dance of Japan, depicted by a 19th-century artist. This dance survives both as a street entertainment and in classical No drama. No actors perfected the art of mime until a mere lift of the mask meant a smile.

times called Thespians. Because the actor wore a mask, the word hypocrite later came to mean a two-faced person—someone who pretends to be what he is not. Yet the Latin word for mask, *persona*, gives us the words "person" and "personality," by which we mean something real, a genuine identity. The drama has always had this dual character of sincerity and pretense.

The development of drama in Japan closely paralleled that in Greece. Again it began with the arrival of a foreign religion—in this case Buddhism, spreading from India through China and Korea. It brought with it ritual dances in which, as in the Greek Comus procession, men wore animal masks and skins. These folk- and temple-dances soon grew much more complex as a result of festivals held in the Buddhist abbeys; they were given their final form in the 14th century through the genius of Kan'ame Kiyotsugu and his son, Ze'ami Motokiyo—who, like the Greek dramatists (p. 256), were both actors, musicians, and dancers as well as playwrights.

As in Greece, these developments were associated with political and social change. In Japan it was the growth of feudalism. The local lord (*daimyo*) and his knights (*samurai*) took over the *No* dramas (as these plays are known) as their exclusive possession, forbidding ordinary people even to witness them. As in Greece, each performance began with religious ritual. Originally performed out of doors, they were—unlike the Greek plays—soon acted exclusively in the palaces of the nobility. The *No* plays are still performed today—the oldest drama in the world with an unbroken tradition of acting. They are short, with subjects usually based upon Japanese history and legend, and are now arranged in sets of three or five. Between each section of the program, farces are played. These are the *Kyogen* ("mad words"). In them, servants make fun of their master, and the gods and Buddhism itself are mocked. In the traditional *No* plays, there are only two masked actors, plus a chorus.

We shall see how Christian drama, like that of Greece and Japan, also grew out of religious ritual. But Christianity, in keeping with its rejection of all other religions, identified masks with the pagan gods. In medieval religious drama, therefore, it was only the devils who were masked. In Europe, the traditional use of masks survived until the 18th century only in Italian improvised comedy, the *commedia dell'arte* (descended from ancient pagan mimes). There it ended. Yet such is the dramatic power of the mask that many modern playwrights have revived its use.

German devil-mask, worn by an actor in a medieval mystery. In Christian drama, masks were reserved for evil roles.

In Italian commedia dell'arte *of the 17th and 18th centuries, masked actors mimed stock characters such as Harlequin.*

Masks still have dramatic power today. Masked actors play the hard-hearted rich in The Caucasian Chalk Circle *by Germany's Bertolt Brecht. Patience Collier played the governor's wife in a 1962 British production.*

The first dramatists

During the sixth century B.C. the little country town of Athens grew into the most important and cultured city-state of Greece. Each year at midsummer, city officials chose the three poets who were to compete the following spring in the Dionysia. This was a festival that Peisistratus, a ruler of Athens, instituted in honor of the wine god Dionysus. The Dionysia was to become the chief festival of the Athenian year; and the three appointed poets each prepared three tragedies for it (comedies were added in later years).

Sometimes, but not always, the three plays were connected in theme (a "trilogy"). Each poet became the official responsibility of a rich citizen who bore the expenses of his plays. To be chosen such a "backer" (*choregus*) was one of the greatest honors Athens could bestow. The plays had to be written on themes taken from the history of Greece or from the legends of her princely families—particularly those incidents described in the poems of Homer (p. 210). Sometimes, however, plays based on more recent events were accepted.

A sacred peace was declared in the city for the five or six days that the festival lasted; no violence was permitted, not even in the action of the plays. On the first day everyone went out in procession from Athens to the village of Eleutherae, where the ancient wooden statue of Dionysus was enshrined. From here they carried the statue back in triumph to the city. In the procession came city officials, priests, important guests, the poets, their actors, the wealthy backers, and the chorus, representing the community of worshipers. During the next three days the plays were acted during the hours of daylight. When all was over, an appointed jury of citizens chose the prize-winning dramatist. The festival closed with *dithyrambs*—choral poems in honor of the god.

Early Greek dramas retold legends of the Trojan War, already over five centuries old. This vase painting (about 540 B.C.) shows Achilles slaying the queen of the Amazons.

The Greek theatre at Delphi, set in a wooded hollow of the hills, was built during the fourth century B.C., restored later by the Romans. With 35 tiers of stone benches, it seated 5000 people, was so well designed that each member of the audience could hear the actors clearly.

A Greek vase painting of Orestes (center) at Delphi, a scene from Aeschylus' tragedy Eumenides. *The play was the third in his great trilogy the* Oresteia, *first performed in 458 B.C.*

These contests were originally held in the city's *agora*, or market place. After the collapse of the wooden seating there in 499 B.C., the event was transferred to a *theatre* ("a place for seeing") scooped out at the foot of the near-by Acropolis hill, close to the temple of Dionysus. There actors performed in a circular dancing place called an *orchestra*. An altar of the god stood in the middle of this space, and the audience sat on the slopes. The actors dressed and put on their masks in a tent on the edge of the orchestra.

The Greek name for the actors' tent was *skene*—our word "scene." In later years the tent was replaced by a wooden building (the *proscenium*), in front of which the actors played on a raised platform. Later still, the wooden building was replaced by an elaborate stone structure. It was here that the poet Aeschylus (525-456 B.C.) had his first successful play performed in 484 B.C. To the single actor originated by Thespis (p. 254) Aeschylus added a second and later a third. He not only acted in his own plays; he also trained the other actors and the chorus.

In 458 B.C. Aeschylus presented his great trilogy, the *Oresteia*. But by this time other, younger poets were coming to the fore. Among them were Sophocles (about 496-406 B.C.), Euripides (about 480-406 B.C.), and Aristophanes (about 448-380 B.C.) To Sophocles the gods gave every gift: wealth, health, long life, talent, and fame. Euripides, on the other hand, was regarded with suspicion as a trouble maker and skeptic. The great comic dramatist was Aristophanes, whose plays mocked everyone from the philosopher Socrates to warmongering politicians.

By 400 B.C. the plays of Athens were famous throughout Greece. They were carried from place to place by professional actors organized in troupes under the protection of Dionysus. After the death of Aeschylus, the older plays began to be revived in his honor and performed at other festivals besides the Dionysia. Theatres were built in every city. But a new kind of comedy was coming into fashion. No longer topical like that of Aristophanes, it was based on a few stock situations and characters: obstinate old men, talkative old women, gay young people, and sly, plotting slaves. The great creative period of Greek drama was over.

We have begun with the Greeks because they have left us our oldest, and some of our best, plays. We also owe to them the basic vocabulary of dramatic art. The word drama itself ("the thing done") was theirs. With the Greeks the drama of the Western world took a recognizable form.

Runaway slaves were stock characters in Greek comedy of the second century B.C. This terra-cotta figure, made at a Greek colony in southern Italy, shows an actor playing a slave seated on an altar, as if seeking refuge.

The actor as entertainer

These acrobats, pictured in an Egyptian royal tomb, performed at court about 2000 B.C. Pharaohs delighted in displays of skill.

Man has sometimes been described as the tool-making animal; he is also an animal that needs to be entertained. We have seen how drama began in magic rites, but it has also served to mock, astonish, and delight. Sometimes the actor is a performer of religious ritual; at other times he is purely an entertainer.

Some entertainers make "magic" and "conjure" (implying the power to perform the apparently impossible). Some have power over wild beasts. Some can swallow swords or fire. Still others live by their personal skill. They can juggle, or they can walk tightropes, or they can swing on a trapeze. In many countries, these activities are now found only in highly organized "circuses," but elsewhere single performers may still be found by the roadside, at fairs, in private homes, and in cabarets and variety theatres.

The clown, or "comic," is an entertainer whose history is closely linked with primitive ritual. Because the "fool" or madman was once regarded as "touched" by the gods, and therefore close to the unseen powers, he was looked upon as a bringer of fertility, a prophet, and a speaker of unexpected truth. He was privileged to go where he pleased and to say what he pleased. If in his travels he crossed the borders of his own country and language, he took to *pantomime* (play without words) and nonsense talk. The clown is an essential figure of medieval drama, the Italian comedy, and the English theatre in Shakespeare's time (p. 260).

Other entertainers—ballad singers, minstrels, tellers of tales—must often know more than one language. Thus, the legends of King Arthur were spread through Europe by multilingual Welsh storytellers.

Comics of the fourth century B.C., shown in an Italian vase painting of the period, parody a scene from the Greek tragedy Amphitryon *in which the god Zeus (left), accompanied by Mercury, visits his mistress Alcmene (center).*

Like the Etruscan boy of the fifth century B.C. (above), 16th-century English comedian Will Kempe (below) relied largely on physical skill. The medieval French showman with his dancing bear (below, left) was a forerunner of 19th-century amusements like this English "Equestrian Circus" (center).

In his great epic poem the *Odyssey*, Homer (p. 210) describes how, at the feast of King Alcinous, the floor was cleared and dancing boys mimed the action of a story as it was being sung by a blind poet, Demodocus. The tale Demodocus told concerned the gods, but it was racy and mocking, telling of the love of Ares and the goddess Aphrodite, and how they were both trapped by her husband, the lame Hephaestus, and exposed before the other immortals. "A fit of uncontrollable laughter seized these happy gods," sang Demodocus.

Hundreds of years later, another Greek writer, Xenophon, relates a similar incident. He tells us that at a banquet given for the philosopher Socrates, an entertainer from Syracuse (in Sicily) told the story of the love of Dionysus and the princess Ariadne. While he related the tale, it was mimed in dance and gesture by a slave boy and girl. Not only did the girl act in the plays, she also performed as an acrobat and sword dancer.

Here for the first time we meet the "actress." For centuries to come, women players belonged *only* to the theatre of entertainment. A woman of low social standing, the actress could take no part in religious ritual, or in the theatre of Dionysus, the *No* plays of Japan, or the Christian drama of the medieval church. Even in the professional theatre of Elizabethan England, young boys played all the female roles.

The episodes described by Homer and Xenophon are almost identical in character with the popular Greek and Roman plays called *mimes*. These were originally danced as silent accompaniment to the singing or recitation of a poet, but the mimes later developed into a spoken dialogue between two, three, or four performers. They became little plays, full of intrigue and realistic or homely detail. Each character was identified by the mask he wore. The gods were presented without reverence and shown in absurd situations; the language was colloquial, the jokes often obscene. These plays were acted on a bare stage made of boards set on trestles or barrels. At the back was hung a divided curtain behind which the players dressed, and through which they popped in and out.

The players tramped the roads from town to town, occasionally patronized by the fashionable world. Eventually some of their unwritten, extemporized plays were written down, or imitated, by literary men in Rome and other leading cities, but few examples have survived. Because of the lack of written evidence, most people are not aware of the great influence of the early theatre of entertainment upon the later development of the drama in the West.

Two masters of mime kept the harlequinade alive in the 19th century: Bohemian-born Gaspard Deburau (above, left), France's most famous clown; and England's great Joseph Grimaldi, portrayed in a scene from pantomime (below).

Supreme among circus clowns of the 20th century was Dr. Adrian Wettach, better known as "Grock." Born in Switzerland in 1880, he delighted audiences for 50 years.

The actor on the road

Throughout history the entertainer has always been uncertain of his place in society—at worst a penniless beggar, at best a favorite of princes. In Shakespeare's play *Twelfth Night*, the steward Malvolio says mockingly that Feste the clown "is gagged" unless people laugh at him. A 20th-century English comedian, Peter Sellers, has been quoted as saying: "You know, people hate a comic. They feel resentment against a comic. They sit there saying: 'Go on, make me laugh.' Once you have a reputation it's easier.... But if they don't know you.... Oh, I've stood up and died."

The people of the road—"rogues and vagabonds," as they were legally termed until the 19th century—have always suffered from both indifference and suspicion. Authority, whether represented by the Senate of ancient Rome, the fathers of the Christian Church, 17th-century Puritans, or 19th-century social reformers, has been against them. The 16th-century Spanish dramatist Lope de Vega and his English contemporary Ben Jonson were both imprisoned. Many others have suffered similarly for their way of life, down to the French playwright Jean Genêt in our own day. In the 17th century, the great French actor-playwright Molière (1622-73) was denied Christian burial. Carlo Goldoni (1707-93), whose plays kept Italy and France laughing for 60 years, died in poverty in Paris.

Many players, however, have won social acceptance—from Roscius in ancient Rome, who became a knight, to the English actor Sir Henry Irving (1838-1905), who, "for the sake of his profession," accepted from Queen Victoria the first knighthood ever offered to an English stage personage. The greatest of French tragic playwrights, Jean Racine (1639-99), left the theatre and took an official post at the court of Louis XIV. He wrote his last plays for the girls of a convent school at St. Cyr near Paris. The greatest of English dramatists, William Shakespeare (1564-1616), bought a coat-of-arms and the largest house in his native town, Stratford-upon-Avon.

Lesser men did the best they could. During the Middle Ages many players managed to gain a place in Church dramas by acting the parts of fools and devils. The good Christians who took the other roles were afraid to play these parts (in case the devil might "claim his own," as legend said he sometimes did). Some traveling actors obtained the reluctant patronage of town authorities and were granted permission to play at fair times, or in a guildhall or town square. A few, like hunchbacked Adam de la Halle (about 1240-86) from the French city of Arras, were lucky enough to be officially appointed as town minstrels.

The devil Astaroth, from a play by Jacob Ruff given in 1539. Traveling actors often took such parts, unpopular with local amateurs. As court fools, actors like Will Summers, below (with Henry VIII), had high social status.

A troupe of 17th-century French actors arrives at an inn, and another company performs on a portable stage nearby. From Comical Romance of a Company of Players *(1676).*

Whenever the city authorities were against them, as was often the case, the actors of the road sought the support of the nobility. At the end of the Middle Ages, Italian traveling companies became fashionable and built up their reputations until splendid troupes with flashy names like the *Confidenti* ("sure to please") were hired to enliven the wedding feasts of princes. In England, at the same period, actors gained rank and some security by taking service with the nobility—becoming, for example, Lord Strange's men, the Earl of Leicester's men, even the king's men. But service with the nobility did not prevent the actors from opening their own public playhouses. And in summer and times of plague they tramped the road as before.

The "life of the road" has been described best by the 17th-century Spanish player Augustin de Rojas Villandrando. His description starts with the humblest kind of performer who entered a village and acted his one or two pieces for a bit of bread and a bowl of soup. Only slightly more elaborate were the two players who went barefoot, but had a drum and a few properties, and even charged a small fee rather than beg. *Gangarilla* was the title given to a company of four actors, which included a fool and a boy to play women's parts. The *Boxiganga*, a larger group, included two actresses, could afford pack mules to carry the luggage, and actually slept in beds. The *Farandula* had perhaps 13 in the troupe, including three women, and traveled in carts. Largest and best equipped of all was a *Compania*, with a repertory of 50 plays, "16 persons who act, 30 who eat, and one who takes money at the door (and God knows what he steals)," says Augustin, slyly.

This satirical print of the late 18th century shows a troupe of traveling players performing a scene from Shakespeare's Macbeth *in an English country barn. A traveling actor is still called a "barnstormer" in some places.*

Two stock figures of Italian commedia dell' arte, *both masked, are shown in a 16th-century French woodcut. Each actor in this unscripted comedy specialized in a particular role, improvising his performance round a simple plot with traditional comic episodes.*

The theatre in the city

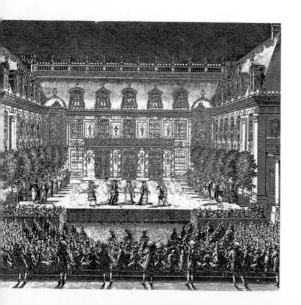

This pageant, pictured by a 17th-century Flemish painter, was held in Brussels, Belgium, in 1615 in honor of Princess Isabella of Spain. Townsfolk looking down from windows or lining the street—a natural setting for public celebrations—had a grandstand view of the passing show. Decorated wooden wagons of the same kind were used in street performances of religious plays given by craft guilds at Corpus Christi or Pentecost.

In its most elaborate form, the theatre has always belonged to the city. In a city there are enough people with money, talent, and resources to put up large buildings and to engage actors, painters, carpenters, musicians, dancers, writers, producers, and architects. The city is the setting for public celebration of victories, coronations, marriages, christenings, and processions of all kinds. In the city, too, live rich and sometimes idle people who require diversions and pastimes: balls and banquets, with "interludes" to amuse the guests.

Clever people from the country come to the city to make their fortunes. Specialists from abroad arrive there with new things to display. The city has academies and societies where people meet to argue, learn new ideas, listen to the wise and famous, criticize, commission new enterprises, and undertake experiments.

The city, however, can assume many attitudes toward the drama. In ancient Athens (around the 4th century B.C.), the drama was both a state ceremony and a religious ritual created for citizens. But the place of drama in the life of ancient Rome was very different. There,

17th-century French engraving depicting a scene from the opera Alceste, *with music by Lully and libretto by Quinault, performed in the open air at the palace of Versailles in 1676.*

conservative opinion saw it as a demoralizing and corrupting spectacle created by foreigners and slaves. The first Roman playwright, Livius, was a Greek slave. Plautus (about 254-184 B.C.) probably came to Rome from the northern province of Umbria, and he began his career by acting in mimes as a *planipes* ("flat-foot" clown). Terence (about 185-159 B.C.) was an African slave, born in Carthage and brought to Rome as the servant of a senator.

All the above men were writers of comedies. (There were many more, but only the plays of these three have survived.) Even about the comedies themselves there is an imported air; Greek costumes were worn, and they were full of Greek names. Many plots were imitated from the Greek comedies of Menander (now lost), but spiced with clowning and sharp, pithy, down-to-earth Latin observations. In Rome, tragedy was never a revered state ceremonial, but the literary activity of a learned minority. The only examples of tragedy that survive—the plays of Seneca (about 4 B.C.-A.D. 65)—were probably not even written for the stage, but were meant to be recited in places of public assembly and in private houses.

While Rome was growing to greatness, there was no permanent theatre in the city; plays were given in the open air at country festivals, or in the courtyards of great men's houses. The first stone theatre was built in 55 B.C. Then, as the empire extended its boundaries, theatres sprang up everywhere, even in the most remote provincial towns. For a time, drama became respectable. Lovers of literature studied playwriting; and it was to two such amateurs (the brothers Piso) that the poet Horace (65-8 B.C.) wrote a letter in verse, the *Epistula ad Pisones*, which later ages took as their textbook for the rules of drama. But all efforts to produce a truly serious Latin drama failed. Shows in the Roman theatres were light-hearted, trivial, and often obscene, though skilful and spectacular, with front curtains and elaborate scenery.

Roman drama, though inferior to the Greek, had a much greater influence. Rome conquered the world and gave it a common language. Latin was inherited, with much else of the Roman world, by the Christian Church. Then, at the end of the Middle Ages, classical Latin was revived as the basis of education and became the recognized international language of men of learning. For generations, the plays of Plautus and Terence were read and acted in schools. And it was the plays of Seneca rather than those of the great Greek dramatists that became the closely studied models for Renaissance writers of tragedy.

Romans enjoyed both Greek drama and sheer spectacle. Above: Greek comedy scene, from a first-century Roman marble. Below: 17th-century reconstruction of a mock sea-battle at the Colosseum.

Carnival processions are still as popular as ever all over the world. This elaborate float, topped by a satellite, was part of a procession at the Estoril Carnival, Portugal, in 1959.

Drama and the church

By the end of the fifth century A.D., the northern half of the Roman Empire had been overrun by Germanic and Celtic tribes. The theatres were deserted, and many fell into ruin. But we know that dramatic activity did not cease entirely. In the records of the monasteries, for example, there are references to traveling actors. From the few non-religious play-texts that survive, we know that these players still wore masks and could do dialogues and perform farces. And the character of their performances remained entirely pagan. This, naturally, provoked the fierce anger of the Church authorities, who took every opportunity to discourage these activities.

The texts of some Roman plays were preserved in monastery libraries, but for 500 years there was little or no organized dramatic activity. By the 10th century, however, a new form of drama began to appear. The Church, softening in its disapproval of play-acting, introduced short scenes as an extension of the Mass to illustrate the Christian story.

On holy days like Easter and Christmas, such scenes —called *tropes*—were acted. In one Easter trope that still survives, a monk, representing the angel at Christ's tomb, asks the three Marys (also played by monks) who come to anoint Christ's body: "Quem quaeritis . . .? [Whom seek ye? He is not here. He is risen as foretold.]" A Christmas trope also has three characters who are searching for Jesus: the shepherds coming to Bethlehem.

Later, the tropes became detached from the Mass and developed into a series of separate little plays. At Easter, for example, Roman soldiers guard Christ's tomb and fall asleep in spite of their boasting. In a trope for Christmas, King Herod, the most famous dramatic "character" of medieval drama, speaks with the three kings seeking the infant Christ.

Phrases and songs in local dialect were added gradually to the Latin texts, and eventually the plays were performed throughout Europe in the different national languages. Platform stages were built—first inside, then outside the church. Various scenic effects were also introduced. With the appearance of shepherds seeking the Christ child, for instance, the star of Bethlehem, hung on wires, would often be drawn before them as they moved down the church nave toward the steps of the high altar, where the figures of Joseph and Mary awaited them.

We know a great deal about the Church drama of the Middle Ages because the texts were preserved and copied by the monks. Many of these texts are very long and include music, stage directions, pictures of scenes and

The Resurrection of Christ. *This English alabaster of about 1400 shows how the scene of Christ rising from the dead was probably portrayed in the Church's early medieval trope dramas.*

In The Death and Assumption of the Virgin, *15th-century Italian artist Gerolamo da Vicenza borrowed ideas from the stage effects used in Church drama of his day. The Virgin rises above a painted landscape (background) flanked by the façades of houses.*

costumes, and drawings of mechanical devices and effects. The trope, which had begun as part of the Church service, had become a show for an audience.

All sorts of dramatic themes were soon drawn from the Bible. The *Mystère d'Adam* (Anglo-Norman, about 1150) has Adam and Eve in the garden, Cain and Abel, prophets and devils. Each abbey and cathedral also had its own playlets for the feast of its patron saint. Of these so-called *miracle plays*—plays based upon a saint's life and miracles—there still survive some on the life of St. Nicholas, written originally for the great Benedictine Abbey of Fleury in France. By the beginning of the 13th century, the St. Nicholas plays had grown to include parts for three thieves who spoke realistic dialogue and had "underworld" names: *Cliquet* (jabberer); *Pincedé* (dice-twister); *Rasoir* (sharper).

By 1300 trade expansion had contributed to the growing size and independence of the towns of Western Europe. To maintain the influence of the Church and ensure the continued religious devotion of the townsfolk, new orders of teaching monks were established. In 1311, a new processional summer feast, *Corpus Christi*, was established. This, with *Pentecost* (Whitsun), became a recognized time for dramatic activity. There were some towns where a procession of decorated wagons carrying actors would stop at a number of points, and at each place a play would be given. More often, the town square was prepared with tiers of benches for the spectators, while, across one end, *mansiones* (houses) for the various scenes were built on a wide raised platform.

In some places plays were given by guilds of craftsmen; in others there were special drama clubs, whose members met throughout the year to prepare the annual performance. The most ambitious clubs engaged professional presenters (p. 272), who could rewrite a script, design scenery and costumes, supervise music, and plan such tricks as making an angel descend from heaven or cutting off John the Baptist's head.

Oldest in origin, but the last form of medieval drama to develop, was the *morality* play. The moralities were often short—like *Everyman* (about 1500), which exists in Dutch, English, and German versions. But they were sometimes very long, like the ambitious English *Castel of Perseverance* (about 1425), which took half a day to perform. Their hero was always Mankind. Sometimes he was tempted by the Seven Deadly Sins, and sought refuge with Wisdom or Charity. In others, betrayed by Avarice, arrested by Death, and tried before the throne of God, he was saved by Mercy and Peace from the horrors of Hell.

The multiple set pictured in this 16th-century miniature by Hubert Cailleau was erected at Valenciennes, France, in 1547, for an open-air performance of the Mystery of the Passion.

265

The actor in the playhouse

From the end of the Roman Empire until the middle of the 16th century (more than a thousand years) not a single permanent theatre was built in Europe. Once a year the religious plays were given in the open air, and elaborate, but temporary, settings were prepared for them. City squares and the courtyards of palaces were filled with scaffolding and stages. Once a year, on the festival of Corpus Christi or at Pentecost (p. 265), the great decorated pageant-wagons went their rounds. But all these things were "insubstantial pageants," as Shakespeare called them, prepared for the occasion and then put away for another year, unless required for a special day of public celebration, such as a royal wedding.

The building of permanent playhouses (which began in the 16th century) was a change that was to have far-reaching results. To build and maintain the playhouses required large sums of money and created many new problems. For instance, as long as actors continued to travel from place to place, a cart could hold their costumes and properties. A repertory of about 20 plays was plenty to offer at the fairs and great houses at which such companies called on their journey. But when a company put up a permanent playhouse, they could not fill it more than two or three times for the same play, even in a large city like London or Madrid, where play-going soon became a popular pastime.

Running a theatre soon changed from an informally run affair into a business. Sometimes this was organized on the basis of what we today might call a co-operative, with sharers. The father of Shakespeare's colleagues Richard and Cuthbert Burbage built the first English playhouse in 1576, and gave it a Greek-inspired name: *The Theatre*. It was erected on leased, not fully owned, ground; and there were so many disagreements with the landlord that, after their father's death, the brothers moved away and built a new playhouse, *The*

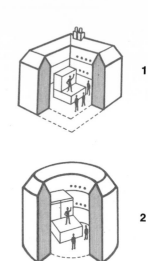

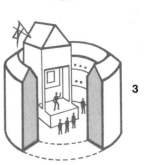

In the Middle Ages traveling actors would often put up their simple stage in the courtyard of an inn (1). The earliest permanent playhouses were constructed on similar lines (2), with spectators either standing round the stage or sitting in galleries. By the end of the 16th century a "machine room" was often built over the stage, from which scenic devices and even actors could be lowered (3).

The theatres of ancient Rome were the model for the Teatro Olimpico at Vicenza, Italy, designed in 1580 by Andrea Palladio.

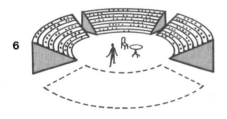

During the 17th century, as more and more indoor theatres were built, staging became increasingly elaborate (4). Painted panels sliding in grooves or on wheels could be arranged to give different backgrounds. Illumination was provided by candles or oil lamps. By the middle of the 19th century the stage was framed by the proscenium arch (5). Gas and, later, electric stage lighting added to the realism of the box set and left little to the imagination of the spectator. Today, the "theatre in the round" (6) brings actors once more into closer contact with audiences.

Globe. It was here that some of Shakespeare's plays were performed for the first time. The Burbage company was a co-operative enterprise, as were the French players at the Hôtel de Bourgogne in Paris and the famous *Comédie Française*, established in the 17th century.

Elsewhere, an actor-manager would engage a troupe of actors to play for a season and pay them weekly wages. He often added extra inducements to the leading players in the form of "benefit nights," when they might choose the play and have all profits. Not until the end of the 19th century were actors engaged "for the run of the piece"— that is, to perform the same play night after night, perhaps for hundreds of performances—for as long, in fact, as there were sufficient people wanting to see it.

There was, naturally, keen competition to choose the best sites for theatres, to build them larger and more sumptuous, and to get the best actors and the best plays. But professional companies were not the only ones to open playhouses. A private patron—a king, prince, cardinal, or rich merchant—might build a theatre of his own (as Cardinal Richelieu did in the Palais Royal in Paris in 1641). A society, corporation, or academy might do the same. For instance, the Accademia Olympica, founded in the northern Italian town of Vicenza in 1556, built the famous *Teatro Olympico* in order to give occasional performances of ancient Greek and Roman dramas. Private patrons, however, rarely maintained their own companies of players; they usually engaged professional companies to play for them when required.

There were many advantages in this system for both patron and players. For example, the patron did not want to keep his theatre open all year round; he wanted only occasional, lavishly staged performances. The actor, on the other hand, was glad to have the support, protection, and prestige that such distinguished patronage gained for him.

But a patron was less likely to be interested in drama than in pageantry and spectacle, for that was what court entertainments had always been based on. The court of a king or nobleman could afford to spend very large sums on machines for stage effects, curtains, and painted scenery, and to engage the best artists to prepare them. So stage scenery, as we know it, began in the court theatres. It then spread gradually, by imitation, into the public playhouses. The actors, who had once stood alone on the stage, the single focus of everyone's attention, and who had relied upon words and gestures alone to set the scene of the dramatic action in the imagination of the audience, found, as time went on, that they were surrounded by increasingly elaborate painted settings.

Covent Garden Theatre, London, in 1804. In the pit, audiences sat on backless benches; auditorium remained lit during performance. Orchestra sat in double row at edge of stage.

Four moods in four words

Four moods—*baroque, classical, romantic,* and *realistic*—predominated in the arts between 1600 and 1900. Among the arts, the drama was often the best public showcase for displaying the characteristics of each mood.

The great 17th-century Italian stage designer Francesco da Bibiena created this baroque setting for an oratorio based on the life of David, performed at the Viennese court.

The word BAROQUE *probably comes from the Portuguese word* barroco *— a large, curiously shaped pearl. Certainly, one characteristic of 17th-century baroque art was its delight in the irregular, odd, and grotesque. As a result of the fierce religious divisions and wars in the first half of the century, man's earlier faith in himself and his powers was badly shaken. Thus, madness, ruin, and death are preoccupations of baroque art and drama. All baroque art is, so to speak, theatrical, but the outstanding dramatic achievements of this period were costly court entertainments (pp. 178 and 262), famous for their lavish spectacle rather than for their literary quality. Here (left) is a typical baroque scene design. Everything, including the archway set at an angle to the stage, is loaded with ornament and is fantastic and a little overpowering.*

This classical stage setting was designed by Italy's Giacomo Torelli for a production of Andromède *(by the great French dramatist Pierre Corneille) in Paris in 1651.*

The term CLASSICAL *(when applied to art) usually means that of ancient Greece and Rome; but it is also used to describe the art produced by a society or period that has decided upon certain fixed values and a code of rules that are accepted as a justifiable discipline. In terms of drama, these rules are the "unities" of time, place, and action (a play must have a single story, set in one place in one day) derived by Renaissance theorists largely from the writings of Horace (p. 262). Disciplined classical art need not be cold; the plays of Racine (p. 260), for example, deal passionately with the deepest human emotions. In the design here (left), the influence of classicism is obvious. Balanced and regular, the scene is placed squarely before the audience. The ornament is simple and dignified, yet elegantly splendid.*

The ROMANTIC artist does not speak for society, but as a rebel. He may well regard civilization as corrupted because it has departed from a "natural" way of life; thus, the past is judged better than the present and the country preferred to the town. The savage is seen as more "natural" than man in civilized society, the child than the adult. The most important experience for a romantic artist is "romantic love," in which the beloved is an unsophisticated "child of nature"—a peasant girl, for instance, or a stranger from a distant land. Romantic drama of the late 18th and early 19th centuries also loved the exotic and remote—above all, the Middle Ages: knights, castles, fair damsels. Romantic drama delighted to show the dramatic face of nature: mountains, moonlight, and storm. At its worst, it escaped from reality and true feeling into the exaggerations of melodrama.

English artist Thomas Grieve created this atmospheric view of Elsinore Castle as one of his romantic stage designs for Charles Kean's London production of Hamlet *(1858).*

REALISM *grew out of romanticism in two ways. Romantic love of the past led to the desire to present past events accurately in the theatre, with convincing period costume, armor, and architecture. Then this painstaking accuracy was transferred from the past to the present, and the "box" set was created, with real doors and windows, furniture, stoves, and properties, and even a real roof, as in this scene of a hut in the Crimea (right). The realist may share the romantic view that civilization is corrupt, but he tries to show the world for what it is, in all its aspects, rather than to escape from it. Thus, playwrights of the late 19th and early 20th centuries claimed the right to speak in everyday language of any subject they chose. Scorning "light entertainment," they gave a new seriousness to the role of drama in modern society.*

This early example of a "box" set was designed by Charles S. James in 1866 for a London production of Ours *by the English realist playwright Tom Robertson.*

The triumphs of realism

Drama has usually aimed to convince audiences that the events happening on the stage are *real*. Medieval players decorated their scenes of Paradise with real oranges and dates, and sometimes with a naked Adam and Eve as well. Actors in the time of Shakespeare stabbed a concealed bladder of pig's blood to make their wounds convincing. But however real Hamlet seemed on the stage, no one expected to meet him in the street.

The theatre is a place of "let's pretend." Once the performance begins, we are no longer in the theatre but, for example, in Venice—because that city is the scene of the play. Whatever we may have read about Miss X, the actress, in the theatre we are ready to believe in her as, for example, an innocent young maiden—if that is her "character" in the play. "Realistic" drama is an art of illusion; it wants the audience to forget that it is pretending, and to believe that for the time being scenes of real life are actually happening on the stage.

Many changes took place in the theatre to make the illusion of realism increasingly possible. First, the stage and audience had to be completely separated (in France, the great writer and prolific dramatist Voltaire achieved this in the 18th century). The actor withdrew behind a proscenium arch (p. 266), which now surrounded the stage setting like a frame around a picture. Gas lighting for the theatre was perfected in the middle of the 19th century. With gas, it became possible to darken the auditorium and concentrate the attention of the audience on the stage. Until then, the audience had always thought of the theatre as a place of rendezvous, where one might eat, drink, talk, and flirt (as people still do in a modern cabaret or in the theatres of China and Japan).

The stage picture had also to be changed. The old scenery had been painted on tall panels called *flats*, between which the actors entered (p. 267). In the mid-19th century a few pioneers like Heinrich Laube (at the Vienna *Burgtheater*) began to build stage settings like real rooms, with windows, doors, furniture, and ceilings. The old style of acting, with its formal gestures, seemed out of place in these surroundings. And so did old forms of stage speech. Solid, sober citizens, sitting in a well-furnished drawing room, could not be expected to speak in verse—because solid citizens never do.

"Verse will find hardly any place worth mentioning in the drama of the near future, for the literary purposes of the future will certainly not be reconciled with it. It will therefore disappear. I myself in the last seven or eight years have hardly written a single verse, but have exclusively cultivated the far more difficult art of writing in the plain truthful language of reality." So wrote Henrik

In medieval drama Adam and Eve were played by actors dressed in white leather or actually naked, as in this 15th-century drawing.

An 18th-century print showing how viewers in candle-lit theatres often ignored the play.

A Parisian audience at a melodrama, pictured by 19th-century French artist Daumier. Gas lighting, introduced into theatres during the 19th century, meant that the auditorium could be darkened, focusing attention on the stage.

Ibsen (1828-1906), whose career sums up the realistic movement. Ibsen began as a romantic poet. He belonged to a small country, Norway, which was ruled by Sweden, and so much dominated by the culture of Denmark that it had no standard language of its own. "Freedom" was one of the great battle cries of romanticism; Ibsen and his generation fought for Norwegian independence. They started a National Theatre at Bergen, and Ibsen became assistant to the director there. His first plays were in verse, on patriotic themes, and set in the Middle Ages—for example, *The Feast at Solhaug* (1855) and *The Vikings at Helgeland* (1860).

Increasingly critical of the narrowness of Norwegian life, Ibsen eventually left Norway, not to return for 27 years. His last verse plays were *Brand* (1865), on religious bigotry, and the magnificent *Peer Gynt* (1867). Then, "in the plain truthful language of reality," he began his series of plays on the corruption of public life and the destructive power of hypocrisy, beginning with *The Pillars of Society* and *A Doll's House* in the 1870s and ending with *Hedda Gabler*, written in 1890. In form these plays are severely classical (p. 268). In them, by constant probing and dramatic revelation, Ibsen gradually strips the motives of the characters bare of all pretense.

The realists broke down the romantic distinction between "beauty" and "ugliness." They argued that because real life contains ugly, coarse, and trivial things, art should contain them too. Nationalism and social reform were great driving forces in realist art. "If civilization is corrupt, let's change it," said the realists.

But realism had to overcome both technical difficulties and public opposition. How can you make boredom interesting and uneventful lives dramatic? If you want to show the surface of life, how can you also tell the audience what is going on beneath the surface? The great realists, like Ibsen, overcame these difficulties by writing freshly and courageously. They made drama matter, as it had not done for a long time.

This drawing (based on an 1891 French production) shows Hedwig's suicide in Ibsen's The Wild Duck. *The Norwegian dramatist's revolutionary realism demanded everyday settings.*

A scene from Konstantin Stanislavski's production (1902) of The Lower Depths *by Maxim Gorki. Stanislavski, the father of the modern Russian theatre, demanded realism in acting as well as in settings and costumes, and he gave meticulous care to detail. He began this production by sending his actors to live in the Moscow slums so that they could convincingly portray beggars.*

French miniature of the 15th century depicting a "presenter," book in hand, directing a performance of The Martyrdom of Saint Apollonia. *Presenters, who fulfilled many of the functions of the modern stage director, were often hired to organize religious plays.*

Enter the director

Until the end of the 19th century, most dramatic companies were organized round a leading actor or actor-manager who chose the plays and allotted the roles. At his worst, the actor-manager was selfish and greedy, quite content so long as his (or her) performance was applauded. On the other hand, many actor-managers were serious artists, and they fulfilled all the functions of the modern director.

There are still actor-managers, like Jean-Louis Barrault and Jean Vilar in France or Sir Laurence Olivier in England. But the controlling personality of a modern theatrical company is likely to be the director. He is responsible for training and discipline, and he must be a man capable of mastering detail, arousing enthusiasm, and communicating ideas. The director, in this sense, is not a new person in the theatre, as some people think. The dramatic poets of ancient Greece, like Sophocles and Aeschylus (p. 256), undertook very much the same role as the modern director, for they rehearsed their actors and dancers and supervised music and costumes, as well as writing and often acting in the plays themselves. The professional *presenters* (p. 264), who organized the elaborate *mystery* and *miracle* plays for the medieval craft guilds and drama societies, were also clearly performing a similar function to that of the director as we know him today.

There was a time when nearly everyone agreed how a play should be written and acted; there were conventions that everyone knew and observed. A tragedy, for instance, had to be in verse and in five acts, and it had to have a prince as its hero. Today, the director chooses among many conflicting conventions. He may be faced with the subtle comedy of the Russian dramatist Anton Chekhov (1860-1904), the swift gusto of an American "musical," or a surrealist farce by the contemporary Eugène Ionesco (born in Romania, 1912). How are actors to be trained for these very different types of play? What kind of stage setting do they need? The director must be a judge not only of drama and acting, but also of other arts, like those of painting, music, and dancing, each of which may contribute much to the theatrical effects he is able to achieve. For a similar reason, he must also master the technical resources of theatrical equipment, such as lighting and stage machinery.

Naturally, there are few people who have had all these talents. From the few who have, let us look at three whose work has been most influential: Jacques Copeau (1879-1949) in France; Konstantin Alexyev (called Stanislavski; 1863-1938) in Russia; and Bertolt Brecht (1898-1956) in Germany.

Actor-managers of the 19th century took great care over the production of plays in which they starred. Sir Henry Irving's long career at London's Lyceum Theatre won him knighthood. Sketch shows 1893 rehearsal.

Jacques Copeau: Copeau was originally a writer. In Paris, at the *Théâtre Libre* (Free Theatre) founded by André Antoine (1857-1943), he saw dramatic realism at its best—and rebelled against it. Copeau converted a building in a Parisian side street, the Rue du Vieux Colombier, into a theatre. Its stage was based upon those of Shakespeare's time and had a simple, permanent setting. There Copeau produced poetic and classical plays, but he was not satisfied with the results. He decided he must train a company who could act together in a unified style and attract playwrights to write for them. From this training emerged the *Compagnie des Quinze* ("Company of Fifteen") directed by his nephew, Michel Saint-Denis. Others who studied with Copeau and later became famous were Louis Jouvet, Charles Dullin, and Valentine Tessier.

Stanislavski: The world-famous Moscow Art Theatre was founded by Stanislavski and his friend and partner Nemirovitch-Danchenko in 1897. In 1898, they presented *The Seagull,* a new play by Anton Chekhov, then virtually unknown as a playwright. Stanislavski was a fine actor and an outstanding director, but he was greatest of all as a teacher. He took exceptional care when producing a play—describing to the actors the lives of the characters they were to act, and often using a year or more of rehearsal for a single production. As a teacher, he sought psychological truth; he wanted the actors to be able to command the mood and effects they needed. The Moscow Art Theatre survived its infancy and the Russian Revolution of 1917 to become the largest and most influential dramatic organization in the world. Stanislavski's influence had a second flowering in America after World War II, with the development of so-called "method" acting in the New York Actors' Studio.

Bertolt Brecht: Brecht began as a playwright in Germany, after World War I, in an atmosphere of defeat, famine, and violence. When the Nazis came to power in 1933, he was driven into exile. In America he continued to write plays in German until after World War II, when he returned to East Berlin and created a new company, the Berliner Ensemble.

Brecht wanted the theatre to be a place of matter-of-fact, not a place of make-believe. Because he hated the atmosphere of magic and illusion, he stripped the stage of painted scenery and encouraged his actors to speak directly to the audience, forbidding them to identify themselves with the characters they played. An actor, he said, must not *become* King Lear, he must *show us* King Lear, remaining always critically detached and encouraging the audience to do so, too.

Russia's renowned Konstantin Stanislavski acting in his own production (1902) of Maxim Gorki's play The Lower Depths.

Jacques Copeau, outstanding among French directors and actors of the 20th century, in La Carrosse de Saint-Sacrement (*1920*).

Germany's brilliant dramatist Bertolt Brecht directing one of his plays. Brecht's rejection of conventional stagecraft in his self-styled "epic" drama has greatly influenced the modern theatre in many countries.

Show business and art theatre

Until the 18th century, even the largest European cities had only a few hundred thousand inhabitants. Such cities could not maintain many permanent theatres. At night the unlighted streets were dangerous, for there were no regular police. Many patrons lived close to the playhouse or came in their own carriages. Others were carried in sedan chairs, accompanied by servants bearing torches or lanterns.

With the rapid growth of industry at the end of the century, cities grew quickly. Street lighting and professional police were introduced. Better roads and, later, railways brought people easily in and out of the cities, carried audiences to the theatres, and bore companies of actors from town to town with their costumes and scenery.

After the middle of the 19th century, theatres began to cluster in favored districts of the chief cities: along the boulevards of Paris, in the West End of London, on Broadway in New York. Improved lighting by gas—and later electricity—and improved building techniques made possible the construction of larger and more comfortable theatres, with cushioned seats instead of wooden benches. Details of performances were published regularly in the new daily newspapers. Eventually, the theatres were able to present plays for a long run, sometimes for hundreds of nights, and then send them on tour to many other cities. Success meant a fortune for those concerned—but failure meant catastrophe.

The commercial theatre has always felt the competition of every novelty of taste and fashion. In the 17th century its chief rival was grand opera; in the 18th century, pleasure gardens with their concerts, fireworks, and other alfresco (open air) entertainments. In the 1850s came the vaudeville or music hall, with its popular songs and knockabout humor. By the 1920s the cinema, at first a novelty in fairground sideshows (p. 282), became a world-wide industry of mass entertainment (and was itself to be threatened after World War II by television).

Through all these changes serious drama has somehow managed to survive. It has been kept alive by the fanatical devotion it inspires in those who love it, by the greatness of its tradition, and by the sense of ritual that goes with it. Going to the theatre is an occasion for most people; it involves effort, choice, and expectation. The actors are your servants, creating something personally for each audience. But the drama can survive only by finding something new all the time—and by training a public to understand and like new things. This the commercial theatre, with its eye naturally on the box office, can rarely do.

The spacious Second Park Theatre, New York (pictured here by artist John Searle), was built in 1821 to seat 2700 people. Many new theatres of this kind sprang up in America and Europe in the early 19th century.

Open-air concert in Vauxhall Gardens, London, in 1784 (from a painting by Thomas Rowlandson). Most European cities had similar pleasure gardens at the time.

London music hall, 1880. Music halls, where audiences ate and drank during performances, developed from tavern entertainments.

Playgoers accustomed to French classical drama rioted (as depicted above) at the first performance of Victor Hugo's romantic play Hernani *in Paris (1830). Experiment was easier for such privately sponsored companies as that founded by Germany's Duke George II of Saxe-Meiningen, who made the sketch below in 1887 to define the crowd movements in Johann von Schiller's* Maid of Orleans.

The triviality of much commercial entertainment long ago produced a movement calling for reform : the so-called "art theatre." The idea of an "art theatre" was rooted in the romantic movement (p. 268), with its contempt for the vulgarity of a world that insufficiently valued the artist and his gift of imagination. When, for instance, the play *Hernani* by Victor Hugo (1802-85) was produced in France in 1830, its romantic, revolutionary character led to rioting in the theatre. In England, at the same period, the actor-manager William Macready was attempting to create a truly national theatre. He commissioned plays by new writers, revived old plays, and freed the text of Shakespeare's plays from the alterations made to them in the past.

But the real fathers of the art theatre were found in Germany, with its ardent theorists and princely patrons, able to finance non-profit-making experiments. In the 18th century Konrad Ekhof (1720-78) and his pupil Friedrich Schröller (1744-1816) set up a National Theatre in Hamburg and the first academy for actors; and they introduced Shakespeare to the German stage. Then, in 1874, Duke George II of the small German state of Saxe-Meiningen, with his actress wife, Ellen Franz, and his stage director, Ludwig Chronegk, founded a theatrical company of a new kind. The company of the "theatre duke" was notable for its discipline, perfection, and polish. In the Meiningen company, rehearsals (unlike those in most theatres of the time) were regular and meticulous. The director supervised everything. Settings, movements of actors, even crowd scenes —all were carefully planned. In 1881, the *Meininger*, as this company were called, began to travel. They were acclaimed wherever they went, setting new standards and inspiring others. The modern art theatres of the Western world are the spiritual inheritors of the *Meininger*.

New times, new plays, new theatres

Dramatic realism (p. 270) produced great masterpieces such as the plays of Ibsen, but at a very heavy price. First of all, it was a wasteful way of working. To be realistic, a play must occupy itself with many theatrically unimportant matters: answering doors, explaining the presence of characters, and serving them food and drink. Realism took away from the actor not only the economy and expressiveness of verse, but also such dramatic forms of prose as rhetoric and declamation. Realism limited the actor's use of his body; he was restricted to the gestures of ordinary life, and he could only dance or sing if the plot gave him a reason for these activities.

The dramatist became worried over minor matters. Anxious to create the appearance of real life, he found himself faced with many technical difficulties, and was constantly plagued with problems of detail. Should characters speak with their backs to the audience, as in real life? Should a character be made to speak in a dialect so authentic that most of the audience would be unable to understand him? Finally, realism was reduced to absurdity in the hackneyed three-act play with its unchanged set: windows to the garden, staircase to the bedrooms, and the inevitable telephone for messages from afar. But the cinema came along and stole the stage's thunder as far as realism was concerned.

Opposition to slavish realism had been growing for a long time. It began in the 1890s. The Swiss designer, Adolphe Appia (1862-1928), went to see the operas of the great German composer, Richard Wagner (p. 156), and was disgusted with the naturalistic way they were staged, with rocks made of wood and canvas, and branches of real foliage. It was his idea to replace these with simple, three-dimensional shapes—which would heighten the effect of the actors' movements, not obscure them. An English designer, Gordon Craig (born 1872), quite independently came to similar conclusions. The task of the drama, he claimed, was to *make*, not to *copy*. The revolutionary scenic effects achieved by both Appia and Craig often relied on the subtle arrangement of bare, uncluttered masses and the imaginative use of color and, especially, lighting. Instead of simply illuminating a painted setting, the newly introduced electric lighting was used as a dramatic element in the total stage picture.

In Ireland, the poet and playwright W. B. Yeats (p. 206) brought a *No* actor from Japan (p. 254) to help him train the actors of the Abbey Theatre in Dublin. Yeats asked Gordon Craig and the French artist Edmund Dulac to design masks, and asked that they should represent "heroic or grotesque types, *keeping always an appropriate distance from life.*"

A scene from The Liars *by the English dramatist Henry Arthur Jones, produced in 1897. The realistic drawing room is typical of late 19th-century stage settings.*

At the turn of the century, the Swiss stage designer Adolphe Appia introduced bold settings with simple forms, dramatic lighting. He designed this striking set for an 1892 production of Wagner's opera The Valkyrie.

The writings and drawings of England's Gordon Craig (born 1872) have been a major influence on the 20th-century theatre. His sketch for Hamlet *(1910) combines bold design with a revolutionary use of lighting.*

In The Dream Play (*1902*), *Sweden's August Strindberg contrasts the wretchedness of man with the innocence of an immortal (right).*

Against background of New England puritanism, Eugene O'Neill retold ancient Greek tragedy in modern psychological terms in his trilogy Mourning Becomes Electra (*1931*).

In Sweden, August Strindberg (1849-1912), who had been a leading dramatist of the realist theatre, began, in his last plays, to write something quite different : plays in short scenes, with generalized characters labeled with general, descriptive titles (The Officer, The Billposter, etc.) instead of individual names. These plays, beginning with *To Damascus* (1899), are filled with the quality of dream and fantasy, uncovering the unconscious motives from which our words and actions spring. This new kind of play developed, especially in Germany and America, into what was called *expressionist* drama. Characteristic plays of this movement are those of Georg Kaiser (1878-1945) and Ernst Toller (1893-1939) in Germany; the later plays of the Irishman Sean O'Casey; works by the Group Theatre playwrights W. H. Auden and Christopher Isherwood in Britain; and in America, some of the later plays of Eugene O'Neill (1888-1953).

In the period since the end of World War II the rival attitudes of realism and expressionism have come closer together. In the theatre there have been many examples of combination and adjustment between the hitherto opposed points of view of actuality and fantasy. Realism has survived because of the great prestige of its masterpieces, and because it has become the common artistic language that everyone understands. But dramatic reality is no longer identified simply with the use of real tables and chairs in real drawing rooms. Realism has learned to moderate its delight in such things, and is now ready to admit that a room with only three walls, however convincing, is still a piece of make-believe. The realist playwrights may now choose an illiterate delinquent for a hero and let him speak words characteristic of his type. But they have also learned to allow an actor a long speech in prose, or even in verse, and are prepared to make use of song and dance.

The best of recent plays unite actuality and the dream on a much deeper level. Such plays as those of Ionesco (p. 272) and Samuel Beckett (author of *Waiting for Godot*) in France, Friedrich Dürrenmatt and Max Frisch in Switzerland, Harold Pinter in England, and Tennessee Williams in America are both fantastic and convincingly *real*.

Rebellion has also affected the stage itself. For some plays, everyone now agrees, the proscenium stage is not the best setting ; and so new types of theatre (for instance, the so-called "theatre in the round") are now being designed. Experiments still continue in the search for more effective theatrical styles—at "an appropriate distance from life," as Yeats said.

Prototype of many modern enigmatic dramas is Samuel Beckett's Waiting for Godot, *written in 1952. It tells of two bewildered tramps whose apparently pointless lives may symbolize the human condition.*

277

Chapter 11

Film

From a scientific novelty, motion-picture making has grown within half a century into a great industry. At first it was simply a matter of taking a motion-picture camera into the street and recording any activity or incident that happened to be of interest. Today, however, it has become a lengthy and highly technical process involving vast sums of money and requiring the collaboration of hundreds of skilled people. There are now film-production centers in almost all countries of the world, and the number of movies that achieve a world-wide showing grows each year.

Is it possible for anything so complex and commercialized to produce works of art? With so many people involved in making a film, can any one of them be singled out as the creative mind behind all this activity? The answer to both questions is yes. Many motion pictures have been outstanding artistic successes; and their success has generally depended on the guiding imagination of one person : the director.

All those whose talents and skills contribute to the making of a film—such as the writers, actors, and camera men—must work in the closest collaboration with the director. It is his planning that gives the film its final shape. Thus he is the key artist in an art that influences almost every aspect of contemporary social life.

The movies are surely the most widespread form of mass entertainment the world has ever known. Moreover, the techniques of the cinema—especially in the way they are able to manipulate the factors of space and time—have greatly influenced the techniques of other arts. But it is in its ability to record and arrange moving images that the art of the "movies" remains unique.

Although motion pictures are no more than shadows cast on a screen, they have a compelling power. They have provided many creative artists of the 20th century with a unique opportunity to reveal new aspects of nature and of life. The film maker may choose to teach or to entertain. He may portray humanity in the mass, pinpoint the individual, or, like the greatest of actor-directors, Charlie Chaplin, in The Gold Rush (1925), *he may brilliantly combine the two.*

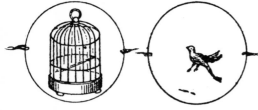

For over nine hundred years Javanese have used shadow puppets to cast moving pictures on a screen.

Birth of the cinema

From earliest times man has wanted to make pictures that move. Prehistoric cave dwellers, seated around a log fire, probably amused their children with finger-shadow faces cast on the rough walls of their caves. One of the oldest forms of mechanical moving pictures still in use is the stick-puppet play of Java. In such plays, silhouette figures manipulated in front of an oil lamp produce moving shadows on a screen. In 19th-century Europe, many kinds of apparatus were invented that tried to produce an impression of *continuous* movement. One such device, which became a popular toy, was known as the *zoetrope*, or "wheel of life." A strip of drawings representing a figure in successive stages of an action—such as jumping a wall or climbing a ladder—was placed on the inside of a drum, in the top of which was a series of slits. As the drum was revolved, a person looking through the slits got the impression that the figure actually moved.

The zoetrope and similar toys depended for their effect upon the fact that our eyes tend to retain an image for a fraction of a second after it has actually passed. Thus, when one image is swiftly followed by another that is only slightly different, we have the impression of seeing both images, superimposed upon each other, as one *moving* image. This so-called "persistence of vision" is the fundamental principle upon which cinematography is based.

But the birth of the cinema as we know it had to wait for two developments. First, there had to be a way of providing a large enough number of pictures to show the progress of really complex actions. Secondly, there had to be a way of showing such pictures to a number of people at once—improving on the early zoetrope, which could be enjoyed by only one person at a time.

The invention of photography provided the beginnings of a solution to the first problem. In 1839, France's Louis Daguerre and Britain's William Fox Talbot independently perfected the first successful photographic processes. Photography could be used to record subjects that would previously have taken a long time to draw or to paint. It was found that the split-second speed of the camera's action was also able to reveal movements too fast for the human eye to detect, such as the beating wings of an insect.

In the 19th century optical toys like the thaumatrope became popular. When the disks were spun, the two images combined.

Boxers painted on this 19th-century zoetrope seemed to perform a series of jerky actions as the drum turned. Natural movement was first analyzed by photographers like France's E.-J. Marey, who shot a sequence of a bird flying.

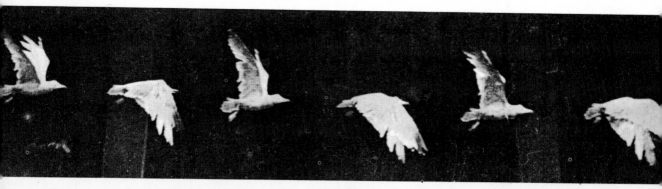

In 1872 Britain's Eadweard Muybridge began to project sequences like the one above by printing photographs onto a revolving disk.

In 1869 the world's first plastic material, Celluloid, appeared on the American market. It was soon discovered that this new material could be made into a transparent flexible film and used, instead of glass, for making photographic negatives and prints. This was a big step toward modern cinematography. The next step was the invention of a camera that could take many thousands of photographs on a strip of film instead of only one at a time.

In 1888 Thomas Edison (1847-1931), the famous American inventor, began experiments with motion-picture devices to be synchronized with the recorded sounds of the phonograph (invented by Edison in 1876). Using strips of Celluloid film, Edison and his young Scottish assistant, W. K. Dickson, achieved success with the kinetograph camera, patented in 1889. The moving pictures produced by this machine were shown in a viewer called the kinetoscope, but could be seen by only one person at a time.

The kinetoscope soon became so popular in amusement arcades that a way of projecting its pictures onto a screen was bound to follow. In America a man named Thomas Armat eventually brought out the vitascope, which did just that. The vitascope's first public screening took place in 1896.

Since then, the cinema's basic tools—a camera and a projector (which works at the same speed as the camera and flashes successive images onto a screen by means of a powerful electric lamp)—have remained fundamentally unchanged.

By 1889 America's Thomas Edison and George Eastman had perfected a flexible Celluloid film strip. It carried a series of transparencies that were moved by teeth that engaged in the perforated frame.

It was a long step from Edison's kinetoscope arcades (above) to the modern cinema projector. Edison's machine produced one-inch images that could be seen only by one person; today's audience may number thousands.

Diagram shows how modern projector works. As each frame of film (1) passes before a beam of light from carbon filament lamp (2), a shadow-image is projected through magnifying lenses (3) onto screen (4). At the same time rotating shutter (5) masks transition between frames. Sound track, converted by photoelectric cell unit (6), is carried through amplifier (7) to loudspeaker behind screen (8).

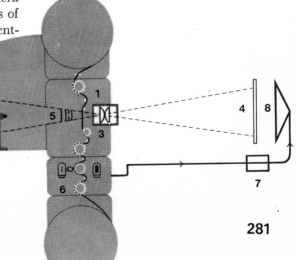

The first films seen by the public were French —short scenes from life (above) shown by the Lumières in 1895. Viewers panicked to see a train apparently steaming toward them.

The early years

At first Thomas Edison regarded his kinetoscope (p. 280) and the other motion-picture machines of the time as little more than passing novelties. Although earning a handsome profit from the hire of kinetoscopes to amusement arcades, Edison felt that if the "living pictures" were seen by more than one person at a time they would soon lose their attraction. Titles such as *What the Boot-black Saw* indicate the trivial character of most of these peepshow movies.

But some of the early pioneers of the cinema were more foresighted. Among them were the brothers Auguste and Louis Lumière, manufacturers of photographic materials at Lyons in southeastern France. In 1895 they patented a motion-picture apparatus of their own invention, the *cinématographe*. This could be adapted for use both as a movie camera and as a projector. Their first film ran for less than a minute, but it had more substance than anything that had been done for the kinetoscope: It showed workers at the Lumière factory leaving for the lunch hour. The public showing of this film, the earliest "actuality" subject of any length, occurred before the first appearance of Armat's vitascope (p. 280). It thus has the distinction of being the first *projection* of moving pictures before a public audience.

In many countries, enthusiastic film makers using simple hand-operated cameras, often of their own making, were soon at work filming similar real-life incidents: street scenes, horse races, the arrivals and departures of royalty and other notables, and—most beloved of all subjects—the local fire brigade galloping off to a fire.

Most of these early films lasted no longer than three or four minutes, and they were usually shown at exhibition halls and charity bazaars. It was left to fair-ground showmen to exploit the new invention and prove that the excitement of seeing pictures that moved was enough to attract a large paying public. Soon moving pictures were a popular attraction in "electric theatre" tents at traveling fairs and circuses. Before long, they also became a regular item on many music-hall and theatre programs.

As the novelty of the new invention wore off, theatre managers and fair-ground exhibitors began asking for films that had a greater variety of dramatic interest. To maintain a regular supply of new films, many film makers now formed companies and began to use teams of cameramen to tour the world in search of exotic subjects. Naturally, many happenings of public interest had already taken place before the cameramen could arrive on the scene. This led some film companies to try something new: They began to film reconstructions of topical

At the turn of the century, film shows were fair-ground attractions presented by traveling showmen. This elaborate booth belonged to Walter Haggar, a leading British exhibitor.

events, with hired actors and scenery. The resultant "fake" newsreels usually gave a highly inaccurate version of the events they claimed to represent, but the public were seldom aware of the deception.

These imitation newsreels are historically important because out of them evolved the first story-telling movies. Often no more than reportage with a minimum of added plot, they were nevertheless a big step forward, since they had a planned beginning, middle, and end. Among the earliest examples were *The Story of a Crime* (made by Ferdinand Zecca in France in 1901) and *The Life of an American Fireman* (made by an Edison cameraman, Edwin S. Porter, in 1902). In the following year Porter made *The Great Train Robbery*. This famous film lasted the then remarkable time of 11 minutes and had a tremendous success. Its story, exciting and easy to follow, did a lot to establish the formula of the American "western": cowboys and crime in the great outdoors.

The earliest artist of the cinema who seized the opportunities the new medium offered to portray the world of the imagination was Georges Méliès, a Parisian conjuror and illusionist. He had been in the audience at a public showing of films made by the Lumière brothers and was eager to start making movies himself. Méliès bought a projector and developed his own camera. Fully equipped, he was soon at work producing films in which many of the trick devices of the modern cinema were used for the first time. In such films as *The India-Rubber Head* (1901), *A Trip to the Moon* (1902), and *A Voyage Across the Impossible* (1904) he created a unique world of lighthearted scientific fantasy.

In his studio, the first of its kind, Méliès threw himself energetically into every aspect of the new art. He wrote his own stories, painted the scenery, acted, and printed and sold copies of the completed film. Today his unique movies may seem naïve, but they are clearly the work of a single controlling imagination. Méliès can be considered one of the first true film directors.

The Great Train Robbery (*Edwin S. Porter, 1903*), *though not actually the first film to tell a story, was the longest and most exciting that audiences had yet seen. Here, robbers force engineers to uncouple the locomotive.*

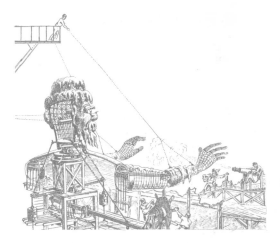

Complicated mechanical tricks characterize the film fantasies of pioneer French director Georges Méliès. This elaborate model of a head and arms (above) represented the giant featured in A Trip to the Pole (1902). *The boat seen below appeared in the hand-colored film* Fairyland, *made in 1903.*

Image, space, and time

In Intolerance (1916), America's D. W. Griffith pioneered the dramatic use of camera angle and movement. Close-up (above) and mid-shot (below) drove home dramatic story.

Griffith filmed this vast Babylonian scene for Intolerance from an anchored balloon. As the balloon descended, the scene narrowed, until the camera finally focused on a single figure.

Many early story films were made to look exactly like stage plays. In some of them a curtain was shown parting to mark the beginning of the "photoplay" and closing at the end. Sometimes the actors were even shown returning and bowing to the unseen audience. But gradually movie makers learned to think of the new medium as something in its own right rather than as a substitute for a "live" performance. And so the film freed itself from theatrical conventions.

Partly because there was as yet no satisfactory way of synchronizing recorded speech with filmed action, early film makers experimented with techniques for telling stories pictorially and without sound. By degrees they learned to separate a story into a *sequence* of incidents and to divide each sequence into *shots* (separate details of the action). They also learned how to take a shot from the position that best explained and emphasized its relation to the dramatic action. In this way—using the camera as a questing as well as a recording eye—the makers of silent movies created a new cinematic art.

The movie maker, like the painter, composes a scene within a shape, or *frame*, of a given size. But in cinematography an important new element is added: The image within the frame moves. Two sorts of movement are possible. The first is the movement of things being photographed. The second is the movement of the camera itself.

The distance of the camera from what it is filming can vary—hence terms like *long shot, medium shot,* and *close-up*. Today the camera can also be made to turn on its axis and to tilt up and down. It can be put on wheels or on a crane to follow the dramatic action of a scene. Fitted with different sorts of lenses, which can narrow

or widen the area being photographed, the camera can see in a way impossible to the human eye. A *wide-angle* lens can make an attic look as spacious as a ballroom; a *long-focus* lens can make people at the far end of a street seem as clearly focused as those in the foreground. Clearly, each camera movement and each change of angle and lens must be planned so that the resulting picture tells the story in the most effective way. The controlling artist of the cinema—the man who makes us look at each scene through *his* eyes—is the *director*.

When all the scenes in a film have been photographed, they are sent to the *editor*. His job is not merely to assemble them in the best possible order, but also—and more importantly—to cut each scene to the length that best relates it to the previous and following scenes. In this way he gives the film a new visual rhythm in addition to that created by the filmed images themselves. This special way of joining scenes together also creates a different sense of time from that which we normally experience.

Actions lasting one minute in actual life can be compressed into a few seconds of film time—or lengthened into five minutes. And this is a moving-picture convention we now take for granted. For example, when a character in a film that is set in Paris says he is going to Brazil, we are not surprised when, a second later, we see him arriving at Brasilia airport. We do not cry out (as people once did) that we are being cheated of part of the film. But having, in a fraction of a second, traveled with him across the Atlantic, we may then follow the character for many minutes, carefully noting everything he does as he walks down a street—again with no sense of surprise at the sudden change of pace.

Classic sequence (right) from The Battleship Potemkin *(1925) bears witness to the brilliant editing of Russian director Sergei Eisenstein. It shows how citizens of Odessa who sympathized with Potemkin mutineers in 1905 were massacred by imperial troops.*

Drawings below represent (1) a shot, *or single frame of film; (2) a* scene, *a piece of continuous action, or a series of shots; (3) a* sequence, *a succession of scenes concerned with one subject.*

1

2

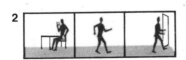

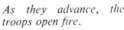

The imperial guards confront the rebellious crowd.

As they advance, the troops open fire.

The crowd turns and flees down the steps in panic.

The soldiers advance relentlessly over the dying.

A wounded man topples down the steps.

A mother stares in horror at the body of her child.

Holding the boy, she defies the guards.

The shadows of soldiers loom over her body.

An old lady turns to one of the soldiers, who slashes her face with his saber.

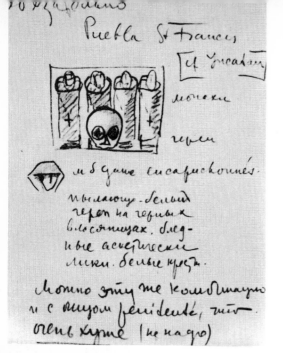

Planning each shot with meticulous care, Russia's masterly director and theorist Sergei Eisenstein achieved rare beauty of line and movement. Sketch and notes (above) made in 1932 for a shot in Que Viva Mexico *produced the dramatic composition below.*

America's great director Robert Flaherty built up his films from largely unrehearsed sequences. He and his team (right) sat by the swamps day after day to film material for Louisiana Story *(1948). The hero (above) was played by a half-wild backwoods boy.*

The director

The film is a synthetic art; that is, it is made by combining the skills and abilities of many people. It is the director who relates these skills to one another, using them as tools to help fashion a movie according to his own particular intentions. When the director has decided on the way he plans to film a given story, his first step is to prepare an *outline*. This outline usually takes a very special form known as a *treatment*. In this, the story to be filmed is written down in dialogue form rather like a play, with technical film terms in place of stage directions. The treatment is next worked out in detail, with descriptions not only of the actors' movements and speeches but also of the exact positioning of the camera for every scene. This final plan is called the *shooting script*. In it the duration of each shot and sequence (p. 284) is marked with great accuracy.

The way a director plans and constructs a film depends on what he is trying to "say." For example, he may feel that the subject calls for a slow, deliberate rhythm, which will allow time for each idea to sink into the minds of the audience. On the other hand, if he is directing a suspense film or a comedy, he may use fast camera movements and rapid editing (p. 284) to keep the audience on the edge of their seats with excitement.

The greatest pioneer in the art of cinematic storytelling was the American director David Wark Griffith (1875-1948). His most famous films are *Birth of a Nation* (1913) and *Intolerance* (1916). Both run for nearly three hours, the latter film telling four separate but linked stories. In these two epics, Griffith may be said to have invented the "grammar" of film making. Using methods that were largely spontaneous and intuitive, he broke new ground in the way he moved his cameras and edited the film they took. As well as scenes of lavish spectacle,

unsurpassed even today, both films include moments in which intimate human emotions are suggested with a remarkable economy of visual details. It was Griffith, for instance, who made the first truly dramatic use of the close-up (p. 284).

Two great Russians—Vsevolod Pudovkin (1893-1953) and Sergei Eisenstein (1898-1948)—developed Griffith's technique still further. Because of its brilliant editing, one particular sequence in Eisenstein's film *The Battleship Potemkin* has been called "the most influential six minutes in cinema history."

Later advances in the art of directing came with the introduction of synchronized sound recording and color photography (p. 290).

The film gradually became a creative medium of almost unlimited possibilities. Thus the modern director has at his disposal a host of techniques with which he can build up and emphasize the dramatic mood of a scene—by the way he uses the cameras, plans the movements of his actors, and supervises the editing of the film. And, unlike the silent-movie director, he can appeal to the ears as well as the eyes of the audience by means of spoken dialogue and with the help of music or natural sound. Finally, by an intelligent use of color, he can strengthen the mood he is striving to create.

Although most directors need to employ the talents of many people to help them, a few—especially directors of documentary films (p. 296)—act as their own writers, cameramen, and editors and are able to create and shape their material with comparatively little assistance. But whether the director works with a small crew or uses the resources of a vast studio, the basic film-making technique is the same. The sequences in a film are usually made up of many separate shots that are very rarely taken in their final order. Each shot will probably last only a few seconds in the completed movie; but to shoot it to the director's satisfaction may entail repeated takes, sometimes 20 or more. Film actors need the help and understanding of the director in order to keep their acting "fresh" in spite of this grinding routine.

Film directors, like other artists, express a personal point of view in their work. The films of a great director clearly bear the stamp of his outlook and interests. One director may wish to tell exciting or amusing stories, another to explore deeply the lives and emotions of individual characters. Others are noted for their understanding and interpretation of social or political problems, historical events, or the beauty and drama of nature. As with other works of art, the work of great film directors has long deserved (and now gets) careful study.

Italy's Luchino Visconti directing Burt Lancaster in a scene from The Leopard (1962).

Directors must be able to handle spectacular sequences as well as intimate scenes. To supervise the filming of the chariot race in Ben Hur *(U.S.A., 1959), director William Wyler rode on the camera truck (right).*

The silent film

Until 1927, when the film found its voice (p. 290) and the "movies" became the "talkies," the appeal of the silent film was international. It told its stories without spoken words, and everyone could understand the panto-mimed action with the help of an occasional explanatory *subtitle*. Such subtitles could be inserted into any motion picture in any language; and so a movie made in Hungary, say, could easily reach mass audiences everywhere.

Before 1914, most European countries had flourishing film studios. Those in Italy were famous for producing historical spectacles like *Quo Vadis* (1912) and *Cabiria* (1914). France, Denmark, Sweden, Britain, and Germany all produced notable films—especially adaptations of famous plays and novels. Then came World War I, and for four years Europe's studios (except in Sweden and Italy) were virtually inactive.

Meanwhile, the American film industry, centered in Hollywood near Los Angeles, grew rapidly. By the end of the war it had gained almost complete control of the world's film market. Attracted by high salaries and the technical resources of Hollywood, many actors and directors left Europe for America. Thus, Sweden's Mauritz Stiller and Greta Garbo, Germany's Emil Jannings and Erich von Stroheim, and Poland's Pola Negri, as well as many other established European directors and stars, were soon as much a part of Hollywood's film industry as America's own Mary Pickford and Douglas Fairbanks.

Undoubtedly the most famous figure of the silent-film era was British-born Charles Chaplin. Arriving in America at the age of 24 as a junior member of a touring music-hall company, he made his first film in 1913. His unique sense of comedy and brilliant pantomime were particularly suited to the medium, and the whole world took "the little tramp" to its heart.

After 1918, however, the most significant developments in the art—as distinguished from the industry—of film-making were made in Russia. There, following the 1917 communist revolution, schools were especially established for training film technicians and directors. In many countries young writers and artists saw the film as a new medium for experimentation. Among the great directors who established their reputations in the 1920s were René Clair and Jean Renoir in France; Fritz Lang, Robert Wiene, F. W. Murnau, and Ernst Lubitsch in Germany; and Alfred Hitchcock in England.

The period before the introduction of sound has often been called the cinema's "golden age." Certainly it was at this time that the film won general recognition as a new and distinctive art.

The Kid, *made in 1921, was Charlie Chaplin's first full-length feature. Playing the title role under Chaplin's direction, the child actor Jackie Coogan (left) became a star overnight.*

Perhaps the most famous silent film made in Italy was Enrico Guazzoni's spectacular Quo Vadis *(1912). Scenes like the chariot race (above) had a universal appeal.*

Slapstick comedies were the speciality of America's Mack Sennett. Tillie's Punctured Romance *(1914) featured Chaplin, the Keystone Cops, and Marie Dressler (above).*

In The Cabinet of Doctor Caligari *(1919), the German director Robert Wiene used stylized costumes and painted sets to evoke the nightmare world of a madman.*

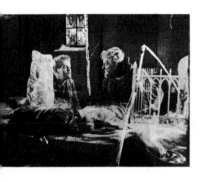

Swedish film makers have always been drawn to symbolism. In Victor Sjöström's Thy Soul Shall Bear Witness *(1920), Death's messenger confronts a drunkard.*

In The Iron Horse *(1924), John Ford portrayed the struggles of early pioneers in the West. The theme has been a constant inspiration to American film makers.*

The Italian Straw Hat, *starring Albert Préjean (right), was made by René Clair in 1927. Satirical— and often farcical—comedy was a speciality of French cinema.*

The German director Fritz Lang drew a grim picture of the future in his Metropolis *(1926). In this scene, a mob tries to wreck a monster-like machine.*

Mother, *starring Vera Baranovskaia (above), was made in 1926 by the Russian Vsevolod Pudovkin. He transformed a Maxim Gorki story into a film of rare beauty.*

In The Passion of Joan of Arc *(1926), the Danish director Carl Dreyer made extensive use of close-ups. The story of Joan's martyrdom is in her tortured face.*

Sound and color

For many years the film itself was silent. But the movie theatres employed musicians to play specially selected music whose mood fitted the action on the screen. The smaller cinemas had just a piano or a pedal organ; larger ones had full-sized orchestras. Where the story was too complex for the actors to explain by mime, printed explanatory subtitles interrupted the flow of the action.

Before 1900, both Thomas Edison (p. 280) and a Frenchman, Léon Gaumont, had separately developed techniques by which sounds recorded on phonograph disks could be made to match the filmed action. The main disadvantage of both processes was that the volume of sound produced was too faint to reach the ears of a whole cinema audience. It was a crisis in the movie industry in the late 1920s that hastened the introduction of talking pictures: Cinema audiences began to decline in numbers because many people preferred to stay home and "listen in" to a new marvel—radio. Film companies, eager to win the public back to the movie theatres, desperately searched for new attractions. One small American company, Warner Brothers, decided to gamble on the success of a new sound-film process invented by engineers of the Bell Telephone laboratories in collaboration with the Western Electric Company. This process made use of vacuum tubes and loudspeakers to increase the volume of the phonograph record.

Using the new process, Warner Brothers made *The Jazz Singer* in 1927. Although silent for most of its length, this now historic movie included short passages of speech and songs on phonograph disks. It was a sensation—and an enormous financial success that also opened a new era in motion-picture production.

In 1928 another American company, Fox Films, introduced a new sound-recording process that actually made sound waves visible and photographed them in the form of a continuous *sound track*. In this way, dialogue recorded in the studio during the shooting of a scene could be printed onto the film, exactly matching actions and lip movements.

Caption from Charlie Chaplin's Shanghaied *(1915).* Dramatic moments in silent films were often interrupted by a subtitle, necessary to give information that could not be conveyed in mime. With the coming of sound in 1927–8, film companies panicked and added awkward, last-minute sound effects to unreleased silent films. Modern sound track (right) informs fully; such effects as coughs, sighs, and outdoor noises heighten reality.

In The Jazz Singer, *first shown on October 6, 1927, in New York, Al Jolson (above) heralded the coming of the talking-film era with the words: "Come on, Ma! Listen to this . . ." Modern directors have developed the artistic use of sound. At the end of Julien Duvivier's* Anna Karenina *(1947), starring England's Vivien Leigh, the thunder of the oncoming train (right) foretells the heroine's fate.*

American director John Huston made dramatic use of color in Moby Dick *(1955), a film version of Herman Melville's novel. At the climax (above) hate-driven Captain Ahab, trapped by the harpooner's ropes, dies on the white whale's flank in a stream of red blood.*

In Gate of Hell *(1953), director Teinosuke Kinugasa recaptures the rich color and design of Japan's medieval paintings. He tells the true story of a wild 12th-century warrior who expiated his crimes by entering a monastery.*

Color can also serve to heighten the reality of a scene. In Le Déjeuner sur l'Herbe *(1959), an idyll of country life, French director Jean Renoir used delicate, natural color that enhanced the film's lyrical mood.*

The talking picture revolutionized the industry. It also created new problems. Some way of retaining the movies' international appeal in spite of the new language barrier had to be found. (Although not entirely to everyone's satisfaction, this problem is now solved either by means of running subtitles that translate the dialogue in condensed form, or by "dubbing in" actual speech that tries as nearly as possible to match the original lip movements.) At first, too, the new interest in dialogue made many movie makers forget the film's unique ability to create *moving pictures.* Temporarily, much of the earlier speed of camera movement and imaginative cutting were neglected as the movies tried to ape the live theatre.

Directors finally realized, however, that sound can also be arranged and edited. They now *select* from the noises of everyday life and the sounds of nature; and they use both spoken dialogue and music equally selectively. The most talented modern directors make sound help to underline dramatic action and mood. They have learned, in other words, how to use sound *as part of the film.* The sound film can not only speak but sing. It can reproduce the music of a full symphony orchestra, or it can hear a pin drop. It can, in effect, listen to a character's unspoken thoughts or the dramatic silence of an empty room.

Another way in which a film may emphasize mood and dramatic action, as well as heighten the effect of reality, is in its use of color. Color has been used in films from their earliest days. Some of the movies made by Georges Méliès (p. 282), for example, had each picture separately colored by hand! An English film showing King George V in India was photographed in color as early as 1911. By the late twenties, a number of film processes that gave reliably accurate color—Technicolor, for instance—were being widely used.

Today the director is able to use color as selectively as he uses images and sounds. Employing color for dramatic effect is often more important than simply being able to photograph objects in natural colors. Like the painter, the film director can use color to stress the personality of a character or the mood of a scene. In the British film of Shakespeare's *Henry V* (1944), for instance, the warm, earthy colors associated with the rougher characters contrasted sharply with the bright, vivid colors used in court scenes. In order to produce such effects, the director must collaborate closely with a team of skilled helpers—in particular, with the art director and with the director of photography, who not only is responsible for the camera work but also controls a large team of lighting technicians.

Above: Director Max Reinhardt surveys model set for A Midsummer Night's Dream *(U.S.A., 1935). Below: Sound recordists and camera crews shoot a scene for* I Thank a Fool *(Britain, 1962), which starred the American actress Susan Hayward (center).*

From script to print

Very large sums of money are needed for the making of a film. The wages of technicians and actors and the cost of electrical apparatus, scenery, costumes, and many other kinds of special equipment all mount up. It is the *producer* who must deal with such business matters. He may work for a large film company or independently. Part of his function is to persuade his company, or his financial backers, that the picture he and the director want to make will not only be good, but that it will earn money at the box office. Thus the producer assists the director simply by protecting him from the financial complications of film making. But he may also collaborate closely in the whole shaping of a given movie.

Working from the final shooting script (p. 286), the *art director* makes many designs for the settings to be used. These must create a suitable visual background for the action. But they must also be carefully planned to fit the composition and movement of each shot. Carpenters and plasterers then translate the art director's designs into three-dimensional reality. Studio settings, often of great size, are prepared with careful attention to detail so as to satisfy the penetrating scrutiny of the camera. Scenes to be filmed out of doors, whether in the streets or in the countryside, must have the right "locations" chosen; and permission to film there must be obtained. When all such matters have been taken care of, the actual filming can start—with a cast assembled by the *casting director* and costumed by expert designers.

Before each shot, while the director rehearses the actors, the director of photography gets the camera into position. With the aid of electricians, he also arranges the lighting. At the same time, the *sound recordist* must carefully place his microphones in such a way that they will be close enough to the actors to pick up their slightest whisper and yet remain out of camera range. "Shooting" a film is a complicated operation, and many things

Actors and technicians working on location in extremes of climate must often tolerate hours of discomfort to film a single shot, and special equipment may be needed. In this scene from David Lean's Lawrence of Arabia *(Britain, 1962), shot in the Middle East, a mirror is being used to soften the dark shadows.*

can go wrong. An actor may forget his lines or speak them too fast. He may move at the wrong speed, preventing the camera from keeping him in focus. A microphone may become visible as it is shifted in order to catch a bit of dialogue. Or the sound of a passing airplane may be picked up by the microphone, spoiling the *take* and requiring a *retake*. It is not surprising that each day's work in the studio usually results in only two or three minutes of final film, or that a full-length feature film may take months to complete.

All the scenes using a particular set or location are shot one after the other, although they may appear at widely separated times in the finished film. When the shots arrive in the cutting room, the editor (p. 284) arranges them in the right order with the aid of the shooting script.

When both director and editor are satisfied that the film has been properly assembled, the next stage begins. This is known as re-recording or "dubbing." Sounds that could not be conveniently recorded in the studio are now added to the sound track. Suppose, for instance, there is a scene in which actors are talking together in a railway carriage. This will probably have been shot in the studio in a specially built replica of a carriage interior. Only the actors' voices will have been recorded at this stage. The sounds of rattling train wheels, locomotive whistles, and so on are added at the dubbing session. If specially written music is to be used, the composer is given the exact number of minutes and seconds to which to fit his score. It is then played in a specially equipped music-recording studio and combined with the other sound tracks by the sound recordist, who adjusts the volume of each sound to suit the action.

In the laboratories the negatives of all sound tracks and pictures are combined together into a "master" copy. From it any number of duplicate positive *prints* may then be made for simultaneous showings in movie theatres all over the world.

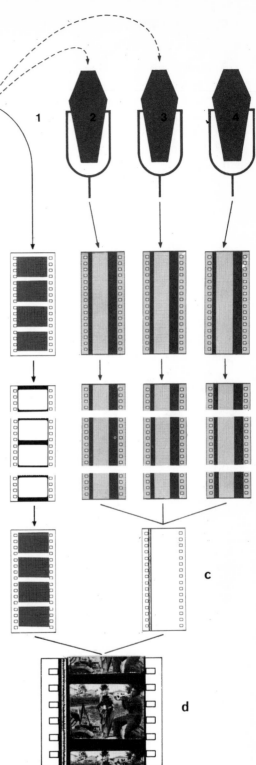

Sound films, such as Federico Fellini's La Strada (*Italy, 1954*), *combine images and separately recorded sounds. Diagram shows how each image (1) is matched with appropriate dialogue (2), sound effects (3), and music (4). Images and sound tracks are synchronized (a), then edited by cutting (b). Negatives of edited film and sound track (c) are combined to print completed film (d).*

Feature films

Though less than 70 years old, the art of the cinema has developed many characteristic forms of its own, and its range of expression has grown very wide. The language of every art is able to perform many tasks. With words, for instance, we can compose a novel or a poem; with musical notation, a symphony or a song. The language of moving pictures has also created its own special world. In the following pages we shall examine some aspects of that world.

Born in the workshops of inventors, the film none the less spent a great deal of its "childhood" in the rowdy atmosphere of fair grounds and variety theatres. There, audiences were accustomed to laughing at simple, boisterous humor, to applauding magicians and jugglers, and to being thrilled by the shallow passions of melodrama.

Each of the many items on a typical variety program lasted only a few minutes. And so, when films were first made to be shown regularly in theatres, they were designed to give a brief moment of amusement to unsophisticated audiences. They ran for about 10 minutes—the length of a single reel of film—and the public at large, who regarded fair grounds and music halls as crude and vulgar, generally considered the early one-reel movies as just one more trashy novelty and took little notice of them. But when well-known stage figures consented to act before the camera, the film quickly gained a new, and slightly self-conscious, respectability.

In 1912 the great French actress Sarah Bernhardt appeared in a four-reel film version of her stage success *Queen Elizabeth*. In the following year an Italian company produced the spectacular *Quo Vadis*, which showed the gory sufferings of early Christians amid the splendors of ancient Rome. This film was made in 12 reels and took the then astounding time of two hours to show. When movies like these were exhibited in European and American opera houses and theatres, they drew huge audiences and stimulated other film makers to undertake

In Lady With a Little Dog (*U.S.S.R., 1959*), *Yosif Heifetz recaptured the romantic mood of a Chekhov story set in imperial Russia.*

Ingmar Bergman's The Seventh Seal (*Sweden, 1956*), *culminating in a grotesque dance of death* (*above*), *was inspired by medieval legend. Tragic realism was the keynote of* La Terra Trema (*Italy, 1948*), *in which Luchino Visconti told of a poor fisherman's family.*

One of the first feature films was The Great Train Robbery *(1903). Audiences were startled by close-up technique.*

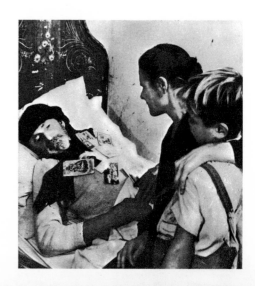

Shin Heike Monogatari (1955) *told of Samurai warriors—a typical Japanese theme.*

A colorful scene from a typically spectacular American musical: Carousel, *made in 1959.*

productions made on an equally ambitious scale.

It now became clear that there was a vast public for serious and ambitious motion pictures. Soon special "cinematograph theatres" were being built in every town and were being regularly supplied with new films. In addition to newsreels, short one- or two-reel comedies, and "thrillers," the programs in such playhouses usually included at least one hour-long film as their main "feature."

The feature film has remained the major item of film production. It can be looked upon as the symphony or the novel of the cinema. Because of its length—now usually two to three hours—the director of such a movie is able to tell as long and complex a story as he wishes. This may be adapted from an existing work of fiction or biography; it may be based upon a stage play; or it may be an original film story, prepared entirely in terms of movie-narrative techniques.

Like *Queen Elizabeth* and *Quo Vadis*, the earliest feature films were often either spectacular or built around the performance of a famous stage actor or actress. Today, the cinema creates many of its own stars; and it can tackle almost any subject-matter—though the "historical spectacle" still remains so very popular that astronomical sums are spent annually to make ever more lavish and spectacular ones. In recent years, the rivalry of television has encouraged film companies to introduce a number of new wide-screen processes that make possible even greater spectacular effects with which the small TV screen cannot compete.

The feature film has developed a number of characteristic forms and conventions. These, like the ever-popular "western" and the "musical," are essentially cinematic —created from the beginning in terms of moving images. As the camera follows galloping horsemen or moves in among a swirling crowd of dancers, it enables us to take part in the proceedings in a way that no other art can duplicate.

The documentary

To most people, the word "movie" suggests simply a pleasant evening's entertainment. There is nothing wrong with this concept, of course. But we should not forget that from their earliest days, films have regularly been used for purposes other than entertainment. In the early 1890s, for instance, a French surgeon was taking moving pictures of his own operations. A little later, a French scientist began to film germs and bacteria as seen through a powerful microscope. In this way he was able to show his colleagues the behavior patterns of these minute organisms.

Today films are used extensively for educational, industrial, and scientific purposes. It is easy to see why. In the classroom, for example, the movies can show how plants grow, or how wild animals live in their natural surroundings. In industry, films can help to train apprentices and to explain new methods of manufacture.

The word "documentary" was first used by a British director, John Grierson, to describe a special type of film pioneered by America's Robert Flaherty (1884-1951). Flaherty was one of the greatest artists of the cinema. His films have been defined by Grierson as giving "a creative treatment of actuality." Whereas a newsreel simply records facts, Flaherty's films are personal and poetic interpretations of reality. His first and best-known work *Nanook of the North* (1922) records the daily struggle for survival of an Eskimo family in the icy conditions of the sub-Arctic. Flaherty's other films—among them, *Moana* (1926), *Man of Aran* (1934), and *Louisiana Story* (1948) —are all characterized by the same awareness of the close relationship between people and nature.

In 1929 John Grierson made *Drifters*, which is regarded as the first British documentary film. In it he showed the life of the fishermen of the Scottish herring fleets and stressed the importance of their work to the rest of the community. A characteristic of the films produced by Britain's influential "documentary movement" was this concern with subjects of social importance. *Housing Problems, Night Mail, Enough to Eat?, Shipyard* —these were typical titles of the years before World War II. A notable feature of all such films was the imaginative use of the sound track, in which an original musical score was often combined with a poetic spoken commentary. The American documentary director Pare Lorentz used a similar technique in *The Plow that Broke the Plains* (1936) and *The River* (1938).

Where does the money come from to make documentary and educational films? Most of them are now sponsored by government agencies or other large public bodies. And many documentary directors have relied on

In 1920–21 America's Robert Flaherty recorded the life of an Eskimo hunter (above) to make Nanook of the North, *a film that is now recognized as the first documentary.*

In 1929 John Grierson pioneered the documentary film movement in Britain with Drifters, *a study of North Sea herring fishermen. Many film makers followed his lead.*

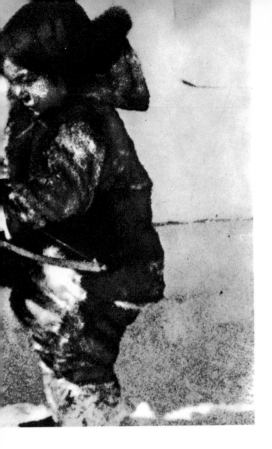

private companies to finance their work. Flaherty, for example, made *Nanook of the North* for a firm of fur importers and *Louisiana Story* for an oil company.

Some documentaries, like the famous American series *The March of Time* (sponsored by a firm of magazine publishers), have been widely distributed in commercial cinemas. Among other commercial successes were such wartime documentaries as the British *Target for To-night,* directed by Harry Watt in 1941, and *The Fighting Lady*, made by America's Louis de Rochemont in 1944. Films like these, often made under conditions of extreme danger, brought home to the public a vivid picture of front-line fighting unmatched by any other medium.

Until recently, most documentaries, apart from the above exceptions, were shown only in schools, colleges, factory canteens, and community centers. Today they have found a vast new audience : In a single screening on television, millions of people can enjoy—and learn from—a movie that would otherwise reach very few people. Most television companies now have permanent documentary film units, and many of these have done outstanding work (such as *The Isle of Favignana*, directed by Alberto Chiesa for Italian television in 1956). The profit from documentary and educational films cannot be assessed in terms of money. It comes in the form of a better educated and more alert community.

In L'Hippocampe (*France, 1934*) *director Jean Painlevé made a scientific film study of sea-horses.*

The Plow That Broke The Plains (*U.S.A., 1936*), *Pare Lorentz' study of effects of soil erosion.*

Spoken verse echoed speeding trains in Night Mail (*1936*), *sponsored by the British Post Office.*

Leni Riefenstahl recorded the 1936 Olympic Games in the lyrical Olympische Spiele (*Germany*).

The simple life of a French farmer's family was the theme of Georges Rouquier's Farrebique (*1947*).

Italian television sponsored Alberto Chiesa's The Isle of Favignana (*1956*), *a story of local tunny fishing.*

297

Drawings that walk and talk

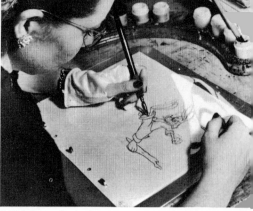

When cinematography was first invented, most early film makers were chiefly interested in using their cameras to record the actions of real people. But a few realized that the motion-picture camera could also be used to photograph drawings and *animate* them in the same way as—but infinitely better than—the old zoetrope (p. 280). Where the 19th-century toys had used only a few drawings, the film camera was able to photograph hundreds. When projected on the screen, the result was an impression of lifelike movement. One of the earliest people to do this was France's Émile Cohl, who made his first cartoon film, *Phantasmagoria*, in 1908.

Because the figures in a cartoon film are invented by the artist who draws them, they can be utterly fantastic, and they can be made to perform all kinds of actions that real people or animals cannot. Drawn figures are not affected by the force of gravity or the limitations of anatomy. The artist can, for instance, make them leap and fly, grow or shrink in size, or vanish altogether, as he wishes. And so a unique technique of the animated cartoon has developed.

In 1909 an American, Winsor McCay, created a cartoon film featuring Gertie, a dinosaur. Four years later came the Russian film *The Grasshopper and the Ant*, made by Ladislas Starevitch. These were the first in a long line of cartoon animal characters—a line that has included Felix the Cat and, most famous of all, Mickey Mouse, who was "born" in 1928. His creator, the American artist Walt Disney, has been responsible for the production of hundreds of cartoon films.

Clearly, such films are not the work of one man alone. In 1923, when Disney established his studios, cartoon-film making was still a comparatively simple, if laborious, process. By employing many artists to produce the thousands of drawings required for a single movie, and by developing new camera techniques, Disney was able to cut down on production time and to undertake more ambitious projects. In 1928, he made *Skeleton Dance*, the first cartoon movie with a synchronized sound track. Then, in 1938, came the first of his many full-length features, *Snow White*.

Above, left: artist's rough drawings for a cartoon character in Walt Disney's Fantasia *(U.S.A., 1940). After checking and polishing, such drawings are traced in ink on Celluloid (above) and colored according to designer's instructions. Finished drawing—in this case, of Disney's famous Donald Duck (below)—is pegged to independently painted background and photographed frame by frame. Using 16 separate drawings per second of screen time, Disney developed a system of highly realistic animation. His style of caricature has influenced cartoon-film makers all over the world.*

In Fumées *(Belgium, 1951), Alexandre Alexeieff photographed a drop of molten glass as it swung from a pendulum (far right). In* Blinkity-Blank *(right), made in 1954, Canada's Norman McLaren drew pictures and sound track directly on film.*

Today, most animated films are short comedies, their stories and style of drawing often modeled on Disney's. In many countries, however, cartoon-film artists have created new, distinctive styles, often influenced by contemporary painting. Moreover, animated films need not always be humorous. Some animated-film makers deal with serious themes or comment satirically upon the real world. Then, too, a number of directors—notably Alexandre Alexeieff in France—have recently tried out entirely new types of animation and have produced remarkable effects of abstract pattern, color, and movement. In the films of Germany's Oskar Fishinger and Britain's Len Lye (all made in the 1930s), as well as in some of those of Canada's Norman McLaren (1950s), abstract designs were painted directly onto strips of film, thus entirely bypassing the use of a camera.

Another kind of animation makes use of tiny puppets. These are made with flexible bodies and limbs that can be moved to reproduce lifelike actions. For each scene the tiny figures are placed in carefully made and often elaborate model settings, and skilfully lighted. Each movement is then filmed, stage by stage, by a special camera. This can be stopped to allow a puppet's arm or head to be moved before taking the next photograph. When the film is projected at normal speed, the puppets appear to move in lifelike fashion.

Many charming puppet films have been made, especially in Holland, Czechoslovakia, and Poland. In 1957, the Czech puppet-film maker Jiři Trnka completed a full-length version of Shakespeare's *A Midsummer Night's Dream*, which has been widely shown with great success. Artists and film makers in many countries are increasingly attracted by the almost unlimited visual possibilities of all types of animated motion picture.

A highly imaginative version of Shakespeare's A Midsummer Night's Dream *was made in 1958–59 by Czech painter and puppet designer Jiři Trnka. In this comic scene, the craftsmen's play, heroine Thisbe is pursued by a lion.*

In 1958 Britain's Richard Williams made his remarkable allegory The Little Island. *It tells how Truth, Good, and Beauty go to live together on a desert island. Good and Beauty (below) fight bitterly until Truth (above) nearly destroys them with the bomb he designs.*

History on Celluloid

An early newsreel, filmed in 1901 by Britain's Joe Rosenthal (above), showed troops fording a river in the Boer War.

All films are a record of past events. Even at the first public showing of a new motion picture, the audience is in fact seeing the selected and assembled record of actions that were filmed months, even years, earlier. In a special way, therefore, the newest feature film is already a fragment of history. The value of the medium as a remarkably vivid kind of historic document is now widely recognized. Nothing else can bring us so closely in touch with the past, or can so completely and informatively "freeze" events of our own time for future viewers, and show them how we of today looked and sounded.

The cinema can also recapture for us something of the art of yesterday's actors and dancers, whose performances would otherwise endure only as long as living memory. Referring to the motion picture, Thomas Edison wrote, in 1894: "I believe that, in coming years, by my own work and that of Dickson, Muybridge, and Marey [p. 280] . . . grand opera can be given at the Metropolitan Opera at New York without any material change from the original, and with artists long since dead."

Unfortunately it took a long time for people to realize the importance of preserving notable films. Most early movies were made purely as entertainment. When they ceased to make money at the box office, they were destroyed or allowed to disintegrate. For unless photographic images are carefully protected, they fade and eventually peel away from the Celluloid on which they

Outstanding among newsreels is the film of the German airship Hindenburg *crashing in flames at Lakeland, New Jersey, in 1937 (above). In 1911–12, British cameraman Herbert Ponting recorded Captain Scott's ill-fated expedition (below) to Antarctica.*

Film of famed ballerina Anna Pavlova dancing the Dying Swan (above) was made in 1936. Directors are often eager to depict great artists at work. In 1956, France's H.-G. Clouzot directed Le Mystère Picasso, a study of the world-famous Spanish painter (below).

When they record momentous events like the space flight of America's first astronaut, Colonel John Glenn (below), in 1962, today's film cameras perform a vital service for both scientists and historians.

are printed. Thus many important early films have been lost for ever. For example, a notable film version of Émile Zola's novel *Thérèse Raquin*, made by the French director Jacques Feyder, won great critical acclaim when first shown in the 1920s. As far as is known, no copy of it now exists.

Today, though, there are film *archives* in many countries. In them films of particular artistic or historic importance are stored under carefully controlled conditions. If the original shows signs of deterioration, a copy print is made. In this way many outstanding movies have been preserved and remain available for public showing. That is why it is still possible for us to see such landmarks of cinema as, for example, the Babylonian scenes in *Intolerance* (1916), the seal hunt from *Nanook of the North* (1922), the trial of St. Joan in *The Passion of Joan of Arc*, made in France in 1928 by the Danish director Carl Dreyer, or the battle on the ice in the Russian film *Alexander Nevsky*, directed by Sergei Eisenstein in 1938.

The main film highway for a backward trip through time is the newsreel. The earliest film makers found a constant supply of subjects for their cameras in very ordinary scenes. It did not matter that the flickering shadows on the screen portrayed nothing more dramatic than *A Cabinet Maker at His Bench* or *A Train Arriving at a Station* (shown on p. 282). It was exciting enough to be able to make pictures that moved. Then the film makers began turning their attention to topical events of special interest. Cameramen often traveled great distances to film a newsworthy subject.

Luckily, many of their early films have been preserved. Through them we can actually be spectators of events that happened before most of us were born. The movies can provide—in a way that no other method of documentation can—an "on-the-spot" impression of major events. They can help us to evoke the mood or atmosphere of a particular moment by capturing on film a revealing gesture or facial expression, as well as more obvious details.

To reconstruct in our mind's eye such a stupendous feat of human effort as, say, the work of building the pyramids in Egypt or the Great Wall of China, we must piece together descriptions written at the time and study the evidence provided by paintings, sculpture, and archaeological research. But when we want to study the way in which Dutch engineers have in recent years succeeded in reclaiming thousands of acres of land from the sea, we can turn to the wealth of material available on film—and actually see the work being done.

The world audience

Few industries have had a more rapid and spectacular growth than the cinema. This was especially true in America. *The Great Train Robbery*, generally accepted as the first American story film, was made in 1903. Only 15 years later, in 1918, the movies were raking in so much money at the box office that film making ranked as America's third most profitable commercial activity.

After World War I, Hollywood-made films dominated most of the world's screens, and audiences everywhere became familiar with the appearance of American life as Hollywood portrayed it. Although America's film makers were often criticized for presenting a false image of their country to the rest of the world, they could—and did—argue that what people saw in American films made them want to buy American goods. In any case, it was true that never before had the world been offered such an inexpensive supply of regular entertainment.

In spite of Hollywood, it soon became increasingly clear that movies could also be a powerful weapon for molding opinion. Way back in 1922, Lenin, the Russian revolutionary leader, said : "Of all the arts, the cinema is for us the most important." He realized that the many different races and languages of Russia presented the new Soviet Government with a problem of communication that the silent movies were ideally suited to solve.

The world-wide growth of the cinema (and, more recently, of television) has made storytelling by means

Today, film is increasingly used in under-develop[ed] countries, both for educational purposes and [for] entertainment. In Ghana (above, left) an educatio[nal] film attracts a large audience. Poster, above, advertis[es] an Indian film that won international acclaim[,] Satyajit Ray's The Music Room *(1958). Below: In [the] West the results of recent scientific research a[re] publicized in films like* The Living Soil *(1960), whi[ch] described new methods of controlling insect pests.*

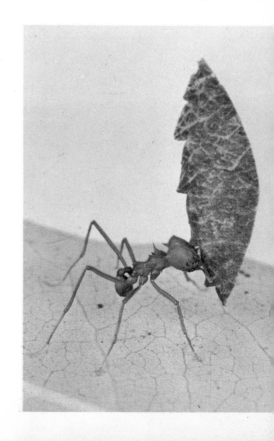

of motion pictures probably the most generally accepted and popular of art forms. This does not mean that the hundreds of films made each year are all works of art. Most are simply conventional film stories whose chief purpose is to make money. Even so, a great director, although his pictures may be unconventional and not widely popular, is able to reach a larger audience than any other type of artist. Compared with a painting that may be seen by only a few hundred people, or a book that may be read by thousands, a film will probably be seen by millions even if it is unusual and hard to understand. It has been estimated that more than 300 million people go to the cinema each week.

Before World War II, more than half the total number of films shown throughout the world were American-made. Today the picture is greatly changed. Hollywood produces fewer and fewer full-length movies each year and concentrates mainly on making television serials; it has been overtaken in the output of feature movies by the studios of Japan, India, and Italy. Outstanding motion pictures from these and other countries reach a wider world audience than at any time since the days of the silent film. By adding translations in the form of subtitles or "dubbing" new voices onto the sound track in place of the original dialogue, a Japanese film may be understood in Norway, or an Indian film in Italy.

Thus it has been possible for notable movies—like *The Seven Samurai* made by the Japanese director Akira Kurosawa; *Bicycle Thieves* directed by the Italian Vittorio de Sica; *Kanal* made by Andrzej Wajda of Poland; and such work of the Swedish director Ingmar Bergman as *Wild Strawberries*—to become known throughout the civilized world.

But there is another, and even larger, potential audience for motion pictures. More than 60 per cent of the world's population is illiterate. In countries where most people can neither read nor write, the cinema is often the quickest and most effective method of instruction. Where education is lacking, especially in such things as hygiene and new methods of agriculture, there will usually be poverty, ill health, and starvation. The United Nations and many national governments are trying to supply films for educational purposes; they are also training people in the underdeveloped countries to make such films for themselves.

The motion picture, then, can do more than merely help countries to exchange entertainment. By aiding the less fortunate people of the world, it may prove to be a vital instrument in bringing all nations together in peace and mutual understanding.

In The Red Balloon *(1956)—a simple film parable that had an international appeal— France's Albert Lamorisse bypassed language barriers by combining color and design so carefully that little dialogue was needed.*

Chapter 12

Art and Idea

All the chapters you have read so far, and the pictures you have looked at, have been attempts to show you some of the ways artists express ideas and emotions. In this final chapter, we shall see if we can find some order in all this variety—unifying qualities that help people to make judgments, to say: "Yes, this is a serious work of art. In fact, it is good." Or to say: "This is a bad work of art."

Looking at a painting, entering a building, listening to a symphony, watching a play—each of these experiences produces a great number of impressions at the same time. When we look at a painting we see a number of separate elements: colors, lines, and textures. These impressions, working together, create the painting's special quality. What unifies these elements is the painting's form.

Form in art is the particular pattern, or scheme, or structure that the artist uses in order to discipline the various components of his work. Though artists never stop experimenting, they generally agree that there are limitations to possible combinations of ideas with certain materials and forms—that, for example, what a dancer can express by the movements of his body will often be an idea or emotion that a poet would find difficult to convey in language, his chosen means of expression. And poets, again, use language differently from novelists.

But we often use the same words to speak of different art forms; ballets, sonatas, buildings may all be called "beautiful," "expressive," and so on. This implies that despite differences in the ways poets, dancers, and other artists go about discovering the best forms to contain their ideas, there are still qualities common to all the arts, and values by which the success or failure of any work can be judged.

Looking up into the central tower of England's Ely Cathedral is like looking into an elegant kaleidoscope. Unlike kaleidoscope forms, the octagonally ribbed pattern is not the outcome of chance but of the way Gothic architects chose to give form to contemporary ideals. Using ribbed vaults to transmit great weight-thrusts down slender piers, they built immensely tall structures, flooded with light, that gave soaring expression to their faith in Christ's heavenly power to redeem those on earth.

Form

We have used the word *form* many times in the preceding chapters. Why is it so important to art? What does it have to do with ideas? If you think for a minute about the ways you use the word "form," you will probably find that you most often use it when you want to talk about the shape of some object or about the way it is made. In this sense, everything that exists has form, though we do sometimes say a thing is "formless" when what we really mean is that its form is defective, badly organized, or appears to have no intelligible purpose.

All the things artists create have some kind of form, whether they are objects we can actually see or touch, like paintings and buildings, or things we experience in some other way, such as poems and symphonies. The end or purpose toward which the artist works is to communicate his ideas by organizing his materials into the forms the rest of us experience.

To take a simple example: think of a spoon. The idea everyone shares about a spoon is that it is an implement with a shallow bowl and a handle, useful for cooking and eating. But the artist-craftsman who makes a particular spoon will add other, more specific ideas: about its material (elegant silver or utilitarian stainless steel?), its workmanship (elaborately carved or perfectly plain?), and its size (to fit a teacup or a large cooking pot?). The maker of the spoon *chooses* from among these ideas the qualities that will govern the final form of the spoon, but his choice is largely determined by the purpose for which the spoon is intended.

One way to get a clear idea of the way purpose determines the forms artists give their works is to take a look at nature. Biologists and botanists have pointed out that forms in nature come about because plant and animal species adapt themselves to particular environments. The forms best suited to a given situation tend to be the ones that survive to eventually become the pattern for all members of a species. Desert-growing cactuses gradually

Forms in nature: Snowflakes, regularly six-pointed and symmetrical, are nevertheless all different. Their complexity and variety suggest clever planning, but such flakes in fact result from chance encounters between ice crystals and dust particles. The form each flake assumes is determined by a combination of temperature and atmospheric conditions.

Though they appear to be cunningly designed, the familiar six-sided storage cells of honeycombs result when hundreds of equal-size cylinders of wax pack closely together, each exerting pressure on its neighbor.

Man-made forms: One stage in the careful planning that went into Mies van der Rohe's design for the Illinois Institute of Technology in Chicago was the model shown above. Plenty of glass allows a flood of illumination for desks and drawing tables. Architects' plans take into account the purposes of buildings, available materials, and personal ideas about beauty.

Vincent van Gogh (p. 44) imposed his personal vision on the forms he observed in the world around him. In The Road with Cypresses he represented the Provence landscape by flame-like shapes that expressed turbulent emotions.

evolved leafless shapes that did not dissipate moisture through leaves into hot, dry, desert air. On the other hand, plants in steamy jungles developed broad, luxuriant leaves that spread themselves to absorb every bit of light that filtered down into the thick undergrowth.

Jungle and desert plants, then, like all living things, have particular forms that result inevitably from the fact that they live in different environments. In the same way, non-living forms—shapes such as you see in eroded rock formations, or in the delicate pattern of ice crystals in a snowflake—result inevitably from natural forces. Aside from general similarities, each snowflake, each formation is unique—the product of a coming together of particular weather or geological conditions. Despite their variety, however, these forms did not result from choice.

We saw that in the design of a spoon, an important element was the maker's choice. In a similar way, a painter may choose from forms in nature. What he chooses depends on how well-suited it is to his purposes in creating a particular picture. Perhaps he chooses to give an illusion of real forms, even though the idea he wants to express is an abstract one. He might take the form of a beautiful woman, for example, and reproduce it in two dimensions on canvas to stand for the idea of springtime, as the Florentine painter Sandro Botticelli (about 1444-1510) did in his painting Primavera.

Or he might use non-representational lines and colors to suggest ideas and feelings more personal and harder to pinpoint than spring. Musicians, of course, nearly always express their ideas through non-representational sound forms. But whatever form an artist chooses, he does so because he wants the best form for his work in relation to the emotions or ideas he wants to communicate.

The more right—we might almost say, the more inevitable—artistic forms seem, the more inseparable they are from the emotions or ideas they contain, the better we say the work of art fulfills the artist's purpose.

Order and balance

Many animal forms seem exactly *right* for their environments: burrowing animals, for example, with their elongated, pointed bodies; swimming animals and fish with their streamlined shapes. Other forms, such as those of horses or dogs, are satisfying too, even though the functional reasons for their particular body-forms may not be immediately apparent. Their shapes nevertheless have a reassuring familiarity, with that symmetry, clarity, and balance that we often call "grace."

A large part of the story of art has been taken up with discovering similarly reassuring qualities for man-made forms. In what often seems to be an unstable and disordered world, men tend to make rules and establish traditions in order to preserve the qualities and forms that they have found to be secure and satisfying. One of the longest-lived attempts at maintaining stable forms in art occurred in Egypt, where men were preoccupied with ensuring the continuation of life after death. Although Egyptian stone portraits are usually recognizable as individual people, sculptors were restricted for over 3000 years to a balanced, static style.

The Greeks looked for forms that would echo the order and harmony that they found in the universe. As Greek philosophers made one discovery after another about the laws of nature, they evolved laws for ideal physical forms as well (p. 56). The philosopher Plato (about 427-347 B.C.) said that *all* three-dimensional forms were variations on certain geometrical solids.

Renaissance painter Piero della Francesca wrote a book applying Euclid's theories to art. Lines superimposed on Piero's Baptism of Christ *(about 1440) show geometric precision of composition. Note dove, representing Holy Ghost, in circle's center (above). With their ordered vistas, 17th-century French gardens like those at Louis XIV's château at Marly, shown below in a painting by J.-B. Martin, were models of elegant classical symmetry.*

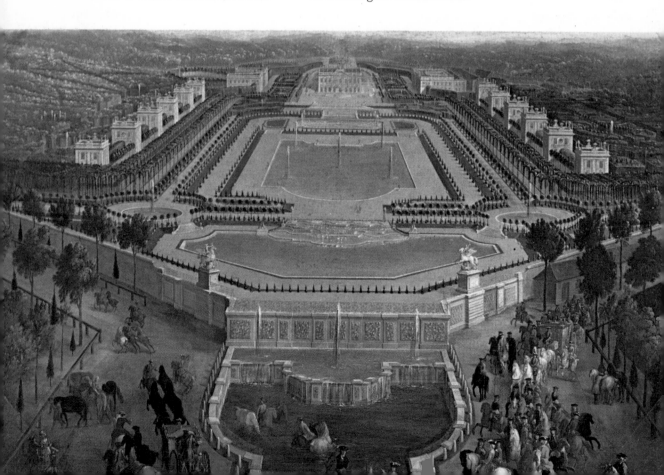

During the Renaissance, artists re-emphasized certain Greek theories of proportion, order, and balance. An example of this is the way painters and architects followed a Greek conception of ideal formal proportions that Renaissance artists called the Golden Section. Interestingly, this mathematically worked-out system is similar to the growth-patterns of many natural forms. A rectangle divided and subdivided according to Golden Section proportions results in a spiral form that resembles that of many sea shells and animal horns.

The most obviously balanced and ordered man-made forms are found in architecture. Someone once called architecture, with its use of columns, windows, and other rhythmically recurring details, "frozen music." We can reverse this comparison to say that music is "flowing architecture." We remember tunes precisely because musicians "build" them with patterns of sound that give them a memorable shape.

Poets use rhythm and repetition, too (p. 144). Every language shapes poetry according to rules about rhyme and meter. These result from attempts to find regular forms, adapted to speech sounds, that help poets to provide a recognized means of communication between them and their audiences. The easily recognized and the familiar all contribute to a sense of discipline and balance that makes artistic communication easier.

A value of artistic innovation is that an artist can call attention to new ideas through new forms. Much innovation seems to consist in the artist's violation of rules about order and balance. Such apparent disorder has value as art, for it may suit an artist's view of life as chaotic and "formless" itself. Or perhaps the artist simply wants to jolt his audience into paying attention to his ideas through his very act of flouting so-called good form, as Picasso did in *The Weeping Woman* (p. 33).

Other painters may apparently abandon all control over their works—as action painters sometimes seem to do (p. 64)—in order to achieve a more direct and spontaneous result. Or musicians may turn to deliberately discordant sounds. But whatever use artists make of their materials, whether they observe traditional rules or experiment, the nature of those materials imposes limits.

Not all art is symmetrical. In ballet Le Coq d'Or, *King Dodon (danced by Dokoudovsky in 1951 Ballets Russes revival) is entranced by the mysterious Queen of Shemakhan, who makes him dance ridiculously (above). Music (adapted from Stravinsky), Fokine's choreography, Gontcharova's designs, all help to suggest king's unbalanced infatuation.*

Carl Christenson motor works plant in Denmark is not symmetrical, but architect Arne Jacobsen balances horizontal lines of main building with tall stack.

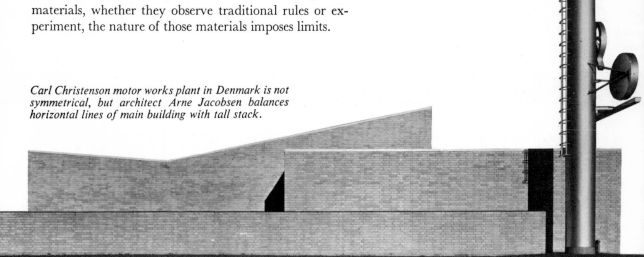

The idea takes shape

Bernini daringly exploited marble to reproduce hair, lace collar, in 17th-century bust (above) of Thomas Baker. Contrast with straight-forward use of chisel in second-century Roman inscription below (top). Sign painters in 19th and early 20th centuries added exuberant flourishes, illusion of depth to classic letter forms as on Dublin shop front (center). Clean lines of contemporary printed type in Swiss architects' journal (bottom) show machine origin.

People often say that an artist "respects his materials." They mean that he is able to create a successful marriage between the materials he chooses to work with and the forms he gives them. This form contains the artist's ideas. Respect for materials consists in the artist's suiting his methods to his material so as to communicate his ideas most effectively.

A film director, for example, may choose a story full of quiet and thoughtful characters. To help us understand what these people think and feel he can concentrate our attention almost entirely on slight changes of their facial expressions seen in close-up, effects that would be unnoticed on a stage. That is why contemporary interest in psychology finds particularly effective expression through the selective lenses of the film camera.

An earlier example of the way materials and form were married to artistic intention can be found in the story of how artists developed techniques of oil painting in the 15th century. Leonardo da Vinci (p. 42) noticed how bonfire smoke often looks very blue. He guessed at what we know to be a fact : that tiny particles of matter diffuse and reflect blue light while letting other colors of the spectrum through—to be absorbed in the darker colors of the background. Leonardo tried brushing light tints out over the darker parts of his paintings. The thinned-out paint turned bluish, giving a delicately pale effect that nevertheless allowed warm tones to show through

AE·NEROTIRA

MULHOLLANDS

from the dark underpainting. This simple technique, with its lifelike color effect, was so well suited to the nature of paint, brush, and canvas that nearly all painters used it until the mid-19th century.

Sometimes artists in different fields have ideas in common, but because they use different materials, the actual expression of similar feelings will be quite different. The architect Le Corbusier (p. 94), for example, used reinforced concrete to achieve the billowing lines of his chapel at Ronchamps in France (p. 120), and the French composer Olivier Messiaen (born 1908) wrote a two-and-a-half-hour work called *Twenty Glimpses of the Child Jesus* for the piano. Both artists wanted to communicate a sense of deep religious conviction.

On the other hand, artists working in the same medium often use similar materials in different ways. All poets use words, but they choose different kinds of words to make different effects. The Irish author Oscar Wilde (1854-1900) described the sky as "that little tent of blue" from the point of view of a prisoner, in his *The Ballad of Reading Gaol*. Keats (p. 196), on the other hand, describes a sky as "the fair and open face of heaven." The title of his sonnet, "To One Who Has Been Long in City Pent," tells us his point of view.

Artists have also often tried to *extend* the range of their materials. The ancient Greeks, for example, developed a technique of stone sculpture by striking marble at right angles with a pointed chisel instead of chipping the stone away in sideways crosscuts. They pitted the marble in this way, leaving finally a fractured, slightly porous texture that reflected light in the same soft way that skin does.

To give the effect of light, shadow, and varying tones, tapestry weavers of the Middle Ages and the Renaissance and some 19th-century painters—instead of mixing colors to duplicate those they found in nature—used small patches of pure colors that blended together when looked at from a distance. Tapestry makers used tiny stitches of dyed wool; painters—notably Georges Seurat (1859-91)—used little "points" of solid paint.

The discovery of a new material often gives rise to the development of new methods and new forms. The invention of motion pictures is a recent example. Instead of showing a succession of scenes as playwrights do, film directors learned to "cut" back and forth between two or more scenes—an innovation D. W. Griffiths pioneered in *Intolerance* (p. 286). New methods like these can even modify the techniques and forms of other arts. Many playwrights, for instance, attempt the kind of simultaneous interweaving of brief scenes that films have made familiar to audiences.

The woven textile above, made in Peru around the 11th century A.D., shows the kind of stylized, flat, two-dimensional design particularly suited to weaving techniques. The object represented is a winged animal, but artist made no attempt at three-dimensional reality.

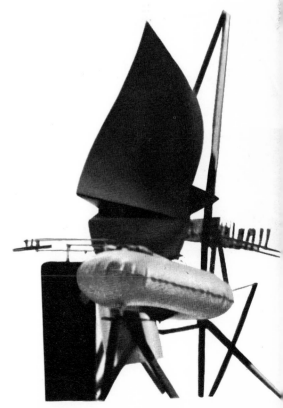

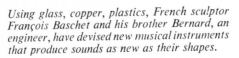

Using glass, copper, plastics, French sculptor François Baschet and his brother Bernard, an engineer, have devised new musical instruments that produce sounds as new as their shapes.

Art and beauty

"Art should be beautiful," people say. But—what is beauty? Does it lie in the subject the artist has chosen: a beautiful woman, a sunset, a flower? Or does it lie elsewhere? Plato (p. 308) believed that beauty existed in an ideal state of pure thought that we cannot hope to attain fully on earth. According to him, beauty could be glimpsed most clearly in truths discovered through logic —that is, the science of well-constructed reasoning.

For Plato, the experience of beauty did not depend on personal like or dislike of an artistic subject, but on intellectual understanding of it. Some Christian thinkers, such as St. Augustine (p. 246) and St. Thomas Aquinas (about 1225-74) believed, like Plato, that truth and beauty were synonymous. A clear understanding of truth —in this case, the truth as revealed by God—would result in the perception of beauty. To try to express this truth in art, they believed, would result in beautiful forms. This was the thinking behind medieval manuscript illuminations, and the great stained-glass windows (p. 48).

But there have always been other artists who preferred to let *emotion* influence their ideas of beauty. Plato, in fact, wanted to banish artists like these from his "ideal republic" chiefly because he thought the use of emotional experiences as the material for art would make people prefer second-hand experience and emotional excitement to that of real life. The idea that a work of art became beautiful if it represented passionate emotions resulted in works of art that enabled audiences to share such feelings without having to assume any actual pain or danger or responsibility.

Much Roman art, such as the *Laocoön* (pp. 80, 82), has this emotional appeal. During the Middle Ages, relief carvings of the Last Judgment, full of agonized figures, showed the faithful the fate in store for unrepentant sinners. In the 19th century, the writings of such poets as Byron, the music of composers like Wagner or Berlioz—and the works of romantic artists generally— all set out principally to excite people's feelings rather than appeal to their powers of reason.

Both these opposing ideas—on the one hand, ideal form, and the expression of strong personal emotion on the other—show that beauty does not necessarily lie in the *subject* of a work of art. Many great artists have portrayed subjects that at first glance seem to be entirely without beauty. The Greek plays of Aeschylus and Euripides (p. 256) are full of violence and death despite their formal, orderly observance of the dramatic unities (p. 268). Rembrandt (p. 42) was unpopular with some of his patrons, despite his acknowledged skill, when he began painting such subjects as the carcass of an ox hanging in

Late 15th-century painter Hieronymus Bosch shows God presenting
Eve to Adam in a scene (left) from
The Garden of Earthly Delights.
Nude figures are not idealized, yet
Genesis story of innocence reigning
in paradise lends beauty to them
and even to the unfamiliar, faintly
disturbing shapes of fantastic plants
and animals. Titian, on the other
hand, took inspiration directly from
ideal Greek beauty for Sacred and
Profane Love (detail, lower left),
painted in the 1520s.

In Still Life with Apples and
Oranges (*reproduced below*), painted in the 1890s, Paul Cézanne
tried to show a beauty in these
objects that went deeper than their
superficial attractiveness. "Painting is not only to copy the object,"
Cézanne said. "It is to seize a
harmony between numerous relations." Here, he harmonizes (*with
careful attention to underlying
structure*) colors, shapes, volumes.

a slaughter house. And Goya (p. 59) did a powerful series
of drawings and etchings about the atrocities that men
commit in wartime. The beauty in these and similar
works is in the skill and appropriateness of the *form* the
artist gave to what he made.

Popular ideas about what is beautiful often depend on
how familiar people are with certain artistic conventions.
Often the so-called beautiful in art is only that kind of art
with which people are most familiar. Fashion drawings
provide a striking example of this. If you analyze them,
you see that seldom are they at all closely related to the
actual forms of the body. Yet most of us accept these distorted drawings without any of the fuss and resentment
that often greet serious experiments in artistic distortion
—such as the furore that greeted Stravinsky's ballet *The
Rite of Spring* in 1913 (p. 184), or Picasso's *The Young
Ladies of Avignon* in 1907 (p. 57).

The fashion drawings of 1913 were dated by 1920;
but we have become used to the innovations of Stravinsky
and Picasso, many of which have been taken up by other
artists. The point, of course, is that a fashion drawing
symbolizes temporary ideas of beauty, and once such
ideas lose their novelty, the drawing ceases to possess
value as something timelessly beautiful in its own right;
it becomes merely a quaint reminder of the past.

Art and imitation

"Art," Plato's pupil Aristotle said, "is imitation." At first hearing, this sounds like good ammunition for people who dislike those types of art, such as abstract painting or 12-tone music, that do not seem to "imitate" anything. Let us see what Aristotle really meant by imitation. When he talked about art and imitation he was referring primarily to the theatre of his day. Was the Greek theatre what any of us would call "realistic" when it imitated life? Its action took place in the open air against a single, stylized setting (p. 256). The actors half spoke, half chanted verse dialogue—hardly an accurate copying of everyday speech! And they recited their lines from behind stylized masks. Evidently Aristotle did not believe that naturalistic reproduction constituted artistic imitation.

A photograph—of a house, for example—represents a second kind of imitation, something that at first glance we would all agree represents reality. But let us look again. A house exists as a three-dimensional object. In a photograph we see, at most, two walls and part of the roof. But because we are so used to photographs, we accept them as realistic. Yet architects' blueprints tell anyone who can read them a good deal more of the real facts about a house than any photograph can. Such plans are not at all "like" the building itself, however much they tell us about it. And to many people, untrained in architectural drawing, they appear meaningless.

The realistic seems to consist, then, of things we can

Left: A Roman tragic actor wears a mask expressing horror, shown in ivory statuette (about A.D. 200). Such masks served to heighten dramatic effect by stylizing facial expression. Patrons of Antonio Canaletto (1697-1768), however, wanted realistic, not stylized, views of Venice (right). To fulfill their commissions, Canaletto often used a camera-like device to help make his paintings accurate.

understand because we have learned to recognize them. Eskimos would probably find the painting of a bowl of unfamiliar fruit on page 313 difficult to understand. On a more sophisticated level, a Japanese audience is likely to find the realistic plays of Henrik Ibsen (p. 270) puzzling just as Europeans find the colorful *No* plays difficult (p. 254). Yet none of the obvious limitations on *universal* comprehension of Cézanne's painting or an Ibsen play prevents either being art. Only if an Eskimo or a Japanese makes himself *familiar* with the conventions of Western painting and drama—or, conversely, if an Englishman learns all he can about *No* drama—can he judge how well they express particular ideas or emotions. People often reject unfamiliar artistic techniques and ideas for their "unreality" when they really mean that they find the fact of their unfamiliarity disturbing.

A third, very important, aspect of imitation is imitation by *analogy*, which we are better prepared to understand now that we know that reality in art goes deeper than the superficial reproduction of familiar forms. Aristotle says that analogy is the very heart of poetry (p. 206). Many artists express their ideas by using something easily recognizable to stand in place of ideas not so easily explained in direct terms. Music is a good example of this. Wagner attached recurring themes to various characters in his operas (p. 156). People who listen to the music closely soon recognize the theme that stands for Siegfried (the hero of the Ring Cycle), for example—and they begin to feel what it was Wagner wanted to say about him. The value of such an analogy is that it makes possible a deeper and more telling expression of ideas than even the most skilfully naturalistic dialogue and staging.

Now we can see why experiments such as Schönberg's adoption of the 12-tone technique in music (p. 168) cause such a stir: They confront people with the unfamiliar. We can also see why such experiments are justifiable as imitation in the Aristotelian sense: They attempt to provide new analogies for the artist's idea.

The English artist-craftsman William Morris (p. 242) echoed St. Thomas Aquinas, advising artists not to "copy nature, but to copy nature's methods." Artists who do this may produce works that are not immediately recognizable to everyone as good, but if they *are* truly in harmony with what are sometimes called the laws of nature, then their worth will be lasting. When we are faced with art that does not seem to resemble any familiar object or is not immediately understandable, a good way to approach it is by trying to see just how it imitates nature in remaining true to the principles of form, order, and balance that we discussed earlier in the chapter.

Beauty of vine-wreathed capitals (above) of columns in England's Southwell Minster is due less to fidelity of surface reality than to insight of medieval artist into essential forms. Below: Italian director Vittorio de Sica created a selective imitation of life by using actual city backgrounds in Bicycle Thieves *(1948).*

Statue of Ramses II (40 feet high) at Abu Simbel, a temple carved 70 yards deep into solid rock by Ramses' artisans in about 1300 B.C. Egyptian sculptors and architects worked almost exclusively for religion and the state.

Art with a message

To some people, moral and social ideals are more important in art than ideas of beauty and form. This is not to say that artists who have a message to get across are always unconcerned with the quality of their art. Vergil (p. 210), for example, filled the *Aeneid* with patriotic passages meant to show that the gods had guided Rome to her predestined magnificence. But on his death bed, he begged that his poem be destroyed because it needed three years' work to make it perfect.

Artists in the Middle Ages created such works as the great cathedrals and illuminated manuscripts to serve what they felt were the truths of religion—following the injunctions of men like the Abbot Suger (about 1081-1151) to execute them "with all outward splendor." In late Renaissance France, Louis XIV built Versailles (p. 102) to glorify the country and himself as its absolute monarch. And he was careful to entrust its design to the greatest French architect of the age, Jules Hardouin-Mansart (1646-1708).

Since that time, however, scientific, political, and social changes have generally been reflected in works in which artists expressed their own individual points of view rather than those of public or private patrons. Such a change of attitude is apparent in the story of Rembrandt's dealings with the company of volunteer soldiers who hired him to paint a portrait group in which each of their faces should have equal prominence. They were greatly annoyed to find that Rembrandt had obscured some of their faces in order to satisfy his idea of a better composition for the picture.

Beethoven's final string quartets met with a similar lack of understanding—the work of a deaf old man, people said. They felt he was being selfishly obscure and so unplayable as to be an insult to the musical amateurs of his day. During much of his career, Goya (p. 59) introduced sly personal comments on his sitters into his portraits, and when he finally painted entirely as he felt, it was in the highly personal style of the strange "black" paintings that he put on the walls of his own house.

The new freedom of the artist to work as he felt was often dedicated to protest or revolt, or to ideals counter, at least at their inception, to those held by society at large. In the 19th century, for example, the novels of authors otherwise as different in outlook as Émile Zola (p. 248) in France and Charles Dickens (p. 232) in England were acutely critical of the social evils of their time.

The experiments of painters have often been protests against traditions that the artists felt were outmoded or lifeless. Sometimes, as with the De Stijl group in Holland (p. 66) or the Bauhaus school in Germany, artists have

To persuade Russian peasants that first five-year plan (1928) and collectivization of farms were beneficial to nation, Soviet director Dovzhenko produced the film Earth *in 1929.*

tried to promote social reforms through their art. The history of modern architecture since the late 19th century has been influenced by architects who want to improve social conditions by providing well-planned housing.

On the other hand, there have always been artists to whom what matters most is the work of art itself. The French painter Cézanne (p. 58) was far less interested in the subjects of his paintings and whether people approved of them than in expressing the structures underlying surface forms and colors. The dancer Isadora Duncan (p. 188) emphasized pure physical movement for the sake of the beauty contained in gestures of the human body. In his films, Jean Cocteau (p. 230) told stories in which carefully composed images were more important than plot.

But neither a strong social purpose nor a dedicated absorption in techniques can guarantee flawless works of art. On the other hand, conscious avoidance of any social meaning or message sometimes results in superficiality and frivolity. Achievement of true harmony, order, form, and balance depends on a deep, full observation of life. In fact, in any really valid and beautiful work of art whose aim is not simply decorative, social and moral ideas and personal emotions are difficult to separate from one another.

Rome was world center of Christianity when Bramante planned St. Peter's in 1506. Michelangelo's dome (1546-81), and Bernini's colonnade (1656-73) symbolize this.

Honoré Daumier (1808-79) was one of the 19th century's foremost satirists of political and social life in his more than 4000 lithographs published in French journals. Drawing reproduced below shows "combat" between the new realism in art (left) and classic idealism (right).

317

Art in the world today

Improvements in transport and communication during the past 100 years have led rapidly to the birth of a general international cultural exchange; despite wars and uncertainty there has been a virtual explosion of technological discovery in every area of human endeavor. These factors have combined to produce such artistic phenomena as the 20th-century look in world architecture that many people call the "international style."

Yet the international exchange of artistic ideas is by no means a new phenomenon. The Romans, for example, borrowed Greek art and in turn diffused their borrowings, stamped by the Romans' own special temperament and technological achievements, throughout their empire. After the fall of Rome, there was a long period when societies lived in relative isolation. But trade and the Crusades opened Europe to ideas from the Orient, and soon after, the Renaissance reawakened interest in the classical world. The great 15th- and 16th-century voyages of discovery revealed even wider horizons.

So, from the late Middle Ages to our own times, world interchange of art and ideas has continued to expand. The introduction of printing and photographic techniques, and later, of recordings, radio, films, and television, has given men the opportunity to familiarize themselves with the history and culture of every country in the world

International festivals, radio, records, television, film, all make the playing of such musicians as cellist Pablo Casals familiar to audiences everywhere.

Today, works of art travel all over the world. Above left, citizens of Warsaw view Delacroix's Liberty Leading the People, *on loan from the Louvre in Paris. Above right, girls tour exhibition of American Alexander Calder's mobiles at London's Tate Gallery.*

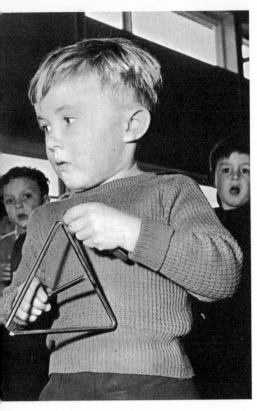

Most schoolchildren learn about the arts by doing—by making music, for example. They gain insight into artists' problems; some will go on to become artists.

without ever going abroad. As important as these mass media of communication, are improved means of transport. Traveling exhibitions, orchestras, ballet, and opera companies bring art works before audiences who 50 years ago would have had no opportunity to experience them.

Is there, perhaps, a danger of "knowing too much" about art? Too many conflicting ideas presented like some spectacular kaleidoscope can confuse both artists and their audiences. Artists may be tempted to imitate artistic forms alien to their own cultures without really understanding them; people may find it difficult to judge unfamiliar works of art, either accepting everything uncritically, or rejecting it in bewilderment. But this need not be so. For one thing, people can learn to understand how the artist and his particular environment interact to produce his art. In addition, with increased leisure, people can actually attempt to express themselves through one of the arts and so experience for themselves something of how the creative process works.

Finally, the vitality of art in the latter half of the 20th century will depend on how well men understand the exciting new ideas, discoveries, and explorations that surround them. The arts must reflect contemporary thoughts and feelings as meaningfully as they did during great periods of artistic creation in the past.

Work on Chandigarh, the new capital of the Indian state of East Punjab, began in 1953 under the direction of a team of Indian, English, and French architects. Above: the concrete façade of the secretariat building, designed by Le Corbusier.

Historical Survey

Throughout this book our attention has chiefly been focused on the "what" and "how" of the arts and on some of the ideas and qualities that they have in common. That is why we have not always followed a strictly historical approach. For the same reason, when we mentioned the names of artists, it was not necessarily because their works are considered great, but because one of them happened to illustrate the particular point under discussion.

On the following pages we take a different approach and, by means of text and pictures, relate the major artists of each age not only to one another but to their society and period as well. Because the arts are expressions of men's thoughts and feelings, they have always been a fascinating and authentic mirror of the society and age in which they were produced. In fact, it is often from works of art that we learn most about the variations in belief and outlook of past ages.

The first four pages survey the great civilizations that flourished between 2000 B.C. and A.D. 1200, and laid the foundations of the modern world. Then, starting with the 13th century, when artists began to acquire a new status in society (and their names, therefore, begin to appear more frequently in the pages of history), we follow the story of Western art until recent times.

On each left-hand page we summarize in words and pictures the trends and characteristics of the period under review. On the right-hand pages, chronological diagrams show the life spans of some of the major artists who were alive at the time. With those life spans are charted some of the significant events through which the artists lived. In this way, artists whom we may know only by their works are seen in a historical perspective that is familiar to us all.

At some time during men's struggle for survival in prehistoric times, they also began making those objects that we today group under the broad category of prehistoric art: paintings, carvings, pottery, metalwork. We do not know the precise function these objects actually had in early societies, but it is doubtful that they were just luxuries made at leisure simply to give pleasure. On the contrary, the urge to shape stone or metal and to make images seems to be a deeply implanted instinct of man. But the history of art as we know it really begins at the time of the first written records: that is, about 3000 B.C. Then, the most important world civilizations existed very close to one another in the Middle East—in Egypt and Sumeria. In Egypt, the absolute power of the pharaohs of the Old Kingdom (from before 3000 B.C. to about 2260 B.C.) determined the basic orientation of artistic activity. This pattern, or style, lasted until about 500 B.C. The major surviving works, built to last "forever," are temples and the tombs of the pharaohs. The character of Egyptian sculpture, reliefs, and paintings is impersonal, static, and subtle. It ranges from delicate naturalistic detail to the symbolic, almost abstract, marks called hieroglyphs. Sumerian culture—less static, less subtle— lasted almost as long as the Egyptian, but as the culture of a region rather

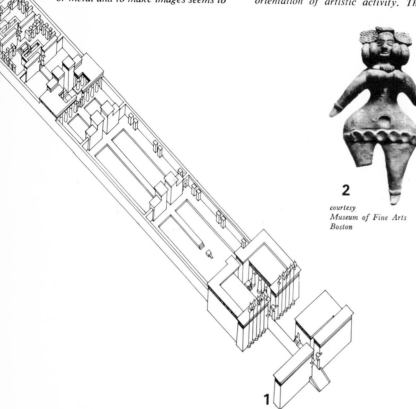

2

courtesy
Museum of Fine Arts
Boston

3

1 Reconstruction of part of the great temple of king Ikhnaton of Egypt (about 1375-58 B.C.).
2 Indian mother goddess Mathura; terra cotta, third or fourth century B.C.
3 Temple carving of the Assyrian King Shamshi-Adad V, from Nimrud (Iraq).
4 View of the Acropolis, Athens dominated by the Parthenon (begun about 480 B.C.).
5 The Pont du Gard—part of the Roman aqueduct near Nîmes (France), begun about 19 B.C.

1

4

5

322

han as an unbroken national style. By contrast, the rise and development of Greek civilization is closer to the modern world in time and feeling. Mathematicians and philosophers flourished; their rigorous logic forms the basis of many of the principles of Western thought. Concepts of democracy and the rights of man were investigated in open discussion. Drawing upon ancient Aegean cultures (particularly that of Crete), as well as that of Egypt, Greek art from the sixth century B.C. explored the world of ideas to create concepts of beauty that directly and indirectly have affected European culture ever since. Greek art forms had a cultivation and subtlety that were not matched by any other ancient culture. The Greeks elevated their poets, sculptors, and playwrights to a social status that artists had never before possessed. The Roman world based much of its own culture upon that of the Greeks and added a practical ability in engineering and social organization that helped them spread their empire and influence over the Western World.

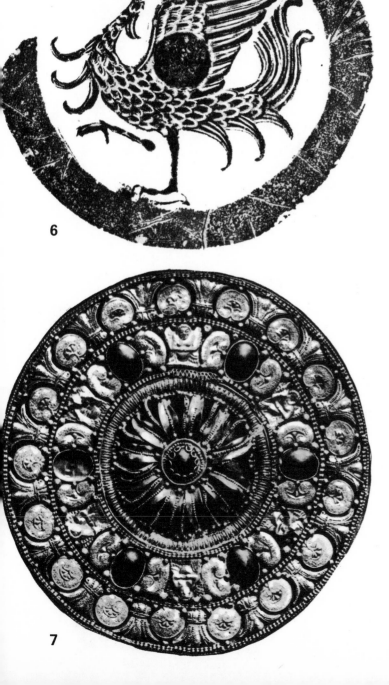

6

Ikhnaton reigned 1375?–1358 Egyptian king
Ramses II reigned 1292–1225 Egyptian king
Moses fl 1200? Hebrew prophet
Homer fl 850? Greek poet
Aesop 620?–560? Greek fabulist
Sappho fl 600? Greek poetess
Lao-tzu 604?–531? Chinese philosopher
Cyrus the Great 600?–529 Persian king
Buddha 563?–483? Indian philosopher
Darius I 558?–486 Persian king
Confucius 551?–479 Chinese philosopher
Pythagoras d 497? Greek mathematician
Aeschylus 525–456 Greek dramatist
Pindar 522?–443 Greek poet
Xerxes 519?–465 Persian king
Sophocles 496?–406 Greek dramatist
Euripides 480?–406? Greek dramatist
Thucydides 471?–400? Greek historian
Socrates 470?–399 Greek philosopher
Hippocrates 460?–377? Greek physician
Pericles d 429 Greek statesman
Democritus b 460? Greek philosopher
Herodotus 5th century Greek historian
Ictinus 5th century Greek architect
Phidias 5th century Greek sculptor
Aristophanes 448?–380? Greek dramatist
Plato 427?–347 Greek philosopher
Diogenes 412?–323 Greek philosopher
Mo Ti 5th–4th centuries Chinese philosopher
Scopas fl 370 Greek sculptor
Demosthenes 385?–322 Greek orator
Aristotle 384–322 Greek philosopher
Mencius 372?–289? Chinese philosopher
Alexander the Great 356–323 Macedonian king
Praxiteles 4th century Greek sculptor
Menander 343?–291? Greek dramatist
Epicurus 342?–270 Greek philosopher
Euclid fl 300 Greek mathematician
Archimedes 287?–212 Greek mathematician
Plautus 254?–184 Roman dramatist
Hannibal 247–183 Carthaginian general
Terence 185–159 Roman dramatist
Marcus Cicero 106–43 Roman orator
Julius Caesar 100–44 Roman general
Lucretius 96?–55 Roman poet
Gaius Catullus 84?–54 Roman poet
Vergil 70–19 Roman poet
Horace 65–8 Roman poet and satirist
Caesar Augustus 63–A.D. 14 Roman emperor
Livy 59–A.D. 17 Roman historian
Vitruvius 1st century B.C. Roman architect
Ovid 43–A.D. 17? Roman poet

6 Rubbing of bronze bowl
decoration, made in China between
202 B.C. and A.D. 220.
7 An Etruscan gold earring
of the sixth century B.C.

7

During the years from the time of Christ to the 13th century, the history of European culture was inevitably linked to the rise of Christianity. This age was also significant in the development of other civilizations in the Middle and Far East—those of China and India, for example. Greek ideas and art forms continued to spread to the outposts of Roman colonization, which linked the West with points as far east as India and as far north as Britain. But as time went on, the power and subtlety of Greek culture was dissipated, and Rome was unable to substitute a real alternative. Outside the major civilizations, there were primitive expressions of great artistic power, but they formed no significant pattern. In A.D. 313, Roman persecution of the Christian religion stopped, and Christianity was established as the official Roman religion. From this time on, the new needs of Christian worship resulted in the adaptation of the Roman public hall into a church. Eventually, the new religion began to neglect sculpture and the pictorial arts, for it feared and rejected the idolatry of pagan worship. A great controversy raged over the use of images in religious art. In the eighth century this resulted in a ban on lifelike religious images in the Eastern, Greek-speaking half of the Roman Empire (centered at Byzantium).

1

3

4

5

1 *Triumphal arch of the Emperor Constantine, built in* A.D. *312 in Rome.*
2 *Verses from a 10th-century Koran written in Kufic script.*
3 *An eighth-century Japanese* gigaku *ritual mask.*
4 *Detail of cup made for Chosroes II, king of Persia,* A.D. *590-628.*
5 *A 12th-century carving from temple of Angkor Wat in Cambodia.*
6 *Earthenware jug made in the Nazca region of* Peru (A.D. *100-600).*
7 *Domed exterior of church of Santa Sofia, Constantinople (built* A.D. *532-7).*
8 *Mosaic portrait of the Emperor Justinian (A.D. 483-565) from the church of San Vitale in Ravenna.*
9 *Initial from the* Book of Kells *(Irish, eighth century).*
10 *Carved dragon's head from an early ninth-century Viking ship.*
11 *Romanesque nave of Durham Cathedral, England (begun 1093).*

6

Stiff, formalized images were permissible, and Byzantine artists worked in a tradition that tended to ignore the natural world. Nevertheless, such limitations did not prevent the Byzantines from creating works of great beauty. They emphasized the splendor and dignity of the Church particularly through the use of mosaics. But the sense of inquiry into nature that had motivated the Greeks was submerged; significant developments in the sciences and philosophy at this time belonged to such cultures as the Islamic and the Chinese. Western Christians (separated from the Eastern Church in 1054) began to use sculpture and the pictorial arts to spread the gospel to predominantly illiterate congregations. By the 12th century, most Romanesque churches and cathedrals contained carved and painted representations of Christian saints and the Christian story. From such works grew the later forms of Gothic art. The illuminated manuscripts produced in the monasteries (where musical traditions were also nourished) preserved a tradition of vivid pictorial and decorative inventiveness everywhere in the West.

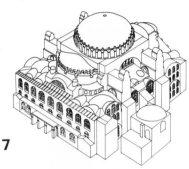

7

8

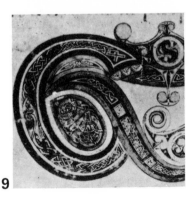

9

10

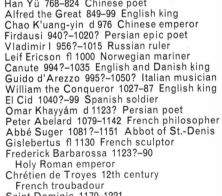

11

Jesus Christ 4? B.C. –A.D. 29?
Saint Peter d 67?
Saint Paul d 67?
Pliny the Elder 23–79 Roman scholar
Lucan 39–65 Roman poet
Martial 40?–102? Roman epigrammatist
Plutarch 46?–120? Greek biographer
Tacitus 55?–118? Roman historian
Juvenal 60?–140? Roman poet and satirist
Hadrian 76–138 Roman emperor
Marcus Aurelius 121–80 Roman emperor
Lucian 2nd century Greek satirist and wit
Ptolemy 2nd century Egyptian mathematician
Constantine 280?–337 Roman emperor
Saint Augustine 354–430 Theologian
Alaric 370?–410 Visigoth king
Attila 406?–53 King of the Huns
Kalidasa 5th century Hindu dramatist and poet
Theodoric 454?–526 Ostrogoth king
Saint Benedict 480?–543?
    Founder of Benedictines
Justinian I 483–565 Byzantine emperor
Saint Columba 521–97 Irish missionary
Pope Gregory I 540?–604
Mohammed 570–632 Founder of Islam
Caedmon fl 670 English poet
Venerable Bede 673–735 English historian
Charles Martel 689?–741 Frankish ruler
Li Po d 762 Chinese poet
Pepin the Short 714?–68 Frankish king
Charlemagne 742–814 Holy Roman emperor
Harun al-Rashid 764?–809 Caliph of Baghdad
Han Yü 768–824 Chinese poet
Alfred the Great 849–99 English king
Chao K'uang-yin d 976 Chinese emperor
Firdausi 940?–1020? Persian epic poet
Vladimir I 956?–1015 Russian ruler
Leif Ericson fl 1000 Norwegian mariner
Canute 994?–1035 English and Danish king
Guido d'Arezzo 995?–1050? Italian musician
William the Conqueror 1027–87 English king
El Cid 1040?–99 Spanish soldier
Omar Khayyám d 1123? Persian poet
Peter Abelard 1079–1142 French philosopher
Abbé Suger 1081?–1151 Abbot of St.-Denis
Gislebertus fl 1130 French sculptor
Frederick Barbarossa 1123?–90
    Holy Roman emperor
Chrétien de Troyes 12th century
    French troubadour
Saint Dominic 1170–1221
    Founder of Dominicans

1200–1400. *The medieval world harnessed all its resources of men, money, and ideas to the building of great cathedrals throughout Europe. The soaring buildings—combining elements of structural logic, symbolism, and fantasy—rose slowly; they were rarely planned ahead in their entirety. Structural problems seem to have been dealt with as the builders came face to face with them. The solutions they found often showed great economy of* means and yet resulted in satisfying forms. In Italy, the rise of the wandering begging orders of friars lent new vigor to the spread of Christian ideas, though the division of the papacy between Rome and Avignon early in the 14th century foreshadowed the division of Christendom. In Italy, toward the end of the 13th century, artists and writers became aware of the near-forgotten antique inheritance surrounding them. As a result artists *began to add the power and poise of ancient art to the Byzantine and medieval traditions they already possessed. This, and the glimpses of the Orient opened up by the Crusades, broadened intellectual as well as artistic horizons; the Renaissance began to dawn over Europe.*

1

1 Dante Alighieri, from a fresco at Orvieto, Italy, by Luca Signorelli (1441-1523).
2 Krak des Chevaliers, a 13th-century castle in Lebanon, built by crusaders.
3 Architectural drawing from sketchbook of Villard de Honnecourt (about 1235).

2

3

The age of the cathedral

These dates tell when the first stones for some great churches were laid. Most took centuries to complete. But the most intense building activity was concentrated in the 13th and 14th centuries.

1072 Lincoln Cathedral
1093 Durham Cathedral
1095 St. Mark's, Venice
1140 Abbey of St. Denis
1163 Notre Dame, Paris
1175 Canterbury Cathedral
1194 Chartres Cathedral
1211 Reims Cathedral
1228 Church of St. Francis, Assisi
1243 Sainte-Chapelle, Paris
1245 Westminster Abbey
1250 Strasbourg Cathedral
1282 Albi Cathedral

4 Fourth Crusade ●1241 Mongols invade ◼279 End of Sung dynasty 1338–1453 Hundred Years' War
pture of Constantinople Poland and Hungary Commencement of Mongol rule in China
●1215 Magna ◼1232? Alhambra ●1258 Mongols Kublai Khan 1216–94 1347–50 The Black Death
Carta of Granada destroy Baghdad 1356–77 Peak of Hanseatic League
●1221 Fifth ◼1245? Siena ◼1266 Salisbury ◼1291 Swiss Confederation
Crusade Cathedral Cathedral 1364 Cracow University
◼1227 Toledo ◼1253? Sorbonne 1368 Ming dynasty
Cathedral University ●1271 Marco Polo travels in China
●1226 Death of ◼1260 Chartres
Saint Francis of Assisi Cathedral

de Honnecourt fl 1230 French architect

Brunelleschi

Robert de Luzarches fl 1220–60 French architect

Giovanni Pisano 1245–1314 Italian sculptor and architect Henry Yevele 1320?–1400? English architect

William Ramsay fl 1325–50 English architect

Donatello

Nicola Pisano 1220–84 Italian sculptor

Ghiberti

Quercia

Fra Angelico

Giovanni Cimabue (Cenni di Pepo) 1240?–1302? Italian painter

Duccio di Buoninsegna 1255?–1319? Italian painter

Giotto (Giotto di Bondone) 1276?–1337? Italian painter and architect

Simone Martini 1283?–1344 Italian painter van Evck

van der Weyden

Pisanello

Uccello

Rublyov

er von der Vogelweide 1170?–1230? German poet and musician

Adam de la Halle 1235?–85? French poet and musician

Guido Cavalcanti 1250?–1300 Italian writer

Dante (Dante Alighieri) 1265–1321 Italian poet

Petrarch (Francesco Petrarca) 1304–74 Italian poet

Giovanni Boccaccio 1313–75 Italian writer

Jean Froissart 1333?–1400? French writer

Eustache Deschamps 1340?–1407? French writer

Geoffrey Chaucer 1340?–1400 English writer

William Langland 1332?–1400? English poet

John Dunstable

Guillaume de Machaut 1305?–77 French composer

1400–1500. *This was the age of the Renaissance, or rebirth, of classical ideas. In Italy, where it began, the aims of medieval culture were not immediately discarded. At first they ran parallel to the rise of humanism (the study of ancient Greco-Roman learning and culture). The Church embarked on a program of church building and decoration whose patrons included the newly prosperous Italian banking families and the civil authorities.*

Architects made a free and inventive use of antique forms in their buildings. Artists used perspective as a means of relating the human figure—increasingly significant in art—to its setting. In both Italy and the Netherlands, painters looked with a clearer vision at the world around them and recorded their observations. A new curiosity about the natural world led to the study of anatomy and the sciences. The Portuguese, Italians, and Spanish

voyaged along new trade routes and opened up a whole new hemisphere to European exploitation. Although artists were still organized in craft guilds, a dramatic broadening of their interests helped to revolutionize their role in society—a process aided by the perfection of movable type and the resulting flood of printed books.

1

2

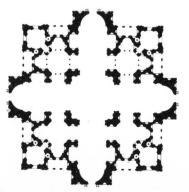

3

5

4

1 *Masaccio's* The Adoration of the Magi *(about 1426).*
2 *Head of St. George, carved by Donatello (about 1416-20).*
3 *Page of first Bible printed from movable type—set by Johann Gutenberg. (Mainz, about 1453-5.)*
4 *The original plan by Donato Bramante for the rebuilding of St. Peter's, Rome (commissioned by Pope Julius II in 1506).*
5 *Turquoise mosaic ornament from Mexico, made by Mixtec Indians in the 15th century.*

1338–1453 Hundred Years' War

● 1455 Wars of the Roses

● 1453 Turks take Constantinople

1480–92
Florence ruled by
Lorenzo de' Medici

● 1492 Catholics take Granada

● 1405 Death of Tamerlane

● 1431 Burning of Joan of Arc

● 1450 Perfection of movable type Johann Gutenberg 1400?–68?

● 1480 Spanish Inquisition

● 1409 University of Leipzig

■ 1478 Canterbury Tales printed by William Caxton 1422?–91

● 1492 Columbus Discovers America

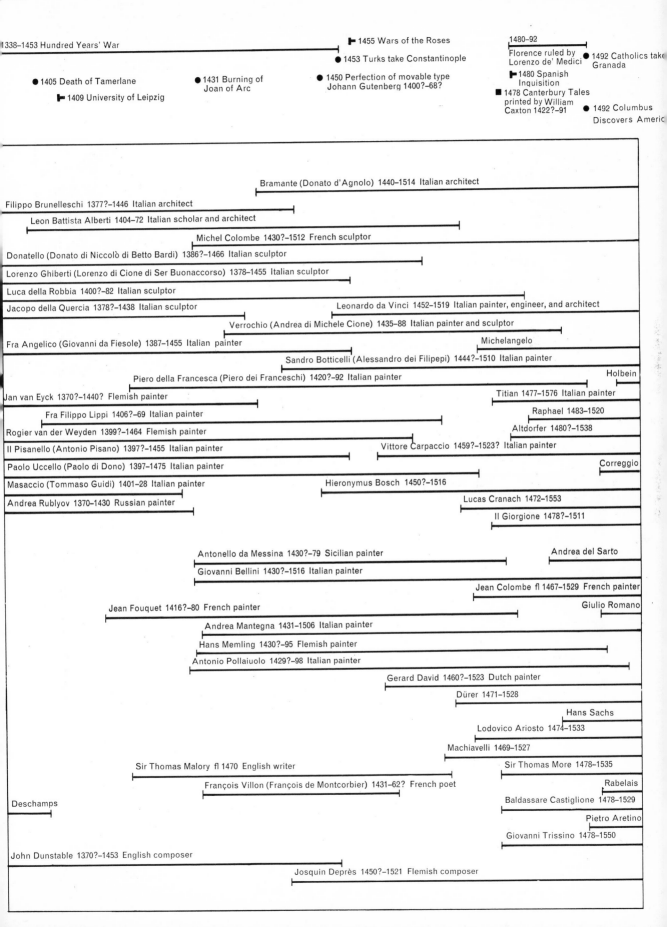

Bramante (Donato d'Agnolo) 1440–1514 Italian architect

Filippo Brunelleschi 1377?–1446 Italian architect

Leon Battista Alberti 1404–72 Italian scholar and architect

Michel Colombe 1430?–1512 French sculptor

Donatello (Donato di Niccolò di Betto Bardi) 1386?–1466 Italian sculptor

Lorenzo Ghiberti (Lorenzo di Cione di Ser Buonaccorso) 1378–1455 Italian sculptor

Luca della Robbia 1400?–82 Italian sculptor

Jacopo della Quercia 1378?–1438 Italian sculptor

Leonardo da Vinci 1452–1519 Italian painter, engineer, and architect

Verrochio (Andrea di Michele Cione) 1435–88 Italian painter and sculptor

Fra Angelico (Giovanni da Fiesole) 1387–1455 Italian painter

Michelangelo

Sandro Botticelli (Alessandro dei Filipepi) 1444?–1510 Italian painter

Piero della Francesca (Piero dei Franceschi) 1420?–92 Italian painter

Holbein

Jan van Eyck 1370?–1440? Flemish painter

Titian 1477–1576 Italian painter

Fra Filippo Lippi 1406?–69 Italian painter

Raphael 1483–1520

Rogier van der Weyden 1399?–1464 Flemish painter

Altdorfer 1480?–1538

Il Pisanello (Antonio Pisano) 1397?–1455 Italian painter

Vittore Carpaccio 1459?–1523? Italian painter

Paolo Uccello (Paolo di Dono) 1397–1475 Italian painter

Correggio

Masaccio (Tommaso Guidi) 1401–28 Italian painter

Hieronymus Bosch 1450?–1516

Andrea Rublyov 1370–1430 Russian painter

Lucas Cranach 1472–1553

Il Giorgione 1478?–1511

Antonello da Messina 1430?–79 Sicilian painter

Andrea del Sarto

Giovanni Bellini 1430?–1516 Italian painter

Jean Colombe fl 1467–1529 French painter

Jean Fouquet 1416?–80 French painter

Giulio Romano

Andrea Mantegna 1431–1506 Italian painter

Hans Memling 1430?–95 Flemish painter

Antonio Pollaiuolo 1429?–98 Italian painter

Gerard David 1460?–1523 Dutch painter

Dürer 1471–1528

Hans Sachs

Lodovico Ariosto 1474–1533

Machiavelli 1469–1527

Sir Thomas Malory fl 1470 English writer

Sir Thomas More 1478–1535

François Villon (François de Montcorbier) 1431–62? French poet

Rabelais

Baldassare Castiglione 1478–1529

Deschamps

Pietro Aretino

Giovanni Trissino 1478–1550

John Dunstable 1370?–1453 English composer

Josquin Deprès 1450?–1521 Flemish composer

1500-1550. *During the age of the High Renaissance in Italy, artists attempted to combine intellectual inquiry with practical architectural and pictorial projects commissioned by an informed and adventurous patronage. The character of these artistic solutions at first stressed classical qualities of balance and symmetry. Later, the tensions arising from the clash of the new learning with old beliefs expressed themselves in exaggerated, mannered styles. Nevertheless an understanding of proportion, anatomy, and perspective was by now common to all painters. In Venice, the use of oil paint, previously explored by Flemish painters, was perfected. The Reformation began in middle Europe, spread throughout the north, and although it did not stop the gradual dissemination of Italian ideas and art forms, the production of religious art slowed down in newly Protestant areas. The Church retained a major role as a patron of the arts, but private patronage—through the courts and nobility—continued to form a pattern that predominated through future centuries. Poets, musicians, and painters enhanced the cultural pretensions of the scores of newly independent principalities whose rulers everywhere sought artists' services.*

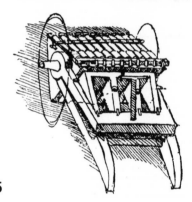

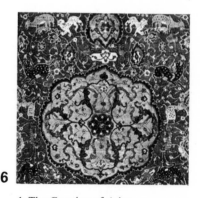

1 The Creation of Adam, *part of Michelangelo's frescoed ceiling in the Vatican's Sistine Chapel (1508-12).*
2 *Detail from* The Ambassadors, *by Hans Holbein the Younger (1533).*
3 *Château of Chambord, France, begun in 1519 for Francis I.*
4 *Martin Luther (1483-1546), from a woodcut by Cranach.*
5 *Leonardo da Vinci's design for a multiple-barrelled gun.*
6 *Detail from a Persian rug woven in Tabriz.*

1503–13 Pope Julius II

1519 Accession
of Charles V

1520 Accession of
Suleiman I

1519–21 Cortes in Mexico

1533 Accession of
Ivan the Terrible

1533 Church of England
founded by Henry VIII

■ 1534 German Bible
Luther 1483–1546

1545–63 Council of Trent

■ 1543 De Revolutionibus
Orbium Coelestium
Copernicus 1473–1543

1508–12 Sistine Chapel painted

1519–22 First circumnavigation of the globe
Magellan 1480?–1521

■ 1516 The Prince, Machiavelli
■ 1516 Greek New Testament, Erasmus 1466?–1536

■ 1536 Institutes of the Christian
Religion John Calvin 1509–64

■ 1539 Society of Jesus
(Jesuits) Ignatius of Loyola 1491–1556

ante

Giacomo da Vignola (Giacomo Barrochio) 1507–73 Italian architect

l Colombe

Andrea Palladio 1518–80 Italian architect

Jean Goujon 1510?–68? French sculptor

Cornelis Floris 1514–75 Flemish sculptor

ardo da Vinci

Jean Bologne (Giovanni da Bologna) 1529?–1608 Flemish sculptor

angelo (Michelangelo Buonarroti) 1475–1564 Italian painter, sculptor, architect, and poet

elli

Il Tintoretto (Jacopo Robusti) 1518–94 Italian painter

Holbein the Younger 1497?–1543 German painter

(Tiziano Vecelli) 1477–1576 Italian painter

ael (Raffaello Santi) 1483–1520 Italian painter

Pieter Brueghel the Elder 1520?–69 Flemish painter

echt Altdorfer 1480?–1538 German painter

El Greco

e Carpaccio 1459?–1523? Italian painter

Paolo Veronese (Paolo Cagliari) 1528–88 Italian painter

ggio (Antonio da Correggio) 1494–1534 Italian painter

Hilliard

nymus Bosch (Hieronymus van Aeken) 1450?–1516 Dutch painter

Cranach 1472–1553 German painter

one

hias Grünewald fl 1500–30 German painter

ea del Sarto (Andrea d'Agnolo di Francesco) 1486–1531 Italian painter

nni Bellini 1430?–1516 Italian painter

Colombe fl 1467–1529 French painter

Romano (Giulio Pippi de' Gianuzzi) 1499–1546 Italian painter and architect

ea Mantegna 1431–1506 Italian painter

Luiz Vaz de Camões 1524–80 Portuguese writer

Il Bronzino (Agnolo di Cosimo) 1502–72 Italian painter

Il Parmigianino (Girolamo Mazzuoli) 1503–40 Italian painter

Cervantes

rd David 1460?–1523 Dutch painter

Pierre de Ronsard 1524–85 French poet

echt Dürer 1471–1528 German painter

Michel de Montaigne 1533–92 French writer

Sachs 1494–1576 German poet and dramatist

vico Ariosto 1474–1533 Italian poet

Tasso

lò Machiavelli 1469–1527 Italian writer

omas More 1478–1535 English writer

ois Rabelais 1494?–1553 French writer

ssare Castiglione 1478–1529 Italian writer

William Byrd 1540–1623

Aretino 1492–1556 Italian poet

nni Trissino 1478–1550 Italian poet

Giovanni Palestrina 1526?–94 Italian composer

in Deprès 1450?–1521 Flemish composer

Orlando di Lasso 1532?–94 Flemish composer

Thomas Tallis 1510?–85 English composer

1550–1600. *Spanish wealth, military power, and court manners continued to affect European-wide cultural patterns. The Catholic resistance to the threat of Protestantism organized itself into the Counter Reformation, a movement that imposed strict rules on artistic activity. Some northern artists, notably Shakespeare and Breughel, made full use of their insight into human behavior, often choosing the lower social classes for their subjects. At the same time, limited and essentially artificial modes of expression were common in much official court art and poetry. In Italy and Spain, certain exaggerated, intensely emotional art traditions continued to be widely influential. The visual arts were expected to conform to a style in which elongated figures and asymmetrical compositions prevailed. In architecture, the authority of the ancient world was formally set out in books explaining the "orders."*

Architects did, however, continue to use antique forms in an inventive rather than historically correct manner. The same basic forms enriched churches as well as palaces and country houses. Out of some of these designs, and the attitudes behind them, arose the Baroque style of the next century.

1 *Court recreations, from a wood engraving by Swiss artist Jost Amman (1539-91).*
2 *Wheel-lock gun, made in southern Germany (about 1560).*
3 *Queen Elizabeth I of England, from a miniature painted by Nicholas Hilliard (1572).*
4 *St. Basil's Cathedral, Moscow, built for Tsar Ivan IV in 1555-60.*
5 *The Villa Pojana, near Vicenza, Italy. Designed by Andrea Palladio.*
6 *Charles V (1500-58), Holy Roman Emperor, from a painting by Titian.*

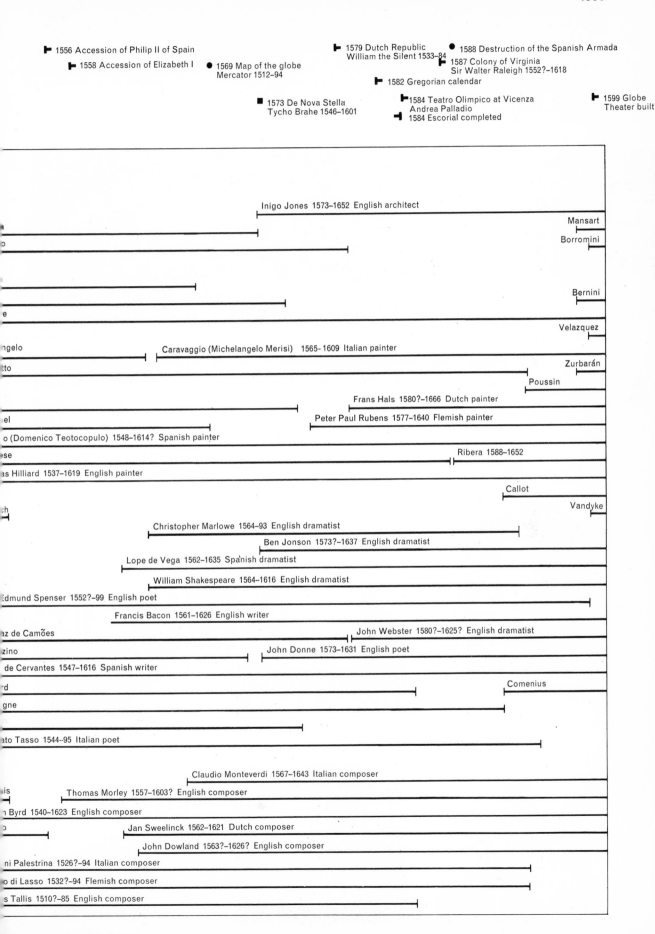

1556 Accession of Philip II of Spain

1558 Accession of Elizabeth I

1569 Map of the globe
Mercator 1512–94

1573 De Nova Stella
Tycho Brahe 1546–1601

1579 Dutch Republic
William the Silent 1533–84

1582 Gregorian calendar

1584 Teatro Olimpico at Vicenza
Andrea Palladio

1584 Escorial completed

1588 Destruction of the Spanish Armada

1587 Colony of Virginia
Sir Walter Raleigh 1552?–1618

1599 Globe
Theater built

Inigo Jones 1573–1652 English architect

Mansart

Borromini

Bernini

Velazquez

ngelo

Caravaggio (Michelangelo Merisi)   1565- 1609 Italian painter

tto

Zurbarán

Poussin

Frans Hals 1580?–1666 Dutch painter

Peter Paul Rubens 1577–1640 Flemish painter

el

o (Domenico Teotocopulo) 1548–1614? Spanish painter

ese

Ribera 1588–1652

as Hilliard 1537–1619 English painter

Callot

Vandyke

ch

Christopher Marlowe 1564–93 English dramatist

Ben Jonson 1573?–1637 English dramatist

Lope de Vega 1562–1635 Spanish dramatist

William Shakespeare 1564–1616 English dramatist

Edmund Spenser 1552?–99 English poet

Francis Bacon 1561–1626 English writer

az de Camões

John Webster 1580?–1625? English dramatist

zino

John Donne 1573–1631 English poet

de Cervantes 1547–1616 Spanish writer

rd

Comenius

gne

ato Tasso 1544–95 Italian poet

Claudio Monteverdi 1567–1643 Italian composer

is

Thomas Morley 1557–1603? English composer

n Byrd 1540–1623 English composer

o

Jan Sweelinck 1562–1621 Dutch composer

John Dowland 1563?–1626? English composer

ni Palestrina 1526?–94 Italian composer

o di Lasso 1532?–94 Flemish composer

s Tallis 1510?–85 English composer

1600–1650. The Baroque age in Italy reflected the heightened emotional climate of the Counter Reformation. The building and decoration of churches and palaces absorbed most of the creative energies of the day. Arguments about artistic styles began to take place on a larger scale than ever before. A new-found interest in the effects of light was used both to reveal forms and to dramatize the subject. The traditions of Italian culture during the preceding 200 years were either modified or disregarded. An emphasis on building plans that had stressed straight lines and right angles was replaced by ones that stressed irregular curves. Ornament became integral to the design rather than something to be applied to a surface. The court patronage of the north favored portraiture of a supremely elegant kind, but the bourgeois patrons of the economically independent Netherlands preferred a precise reflection of their domestic surroundings. Interest in Greek and Roman literature was one of the causes behind an upsurge of dramatic activity in Spain, Italy, France, and England. In Italy, musicians experimented with drama and music.

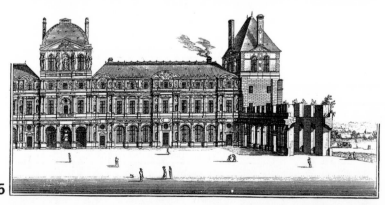

1 Title page from first edition of Shakespeare's King Lear (1608).
2 The Anatomy Lesson of Dr. Tulp by Rembrandt (about 1632).
3 An engraving by Jacques Callot, from a series called Beggars and Vagabonds.
4 The Fountain of the Moor, Rome, designed by Giovanni Bernini.
5 Courtyard façade of the Louvre, Paris (1546-1654).

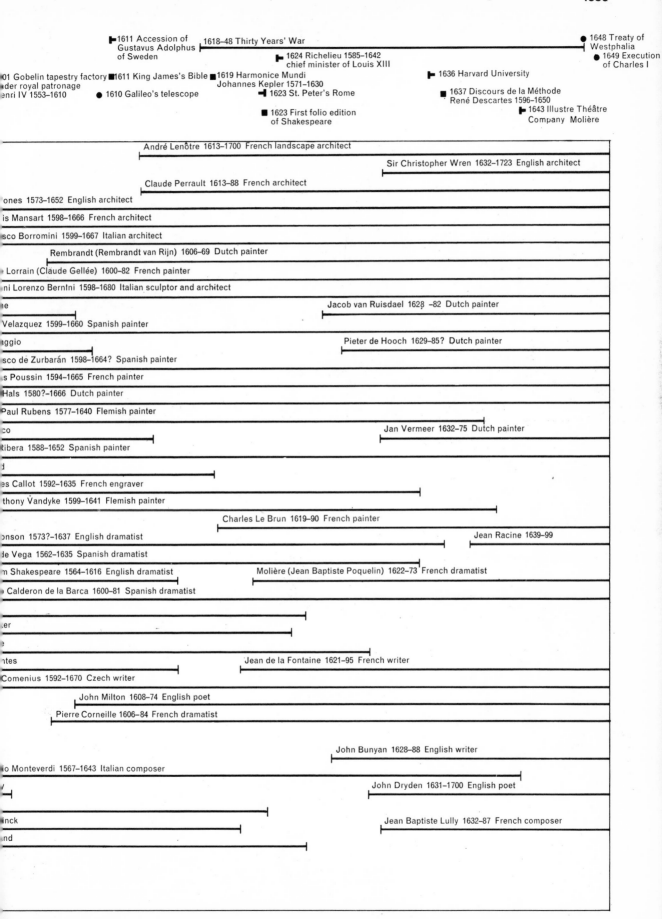

⊢1611 Accession of
Gustavus Adolphus
of Sweden

1618–48 Thirty Years' War

●1648 Treaty of
Westphalia

1624 Richelieu 1585–1642
chief minister of Louis XIII

●1649 Execution
of Charles I

01 Gobelin tapestry factory ■1611 King James's Bible ■1619 Harmonice Mundi
der royal patronage
Johannes Kepler 1571–1630

■1636 Harvard University

enri IV 1553–1610   ● 1610 Galileo's telescope

⊣1623 St. Peter's Rome

■1637 Discours de la Méthode
René Descartes 1596–1650

■1623 First folio edition
of Shakespeare

⊢1643 Illustre Théâtre
Company Molière

André Lenôtre 1613–1700 French landscape architect

Sir Christopher Wren 1632–1723 English architect

Claude Perrault 1613–88 French architect

ones 1573–1652 English architect

is Mansart 1598–1666 French architect

sco Borromini 1599–1667 Italian architect

Rembrandt (Rembrandt van Rijn) 1606–69 Dutch painter

Lorrain (Claude Gellée) 1600–82 French painter

ni Lorenzo Bernini 1598–1680 Italian sculptor and architect

Jacob van Ruisdael 1628 –82 Dutch painter

Velazquez 1599–1660 Spanish painter

aggio

Pieter de Hooch 1629–85? Dutch painter

sco de Zurbarán 1598–1664? Spanish painter

s Poussin 1594–1665 French painter

Hals 1580?–1666 Dutch painter

Paul Rubens 1577–1640 Flemish painter

co

Jan Vermeer 1632–75 Dutch painter

Ribera 1588–1652 Spanish painter

es Callot 1592–1635 French engraver

thony Vandyke 1599–1641 Flemish painter

Charles Le Brun 1619–90 French painter

nson 1573?–1637 English dramatist

Jean Racine 1639–99

de Vega 1562–1635 Spanish dramatist

m Shakespeare 1564–1616 English dramatist

Molière (Jean Baptiste Poquelin) 1622–73 French dramatist

Calderon de la Barca 1600–81 Spanish dramatist

er

e

ntes

Jean de la Fontaine 1621–95 French writer

Comenius 1592–1670 Czech writer

John Milton 1608–74 English poet

Pierre Corneille 1606–84 French dramatist

John Bunyan 1628–88 English writer

o Monteverdi 1567–1643 Italian composer

John Dryden 1631–1700 English poet

inck

Jean Baptiste Lully 1632–87 French composer

nd

1650–1700. *Baroque architecture, in which architectural space and painted surfaces were designed to give the effect of a unified whole, flourished. Illusionistic effects in painted surfaces, although by no means new, were exploited in order to heighten emotional effect, while sculpture, too, took a part in the complex designs. Although primarily a religious style, the Baroque in France was used in the service of the state under a supremely powerful monarchy. The character and treatment of the Baroque in France differed considerably from that in Italy, though the intentions and scale were often similar; in Protestant countries the style was not so widespread. But as well as these exuberant and exciting displays of pomp and grandeur, artists produced deeply humane and maturely thought-out works either as personal statements or in response to philosophical inquiry. Some painters incorporated poetic nostalgia for the ancient world into landscape painting, while other artists stressed the dramatic and atmospheric possibilities of both land- and sea-scapes. Poets and writers expressed themselves with clarity, guiding themselves by rational attitudes toward the natural world. In this, they anticipated later trends.*

1 *Park façade of the Palace of Versailles, France. Designed by Jules Hardouin-Mansart (about 1684).*
2 *Bronze cannon cast by Giovanni Mazzaroli (Venice, 1688).*
3 *Japanese lacquer box inlaid with mother-of-pearl. By Korin (1658-1716).*
4 *Engraving showing French dramatist and actor Molière in the role of Sganarelle.*

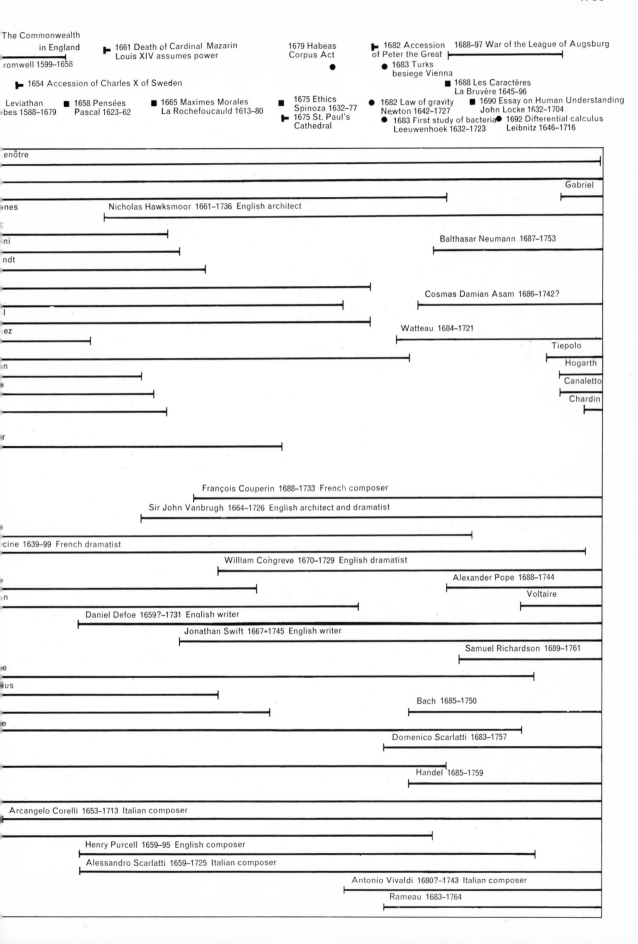

The Commonwealth
in England
romwell 1599–1658

1661 Death of Cardinal Mazarin
Louis XIV assumes power

1679 Habeas
Corpus Act

1682 Accession
of Peter the Great

1688–97 War of the League of Augsburg

1654 Accession of Charles X of Sweden

1683 Turks
besiege Vienna

1688 Les Caractères
La Bruyère 1645–96

Leviathan
bes 1588–1679

1658 Pensées
Pascal 1623–62

1665 Maximes Morales
La Rochefoucauld 1613–80

1675 Ethics
Spinoza 1632–77

1675 St. Paul's
Cathedral

1682 Law of gravity
Newton 1642–1727

1683 First study of bacteria
Leeuwenhoek 1632–1723

1690 Essay on Human Understanding
John Locke 1632–1704

1692 Differential calculus
Leibnitz 1646–1716

enôtre

Gabriel

nes — Nicholas Hawksmoor 1661–1736 English architect

ni

Balthasar Neumann 1687–1753

ndt

Cosmas Damian Asam 1686–1742?

ez

Watteau 1684–1721

Tiepolo

n

Hogarth

Canaletto

Chardin

r

François Couperin 1688–1733 French composer

Sir John Vanbrugh 1664–1726 English architect and dramatist

cine 1639–99 French dramatist

William Congreve 1670–1729 English dramatist

Alexander Pope 1688–1744

n

Voltaire

Daniel Defoe 1659?–1731 English writer

Jonathan Swift 1667–1745 English writer

Samuel Richardson 1689–1761

e

ius

Bach 1685–1750

e

Domenico Scarlatti 1683–1757

Handel 1685–1759

Arcangelo Corelli 1653–1713 Italian composer

Henry Purcell 1659–95 English composer

Alessandro Scarlatti 1659–1725 Italian composer

Antonio Vivaldi 1680?–1743 Italian composer

Rameau 1683–1764

1700–1750. *Many of the characteristics of the 17th century continued into the 18th and changed only imperceptibly by mid-century. The persistence of powerful monarchies and the rise of new ones emphasized the gap between rich and poor, although a new rationalism began to emerge in scientific and philosophical inquiry. Southern Germany and Austria, predominantly Catholic, developed still further the ideals of the Baroque, achieving a rare fusion of architecture, sculpture, and painting. In France, a more delicate, lighthearted version of the Baroque emerged, called Rococo, found everywhere in French furniture and decoration of the period. Playwrights, artists, and writers turned their gaze on social conditions of the time, often commenting with great insight and power. Oratorio, opera, and instrumental music reflected the tastes of the time, ranging from elegant diversions to works of deep religious feeling. In England, architects and patrons renewed their interest in the classicism of the Renaissance and began to adapt 16th-century formulas to contemporary needs. In addition, as the need for defensive walls disappeared, the planning of towns and cities was conceived in a more spacious way.*

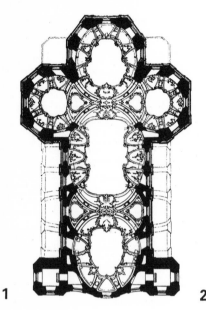

1

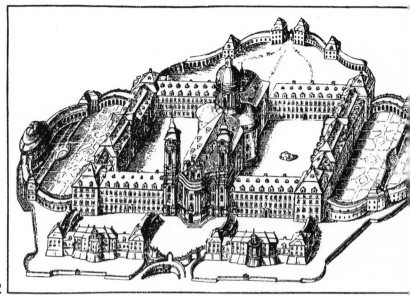

2

3

4

5

1 *Balthasar Neumann's plans for vaults of Vierzehnheiligen, church in southern Germany.*
2 *Design (1723) for rebuilding Benedictine abbey at Weingarten, Germany.*
3 *Recruiting appeal issued by the German Prince of Anhalt.*
4 *German visiting carriage.*
5 *Contemporary cartoon showing Daniel Defoe playing leapfrog with the devil.*

01–14 War of Spanish Succession ● 1713 Treaty of Utrecht

┡ 1715 Accession of Louis XV

┡ 1740 Accession of
Maria Theresa of Austria

┡ 1740 Accession of
Frederick the Great of Prussia

■ 1710 A Treatise concerning the Principles of Human Knowledge
George Berkeley 1685–1753

┡ 1733 Mechanization of English cotton industry

■ 1711 Spectator
Joseph Addison 1672–1719
Sir Richard Steele 1672–1729

■ 1721 Lettres Persanes
Montesquieu 1689–1755

■ 1739 A Treatise of Human Nature
David Hume 1711–76

■ 1725 Scienza Nuova
Giovanni Vico 1668–1744

Thomas Chippendale 1718?–79 English furniture designer

Georges Jacob 1739–1814

ues Ange Gabriel 1698–1782 French architect

smoor

Robert Adam 1728–92 Scottish architect

asar Neumann 1687–1753 German architect

Giambattista Piranesi 1720–78 Italian architect and engraver

Houdon 1741–1828

as Damian Asam 1686–1742? German painter and architect

Francisco Goya

ine Watteau 1684–1721 French painter

Thomas Gainsborough 1727–88 English painter

anni Battista Tiepolo 1696–1770 Italian painter

am Hogarth 1697–1764 English painter

nio Canaletto 1697–1768 Italian painter

Baptiste Chardin 1699–1779 French painter

François Boucher 1703–70 French painter

Francesco Guardi 1712–93 Italian painter

Sir Joshua Reynolds 1723–92 English painter

George Stubbs 1724–1806 English painter

erin

David

rugh

Alfieri

Carlo Goldoni 1707–93 Italian dramatist

greve

ander Pope 1688–1744 English poet

aire (François Arouet) 1694–1778 French writer

e

Goethe

uel Richardson 1689–1761 English novelist

Henry Fielding 1707–54 English novelist

Laurence Sterne 1713–68 Irish writer

ann Sebastian Bach 1685–1750 German composer

Samuel Johnson 1709–84 English writer

enico Scarlatti 1683–1757 Italian composer

Jean Jacques Rousseau 1712–78 French writer

rge Frederick Handel 1685–1759 German composer

Christoph Willibald Gluck 1714–87 German composer

elli

Karl Philipp Emanuel Bach 1714–88 German composer

Giovanni Battista Pergolesi 1710–36 Italian composer

sandro Scarlatti 1659–1725 Italian composer

Joseph Haydn 1732–1809 Austrian composer

ldi

Philippe Rameau 1683–1764 French composer

1750–1800. *Certain events of this period were to have far-reaching historical and cultural implications, although their immediate effect upon the arts was less obvious. The beginnings of the Industrial Revolution, the American War of Independence, and the French Revolution all helped to form a climate in which traditions were questioned and new solutions sought. The rise of the neo-classic movement, especially in architecture, stemmed* from the realization that Greek art forms inspired those of Rome and the Renaissance, and was intensified by new archaeological discoveries. In practice, neo-classic art was used to glorify national ideals during the French Revolution and the Napoleonic era. Neo-classicism was international, but local traditions were kept alive. New academies, both of the arts and the sciences, served to preserve traditions as well as to provide channels *through which new discoveries could be transmitted. New educational principles arose, which, in combination with the ideas of philosophers, were to lay the foundations of modern thought. In music, the formal sophistication and inventiveness of the age merged with the beginnings of Romantic feeling.*

1

3

1 *Chair design from Thomas Chippendale's* Gentlemen's and Cabinet-Makers' Directory (1762).
2 *Official stamp of the* Comité de Salut Public, *from an edict issued in 1794 during the French Revolution.*

2

4

5

3 *Plate from Volume III of Diderot's* Encyclopédie *(1751-72). It shows a cutler's workshop.*
4 *French philosopher Jean Jacques Rousseau, from a contemporary engraving.*
5 *English actor David Garrick (1717-79) as King Lear.*
6 *Jasperware plaque inspired by ancient Roman paintings. Designed by Josiah Wedgwood (English, 1730-95).*

6

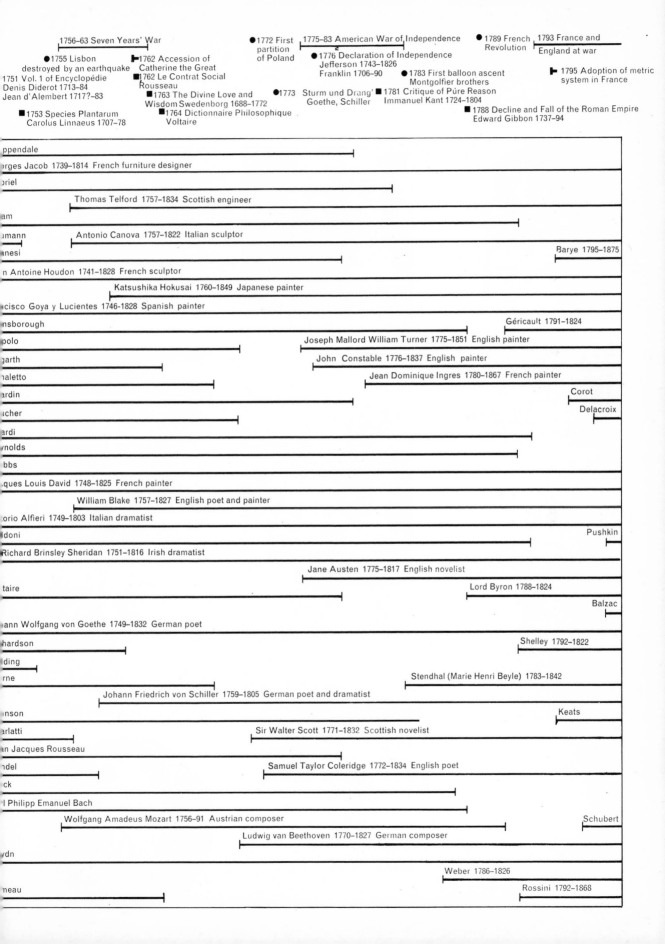

1756–63 Seven Years' War

●1755 Lisbon
destroyed by an earthquake
1751 Vol. 1 of Encyclopédie
Denis Diderot 1713–84
Jean d'Alembert 1717?–83

■1753 Species Plantarum
Carolus Linnaeus 1707–78

●1762 Accession of
Catherine the Great
1762 Le Contrat Social
Rousseau

1763 The Divine Love and
Wisdom Swedenborg 1688–1772

1764 Dictionnaire Philosophique
Voltaire

●1772 First
partition
of Poland

●1773 Sturm und Drang'
Goethe, Schiller

1775–83 American War of Independence

●1776 Declaration of Independence
Jefferson 1743–1826
Franklin 1706–90

1781 Critique of Pure Reason
Immanuel Kant 1724–1804

●1789 French
Revolution

1793 France and
England at war

●1783 First balloon ascent
Montgolfier brothers

1795 Adoption of metric
system in France

1788 Decline and Fall of the Roman Empire
Edward Gibbon 1737–94

ppendale

rges Jacob 1739–1814 French furniture designer

riel

Thomas Telford 1757–1834 Scottish engineer

am

umann

Antonio Canova 1757–1822 Italian sculptor

nesi

Barye 1795–1875

n Antoine Houdon 1741–1828 French sculptor

Katsushika Hokusai 1760–1849 Japanese painter

cisco Goya y Lucientes 1746-1828 Spanish painter

nsborough

Géricault 1791–1824

polo

Joseph Mallord William Turner 1775–1851 English painter

garth

John Constable 1776–1837 English painter

naletto

Jean Dominique Ingres 1780–1867 French painter

ardin

Corot

ucher

Delacroix

ardi

ynolds

bbs

ques Louis David 1748–1825 French painter

William Blake 1757–1827 English poet and painter

orio Alfieri 1749–1803 Italian dramatist

ldoni

Pushkin

Richard Brinsley Sheridan 1751–1816 Irish dramatist

Jane Austen 1775–1817 English novelist

taire

Lord Byron 1788–1824

Balzac

ann Wolfgang von Goethe 1749–1832 German poet

hardson

Shelley 1792–1822

lding

rne

Stendhal (Marie Henri Beyle) 1783–1842

Johann Friedrich von Schiller 1759–1805 German poet and dramatist

nson

Keats

arlatti

Sir Walter Scott 1771–1832 Scottish novelist

n Jacques Rousseau

ndel

Samuel Taylor Coleridge 1772–1834 English poet

ck

l Philipp Emanuel Bach

Wolfgang Amadeus Mozart 1756–91 Austrian composer

Schubert

Ludwig van Beethoven 1770–1827 German composer

dn

Weber 1786–1826

meau

Rossini 1792–1868

1800–1850. *The reshaping of Europe after Napoleon's defeat changed traditional political and social conditions. New sources of power and the rapid growth of industry increased the populations and the wealth of towns, creating both a prosperous new middle class and hardships for the poor. Machines took over much of the work previously done by hand. Better communications and improved transport broadened the range of ideas and experiences open to artists. In response to these changes, artists began to develop a new sense of identity and to create the cult of the artistic genius. This pervading undercurrent of ideas and feelings surfaced as Romanticism —a movement that drove artists to adopt new attitudes and seek new subject matter, either from literature or the natural world. Most of them rejected traditional classic themes, and artists who did continue the neo-classic tradition often colored it with romantic feeling. Architects widened their use of historical forms to include Oriental and Gothic as well as the traditional Greek and Roman. Poets celebrated nature. On the other hand, some novelists wrote realistically about the new shapes society took, often campaigning against social evils.*

1

1 Is There no Remedy?—*from a series of etchings by Goya called* The Disasters of War.

The Industrial Revolution, aided by late-18th-century ingenuity in harnessing steam and inventing new machines, was in full swing by the early 19th century. Some of the period's remarkable technological advances are listed below.

1804 First screw propeller designed by John Stevens; first steam locomotive built by Richard Trevithick; J. M. Jacquard perfects mechanical loom for weaving patterns into textiles.
1807 Robert Fulton's Clermont— *the first successful steamship.*
1830 Barthélemy Thimonnier's sewing machine.
1831 Michael Faraday discovers principle of the electric dynamo; Cyrus McCormack's automatic reaper.
1838 First crossings of the Atlantic entirely by steam power— the ships Sirius *and* Great Western.
1844 Samuel Morse transmits the first telegraphic message.

The romantic outlook is reflected in these literary and musical works. The movement's roots were in the 18th century, but its full flowering came in the 19th.

1807 Wordsworth's Poems
1808 Beethoven's "Pastoral" Symphony (No. 6)
1816 Coleridge's Christabel
1818 Keats's Endymion
1819 Scott's Ivanhoe
1820 Lamartine's Méditations; *Irving's* The Sketch Book
1821 Weber's Der Freischütz
1822 Schubert's "Unfinished" Symphony (No. 8)
1824 Byron's Don Juan
1826 Manzoni's I Promessi Sposi; *de Vigny's* Cinq-Mars
1827 Heine's Book of Songs
1829 Chopin's Piano Concerto in F Minor; *Rossini's* William Tell
1830 Berlioz's Symphonie Fantastique; *Hugo's* Hernani
1832 Pushkin's Eugene Onegin
1833 Mendelssohn's "Italian" Symphony (No. 4)
1834 Schumann's Carnaval
1836 Leopardi's I Canti
1840 Poe's Tales of the Grotesque and Arabesque
1843 Wagner's The Flying Dutchman
1847 Verdi's Macbeth
1849 Liszt's Piano Concerto in E flat (No. 1)
1850 Hawthorne's The Scarlet Letter

2

2 Rain, Steam, and Speed *by J. M. W. Turner (1844).*

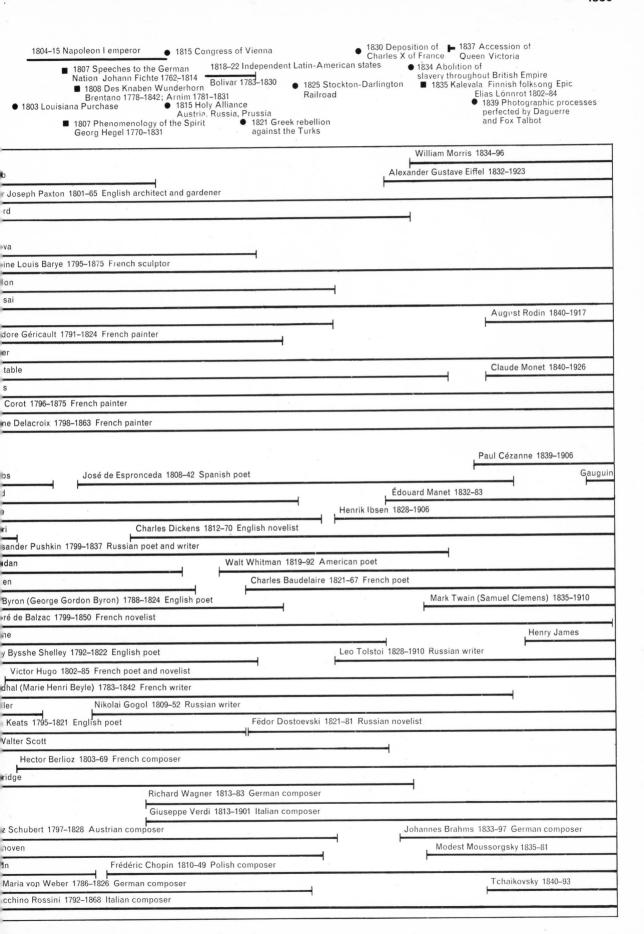

1804–15 Napoleon I emperor ● 1815 Congress of Vienna   ● 1830 Deposition of   ┣ 1837 Accession of
    Charles X of France   Queen Victoria

■ 1807 Speeches to the German   1818–22 Independent Latin-American states   ● 1834 Abolition of
Nation Johann Fichte 1762–1814   Bolivar 1783–1830   slavery throughout British Empire

■ 1808 Des Knaben Wunderhorn   ● 1825 Stockton-Darlington   ■ 1835 Kalevala Finnish folksong Epic
Brentano 1778–1842; Arnim 1781–1831   Railroad   Elias Lönnrot 1802–84

● 1803 Louisiana Purchase   ● 1815 Holy Alliance   ● 1839 Photographic processes
Austria, Russia, Prussia   perfected by Daguerre

■ 1807 Phenomenology of the Spirit   ● 1821 Greek rebellion   and Fox Talbot
Georg Hegel 1770–1831   against the Turks

William Morris 1834–96

Alexander Gustave Eiffel 1832–1923

Joseph Paxton 1801–65 English architect and gardener

…rd

…va

…ine Louis Barye 1795–1875 French sculptor

…on

…sai

August Rodin 1840–1917

…dore Géricault 1791–1824 French painter

…er

…table

Claude Monet 1840–1926

…s

Corot 1796–1875 French painter

…ne Delacroix 1798–1863 French painter

Paul Cézanne 1839–1906

…os   José de Espronceda 1808–42 Spanish poet   Gauguin

…d   Édouard Manet 1832–83

…e   Henrik Ibsen 1828–1906

…ri   Charles Dickens 1812–70 English novelist

…sander Pushkin 1799–1837 Russian poet and writer

…dan   Walt Whitman 1819–92 American poet

…en   Charles Baudelaire 1821–67 French poet

Byron (George Gordon Byron) 1788–1824 English poet   Mark Twain (Samuel Clemens) 1835–1910

…ré de Balzac 1799–1850 French novelist

…ne   Henry James

…y Bysshe Shelley 1792–1822 English poet   Leo Tolstoi 1828–1910 Russian writer

Victor Hugo 1802–85 French poet and novelist

…dhal (Marie Henri Beyle) 1783–1842 French writer

…ler   Nikolai Gogol 1809–52 Russian writer

…Keats 1795–1821 English poet   Fëdor Dostoevski 1821–81 Russian novelist

…Walter Scott

Hector Berlioz 1803–69 French composer

…ridge

Richard Wagner 1813–83 German composer

Giuseppe Verdi 1813–1901 Italian composer

…z Schubert 1797–1828 Austrian composer   Johannes Brahms 1833–97 German composer

…hoven   Modest Moussorgsky 1835–81

…n   Frédéric Chopin 1810–49 Polish composer

…Maria von Weber 1786–1826 German composer   Tchaikovsky 1840–93

…cchino Rossini 1792–1868 Italian composer

1850–1900. *Many of the problems of the modern artist as well as of modern society arose during this period. Free of major wars, the age was absorbed by problems of material expansion. It saw the publication of Darwin's theory of evolution and the political ideas of Marx. Conventional ways of seeing the world were assaulted by both photography and more rapid, direct painting techniques. Impressionism and the movements that came after rejected subjects with literary meaning and concerned themselves with optical effects and the treatment of picture surfaces. Preoccupation with line, form, and composition spurred artists to look beyond Europe to seek inspiration from Japanese prints and primitive art forms. In addition, artists adopted new approaches to the use of color. Galleries of independent art dealers and group shows organized by artists themselves began to replace academy exhibitions. Architects joined engineers in developing new attitudes toward structure and materials, although most buildings were built in borrowed styles. Many artists showed social concern, but in the 1890s a self-conscious "art-for-art's-sake" attitude underlined a general quest for fresh art forms.*

1

2

3

4

5

1 *The Crystal Palace, London, from the catalogue for the Great Exhibition of 1851.*
2 *Honoré de Balzac, sculptured in bronze by Auguste Rodin.*
3 *Richard Wagner, from a warrant for his arrest for involvement in one of the revolutionary upheavals that ushered in the half-century.*
4 *Detail from* Regatta at Argenteuil *by Claude Monet.*
5 The Black Cape, *illustration by Aubrey Beardsley (1872-98) for Oscar Wilde's play* Salomé.

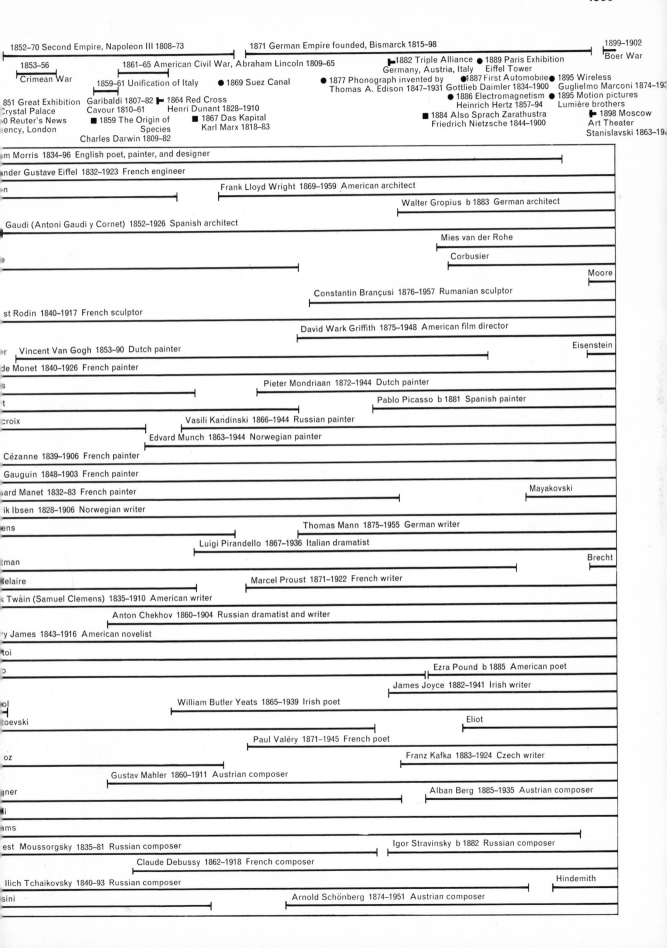

1852–70 Second Empire, Napoleon III 1808–73

1853–56
Crimean War

1851 Great Exhibition
Crystal Palace
0 Reuter's News
ency, London

1871 German Empire founded, Bismarck 1815–98

1861–65 American Civil War, Abraham Lincoln 1809–65

1859–61 Unification of Italy ● 1869 Suez Canal

Garibaldi 1807–82 ▬ 1864 Red Cross
Cavour 1810–61   Henri Dunant 1828–1910
■ 1859 The Origin of   ■ 1867 Das Kapital
        Species   Karl Marx 1818–83
Charles Darwin 1809–82

▬1882 Triple Alliance   ● 1889 Paris Exhibition
Germany, Austria, Italy   Eiffel Tower
● 1877 Phonograph invented by   ●1887 First Automobile● 1895 Wireless
    Thomas A. Edison 1847–1931 Gottlieb Daimler 1834–1900 Guglielmo Marconi 1874–19
              ● 1886 Electromagnetism ● 1895 Motion pictures
                 Heinrich Hertz 1857–94   Lumière brothers
     ■ 1884 Also Sprach Zarathustra   ▬ 1898 Moscow
        Friedrich Nietzsche 1844–1900   Art Theater
                                  Stanislavski 1863–19

1899–1902
Boer War

m Morris 1834–96 English poet, painter, and designer

nder Gustave Eiffel 1832–1923 French engineer

n   Frank Lloyd Wright 1869–1959 American architect

Walter Gropius b 1883 German architect

Gaudi (Antoni Gaudi y Cornet) 1852–1926 Spanish architect

Mies van der Rohe

Corbusier

Moore

Constantin Brançusi 1876–1957 Rumanian sculptor

st Rodin 1840–1917 French sculptor

David Wark Griffith 1875–1948 American film director

r Vincent Van Gogh 1853–90 Dutch painter

Eisenstein

de Monet 1840–1926 French painter

Pieter Mondriaan 1872–1944 Dutch painter

Pablo Picasso b 1881 Spanish painter

croix   Vasili Kandinski 1866–1944 Russian painter

Edvard Munch 1863–1944 Norwegian painter

Cézanne 1839–1906 French painter

Gauguin 1848–1903 French painter

ard Manet 1832–83 French painter

Mayakovski

ik Ibsen 1828–1906 Norwegian writer

ens   Thomas Mann 1875–1955 German writer

Luigi Pirandello 1867–1936 Italian dramatist

tman

Brecht

elaire   Marcel Proust 1871–1922 French writer

Twáin (Samuel Clemens) 1835–1910 American writer

Anton Chekhov 1860–1904 Russian dramatist and writer

y James 1843–1916 American novelist

toi

o

Ezra Pound b 1885 American poet

James Joyce 1882–1941 Irish writer

ol   William Butler Yeats 1865–1939 Irish poet

toevski

Eliot

Paul Valéry 1871–1945 French poet

oz

Franz Kafka 1883–1924 Czech writer

Gustav Mahler 1860–1911 Austrian composer

gner

Alban Berg 1885–1935 Austrian composer

li

ms

est Moussorgsky 1835–81 Russian composer

Igor Stravinsky b 1882 Russian composer

Claude Debussy 1862–1918 French composer

Ilich Tchaikovsky 1840–93 Russian composer

Hindemith

sini

Arnold Schönberg 1874–1951 Austrian composer

From 1900 onward. *The unrest and anxiety stirred by two world wars has led artists to experiment in all fields. Technological and scientific advances have tended to isolate many artists and divorce their concerns from those of society at large. But running counter to these tendencies, there has also been an increase in the artist's public through modern means of communication. Many of these changes, heralded in the 19th century, have developed so* *rapidly during recent times that they have radically altered cultural patterns. Compelling visual images now confront a larger number of people than ever before mainly through the use of film and television. New materials and techniques in architecture have developed, partly in response to a desire for change, partly in accord with technological progress—of which prefabrication and a wide use of concrete, glass, steel, and plastics are* *characteristic. European-based art forms have tended to give way to international styles. Direct contact between patron and artist has been progressively limited by the rise of the art "market" and the growth of advertising. Few individual demands are made by the mass audiences that now exist for all forms of art.*

3

4

1

2

1 *Model by Mies van der Rohe for glass skyscraper (1919).*
2 *Fuselage of a French jet-powered fighter plane.*
3 *Scene from* October, *Eisenstein's study of the 1917 revolution (U.S.S.R., 1927).*
4 *Scene from* The Cabinet of Dr. Caligari, *directed by Robert Wiene (Germany, 1919).*
5 *Inside the Body drawn by Paul Klee (1879-1940) in 1940.*

5

1904–05 Russo-Japanese War

1914–18 World War I ● 1919 Treaty of Versailles ● 1929 Wall Street crash 1939–45 World War II ● 1948 Berlin blockade

Interpretation of Dreams and Freud 1856–1939 ● 1917 October Revolution Nikolai Lenin 1870–1924, Leon Trotsky 1877–1940 1936–39 Spanish Civil War ● 1945 Atomic bombs dropped on Japan

quantum, ■ 1906 Creative Evolution ● 1914 Panama Canal ● 1933 Election of Franklin D. Roosevelt ┣ 1947 Indian independence Mahatma Gandhi

Max Planck Henri Bergson 1859–1941

● 1903 First powered flight Wright brothers ● 1916 General theory of relativity Albert Einstein 1879–1955 ● 1928 Discovery of penicillin Sir Alexander Fleming 1881–1955

■ 1903 La Critica Benedetto Croce ■ 1910 Principia Mathematica Russell and Whitehead ┣ 1919 Experiments with the atom Ernest Rutherford 1871–1937 ● 1931 First ascent into the stratosphere Auguste Picard b 1884 ┣ 1945 United Nations UNESCO

Marcel Breuer b 1902 Hungarian architect and designer

Mies van der Rohe b 1886 Dutch architect

busier (Charles Jeanneret) b 1887 Swiss architect

Moore b 1898 English sculptor

Ingmar Bergman b 1918 Swedish film director

Eisenstein 1898–1948 Russian film director

Jackson Pollock 1912–56 American painter

Salvador Dali b 1904 Spanish painter

mir Mayakovski 1893–1930 Russian poet

Samuel Beckett b 1906 Irish dramatist

Brecht 1898–1956 German dramatist

Eugène Ionesco b 1912 French dramatist

Wystan Hugh Auden b 1907 English poet

Albert Camus 1913–60 French writer

as Stearns Eliot b 1888 English poet

John Cage b 1912 American composer

Olivier Messiaen b 1908 French composer

Copland b 1900 American composer

Pierre Boulez b 1925 French composer

Hindemith b 1895-1963 German composer

Index

Page numbers in *italics* indicate illustrations, diagrams, maps, or their captions. Page numbers in **bold** type denote items dealt with at some length in the text.

Note that all text references for each unit of facing pages are indexed to the left-hand page only. Page numbers for illustrations and captions, however, refer to the exact page on which they occur.

The body of this book is designed in two-page units. Text references for each such unit are indexed to the left-hand page only.

Barye, Antoine Louis (sculptor), 341

Baschet, François (sculptor), *311;* Bernard (engineer), *311*

Bas-relief, 82

Bass drum, 160

Bassoon, 160

Battle of the Centaurs (Michelangelo), 70

Battleship Potemkin, The (film), *285,* 286

Baudelaire, Charles (poet), 343

Bauhaus art school (Germany), 316

Beardsley, Aubrey Vincent (illustrator), *The Black Cape, 344*

"Beat" poets, 209, 221

Beaujoyeulx, *see* Belgiojoso

Beauty: art and, 202, **312;** physical, 56, 80; usefulness and, 132

Beckett, Samuel (dramatist), 276, *277,* 347

Beethoven, Ludwig van (composer), 148, **150,** *150,* **158,** 341; *Battle Symphony,* 26; *Fidelio* (opera), 156, 158; last string quartet of, **316;** piano sonatas by, 154; quoted, 142; *The Ruins of Athens* score, 29

Beggar's Opera, The (Gay), **164**

Behrens, Peter (industrial designer), *132*

Belgiojoso, Baldassarino da (musician), 178, *178*

Belle Hélène, La (Offenbach), 154

Bellini, Giovanni (painter), 329

Ben Hur (film), *287*

Beni Hasan (Egypt), tomb at, 92

Benin (W. Africa), modeling and bronze casting in, 76, *77;* bronze cock, 76

Benois, Alexandre (painter), 184

Beowulf (epic poem), 199, 210, 226

Berg, Alban (composer), *Wozzeck,* **156,** 168, *169,* 345

Bergman, Ingmar (film director), *294,* 302, 347

Berlioz, Hector (composer), 150, **158,** 343; caricature, *159*

Bernhardt, Sarah (actress), 294

Bernini, Giovanni Lorenzo (sculptor and architect), 74, *75,* 82, 106, 333; bust of Thomas Baker, *310;* colonnade, *317; Fountain of the Moor, 334*

Bewick, Thomas (engraver), *51*

Bharata natyam (Hindu dance), *176*

Bibiena, Francesco da (stage designer), *268*

Bibiena, Giuseppe da (stage designer), *180*

Bible: Gutenberg's, *328;* King James version, 204, 335; pictures in, 40, *51,* 224

Bicycle Thieves (film), 302

Binary form (music), **148**

Biography, 58, **244-5;** in pictures, *244*

Birth of a Nation (film), **286**

Blake, William (artist and poet), 341; "Infant Joy," *206*

Blank verse, 204, *204, 205*

Blasis, Carlo, *Code of Terpsichore,* **182**

Blaue Reiter, Der, 66

Bleak House (Dickens), 234

Blinkity-Blank (film), *298*

"Blues" (Negro songs), *208*

Boating by Moonlight, 41

Boccaccio, Giovanni (writer), **228,** *234,* 327

Boccioni, Umberto (sculptor), 86

Bohème, La (Puccini), 156

Boileau, Nicholas, *The Poetic Art, 197*

Bolm, Adolph (ballet dancer), 184

Bologne, Jean (sculptor), 331

Bolshoi Ballet, *173*

Bonnard, Pierre (painter), 215

Book of Kells, The, 324

Boris Godunov (Moussorgsky), 156

Borodin, Aleksandr (composer), 150

Borromini, Francesco (architect), 106, 333

Bosch, Hieronymus (painter), 329; *The Garden of Earthly Delights,* 313

Boswell, James (writer), 244, *245*

Botticelli, Sandro (painter), 329; *Primavera,* 306; *The Sky of Mercury,* 201

Boucher, François (painter), *136, 339*

"Boule de Suif" (Maupassant), *233*

Boulez, Pierre (composer), 347

Bournonville, Auguste (balletmaster), 182, **186**

Boxiganga (actors' troupe), 260

Bradbury, Ray (writer), **242,** *243*

Brahms, Johannes (composer), 150, *150,* 158, 186, 343; *Requiem, 161*

Bramante, Donato d'Agnolo (architect), *318,* 328, 329

Brancusi, Constantin (sculptor), 75, *132,* 345

Brand (Ibsen), 270

Brandenburg, Margrave of, 158

Branle (dance), 176, *177*

Brant, Sebastian (poet), *The Ship of Fools,* 218

Braque, Georges (painter), 64, 184; *Still Life with Playing Cards,* 39

Brasilia, plan of, 94, *95*

Brass band, *165*

Brass instruments, 158, **160,** *160*

Brave New World (Huxley), 242

Brecht, Bertolt (playwright), 212, 216, 220, **272,** *273,* 345; *The Caucasian Chalk Circle,* 255

Breton, André (poet), 220

Breuer, Marcel (architect), 134, 347

Brick buildings, 92, 108, 112, *115*

Bridges, *111,* **124,** *124,* 132

Brighton Rock (Greene), **238,** 248

Britten, Benjamin (composer), 168

Brontë, Charlotte (writer), **238**

Brontë, Emily (writer), 232, 238; *Wuthering Heights,* 241

Bronzino, Il (painter), 331

Brothers Karamazov, The (Dostoevski), 232

Brueghel, Pieter, the Elder (painter), *62, 177, 198,* 331

Brunelleschi, Filippo (àrchitect), 327

Buddenbrooks (Mann), 232

Buddhism, 52, 54, 72, 84, *84,* 100, *224,* 254, 323

Buildings: cost of, 104; new, for new needs, **116;** permanent, **102;** public, 102, 104, 106; symbolism of, **100;** *see also* Architecture

Bull, John (composer): *The King's Hunt,* 154

Bullfight, The (Goya), 51

Bunning, James Bunsten (architect), 112

Bunyan, John (writer), **228,** *228,* 335

Bunyan, Paul (folk hero), 230

Buoninsegna, Duccio di (painter), 327; *The Virgin and Child with Saints,* 45

Burbage, Richard and Cuthbert (actors), 266

Burghers of Calais (Rodin), 72

Burial at Ornans (Courbet), 60

Burns, Robert (poet), 208, 209, 214

Butler, Reg (sculptor), 86

Buttresses, 110, *111,* 112

Buxtehude, Dietrich (composer), 154, *154*

Byrd, William (composer), 152, **154,** 331

Byron, George Gordon, Lord (poet), *213,* 341; *Don Juan,* 200; *Manfred,* 212; *Tasso,* 150

Byzantine art, 324; architecture, 100, 114; painting, 40; sculpture, 84

Cabinet Maker at His Bench, A (film), 300

Cabinet of Doctor Caligari, The (film), *289,* 346

Cabiria (film), 288

Caesura (metrical division), 196

Cailleau, Hubert (painter), *265*

Cairo Opera House (Egypt), 24

Calder, Alexander (sculptor), 86, *86, 318*

Calderón de la Barca, Pedro (dramatist), 335

Callicrates (architect), 104

Callot, Jacques (engraver), 333, *334*

Camargo, Marie Anne de (ballerina), **180,** *180*

Camera: design of, *124;* motion-picture, 280, 284, 286

Camões, Luiz Vaz de (poet), *Lusiads,* 210, *210,* 331

Camus, Albert (writer), 248, 347

Canaletto, Antonio (painter), *314, 337*

Candide (Voltaire), **228,** *228*

Canon, 152

Canova, Antonio (sculptor), 80, 341

Cantabile, 162

Cantar de Mio Cid (epic poem), 210

Canterbury Tales, The (Chaucer), 210, *211,* 218

Cantilevers, 112

Caravaggio, Michelangelo da (painter), *49,* 333

Caravelle (jet aircraft), *140*

Carnivals, 24, *25,* 166, *263*

Carousel (film), *295*

Carpaccio, Vittore (painter), 329

Carroll, Lewis (writer): *Alice's Adventures in Wonderland,* **224,** *237;* "Father William" parody, 218, *219;* "Jabberwocky," 218

Carrosse de Saint-Sacrement, La (play), *272*

Cary, Joyce (writer), **28**

Casals, Pablo (cellist), *318*
Castel of Perseverance (play), 264
Castiglione, Baldassare (writer), 329
Castle, The (Kafka), 240
Castles, 98; Harlech, *98;* Krak des Chevaliers, *326*
Cathedrals, *40,* 94, **102,** 104, 112, 316; Amiens, *106;* Autun, *83;* Chartres, *48,* 78, *79;* Durham, *324;* Ely, *304;* Exeter, *104;* markets in front of, 96; Moscow, St. Basil's, *332;* medieval construction of, **326;** Pisa *106;* Salisbury, *115;* Southwell Minster, *315;* Ulm, *110*
Catullus, Gaius (poet), 208, 323, *196*
Cavalcanti, Guido (poet), 214
Cavalieri, Emilio de' (composer), *153*
Cave pictures, 22, *36,* 64, 138, *172;* art first recorded in, **22,** 24
Cellini, Benvenuto (sculptor), *246;* autobiography of, 246; *Perseus,* 76
Cello, *see* Violoncello
Cerrito, Fanny (ballerina), 180, *181*
Cervantes Saavedra, Miguel de (writer), **232,** *236,* 331
Cézanne, Paul (painter), 58, 64, 66, 68, 86, *314,* 343; art of, *316; Le Lac d'Annecy, 63; La Montagne Sainte Victoire, 43; Still Life with Apples and Oranges, 313*
Chagall, Marc (painter), *The Poet, 204; Dead Souls,* illustration, *228*
Chalon, A. E. (painter), *181*
Chamber music, **154,** *155,* 168
Chambord (château), 104, *116, 330*
Champion, Pierre (writer), 244
Champs-Elyseés Theatre, *109*
Chandigarh, East Punjab capital, *101, 319*
Chandler, Raymond (writer), *249*
Chants, 146, 152; *see also* Plainsong
Chaplin, Charles (film actor-director), *278,* **288,** *288, 289, 290*
Chardin, Jean Baptiste (painter), 337
Charlemagne, legends of, 226
Charles V, Holy Roman Emperor, *332*
Charleston (dance), 188
Chartres Cathedral (France), *48;* sculpture in west front, 78, *79*
Chase Manhattan Bank building (New York), 118
Châteaux, 104, *116,* 308, *330*
Chaucer, Geoffrey (poet), 327; *Canterbury Tales,* 210, *211, 218*
Chekhov, Anton (dramatist), 232, *232,* 250, 272, *294,* 345
Cheops, Great Pyramid of (Egypt), 102
Chiaroscuro, 48
Chichén Itzá (Mexico): shrines at, *102,* 202; statuary at, *73*
Chiesa, Alberto (film director), 296
China:
artists, 42, 62; bowl rubbing, *332;* building, *114;* culture, 324; dancing, 174, 176; pagodas, *100;* painting, *41;* ritual caldron, *24;* sculpture, 76; stonework vase, *138;* terra-cotta horse, *77;* theatres, 270; vase, *126;* woodcuts, *244*
Chippendale, Thomas (furniture designer), 130, *134,* 339, *340; Directory of Designs,* 130
Chirico, Giorgio di (painter), 64
Chopin, Frédéric (composer), *151, 154,* 343
Chorales, 152
Choreography, **178,** 180, **184,** 186, 188; recording of, **190,** *191;* Russian, **186**
Chorus:
conductor of, **162;** Greek, *196,* 254; opera, 156; orchestra and, *161, 169*
Christian art, **324;** architecture, 100, **102;** dancing, 174, *174;* drama, 254, 258, 260, **264,** *264,* 266; music, 146, **152;** painting, 40, 44, 45, **52,** *53;* sculpture, 72, 82, **84,** *85,* **324**
Chronegk, Ludwig (stage director), 274
Churches, **102,** 104, 328; Byzantine, 100; paintings in, 40; sculpture in, 78, 82; stained glass in, 48
Cibber, Colley (playwright), *246*
Cimabue (painter), 327
Cinderella, **224,** *224,* 226
Cinématographe, 282
Circuses, 258, *258*
Clair, René (film director), 288, *289*
Clarinets, 154, 158, 160, *160*
Classical art, 104, 150, 268, *268*
Claude Lorrain (painter), *63,* 335
Clavichords, 154
Clemens, Samuel, *see* Twain, Mark
Close-up (filming), 284, *284,* 294
Clouzot, H.-G. (film director), *301*
Clowns, 258, 260, 262
Cocteau, Jean (author), *168,* 186, 230, 316
Code of Terpsichore (Blasis), **182**
Cohl, Émile (film cartoonist), 298
Coleridge, Samuel Taylor (poet), 341; "The Rime of the Ancient Mariner," 198
Collage, 50
Colleoni, Bartolommeo, Verocchio's statue, 72, *72*
Collier, Patience (actress), *255*
Collins, Wilkie (writer), 234
Cologne Bible, the (1478), *51*
Colombe, Jean (painter), 329
Colombe, Michel (sculptor), 329
Color in motion pictures, 290, *291, 303*
Color in painting, **44,** 48, 50, 66; formless, *47;* light's influence on, 47, 48
Colosseum (Rome), 98, *114, 263*
Columns (architecture), **92,** 106, 110, 112, *113,* **114,** *114, 115*
Comédie Française (Paris), 266
Comédie Humaine, La (Balzac), *235*
Comedy, 256; classical, **262;** film, *289,* 294; origin of word, 254
Comenius, John (writer), 333
"Comic" entertainers, 258, *258,* 260
Comic operas, **218**
Comic strip, *251*
Comic verse, **218**
Comical Romance of a Company of Players (1676), 260
Commedia dell'arte, 76, 254, *255, 261*
Commedia harmonica, 212
Compagnie des Quinze, la, 272
Compania (actors' troupe), 260
Composers, **150;** classical and classical-romantic, 150; film music, 292; modern, **168;** opera, **156;** religious, **152**
Comus processions, Greek, 254
Concerto Barocco (ballet), *186*
Concerto, 148, 158, **162**
Concrete, **108,** *109,* 120, 346; *see also* Reinforced concrete
Confessions, The (Rousseau), **246;** *Confessions, The* (St. Augustine), **246**
Confidenti (actors' troupe), 260
Congregation of the Oratory, the, **152**
Congreve, William (dramatist), 337; Dr. Johnson's Life of, 244
Conrad, Joseph (author), 238, 248; *Typhoon,* **240**
Constable, John (painter), 51, 64, *65,* 341; quoted, 62
"Constance" Missal, *250*
Constantine the Great, triumphal arch, *324*
Constructivist movement, 66, **86**
Coogan, Jackie (film actor), *288*
Copeau, Jacques (stage director), **272,** *272*
Copland, Aaron (composer), 347
Coq d'Or, Le (ballet), *184,* 309
Cor anglais, 160
Corbusier, *see* Le Corbusier
Cordier, Baude (composer), *152*
Corelli, Arcangelo (composer), 148, *149,* 154
Corinthian order, *93*
Corneille, Pierre (dramatist), 268, 335
Corner of the Artist's Studio (Delacroix), *69*
Cornerstone, The (Oldenbourg), 242
Corot, Jean (painter), 341
Correggio (Antonio Allegri) (painter), 329
Corso, Gregory (poet), 220
Costa, Lorenzo (painter), *142*
Costa, Lucio (architect), 95
Cotillion (dance), *177*
Counterpoint (*see also* Polyphony), 146, 150, 152, 154, 166, 168
Couperin, François (composer), 148
Courbet, Gustave (painter), *60*
Covent Garden Theatre, *156*
Cover Girl (film), 190
Craftsmen, 34, **130,** *130, 131*
Craig, Gordon (stage designer), **276,** *276*
Cranach, Lucas (painter), 329, *330*
Crane, Hart (poet), "To Brooklyn Bridge," 206
Création du Monde, La (ballet), *188*
Creation of Adam, The (Michelangelo), *330*
Crucifixes, 72
Crucifixion, paintings of the, *32, 53*
Cruikshank, George (illustrator), *231*
Crystal Palace, the, 108, 112, 345, *344;* concert in, *159*
Cubist painters, *39,* **64,** 66, 86
Cummings, E. E. (poet), **202,** 214
Cymbals, 160

The body of this book is designed in two-page units. Text references for each such unit are indexed to the left-hand page only.

Metropolis (film), *289*
Mexico:
architecture in, **102**, *102;* painting in, 60
Michaux, Henri (poet), 220
Michelangelo Buonarrotti, 80, 329; dome of St. Peter's, *317;* fresco in Sistine Chapel, *330;* independence of, 68; on modeling, 74, 76; paintings by, 26, 40, *41,* 44, 56; sculpture by, *70,* 80, *81;* sketch for Libyan Sibyl, *27*
Mickey Mouse (film series), 298
Middle Ages, the:
architecture in, 96, 102, 110, 112, 120, **326;** biography in, **244** defensive walls, 98; drama in, *266, 270;* furniture design in, **134;** organs in, 154; painting in, 40, 64, **68;** poetry in, **214;** romantic appeal of, *269;* sculpture in, 74, 78
Middlemarch (Eliot), 232, **240**
Midsummer Night's Dream, A (films), *292,* 298, *298*
Mies van der Rohe, Ludwig (architect), 120, *307,* 345, *346*
Milan (Italy), ballet in, 178
Milhaud, Darius (composer), 168 *168*
Millais, Sir John (painter), *Bubbles, 34*
Miller, Max (comedian), *227*
Milton, John (poet), 244, 335; *L'Allegro,* 196; *Lycidas,* 196; *Paradise Lost,* 204, *205,* **216;** *Samson Agonistes,* 204
Mimes, *175,* 176, 180, **186;** Greek and Roman, **258,** 262; Japanese, *254;* origin of word, 254
Mimesis, 254
Minnesingers, 208, *208,* 226
Minor scale, 146, 162, 168
Minstrels, medieval, 200, *200,* 208, 218, 226, 258
Minuet (dance), 148, **176,** *190*
Miracle of the Mass, The (Raphael), *43*
Miracle plays, 264, 272
Miró, Joan (painter), 64, **67**
Mitchell, Margaret (writer), 242
Moana (film), 296
Moby Dick (Melville), 232; film version, *291*
Modernist painters, 66
"Modulor" proportional system, *105,* 106, *107*
Moe, Jörgen (folk tale collector), 230
Molière (J. B. Poquelin) (dramatist), 260, 335, *336*
Monasteries:
drama records in, 264; musical traditions preserved in, 324; paintings in, 40
Mondriaan, Pieter (painter), 66, *66,* 345
Monet, Claude (painter), 46, *47,* 343; *Regatta at Argenteuil, 344*
Monreale Cathedral (Sicily), *40*
Montagne Sainte Victoire, La (Cézanne), *43*
Montaigne, Michel de (author), 331
Monteverdi, Claudio (composer), 156, *156,* 158, 333
Monumental sculpture, 74, 76, 84
Moore, Henry (sculptor), **86,** *87;* reclining figure, *81*

Morality plays, 264
More, Sir Thomas (statesman and writer), 329
Morley, Thomas (composer), 333
Morning Dew in the Moonlight (Miró), *67*
Morris, William (poet and designer), **242,** 343; quoted, 314
Morte d'Arthur, 225
Mosaics, 40, **48,** *48,* 78, 115, 324, *324*
Moscow Art Theatre, 272
Mosque (Isfahan), *115*
Mostel, Zero (actor), *237*
Mother Goose Tales (Perrault), 231
Mother (film), *289*
Motion pictures, *see* Film
Motokiyo, Ze'ami (playwright), 254
Mourning Becomes Electra (O'Neill), 277
Moussorgsky, Modest (composer), 156, 343
Mozart, Wolfgang Amadeus (composer), 26, 148, *149,* **150,** 154, 341; operas by, **156,** *156,* orchestral combinations of, **158**
Mrs. Dalloway (Woolf), 234, 240
Mudras (temple dancers' gestures), 172
Munch, Edward (artist), 345; *The Cry, 198*
Mural paintings, 40, 78
Murnau, F. W. (film director), 288
Music, 142-69, 340; "architecture is frozen," 308; ballet, 178; broadcasts, *159;* canon, *152;* court concert, *148;* folk, 30, **150,** **166;** form in, **148;** funeral, *162;* instrumental, 154, 160; interpretation of, *162;* light, **164;** modern, **168;** notation, *147, 168;* oratorio, **152,** *152, 153;* orchestral, **158-61;** primitive, **142;** printed, *146,* 162; recorded, *159;* storytelling's connection with, 226; theatre, 272, 334; vocal, **152;** wedding, *148*
Music halls, 164, 226, 274, *275*
Music Room, The (film), *302*
Musical comedies, 164
Musical films, 294, *295*
Musical instruments:
154, 160; families of, *145, 160;* maker's workshop, *145;* new, *159; see also* names of specific instruments
Musical plays, 186, 188, 272
Musique concrète, 168
Mystère d'Adam, Le (Biblical drama), 264
Mystère Picasso, Le (film), *301*
Muybridge, Eadweard James (photographer), *281,* 300
Mycenae (Greece), Treasury at, 100
Mystery of the Passion (play), 265
Mystery plays, 255, 272
Mythology, 230; painting and, 54, 56, 60

Nanook of the North (film), 296, *296,* 300
Napoleon I, Emperor, 340, 342, 343; *Life* of (Ludwig), 244; portrait of (David), *58;* retreat from Moscow, *241*
Napoli (ballet), 186

Narcissus (Caravaggio), *49*
Narrative poetry, 208, **210,** 226
Nashe, Thomas (poet), **208**
Naturalism in novels, 248
Natya Sastra, 173
Negri, Pola (film actress), 288
Negroes:
dancing and, 176, **188,** *188;* bands in New Orleans, *166;* songs of, **166,** 208
Nemirovitch-Danchenko, Vladimir (stage director), 272
Neo-classical art, 80, **340,** 342
Nervi, Pier Luigi (architect), *119,* 120
Netherlands, the:
architecture, 108; chair design, 15th-century, *134;* films from, 298; painting in, *47,* 58, **60,** 62, 66, 316, 328, 334
Neumann, Balthasar (architect), 337, *338*
New Lanark, *118*
New York City:
Broadway, 274; buildings in, 98, **118;** Chase Manhattan Bank, 118; Lever House, 102, 118; Lincoln Center, *99;* Museum of Modern Art, *54, 57,* 112; Radio City, *190;* Second Park Theatre, 274
New York City Ballet, 186
"New York School" of painting, 67
Newman, Cardinal, autobiography of, 246
News from Nowhere (Morris), 242
Newsreels, film, 282, 294, 296, **300,** *300*
Nibelungenlied (epic poem), 210
Niemeyer, Oscar (architect), 95
Night Journey (ballet), *189*
Night Mail (film), 296, *297*
Nijinsky, Vaslav (ballet dancer), 184
Nîmes (France), theatre and amphitheatre at, 98
Nineteen Eighty Four (Orwell), 242
Njala (Norse saga), 226
No dramas (Japan), **254,** *254,* 258, 276, 314
Nolhac, Pierre de (writer), 245
Non-representational art,
painting, 34, 46, **66,** *67;* sculpture, 86
Nonsense verse, 218, *219,* 220
Notation (musical), **146,** *146,* 294
Notre Dame de Paris (Hugo), 240, 242
Novels, 228, 230, **232,** 342; characters in, **236;** modern, **248;** past and future in, **242;** plot of, 224, **234**
Noverre, Jean Georges (choreographer), **180,** *180*
Nutcracker, The (ballet), 182, *183*

Oboe, 154, 160
O'Casey, Sean (playwright), 276
October (film by Eisenstein), *346*
Odes, 208
Odyssey, The (Homer), 210, 234, 258
Offenbach, Jacques (composer), **164,** *164*
Oil painting, 50, 310, 330
Old Possum's Book of Practical Cats (Eliot), *219*

The body of this book is designed in two-page units. Text references for each such unit are indexed to the left-hand page only.

The body of this book is designed in two-page units. Text references for each such unit are indexed to the left-hand page only.

The body of this book is designed in two-page units. Text references for each such unit are indexed to the left-hand page only.

Illustration Credits

Key to picture positions

(T) top (C) center (L) left (B)
bottom (R) right and combinations; for example, (TC) top
center, or (CR2) second picture,
center right of page.

Page

Drawings on introductory pages:
Hans Erni
18 Hans Erni
21 Photo Herdeg
22 (TL) Herdeg and Weider
(TR) Naturhistorisches Museum,
Vienna/Photo Archives Photo-
graphiques
(B) Colorphoto Hinz, Basle
23 (T) Photo Herdeg
(B) Musée du Louvre, Paris/
Photo Giraudon
24 (BL) John Sparks Limited,
London
(BR) From Franz Boas,
Primitive Art
25 (TL) Axel Poignant
(B) By courtesy of the Belgian
National Tourist Office
26 (B) Roger Mayne
27 (T) Metropolitan Museum of
Art, Purchase, 1924, Joseph
Pulitzer Bequest
(B) Cappella Sistina,
Rome/Colorphoto Hinz, Basle
28 (T) Eric Jelly, Photography
Thirty-Three
(BL) National Library of
Ireland, Lawrence Collection
(CB) Noel Moffett—Architect
(BR) Courtesy Mrs. Augustus
John
29 (TL) British Museum
(B) Photographer: Morley Baer;
courtesy Skidmore, Owings &
Merrill, Architects
30 (T) *Alt-Amerika* (Kunst der
Welt), Holle-Verlag, Baden-
Baden
(B) Victoria & Albert Museum,
London/Photo Freeman
31 (T) Courtesy of the Italian
Institute for Foreign Trade/
Photo Freeman
(B) American Museum in
Britain/Photo Desmond Tripp,
A.I.B.P., F.R.P.S.
32 (T, C, and B) Mansell/Alinari
33 (T) Mansell/Alinari
(BL) Private collection, London/
Photo Brompton Studios
(BR) Photo Theo Bandi and
Emil Schulthess
34 (T) Reproduced by kind
permission of A. & F. Pears
Limited
(C) British Olivetti Ltd.
(B) Citroen Cars Limited
35 (T) Ray Green of *The Observer*
(C) Photo Gerald Howson
(B) Putnam and Co. Ltd. and
Dobson Books Ltd. for per-
mission to reproduce the draw-
ing by Gerard Hoffnung

Page
37 National Portrait Gallery,
London/Photo Freeman
38 (T) Reproduced from the
Ordnance Survey Map with the
sanction of Her Britannic
Majesty's Stationery Office,
Crown Copyright Reserved
(B) Galleria Nazionale della
Marche, Urbino/Photo Man-
sell/Alinari
39 (TL) Ehem. Staatliche Museen
Berlin, Museum Dahlem, Gem-
äldegalerie
(TR) Victoria & Albert Museum,
London. British Crown Copy-
right
(BL) Musée National d'Art
Moderne, Paris/Photo Caisse
Nationale des Monuments
Historiques
40 (T) Scala—Istituto Fotografico
Edi.
(BL) Musée du Louvre,
Paris/Photo Giraudon
(BR) Kunsthistorisches
Museum, Vienna/Photo Meyer
41 (T) British Museum
(B) Cappella Sistina,
Rome/Photo Mansell/Alinari
42 (T) Royal Collection, Windsor
Castle, Copyright Reserved
(CL) Victoria & Albert Museum,
London/Photo Freeman
(CR) Victoria & Albert Museum,
London. British Crown Copy-
right
(B) Courtesy Peter Swann
43 (T) Devonshire Collection,
Chatsworth, reproduced by
permission of the Trustees of
the Chatsworth Settlement
(TR) Amsterdam,
Rijksprentenkabinet
(BL) Courtauld Institute of
Art, London
(BR) The Tate Gallery, Lon-
don; © S.P.A.D.E.M., Paris,
1964
44 (T) Musée National d'Art
Moderne, Paris/Photo Girau-
don; © S.P.A.D.E.M., Paris,
1964
(B) National Gallery,
London/Photo Freeman
45 (T) Collection: O'Hana Gallery
(BL) National Gallery,
London/Photo Freeman
(BR) Kröller-Müller Museum,
Otterlo, Holland
46 (T) Museum Boymans/van
Beuningen, Rotterdam
(B) Santa Maria della Grazie,
Milan/Photo Mansell/Alinari
47 (TL) National Gallery, London
(TR) Barber Institute, Birming-
ham University/Photo Lefevre
Gallery
(B) Carnegie Institute, Pitts-
burgh; © S.P.A.D.E.M., Paris,
1964
48 (TL) Scala—Istituto Foto-
grafico Edi.
(R) Photo Giraudon
49 (TL) Museo di San Marco,
Florence/Photo Mansell/Alinari
(TR) Galleria Nazionale,
Rome/Photo Mansell/Alinari
(BR) Nationalmuseum, Stock-
holm; © S.P.A.D.E.M., Paris,
1964

Page
176 (T) Arthur Tarnowski
(C) British Museum/Photo
Freeman
(B) Public Relations Office, The
Royal Thai Embassy, London
177 (TL) British Museum/Photo
Freeman
(TR) From the collection of the
Detroit Institute of Arts
(B) British Museum/Photo
Freeman
178 (T and B) British Museum
179 (TL) British Museum/Photo
Freeman
(TR and B) Bibliothèque
Nationale, Paris
180 (BL) Reproduced by permission
of the Trustees of the Wallace
Collection/Photo Freeman
(TR and BR) British Museum/
Photo Freeman
181 (B) Photo Freeman
182 (TL) Marius Borisogleb-
sky, *Materials for the History of
Russian Ballet*, Leningrad, 1938
(BL and BR) Joan Lawson
Collection, London
183 (BL and BR) Joan Lawson
Collection, London
184 (T) L. Courtin, Dour
(BR) Wadsworth Atheneum,
Hartford, Connecticut; The
Ella Gallup Sumner and Mary
Catlin Sumner Collection
185 (C) © S.P.A.D.E.M., Paris,
1964
(B) © S.P.A.D.E.M., Paris,
1964
186 (T) Photo Baron
(C) Photo Paul Wilson,
A.R.P.S.
(B) Roger Wood, London
187 (T) Action Photograph, Roger
Wood, London
(C) Photo Baron
188 (BL) Action Photograph,
Roger Wood, London
(TR) City Center of Music and
Drama, Inc.
(CR) Photograph by courtesy
of MGM
(BR) Collection Anne Lejard,
taken from *Le Ballet*, by Boris
Kochno and Maria Luz, Arts
du Monde, Hachette, Paris,
1954; © S.P.A.D.E.M., Paris,
1964
189 (TL) Action Photograph, Roger
Wood, London
(CL) © S.P.A.D.E.M., Paris,
1964
(B) Photo Philippe Halsman
190 (TR) Bibliothèque Nationale,
Paris, taken from *Le Ballet*, by
Boris Kochno and Maria Luz,
Arts du Monde, Hachette,
Paris, 1954
(CR) British Museum
(LR) Dance Notation Bureau,
Inc., New York
(B) Radio City Music Hall
191 (TL) Action Photograph,
Roger Wood, London
(TR) Still from Martha Gra-
ham's film *A Dancer's World*,
distributed by Contemporary
Films, London
(BR) United Artists
193 Courtesy Museum of Modern
Western Art, Moscow

Page
194 (T) Radio Times Hulton
Picture Library
(B) British Museum
195 (T) Biblioteca Apostolica
Vaticana
(B) British Museum/Photo
Freeman
196 (T) British Museum
197 (B) Drawn by Ernst Haeckel
from *Report on the Scientific
Results of the Voyage of H.M.S.
Challenger during the years 1873-
76*, courtesy of the publishers,
Her Majesty's Stationery Office,
London, 1887
198 (T) Nasjonalgalleriet, Oslo
(B) Museum Mayer van den
Bergh, Antwerp; © A.C.L.
Brussels
199 (T and B) British Museum
200 (TR) Bibliothèque Nationale,
Paris
(BL) British Museum/Photo
Freeman
201 (TC) Victoria & Albert Museum,
London/Photo Freeman
(TL) British Museum/Photo
Freeman
(BC) Staatliche Museen, Berlin
202 (T) British Museum/Photo
Freeman
(B) Istituto Grafico Tiberino,
Rome
203 (T) Guillaume Apollinaire,
Calligrammes; © Éditions Gal-
limard, Paris, 1925; Harvill
Press Ltd., London; Ugo
Guanda Editore, Parma; and
from *Selected Writings*, etc. All
rights reserved. Reprinted by
permission of New Directions,
New York
(C) © Éditions Seghers, Paris
(B) Dylan Thomas, *Collected
Poems*, J. M. Dent & Sons Ltd.,
London, 1952, and © New
Directions, New York, 1957
204 (T) Philadelphia Museum of
Art, The Louise and Walter
Arensberg Collection
(BL) © Éditions Messein, Paris
205 (T) Victoria & Albert Museum,
London/Photo Freeman
(BL) British Museum/Photo
Freeman
(BR) Society for Cultural
Relations with the U.S.S.R.
206 (BL) British Museum/Photo
Freeman
(T) © Société d'Édition de
Dictionnaires et Encyclopédies,
Paris
(BR) British Museum/Photo
Freeman
207 (T) National Portrait Gallery,
London
(B) British Museum/Photo
Freeman
208 (T) National Museum, Athens/
Photo L. Frederic, Rapho
(C) Universitätsbibliothek,
Heidelberg
(B) Radio Times Hulton
Picture Library
209 (T) British Museum/Photo
Freeman
(C) National Portrait Gallery,
London
(B) © Fred W. McDarrah,
from *The Beat Scene*

Page
210 (T) British Museum
(B) British Museum/Photo
Freeman
211 (T) Foto ATA., Sweden
(C and B) British Museum/
Photo Freeman
212 (BL) British Museum/Photo
Freeman
(T) Biblioteca Nacional,
Madrid
(BR) British Museum
213 (TL) Nationale Forschungs-und
Gedenkstätten der Klassischen
Deutschen Literatur, Weimar
(CL) Federico García Lorca:
courtesy of Aguilar, S.A. de
Ediciones, Madrid
(BL) Photo John Vickers
(CT) British Museum/Photo
Freeman
214 (BL) Photo Giraudon
(R) British Museum
215 (T) Victoria & Albert Museum,
London
(B) © S.P.A.D.E.M., Paris,
1964
216 (T) British Museum/Photo
Freeman
(B) Courtesy The Gehenna
Press, Northampton, Mass.
218 (T) © Bibliothèque Royale,
Brussels
(C and B) British Museum/
Photo Freeman
219 (T) British Museum/Photo
Freeman
(C) Reproduced from the
Tenniel illustration in *Alice's
Adventures in Wonderland* by per-
mission of Macmillan & Co.,
Ltd., London, 1865
(B) Reproduced from T. S.
Eliot's *Old Possum's Book of
Practical Cats* by permission of
Faber and Faber Ltd., London,
1940
220 (C) The New York Public
Library, Spencer Collection;
Courtesy Jean Arp
(B) Robert Capa—Magnum
221 (T) © Fred W. McDarrah,
from *The Beat Scene*
(B) Novosti Press Agency
(APN), Moscow
223 British Museum/Photo
Freeman
224 (TR) British Museum/Photo
Freeman
225 (TR) Musée Th. Dobrée/Photo
G. Madec
(CR) British Museum/Photo
Freeman
226 (T) N. R. Farbman—courtesy
Life Magazine © 1955 Time
Inc.
(B) British Museum
227 (T) Mansell Collection
(B) B.B.C. Photo
(TR) British Museum/Photo
228 Freeman
(BL) Klee, from Voltaire, *Can-
dide*, courtesy Random House,
Inc., New York
(BR) © A.D.A.G.P., Paris
229 (TR) Reproduced from the Col-
lection of the Library of Con-
gress
(BL) Drawn for *Radio Times* by
Eric Fraser
(BR) 20th Century-Fox